Endorsements

"I connected deeply with the Queer Superpowers section of *Queer Flourishing*. It was empowering to think of my queerness as a great asset, especially when many of us have been subjected to negative depictions of "fussiness" or "flamboyance." I also appreciate the concept of using different superpowers/different selves at different times in our lives. Often inner work equates personal growth with leaving our past selves behind. In *Queer Flourishing*, we see the value in embracing and relying upon all aspects our personalities."

Chiedu Egbuniwe
Diversity, Equity, and Inclusion Strategist

"In the modern world, there are millions of technologically enhanced maps for you to get from here to there, but there are fewer and fewer maps that help us arrive at our full potential, or find our way to wisdom. Longo's book charts a profound and powerful map for Queer Flourishing. Showing that the journey is both deeply personal and also has patterns that enable others to find their way to their Queer Superpowers, Longo's book itself will be a friend and mentor to those who read it. As a cisgender, straight developmentalist, I loved learning deeply from Longo's theories and experiences and putting some of them in practice in my own life. A book that will change your life!"

Dr. Jennifer Garvey Berger
CEO, Cultivating Leadership

"Thanks to Flourishing Gays, I've grown a great deal as a person and a leader, as a gay diplomat, author, and journalist. I am now more confident, resilient, and assertive, with a larger capacity for making a positive difference in such a convoluted world as the one we are living in these days. *Queer Flourishing* is a book that transcends cultural, ethnic, social, and economic barriers and talks to the queerness in every single one of us."

Ambassador Diego Gómez Pickering
Journalist and Diplomat

"As a DEI [Diversity, Equity, and Inclusion] practitioner for nearly two decades, and especially as a member of the LGBTQ+ community, I've noticed a conversation missing. We should be talking about our own leadership development, and the untapped potential of queer leaders to set a new course for leaders of ALL identities, creating a new, more inclusive paradigm. Dominic's work beautifully lays out the case for this investment. He explains why it can and should be made by individuals and organizations, and elegantly differentiates between being "out," and flourishing. As we shift the workplace conversation to a focus on unleashing human performance through belonging, we shouldn't stop there—but pursue *actual flourishing*, implying that being "out" isn't the only destination, or destiny, of so many leaders. His frameworks, like the ten Queer Superpowers, celebrate the talents and resilience of the LGBTQ+ community, and provide a roadmap to inspire big shifts and openings for new kinds of leaders to rise."

Jennifer Brown
CEO, Jennifer Brown Consulting

"I have been reflecting on the Queer Superpowers since participating in Dominic's Heroes Journey program and revisited them while reading this book. His work brings communities together, through bonding over growing up feeling othered and sharing how that has shaped us as queer adults. It gave me the tools to recognize the obstacles I create for myself and find ways to begin breaking them down. If you are looking to improve how you manifest and execute the life you are living, also known as flourishing, I highly recommend reading this book reflectively and signing up to become a part of the Heroes Journey program."

Jason Mitchell Kahn
Entrepreneur

"As I grow in my own leadership journey, I found *Queer Flourishing* to be a clear articulation of the transformations of leadership presented in a relatable, gay man's context. It is the first book I have seen that is focused on the queer journey from assimilation to independence and offers interesting personal examples of fitting in, finding one's tribe, and coming of age."

Dan Chen
Product Strategy, Google

"Dominic is someone who brings a strong commitment to fostering queer community and a deep knowledge of adult development, marrying the two to create a unique message about how queer folks can grow and thrive. *Queer Flourishing* is a guide to making your queer way through an often confusing, sometimes hostile world."

Sasha Aickin
Software Engineer and Tech Founder
Former Chief Technology Officer, Redfin

"At the heart of Longo's beautifully written book is the human need for love and personal growth. From the experience of having to live outside the conventional mindset of what it means to be a sexual being, Longo shows how marginalized individuals and communities can develop unique ways towards wholesome self-affirmation.

I especially appreciated Longo's understanding of human development that follows predictable phases in identity formation. He outlines how LGBTQ+ people can become skilled at navigating the often-hostile territory they live in and develop increasing self-acceptance and well-being. While it is a developmental task for all of us to find a balance between belonging (connection) and separateness (autonomy), Longo chronicles this journey towards flourishing for his community.

This insightful and hopeful book about queer flourishing should be required reading for all struggling to find meaning in their otherness and for those who grapple with how best to support LGBTQ+ people in their quest for wholeness, connection, and love and their capacity to powerfully contribute to society."

Dr. Susanne Cook-Greuter
Independent Scholar

QUEER
FLOURISHING

QUEER FLOURISHING

A Guide to Personal Growth and Greater Aliveness for LGBTQ+ Adults

BY

F. Dominic Longo, Ph.D.

Copyright (C) 2024 Dominic Longo. All rights reserved.

No part of this publication shall be reproduced, transmitted, or sold in whole or in part in any form without prior written consent of the author, except as provided by the United States of America copyright law. Any unauthorized usage of the text without express written permission of the publisher is a violation of the author's copyright and is illegal and punishable by law. All trademarks and registered trademarks appearing in this guide are the property of their respective owners.

For permission requests, write to the publisher, addressed "Attention: Permissions Coordinator," at the address below.

Publish Your Purpose
141 Weston Street, #155
Hartford, CT, 06141

The opinions expressed by the Author are not necessarily those held by Publish Your Purpose.

Ordering Information: Quantity sales and special discounts are available on quantity purchases by corporations, associations, and others. For details, contact the author at info@flourishinggays.com.

Edited by: Blue DeLac, Lily Capstick, Michael Pettinger
Cover design by: Nelly Murariu
Typeset and ebook design by: Amit Dey

ISBN: 979-8-88797-136-0 (hardcover)
ISBN: 979-8-88797-137-7 (paperback)
ISBN: 979-8-88797-138-4 (ebook)

Library of Congress Control Number: 2024914453

First edition, January 2025

The information contained within this book is strictly for informational purposes. The material may include information, products, or services by third parties. As such, the Author and Publisher do not assume responsibility or liability for any third-party material or opinions. The publisher is not responsible for websites (or their content) that are not owned by the publisher. Readers are advised to do their own due diligence when it comes to making decisions.

Portions of Chapter 2 have been adapted from a previously published form in F. Dominic Longo, "Taking a Developmental Approach to Coaching Gay Men," Coaching Wisdom: Voices of the Gay Coaches Alliance (Gay Coaches Alliance, 2022). Re-published with permission from Gay Coaches Alliance.

Publish Your Purpose is a hybrid publisher of non-fiction books. Our mission is to elevate the voices often excluded from traditional publishing. We intentionally seek out authors and storytellers with diverse backgrounds, life experiences, and unique perspectives to publish books that will make an impact in the world. Do you have a book idea you would like us to consider publishing? Please visit PublishYourPurpose.com for more information.

To all those who have entrusted me with permission to companion them on their journey into flourishing,

To all those whose love makes possible my greater aliveness, especially Martin,

and

To all those yearning to flourish and step into greater aliveness—may reading this book help you find your way.

Table of Contents

Preface . . . . **xix**
    Growing Into Ourselves xix
    How This Book Is Structured xxiv
    Origins xxvii
    Predecessors to This Book xxxvi

Dramatic Pause: Setting the Stage for Queer Flourishing . .xlv

Introduction: Foundations for Queer Flourishing **1**
    Stages of Development 1
    Subject and Object 7
    Inner Diversity and Inclusion 9

PART I **13**

Chapter 1: Discovering Queer Superpowers **15**
    Growing Into Queer Flourishing 15
    Queer Superpowers of Inner Diversity and Inclusion . 20

Chapter 2: Teenage Superpowers **37**
    Proud Distinction 37
    Socializing 41

  Jagged Development 45

  The Best Little Kid 52

  School Mind 65

  Teen Cool 75

  Growing Up and Growing into Gender 80

Chapter 3: Dark Sides 91

  Powers and Pitfalls 91

  The Boys in the Band 97

  Creature of the Night 105

  GRIEF and Alejandro 110

  Rise and Fall of the Golden Boy 115

  Charting a Course to College 118

PART II 121

Chapter 4: Queen Rising 125

  My Great Sending Off 125

  Queenly Self-Authoring 127

  Climbing the Ivory Tower to Straight
    Self-Authoring 133

  Life as a Queen 139

  The Queen's Dilemmas and Defenses 145

  Carly 150

  Transgressive Titillations of a Young Catholic
    Intellectual 165

  Queen Harold 174

  "Thus play I in one person many people" 177

  Flourishing into Personal Greatness 180

PART III 183
Chapter 5: Into the Desert 187
Humpty Dumpty Had a Great Fall 187
Becoming Adult All Over Again 194
Redefining Ourselves Beyond Convention 201
Cairo, the Pressure Cooker 206
A Controlled Coming Apart 210

Chapter 6: Spiraling 219
Keifo 219
Curfew in the Barracks 222
Developmental Focus 230
The Stories We Tell.......................... 232
Fallback................................... 246
The Sinking Ship............................ 249
There and Back Again....................... 255
Therapeutic Thawing........................ 263
Trauma Recovery 267
A Queer Cycle of Violence.................... 274

PART IV 281
Chapter 7: Returning and Retrieving............ 285
Developmental Defenses...................... 286
The Closeting–Coming Out Continuum 290
Self-Protective Opportunist Queer Superpowers ... 297
"Itsasecretia" 305
The End of Eddy........................... 310

    Finding Flourishing for Our Self-Protective
        Opportunist Self.......................... 312
    No Longer Afraid of Our Shadow.............. 315
    The Cycle Continues......................... 320

Conclusion: Languishing, the Diminishment of Love That Deadens......................... 335
    Heroes Journey from Languishing to Flourishing... 357

What's Next? Let's Journey on Together......... 361

Glossary for Queer Flourishing............... 365

Bibliography............................. 385

Endnotes................................. 391

Acknowledgements....................... 401

Hire Dominic to Speak..................... 405

Bring Queer Superpowers for Leaders to Your Organization............................. 407

Heroes Journey Program for Gay, Bi, and Queer Men.. 409

What Heroes Journey Alumni Say.............. 411

Actionable Allies Program.................. 413

Bring Dominic to Your ERG................. 415

About the Author......................... 417

List of Tables

1. Developmental Mindsets and Queer Superpowers ... 28
2. The Queer Superpowers 32
3. Queer Superpowers of Socialized Mind 34
4. Developmental Stages as Named by Researchers 66
5. Developmental Stages of Diversity and Inclusion 70
6. Focus on Queer Superpowers of Socialized Mind 95
7. Queer Superpowers of Early Self-Authoring 122
8. Queer Superpowers of Early Post-Conventional Stages 184
9. Queer Superpowers of Self-Protective Opportunist .. 282
10. The Queer Superpowers Revisited 354

PREFACE

Growing Into Ourselves

Personal growth, from a queer perspective, finds love as its source.

Love brings us to life. Whether a coupling that makes two lovers parents or a kind embrace in a downtrodden moment of anguish, love enlivens. The very nature of love sparks ever more life. Indeed, the love that flows through us outlives even death.

Queer people love differently and so we live differently. As we let love flow into and out of us, not only do we grow into fuller **aliveness**, we become ourselves more fully. Love powers the quest to become ourselves, as fully alive as possible.

Naturally, our individuality shapes who and how we love, as does our sex. *Male or female, woman or man?*

> **Aliveness:** Beyond biological life, aliveness refers to awareness, activation, and integration of the diverse parts of the Self. Encompassing the light and joyful aspects of human experience as well as the heavy and painful aspects, aliveness can be extremely difficult and taxing at times. The opposite of aliveness is a deadened, numbed state of half-awake avoidance.

Beyond or between or crisscrossing the binary—intersex or transgender or non-binary. *What is the sex in us? What is the sex we yearn to have? Gay or straight or lesbian or queer or asexual or something else besides?* Becoming ourselves—thanks to the aliveness made possible by love—includes coming to know our sex and all else in our depths and our flesh. In our aliveness, we unfold. More of our being becomes human. We become bigger versions of ourselves. The quest to grow as a human being expresses the aliveness made possible by love. In growing, we flourish.

Unfortunately, too few resources support LGBTQ+ people in this quest to grow and **flourish**.

Perhaps the most famous guidance for personal growth points us *to know ourselves.* In trying to follow this guidance from the ancient oracle of Delphi, we encounter many surprises—roadblocks, diversions, and pitfalls, as well as treasures, secret compartments, and even wonders of the world. The frontiers within the Self make for great adventures! The timeless wisdom of the Delphic oracle's command "Know thyself!" has propelled the quests of countless quotidian heroes. Yet no ancient treasure map of lost riches or Sufi handbook of spiritual knowledge can provide enough guidance to make straightforward the quest to know ourselves. The structures within human beings shift and morph as the world evolves. Inner realms reflect outer realms. To know

> **Flourishing:** In the context of human development, flourishing refers to a condition of holistic well-being that continues to expand, grow, and generate in a dynamic process. Derived from the Latin *florere*, meaning to bloom, to blossom, to flower. See Glossary for further explanation.

oneself always entails adventure into vast, previously uncharted territory.

The Delphic oracle's famous imperative and other voices of wisdom recognize every life journey as both universal and unique. Yet queer people find much missing from the wisdom passed down from ancient and modern cultures to direct wayfarers on their quests. Between sages of the ages, ancient philosophers and mystics, gurus and soothsayers, none of them contemplated the inner lives or social realities of queer people as we are today. How could they? So many guides to personal growth assume heteronormativity without even thinking about it. Queer lives elude conventional wisdom. **LGBTQ+** people, consequently, miss out on some of the benefits that straight people gain from these rich resources.

Queer Flourishing aims to address the needs of contemporary wayfarers in the quest to know ourselves. Gay, bi, and queer men might find most relevance in *Queer Flourishing*, but I hope and expect readers who identify otherwise, whether **queer** or straight, to find resonance. Of course, no one else's instructions can tell you how to undertake your own version

LGBTQ+ or LGBTQIA+: Acronym for lesbian, gay, bisexual, transgender, queer, questioning, intersex, asexual, and other non-standard sexual orientations and gender identities.

Queer: Once a derogatory slur, today "queer" is commonly used to describe sexual orientations and gender identities that differ from standard straight norms and the gender binary. The word is used by some (not all) individuals across the LGBTQ+ spectrum, more by younger generations than older. See Glossary for further explanation.

of the archetypal hero's journey. No tips or tricks can speed you through the adventure of knowing and becoming yourself. Only you can find your way through the swamplands of the soul.[1] Nonetheless, I hope and expect this book to serve as a resource for you as you move forward on your journey.

Of course, we need not be on a journey of **personal growth** and expansion. While human life by its nature keeps unfolding and growing beyond its current limits, many alternatives present themselves.

> **Personal growth:** The process of becoming oneself more fully, through unfolding more of one's unique human potential. As we grow, how we make sense of reality changes and expands to encompass more of its complexity. See Glossary for further explanation.

We might grow to a certain point and then reach a version of ourselves that suffices. We might not find the motivation or reason to become anything more than we already are. You may find yourself thinking: *Life is hard enough already, without having to delve into my inner workings! I am comfortable, so I just think I'll enjoy that and keep on with my life.* Or we might get waylaid by a tragic setback that saps our strength and drains our verve. *I just can't—at least not now.* Curiosity and desire gloss over or dull down to such an extent that we might take refuge in a routine or in some corner of the world, without any interest in breaking out of it into anything else.

While some adults stop learning, growing, or changing by choice, I reckon most have just lost sight of the possibility. The busyness or the heaviness of life brings their attention elsewhere. Problems at work and home pile up and cover over whatever else might be there. Or they might put their energy and attention towards a different kind of quest, such as the quest for money. *Once I have such and such amount of money, then I shall start to live the life I really want! It might be a slog or require crafty savvy, but if I can manage it, my dreams will come true!* Another common quest seeks recognition, perhaps not grand fame, that ticket to immortality, but renown in certain circles for being or doing something admirably. *"She's a highly competent Vice President of Sales, ably handling both clients and strategy." That's what they'll say about me!* Or, *"He's the longest-serving coach in the league, and the kids all love him."* Less commonly, adults devote themselves to excellence in some realm, without much care about recognition. The technical and creative aspects of some craft consume those on such a quest.

Quests for fame, fortune, excellence, or even pausing for rest and recovery can all make part of a life of flourishing. However, these scenarios can also take us off the path of increasing aliveness and into a stagnant state of **languishing**. So, what's the big deal? However much we grow, we can be and do good, or be and do evil. So, what do we lose out on if we stop growing? When we move forward on the journey of life through growing and expanding, we become bigger people in the sense that we see and hold and handle more of reality, in all its mess and glory. Continuing to grow might not lead to goodness, but it is the path of greatness. No trophy

> **Languishing:** A middle ground in mental health between flourishing and depression. Somone languishing may describe themself as aimless, joyless, empty inside, blah, ho-hum, stuck, stagnating, and/or discontented. Sticking to the routines of life, a person who's languishing might maintain normal function, but feel exhausted and drained, even lifeless. See Glossary for further explanation.

awaits at the end of this quest. Growing does not (necessarily) make us a better person, just a bigger person—a more expansive person. The journey of becoming ourselves more fully is its own reward. This dynamic movement is the aliveness made possible by love called flourishing.

How This Book Is Structured

This book is structured to empower you to see the developmental journey that you yourself are on. I believe that if you are able to see your life developmentally, you will more easily find your way to flourishing. Yet seeing ourselves developmentally requires practice. Normal life in society does not typically equip us to look at our lives this way. Since we are always still on the path of development, we find it difficult to somehow find distance between our looking and our living.

You will encounter a novel mix of theoretical, autobiographic, and literary material while you read this book. The mix of material might even surprise you at times. It aims, after all, to spur shifts and changes in you, so I encourage you to welcome any experience of strangeness as an invitation for you to expand. Should you feel disoriented, reflection questions before and after most sections of the book point you to the main thread of the book.

Adult development theory: Field of scholarly research focused on the ongoing process, after reaching physical adulthood, of human beings expanding their capacities and realizing their potential. See Glossary for further explanation.

You'll encounter theoretical material, because I believe it can help you plot your own journey and find your way. The psychological research field of **adult development theory** has found a number of features anyone can expect to encounter in the journey of becoming themselves. Neither our individual genetic make-up nor our personality crystallizes a certain way of making sense of what we experience that we keep throughout our life. Instead, adult development theory sketches out a sequence of developmental stages of meaning-making. Each person's journey only traverses a certain expanse of territory. We each only reach a certain stage at the furthest limits of our development. While not every wayfarer will reach every known developmental stage, the theory provides a useful map pertinent to everyone, if only partially and schematically.

In *Queer Flourishing*, I bring my queer eyes to this map of adult development. I translate some of the guidance from adult development theory into queer language, and I add to the theoretical map of human development ten features common in queer lives, which I call "**queer superpowers**." The main body of the book is organized into four parts, according to which queer superpowers are the focus.

The table of queer superpowers is repeated as a tracker at the beginning of each of these four parts of the book, highlighting those particular powers that shall be the focus in that part. Our exploration of these superpowers aims to help you recall territory you have already traversed, see the terrain you are presently traveling, and look forward to what could lie ahead. Not every LGBTQ+ person takes on every one of these ten

> **Queer superpower:** A posture or pattern commonly appearing in LGBTQ+ people in order to handle the particular constellation of personal and social challenges of their lives at a given developmental stage. Queer superpowers are creative adaptations that ingeniously empower LGBTQ+ people with heroic capabilities, yet each superpower also brings treacherous pitfalls. See Glossary for further explanation.

patterns and postures, but even if you haven't personally, you will probably recognize them from others in your circle.

The book is further organized into seven chapters, according to thematic material, and each chapter is divided into a number of sections. At the beginning and end of most of these sections, you'll find reflection questions that aim to slow you down and look at some aspect of your life through a specific lens, to help you apply what you're reading to yourself.

Throughout the book I use a number of terms from the field of adult development and create some new ones. The Glossary in the back of the book provides explanations of about 45 of these terms to which you can refer as needed. Names for developmental stages and the queer superpowers are in bold throughout the book. Other terms in the Glossary are bold-faced just once in the main text, with a call-out box offering a brief definition.

These pages also invite you into my own personal story. While no famed wayfarer like Ibn Battuta or Marco Polo, I lay bare the contours of a single queer life in the hope that my travelogues benefit you on your unique path. My stories can offer nothing more than I am—a gay, Italian-American, upper middle-class, cisgender man—among many other things. I take you through territory I have traversed, with commentary on how that journey went, so you can witness how I see myself developmentally. In a few places, you will see quotes from journal entries and other pieces I wrote many years ago showing how I used to see myself and how I made sense of certain crucial experiences as I went through them. In sharing my story, I do not mean for my life to be a model for yours. Instead, I put forward my story so that you can better see your own. I intend to model the honesty, vulnerability, self-awareness, and compassion that I hope you bring to yourself.

Reading has always served my own wayfaring. Others' stories help us read our own with greater understanding. Myths and novels, plays and memoirs, epics and lore pass onto us great learning derived from our forebears' lived experience and thoughtful reflection. More recent works can do the same, such as Mart Crowley's play *The Boys in the Band*,[2] and French author Edouard Louis's novels, published in English as *The End of Eddy* (2017)[3] and *History of Violence* (2018)[4]. To give you practice seeing with compassion the vagaries of queer developmental journeys, we will consider the queer superpowers as they show up in these and other queer stories. They will introduce you to characters who are queer in a variety of senses and bring you to other historical periods, cultures, and lands—some real and others completely fictional. Because of copyright issues with extensive citations, in a few instances you'll be directed to the Flourishing Gays website for the full exploration of how the queer superpowers pertain to these literary works.

Ultimately, neither my story nor those in these literary sources is the point here—yours is. I hope that reading these stories helps you explore your own. I hope that *Queer Flourishing* helps you to better know yourself. I hope that reading this book helps you read the story of your life with more compassion and new understanding, so that you can fill your next chapters with greater flourishing.

Origins

Promoting human flourishing has come to animate my life and work. This quest feels ample enough to hold virtually all the goods that I value. The enterprise I founded, Flourishing Gays, allows me to pursue this animating quest by bringing LGBTQ+ perspectives to **leadership development** and coaching. I help individuals, groups, and organizations explore, uncover, and

> **Leadership development:** The part of personal growth that relates to having an impact in the world. Since all human beings have some degree and kind of impact on the world around them, everyone is a leader, to whatever extent of consciousness or efficacy. Leadership development thus refers to the process of growing in the capacity to have greater and more intentional impact in the world.
> See Glossary for further explanation.

cultivate the possibilities they hold within so that they can grow into fuller versions of themselves.

The book you hold has emerged from Flourishing Gays. With it, I aim to instigate flourishing in as many people as possible, beyond the limits of those I ever meet or work with in person. I mean for your experience reading this book to be quite personal. So that you might grow as a whole person, I address personal questions to you for reflection and inquiry. To model the kind of vulnerable introspection that could help you grow, I share quite personal anecdotes and stories from my life. That may raise some questions, such as, Who am I, addressing you with these words and ideas? What credibility do I have for writing a book that purports to stimulate your growth and development as a person? So let me begin with the story of Flourishing Gays and how it came out of my life journey.

I never set out to be a coach or an entrepreneur or to work in personal development. Nor did I see a place for myself in the field of diversity, equity, inclusion, and belonging. Growing up, I imagined myself in diplomacy or international business or teaching and doing research as a university professor or even as a Jesuit priest. From an early age, I had keen curiosity about the larger world beyond the one I experienced daily. I also took delight in learning—not just school stuff, but athletic skills and politics. I explored imaginary worlds through science fiction or fantasy. At some point in high school, through some combination of the Jesuit approach to educating the whole person and talking with my mother about her self-help books like Scott Peck's *The Road Less Traveled*, I heard about "personal growth."

Personal growth gradually gained immense importance in my personal values and priorities. Throughout my 20s and 30s, I consciously made my major life decisions about where to live, what to study, and what work to do based on what would most contribute to my personal growth and development. My quest for growth brought me from my hometown of Omaha, Nebraska, to college in Boston, and to volunteer teaching in Cairo, Egypt. In the following years, I worked as an educator, manager, and consultant in the Middle East and the USA.

The ambition and excellence of Harvard University drew me there, at the cusp of 30 years old, for a Ph.D. program in Arabic and Islamic Studies. This program typically took students eight years to complete, and I worried that it would only grow me intellectually while other dimensions of myself might languish. I had seen this happen with other graduate students I had known. Consequently, I sought a way to mix more professional experience into these years of study. Happily, I found an opportunity at McKinsey & Company, the strategic consulting firm, in their Middle East office. McKinsey bills itself as "a leadership factory," growing academic overachievers into eminently competent problem-solvers.

The academic and professional contexts at Harvard and McKinsey posed temptations to prioritize prestige over anything deeper. But thanks mainly to an ongoing practice of reflection in the midst of all the action of life, I managed to keep true to my commitment to personal growth and development. I found great joy in learning and exploring the world through studies and travels, which in turn built my capacity for service to others, which I came to see as a way to find meaning in life. Reflecting on my experience, I have in recent years reframed my commitment to personal growth within a more expansive pursuit of promoting human flourishing.

At McKinsey, I also discovered that, regardless of the industry, consulting projects that required leadership development and capability building for the client held the greatest interest for me. Eventually, I left McKinsey and did formal training and certification as a coach so that I could expand my capacity to help others to grow. I found a tenure-track position as a university professor, through which I brought everything I knew about growing leaders to my work with undergraduate and graduate students. Then, in 2018, I left my university job directing the Muslim-Christian Dialogue Center at the University of St. Thomas in Minneapolis-St. Paul, Minnesota, and I founded Flourishing Gays.

In all my previous leadership development—whether designing leadership development programs, facilitating workshops, teaching courses, or coaching someone individually—I had grown increasingly aware that what helped a person to grow was affected by their particular constellation of personal and social identities. I noticed patterns that showed up for women differed from those of men, patterns for immigrants differed from those living in their home language and country, and patterns for people of color differed from those of white folks. My clients' particular positions within structures of power and privilege affected their developmental needs and opportunities.

This was true for people of all ages. For example, in one small Arab country where I spent the better part of a year building capacity in the education system, I noticed how leaders' gender, native language, and religious identity as Sunni or

Shiite affected them. In that society men held power and privilege over women, Arabic speakers over Persian speakers, and Sunnis over Shiites. In coaching and mentoring of clients in that cultural context, I learned to appreciate how cultural identities interact with patriarchal structures to generate different obstacles and possibilities for development—as well as coping strategies.

In truth, I had first learned about such patterns as they showed up for my mom—a divorced, white, Irish Catholic woman making her way to partner in a big law firm in Nebraska. As I observed her, I came to appreciate how the interplay of gender, sexual status, and cultural identities present specific challenges as well as resources for someone's journey of growth. No surprise then, that I was especially inspired by the way women's leadership programs, at McKinsey and elsewhere, worked with these patterns of challenge and opportunity to help participants grow and learn.

In developmental spaces exclusively for women, participants would find easy understanding and compassion for their particular struggles and joys that related to womanhood. From bodily experiences to structural sexism and misogyny to family dynamics and their position in patriarchal cultural, religious, legal, and societal structures, women share a collective store of knowledge and wisdom—as well as familiarity with a range of coping mechanisms!

The position in the patriarchy of gay, bi, and queer men differs from women's, and we find different challenges and opportunities. However, we face similar pressures and prejudice from patriarchal cultural, religious, legal, and societal structures. We too share a collective store of knowledge, wisdom, and coping mechanisms. While leadership programs customized for women have existed for decades, no leadership development program in the world, so far as I knew, addressed gay, bi, and queer men's social identities specifically or made use of our collective store of experience to help us learn from each other and grow as human beings. The gay, bi, and queer men I knew who had moved from their native lands in every corner of the globe to the big cities of the United States, Europe, and the Middle East seemed especially underserved by the professional and personal development offerings presently available. This gap presented me with an opportunity to meet a vital need in the world. I founded Flourishing Gays first of all to fill it.

What might be possible when a group of LGBTQ+ men come together in a context of personal growth and mutual support? To seek answers to this question, I put on a set of experimental workshops for gay, bi, and queer men of all ages in Boston, Barcelona, and New York. Participants marveled at how refreshing it was to be in a space that fostered vulnerability and intimacy for gay men in a non-sexual context, without alcohol or other drugs. They said they had never encountered such a space anywhere before. Gay men's group therapy, support groups for coming out, and recovery from addiction do create containers for non-sexual intimacy and vulnerability. However, in Flourishing Gays workshops we focused not on healing from hurts, but rather on moving from good to great, from ho-hum to thriving. The response was enthusiastic.

After these first experiments, I put on my ex-McKinsey hat and began crafting a business strategy for a social enterprise where I could earn my livelihood by addressing this need that I had identified. While the one-off workshops generated excitement as participants caught a glimpse of new possibilities, I yearned to go much further for my clients. I wanted to help them catalyze personal transformations to move into lives of greater meaning, connection, and depth.

I began hatching a vision to bring together small groups of gay, bi, and queer men for a leadership development program. I imagined these small groups as microcosms of a new kind of gay community—one founded on vulnerability and mutual support for the sake of personal growth and flourishing. I would work with participants individually and as a group to facilitate their gaining new perspectives on the challenges and opportunities they face in their personal and professional lives. This deeper work could especially support men who found themselves at the crossroads of life transitions, such as after a job promotion, or before fatherhood, or when yearning welled up within them for greater meaning and purpose in life.

From this vision, I created a program called Heroes Journey—a name that alludes to the archetypal quest that myths describe. Instead of accentuating our individualistic tendencies, however, I envisioned creating a community in which *heroes journey together*. We need each other in order to become ourselves. The six-month program starts with a preparation phase customized to each participant's particular needs. Through a series of psychometric assessments and reflective exercises, each participant gains clarity on what growth and development presently entail for him. Once each participant articulates his personal development plan, the cohort of five to eight members starts meeting in "mastermind" sessions, where they take turns sharing challenges and opportunities to gain feedback and insights from each other.

Running this program over the past several years, I see every participant enjoying remarkable benefits. They clarify their vision for their lives and the creative contribution that they wish to make to the world. They become able to pursue this vision more fervently and joyfully by tapping into their passions and sense of purpose. Through the mastermind sessions, they increase their capacity for listening deeply and empathetically. This, in turn, not only allows them to deepen interpersonal relationships but also gain new perspectives that prompt them to reconfigure patterns of thought and behavior. Through our coaching and their reflection, they identify limiting beliefs and assumptions about themselves, others, and the world. They gain freedom from these limits, and more consciously discern the principles by which they wish to live. All of this serves to increase their efficacy and impact in the world. In short, they find their way to a personal transformation through which they become themselves more fully.

The path I've travelled has wound its way around many parts of the world and delved into many deep places in myself. This has all prepared me for an entrepreneurial adventure where I do work that matters to me, helping others explore themselves and empowering them to expand their worlds. Building on all I've experienced and learned, I've written a book which I would have wanted to read. I hope and expect that—whatever your gender, sexual orientation, and other identities—you will gain from reading these pages.

In my work coaching and creating leadership development programs for gay, bi, and queer men as well as straight women and men, I tap into a deep collective yearning for trust, acceptance, and intimacy. I believe this yearning is shared by all people, though it has its own character in the queer community. For example, though gay men fall in love with other men, our trust in each other—and in ourselves—is all too often sharply limited. We seem to share a collective memory of being burned for showing up too genuinely or vulnerably. We flinch. We shield. We withdraw. While queer people are not unique in experiencing betrayals and hurts, certain patterns that are unique to our community show up in the ways we undergo these experiences.

Opportunities to be seen and known seem all too scarce for gay, queer, and trans people. Even scarcer are the spaces and communities where we can be supported and encouraged to find fulfillment and capaciousness. I write this book to provide some of the insights or 'Aha!' moments, and heart knowledge that my clients experience through Flourishing Gays. I mean to help LGBTQ+ readers—and those who love us—to see and know more of what flourishing is possible for all of us. In my role as author and narrator, I intend to show up vulnerably and genuinely despite the risks this entails, so as to model a way of being in the world that makes possible self-awareness, intimacy, and growth.

As I tell my story, I hope that you find or remember more of your own story on two levels. First, we increase our self-awareness by remembering our backstory, that is, the historical, in-the-world happenings of our lives. But we also deepen our self-knowledge by acknowledging our "**understory**," that is, the ways we make sense of ourselves, others, and the world. Normally, our understory lies mostly in shadow, bubbling to the conscious surface of our minds through dreams, intuitions, reveries, somatic experiences, and 'Eureka!' moments. However, with reflection, we can notice our own sensemaking. Indeed, only by noticing our own

Understory: The partially conscious, inner story we hold within ourselves to make sense of ourselves, others, and the world. Whereas someone's backstory tells what external events happened earlier in their life—the when, where, what of their history, a person's understory relates the why and how of who they are today. See Glossary for further explanation.

meaning-making can we more consciously choose what sense to make of ourselves, others, or the world. I hope that reading *Queer Flourishing* catalyzes a bubbling up of many parts of yourself and inner processes by which you make sense of the world. I also hope that reading this book prompts you to engage more consciously in the writing of the story of you, which even now is still to some extent being written by other characters in your life, by scenes in which you find yourself, and by cultural and historical forces beyond your control. In other words, I hope that you gain greater capacity *to author* in new and more lifegiving ways the unfolding story of yourself.

You will hear much of my story of becoming myself—as a man and as a gay person in particular. In telling you my backstory and understory, I mean to coax, direct, and guide you toward seeing your own story anew. You will also learn about what researchers of adult development have to say about the process of growing as human beings, especially about the stages of human development. Exploring this theory will help to give you new ways to see your journey of life.

Predecessors to This Book

Before going any further, I want to situate *Queer Flourishing* amidst other books. If you are up for getting bookish, this section is for you! In writing this book over the last five years, I have realized that my personal growth and development have been nurtured primarily through three avenues: introspection, interpersonal relationships, and reading. While most of *Queer Flourishing* deals with our inner lives and our relationships with others, the vistas afforded by reading have their place here too.

Books have whisked me away to far off lands. They have given me out of body experiences across time and space. They have let me shapeshift, taking the form of other people in other bodies. Ancient and modern myths, epic poems, novels, plays, travelogues, and mystical journals have all transported me into scenes that otherwise I could never have experienced. Thanks to reading, I have lived many lives. In these pages, I will occasionally endeavor to bring you into worlds created by a few of these texts. I will offer you a reading of small portions of them in order to expand our exploration of flourishing beyond the borders of my life and yours.

Meanwhile, in this section, I address books in a different way. Here I describe a few previous books that resemble in one way or another the book that you are now reading to situate it amidst other writings that pertain to queer developmental journeys. I hope this brief bookish discussion gives you some reading ideas that appeal to you, while also helping you see more clearly what I am up to in this volume. If you are not in a bookish mood, skip this section, and perhaps come back to it some other time.

Queer Flourishing is not by any means the first book written to help LGBTQ+ people, and especially gay men, with their personal growth. However, to my knowledge, it is the first to engage with contemporary research on adult human development from a queer perspective. Previous books, most famously, *Velvet Rage*, take a narrower view of personal growth and development for gay men, while my work looks at queer development more holistically. These previous books have left a gap which I mean to fill. Nevertheless, I feel grateful for the books that experts of various kinds have written in order to serve the personal growth and development of LGBTQ+ people and specifically gay, bi, and queer men.

Ever since Oprah Winfrey had gay psychologist Alan Downs on her talk show in 2005, thousands of gay men have found their way to his book, *Velvet Rage: Overcoming the Pain of Growing Up Gay in a Straight Man's World* (Da Capo Press, 2005; 2012). Highlighting shame as the hallmark of gay men's lives, Downs situates the journey from closeting to coming out and finding fulfillment in three stages: Overwhelmed by Shame, Compensating for Shame, and Cultivating Authenticity. He expresses his belief that this "simple three-stage model . . . . is likely to be universal to all gay men in the western world and perhaps across the globe."[5] Countering glossy happy-go-lucky images of gay life, Downs emphasizes the pain, the rage, and the shame of gay men's lives, starting with the trauma of growing up gay in a straight world. *Velvet Rage* makes a clear-cut diagnosis and uses it to explain gay men and gay culture. Using brief, anonymized anecdotes throughout his book to profile his gay clients in West Hollywood, Downs works up to a chapter with clear directions on what gay men need to do in order to reach contentment and an authentic life. In line with the cognitive behavioral therapeutic (CBT) and other approaches that he uses with clients, Downs explains to readers what "skills" to practice in order to find their way to a life of authentic meaning and fulfillment.

Much more recently, *Out of the Shadows: Reimagining Gay Men's Lives* (2019) by Bay Area psychologist Walt Odets also aims to provide insight into the inner dynamics of gay men so that they can find their way to more fulfillment.[6] Like *Velvet Rage*, *Out of the Shadows* makes much of shame and its effects, even despite recent legal victories and other advances in society and culture towards protection and acceptance of LGBTQ+ people. Odets argues that homophobia stubbornly persists, despite appearances to the contrary. As in *Velvet Rage*, Odets also devises a three-part framework that he applies to gay men for the purpose of better explaining the challenges of their lives.

Whereas the framework in *Velvet Rage* relates to how gay men handle shame, the framework in *Out of the Shadows* divides gay men into three generations according to their relationship to the HIV/AIDS epidemic.

Whereas *Velvet Rage* has been criticized for overgeneralizing and oversimplifying the complexity of gay men's lives, *Out of the Shadows* attends carefully to the nuance and depth of the human psyche. Odets's book is high-brow and intellectual, with ample references to psychological theory and method. Indeed, at many points in *Out of the Shadows*, Odets seems to be writing primarily for other gay psychotherapists.

I find both of these books to be most compelling when the authors write with the authenticity that they encourage other gay men to embrace. Odets appends to his book a final chapter, "The Life and Times of Mattias Johnston," which presents a moving autobiographical narrative about his relationship with a lifelong friend and lover. In the second edition of *Velvet Rage*, Downs adds a sketch of his own story in an epilogue, "This Peter Pan Grows Up," starting from the moment he received his HIV diagnosis at the age of 26.

An earlier book, *Uncharted Lives: Understanding the Life Passages of Gay Men* (New York: Dutton, 1994) was written primarily by gay psychologist Stanley Siegel, with the help of straight friend, journalist Ed Lowe, Jr. It integrates the author's own story with the presentation of a stage model of gay men's lives. Gay Catholic priest and theologian James Alison graciously recommended *Uncharted Lives* to me during an evening of conversation the summer of 2023 in Madrid as I was working on final revisions of *Queer Flourishing*.

Siegel and Lowe's book may have had a greater influence on my writing had I encountered it earlier in the process, but, in any case, I appreciate *Uncharted Lives* tremendously and find numerous points of resonance in our understanding of gay men's developmental journeys. At the same time, in the thirty years since *Uncharted Lives*, the legal, cultural, and societal contexts for gay men in the United States have changed to such a degree no one could have imagined in the 1980s or 1990s, when Siegel was going through the process of divorcing his wife and stepping into life as a gay man. Sigel and Lowe do not draw on general research on adult development, but on homosexual identity formation. Fitting for the time when written, Siegel and Lowe concentrated on coming out as the culmination of gay men's development. The stages into which *Uncharted Lives* is divided are: Pre-emergence, Self-acknowledgement, Self-identification, Assuming a Homosexual Identity, Accepting Homosexuality, Celebrating Self-expression, Reevaluation and Renewal, and Mentoring.

Other books address leadership development for LGBTQ+ readers with a focus solely on professional life. Two relatively recent books focus on bringing queer perspectives to workplace leadership. Kirk Snyder based his book *The G Quotient* (2006) on extensive empirical research. His findings highlight seven elements of leadership exemplified by gay male executives which he promotes as a model for business leaders of all genders and sexual orientations. In *Pride Leadership* (2019), author Steven R. Yacovelli similarly focuses on six leadership competencies, which he explicitly aligns with the seven named in *The G Quotient*, which Yacovelli applauds in 2019 as still the only book-length academic treatment of the leadership effectiveness of LGBTQ+ folks. In his own book, whose approach and tone are not at all academic, Yacovelli critiques the use of narrow binaries, namely, gay/straight and man/women in Snyder's research.

Many other queer autobiographies and memoirs make up an ever-increasing treasure trove of texts that allow us to follow vicariously the developmental travails and triumphs of LGBTQ+ people. To expand beyond my own context and foibles, I bring up two, Andrew Tobias's *The Best Little Boy in the World* (1973) and Mohsin Zaidi's *A Dutiful Boy* (2020).[7] Other queer works have come out in the hybrid genre of "autofiction," in which authors tell their truths in a freer literary form than pure autobiography. As noted above, I will make use in these pages of two such works by French author Edouard Louis, which in English were published as *The End of Eddy* (2017) and *History of Violence* (2018). American author Sam Lansky followed his 2016 coming-of-age memoir of addiction, *The Gilded Razor*,[8] with an autobiographical novel named *Broken People* (2020) whose protagonist—like its author—is a sober 28-year-old gay male writer living in Los Angeles.[9] The recently published spiritual memoir, *I Came Here Seeking a Person: One Gay Man's Spiritual Journey* (2023) by my friend William D. Glenn points from autobiography to another corpus that has influenced me deeply, namely, the realm of queer theology.[10]

While this is not the place for me to put forward some long list of reading recommendations in that realm, I want to note three titles from this field that weave together (auto)biographical narratives with theological inquiry: *Indecent Theology: Theological Perversions in Sex, Gender and Politics* (2000) by Marcella Althaus-Reid,[11] *The Silence of Sodom: Homosexuality in Modern Catholicism* (2000) by Mark D. Jordan,[12] and *Living Out Islam: Voices of Gay, Lesbian, and Transgender Muslims* (2014) by Scott Siraj al-Haqq Kugle.[13] (Auto)biographical and theological reflections by queer scholars of religion have a great deal of relevant wisdom for anyone today seeking to find their flourishing. These works have touched me deeply.

A non-fiction book that contributed early on to my reflection on the inner resources distinctive to queer people is *The*

Soul Beneath the Skin: The Unseen Hearts and Habits of Gay Men (2002) by David Nimmons, who portrays some of the wonderful aspects of gay male culture.[14] Verging at times on queer theology, Nimmons grounds his account in a comparison of gay men to an "order of devout monks":[15]

> many of the customs of gay enclave cultures echo traditions of Judeo-Christian brotherhoods and intentional communities.... Queer-inspired practices, from Radical Faerie gatherings to AIDS volunteer buddy teams, shimmer with notions of communal caretaking and altruism. At their best, they recall nothing so much as New Testament teachings of *agape* and *caritas*, male embodiments of service and nurture, nonviolence and gender peace, brotherhood and friendship, all spiced with equal dollops of sexuality and spectacle. Only in this case, the apostles are wearing Calvins or Abercrombie and Fitch...and sometimes not even that. Yet look at the soul beneath the skin, and you see we are rewriting the defaults of what a culture of men can be with and for each other.[16]

Nimmons treats multiple positive characteristics of gay male culture while grounding his work in social science research and writing in a narrative voice that often adopts the campy irreverence and wit embraced by much of gay culture. Drawing on crime statistics, his chapter "Our Peaceable Kingdom" marvels at how little violence gay men do. To flip the negative stories that gay men tell about themselves collectively, Nimmons highlights the altruism, responsibility, and care expressed through our mitigating risks of HIV transmission via condom use and other safer sex practices. In a chapter based on the metaphor of "sexual Madagascar," Nimmons celebrates gay men's "erotic innovations":

> Our Fantasy Island was just isolated enough from the mainstream so that a vast profusion of sexual variants could evolve. Far up in the hidden canyons of gay world, an astonishing range of diverse sexual species began to flourish. We developed our own erotic Madagascar, a largely unseen erotic ecosystem. In that libidinal landscape blooms a profuse flora and fauna of fantasy, fucking, and fun.[17]

Resonating with my own reflection on queer flourishing, Nimmons argues that gay male culture makes powerful and important contributions to mainstream culture. For example, in the caring and thoughtful ways that gay male couples practice non-monogamy, Nimmons argues that "we have clearly elaborated a parallel set of acceptable cultural norms."[18] I'm grateful for how Nimmons's book furthered my appreciation of the valuable resources that can be found in queer cultures. His book helped me see the ways we can access queer cultural resources—such as individual and collective memories, experiences, and role models—to support learning and development.

In different ways, each of the books I've mentioned in this bookish section illuminates the distinctive struggles of queer people in the effort to flourish. Likewise, each of these valuable books adds to the resources of queer culture to help anyone to flourish more fully.

DRAMATIC PAUSE:

Setting the Stage for Queer Flourishing

B efore you read on, take a moment to reflect:

In what ways do you see yourself and others as performers or actors who, throughout life, play many parts?

Facing a reflection question like this at the start of a book, you might be tempted to ponder only briefly. However, you'll gain much more if you find a way to engage more deeply with this and the many other reflection questions posed throughout this book. The Preface, this Dramatic Pause, and the Introduction aim to prepare you in various ways to gain as much as possible from the main sections of the book. With the pause here, I mean to prepare you to intermix your reading with reflection and even some writing.

Perhaps get yourself a journal where you can record what comes up for you in response to this first reflection question and the many that follow, or bring the question to a conversation with a friend, or go for a reflective walk in a garden or a jog along a river as you ponder. Like tilling before planting, these moments of pause prepare the ground for new learning by prompting you to take stock of your preexisting beliefs, understandings, and experiences connected to the topics to come.

To set the stage for learning how modern research looks at the stages of life, let's dip into drama for a wider, more humanistic view. Long before the contemporary research on adult human development, which you'll begin to hear about in the Introduction, thinkers have been reflecting on the stages of life. Drawing on this tradition, Shakespeare composed these famous lines, from his play *As You Like It* (Act II, Scene vii).

> All the world's a stage,
> And all the men and women merely players;
> They have their exits and their entrances;
> And one man in his time plays many parts,
> His acts being seven ages.

In this monologue by the character Jacques, the bard brings existential perspectives to his stagecraft and theatrical perspectives to our lives. The "seven ages" relate the stages of a man's life, from entrance to exit.

> At first the infant,
> Mewling and puking in the nurse's arms;
> And then the whining school-boy, with his satchel
> And shining morning face, creeping like a snail
> Unwillingly to school. And then the lover,
> Sighing like furnace, with a woeful ballad
> Made to his mistress' eyebrow.

In a series of vignettes, Jacques presents the first stages of life, all centered on relationships—the nurse, the school, the beloved. Relationships like these are absent from the stages of adulthood that follow, which focus instead on what the man says and how he holds himself.

Considering these stages and ages, what do you notice about your own mental model of the stages of life? What do you believe marks the transition from one stage to the next?

> Then a soldier,
> Full of strange oaths, and bearded like the pard,
> Jealous in honour, sudden and quick in quarrel,
> Seeking the bubble reputation
> Even in the cannon's mouth. And then the justice,
> In fair round belly with good capon lin'd,
> With eyes severe and beard of formal cut,
> Full of wise saws and modern instances;
> And so he plays his part.

The hot-headed soldier and self-satisfied justice bring focus to what the man says and how he holds himself. Bodily diminishment epitomizes the sixth and seventh stages, as the player exits into oblivion.

> The sixth age shifts
> Into the lean and slipper'd pantaloon,
> With spectacles on nose and pouch on side;
> His youthful hose, well sav'd, a world too wide
> For his shrunk shank; and his big manly voice,
> Turning again toward childish treble, pipes
> And whistles in his sound. Last scene of all,
> That ends this strange eventful history,
> Is second childishness and mere oblivion;
> Sans teeth, sans eyes, sans taste, sans everything.

Shakespeare's stage metaphors hold much value for us as we reflect on our own relationship to life stages as framed by contemporary adult development theory. In the appearances and disappearances of actors playing roles, the speech implicitly turns to the audience: *What kind of character are you playing? How long will you stay on stage before your plotline ends?*

As you read on, you will find spaces with a range of moods and scenes, with various characters showing up and reappearing. Focus will turn from one character's story to the next, especially my story and yours. I will continually invite you to enter these spaces, play your part, and through personal reflection ultimately set your own scenes. Whether reading by yourself, with a companion, or in a community, each time you read, you get to decide and design how you show up. You choose your response to the drama—what questions you ask yourself and others, what speeches you give, what actions you take, your interactions with various characters—here and in your life outside these pages.

As we conclude this brief but dramatic pause, notice what happens for you when you regard the scenes of your life up till now as a play. Besides looking back, try also looking ahead:

> *What might it take to allow yourself to see your life as a stage play where you get to perform yourself?*

INTRODUCTION:
Foundations for Queer Flourishing

Stages of Development

As a first introduction to the map that charts the journey of personal growth as seen by contemporary theory, this section presents a very brief description of the **stages of adult development.** The Glossary similarly offers succinct definitions and explanations for these stages and other technical terms and concepts that I believe are most important for you to grasp to see personal growth and development from LGBTQ+ perspectives.

Stage of development, or developmental stage: A way of making sense of reality, including oneself, others, and the world. Synonymous with **form of mind** and **developmental mindset.** Each stage represents a major step in the capacity for noticing and responding to greater levels of complexity. Stage describes a kind of meaning-making; it doesn't describe any individual. Actual human beings operate from multiple stages of development at any given point in life. See Glossary for further explanation.

Adult development is a field of empirical research and theory that focuses on how we each *make sense* of ourselves, others, and our world. This field is based in a constructive-developmental view of human nature. Adult development theories are *constructive* because they attend to how we each *make sense*, that is, how we create meaning and *construct* our own reality. They are *developmental* because they regard each person as prone to changing with the "unfolding of human potential towards deeper understanding, wisdom and effectiveness in the world."[19] The field grew out of developmental psychology, which began with its attention squarely on the various transformations of children's consciousness as they grow up physically.

Apparently, developmental psychologists in the early 20th century had little interest in adults' consciousness. They figured that when the body was fully developed sexually and otherwise, consciousness was as well. In contrast, they were fascinated by the radical transformations of mind that they saw as a typical human grew from infant through the completion of adolescence. In the second half of the 20th century, scholars such as Jane Loevinger became interested in the changes of consciousness in people during their lives after full sexual maturity. Since then, several generations of researchers have discovered transformations of consciousness as radical among adults as among children. People are typically much less aware of the different kinds of consciousness among adults compared to the tremendous variation in the capacities of children. You don't need to be a scientist to see that a 1-year-old cannot manage what most 9-year-olds can do easily, or that 16-year-olds typically have much greater self-awareness and scope of understanding than most 9-year-olds.

One way developmental psychologists demarcate the line between children and adults has to do with becoming members of society. This isn't the kind of membership signified by registration on some official roster, but rather the internalization of some particular society's implicit categories, rules, habits, beliefs, and assumptions. I see this process of "socialization" as akin to natural language acquisition. In both cases, the process occurs mostly unconsciously through interactions with other members of a community. Socialization, however, is not about learning to speak some language; it is rather about knowing implicitly what emotion is appropriate when, or what a person is supposed to do in a certain situation, shared expectations, and the like.

Researchers regard the beginning of adult development as a kind of consciousness which they call "**Socialized mind**." After all the extraordinary changes of childhood, here we finally grow the capacity to internalize the conventions, norms, and expectations of others, especially certain "**important others**" who most influence us. (Incidentally, we shall use interchangeably the terms "**form of mind**," "**developmental stage**," and "**mindset**.") With **Socialized** mind, we become "normal." In early **Socialized** mind, called the **Conformist** stage of meaning-making, we notice and

> For further explanation of **Socialized mind** and all the stages of adult development, see the Glossary. The names of these stages will be boldfaced throughout the entire text.
>
> **Important others:** Socialized mind imprints on certain people as role models and authorities. The worldview, values, manners, and even personal styles of these important others especially influence the person who holds them as such. Important others might be family members, mentors, peers, or public figures or celebrities whom the person has never even met.

3

internalize societal conventions. In later **Socialized** mind, called the **Expert** stage, we focus on distinguishing ourselves within society, especially through knowledge and skill.

Besides **Socialized** mind and what comes after, in this book we will also pay attention to what comes just before, namely, **Self-Sovereign** mind. This stage at the end of child development immediately precedes psychological adulthood. In **Self-Sovereign** mind, we have not yet internalized the conventions and rules of society. This so-called 'pre-conventional' **Self-Sovereign** mind includes the **Self-Protective Opportunist** stage, in which we do what we need to get our basic needs met and keep from harm.

> **Pre-Conventional:** Developmental period before a person gains the capacity to internalize societal conventions. In this period of psychological childhood, cultural and societal norms, values, expectations, and rules have not yet become rooted in a person's inner world. See Glossary for further explanation.

It's worth pointing out that a relatively small number of people never leave **Self-Sovereign** mind but stay in the **Self-Protective Opportunist** form of mind. Similarly, many adults who reach a **Socialized** form of mind keep that as their primary way of making sense of the world for the rest of their lives. For some people, however, from the range of options presented by conventional society, they increasingly choose their own values, beliefs, and assumptions for themselves. Sequentially following **Socialized** mind, the next two stages are thus together "**Self-Authoring**" mind, in which we begin to claim ultimate *authority* in our lives. This marks a shift from looking outwards to societal norms for direction in life to looking inwards to oneself. While still "normal," we begin to find our way to a kind of "natural," that fits our individuality. In early **Self-Authoring**, called the **Achiever** stage, we differentiate and include our own personal vision and goals, which become our most important focus. Researchers consider the **Achiever** stage as a **conventional** form of mind, since here we are still powerfully subject to societal and cultural conventions.

> **Conventional:** Developmental period encompassing the Conformist, Expert, and Achiever forms of mind. Conventional sense-making is characterized by a person's capacity to internalize the conventions of their cultural milieu. This capacity marks the beginning of psychological adulthood and the possibility of joining a society as a full member. See Glossary for further explanation.

This stage represents an important high point in the process of *individuation*, which is one way of naming all of the human development up to this point that started with the (con)fusion of the infant within the mother as a holding environment. To differentiate themselves into becoming an 'individual' ever more fully, the person first separated themselves in significant ways from mother and the family, and eventually also found some measure of autonomy apart from social norms and expectations. Now, they *author* their own worldview.

Next, at some point, maybe, just maybe, we may begin to call into question all the cultural conventions and norms that we previously internalized. This makes possible a stage of more profound self-authoring called **Redefining** mind. We continue becoming ourselves even more fully as this form of mind shakes our very foundations and tips us into the first form of so-called '**post-conventional**' consciousness. The last stage of adult development that we shall explore goes even further in the move from *normal* to *natural*, by putting focus on the very

> **Post-Conventional:** Developmental period encompassing multiple stages of meaning-making or forms of mind marked by a greater capacity for seeing and navigating complexity, within oneself and out in the world, thanks in part to significant subject-object shifts in the realm of societal and cultural conventions. See Glossary for further explanation.

process of learning, changing, and development. In **Self-Transforming** mind, the developmental adventure itself captures our attention.[20]

While we can avoid growing and developing, staying primarily in one of these stages of meaning-making for most of our adult life, according to the research no one ever skips a stage in this sequential order. While all earlier forms of mind remain within us (and at times even take over our meaning-making), we cannot grow into a later stage until we have grown into the one before it. At the same time, actual development is neither linear nor predictable. What will elicit growth for someone in a particular instance cannot be known ahead of time. In some cases, what causes personal growth might stay unknowable even looking back after that growth has occurred. Major life experiences can leave someone unchanged in their meaning-making, while seemingly minor factors can sometimes yield extraordinarily significant consequences within our structure of mind.

For that reason, the autobiographical pieces of this book will at times spiral forward to later stages and at times backward to earlier stages, while the theoretical abstraction, the descriptions of stages, will afford us a macroscopic view and help us keep our bearings. The map created by adult development theory translates the vast territory of personal growth and development—with all of its hills and valleys, twists and turns, bogs and jungles, sinkholes and geysers—into neat and clean points of reference in a linear sequence. Like any map, this linear sequence of developmental stages will provide valuable points of reference as you make your way through this book. But the nonlinear set of investigations, explorations, and interventions must reflect the complex messiness of personal development. I hope reading this book brings new parts of you to life and prompts you to revisit younger forms of meaning-making that have long operated within you.

Subject and Object

Despite its brevity, this account of developmental stages might already have generated new perspectives through which to see your life journey. Those new perspectives are what this book is structured to generate. The most basic and fundamental step of personal growth comes down to a shift of perspective. Of course, not every shift of perspective amounts to a step in our development. Rather, developmental steps involve what theorists call a **subject-object shift**. Of the handful of technical terms and concepts I will introduce you to, this one is least self-explanatory and most deserves our mutual attention.

> **Subject-object shift:** A change in consciousness or sense-making that can be described as the most basic unit of human development. See Glossary for further explanation.

Think of subject and object as the background and figure, respectively, in a sketch or painting. As what formerly grounded our perspective becomes a figure on which we can focus our gaze, our consciousness grows. This shift of perspective from ground to figure, subject to object makes for the fundamental step or unit of personal growth, as I understand it.

The term "subject" in this context refers to the ground of our reality, as we see it at some point in time. Subject makes for the kind of consciousness we project outwards to structure our world and inwards to structure ourselves.[21] Many beliefs, ideas, values, categories, and assumptions comprise this ground, and we are *subject to* these realities at each moment in our development. That to which we are subject weaves the context of our lives and the reality in which we are currently embedded. It is the ground on which we stand, the stage on which we play, the background for the scenes of our lives. When we are subject to something, it defines us and our knowable world. In a sense, we are a subject *of* that thing, that reality. It *subjects* us, and we are subjected to it. It makes us who we are. It makes us *a subject* and shapes our *subjectivity*. When we are subject to something, it has power over us that we cannot overcome, because we are not even able to truly see it as "a thing."

To illustrate the shift of subject to object, let's take an example. As mentioned in our brief account of the stages, in the **Self-Protective Opportunist** mindset, we are subject to our basic needs for safety and to brute power. **Self-Protective Opportunist** mind zeroes in on how power differentials between ourselves and others affect our getting what we need. In **Conformist mind,** we no longer see the world through the lens of these basic needs and power differentials. Rather, these concerns become figures or items, which we can regard as such. Basic needs and power differentials no longer *structure* our consciousness, but rather become part of its *content*.

Human development theory uses the term "object" for the contents of our consciousness. What are objects for us are figures set against the background that frames and structures our consciousness. We grasp these objects as separate from us. We hold objects in front of us and know that they are not us. What we are subject to defines us and our reality. What we hold as object populates our inner and outer reality, but does not define it. We can behold objects and accept or reject them. At each subsequent stage, a person's purview expands, as that to which we were subject now becomes objects which we *have*. In this way, our awareness can embrace more of reality, including more aspects of both our inner complexity and of the world outside ourselves. This so-called "subject-object shift" reorganizes, expands, and complexifies the reality that we construct through our meaning-making.[22]

Inner Diversity and Inclusion

Reflecting on my own developmental journey and those I witness among my clients, I have come to appreciate how much our experience of the world reflects our inner life. This observation relates to constructivist psychological theories that we each construct the reality we experience through "making sense" of it all. The categories and distinctions that hold us as subject *shape* our world and our entire view of reality. The categories and distinctions that we hold as object *populate* our world. Together, subject and object determine what is possible for our "sense-making" and determine what we can integrate into ourselves and our worldview.

Bringing LGBTQ+ perspectives to the work of leadership development and coaching over the years, I have found myself situated in the emerging professional field called by many names—Diversity and Inclusion (D&I); Diversity, Equity, and Inclusion (DEI); and Justice, Equity, Diversity, Inclusion, and Belonging (JEDIB). From this vantage point, I've gained a number of new perspectives on personal growth and human development. Diversity & Inclusion has become a familiar business function, often managed by the Human Resources department. *Recruit, retain, and promote employees from varied backgrounds. Create an organizational culture where people from many walks of life can feel at home and do their best work.* Leaders with all sorts of political perspectives have come to embrace D&I mandates like these as vital to organizational culture and performance.

> **Inner diversity and inclusion:** A concept that evokes integration of key concepts from the fields of DEI and adult development. The process of human development can, for example, be described as an ongoing increase of diversity of realities and perspectives within a person's consciousness as well as an increase of fuller inclusion and integration of these realities into that person's consciousness, rather than ignoring, avoiding, or marginalizing those diverse realities. See Glossary for further explanation.

However, diversity and inclusion can be more than an HR function, one that looks "out there" at the headcount of a company or the members of an organization. The very process of growing and developing as human beings can properly and appropriately be framed as a journey of **inner diversity and inclusion**. Just as organizations gain more perspectives as they hire and retain more diverse employees, so does any individual increase their perspective-taking capacity by seeing and honoring more parts of themselves. Just as organizations which embark on Diversity & Inclusion journeys grow in the capacity to empathize with clients or customers, so do individuals gain in empathy for others as they consciously embrace more of themselves. Just as organizations can more creatively solve problems when they bring more voices into the conversation, so do individuals multiply their pathways for handling whatever comes their way as they honor the various voices inside themselves. As we make more subject-object shifts, we diversify the realities we can notice, include, and integrate into ourselves and our known world.

At the same time, giving too much emphasis to either diversity or inclusion can create dysfunction. Diversity and inclusion move in opposite directions. Too much diversity without harmony or integration produces cacophony within an organization, and confusion or even schizophrenia in an individual. Too much inclusion and belonging without diversity or variation produces groupthink within organizations, and makes individuals bored and boring, stuck in ruts of robotic mimicry. Both organizations and individuals require diversity and inclusion as an interdependent pair that operate in tension with each other—a polarity. If we become too separate, too different, too independent, we find ourselves unconnected, lonely, and disoriented. And if we lean too far towards belonging, we lose our sense of self, becoming mere members of a "hive mind," like the Borg in Star Trek, or components in a machine in which some collective controls our freedom and agency.

Though I've not seen anyone else make this connection between adult development and DEI, some researchers have described the growth and maturation of a human being as an ongoing effort to find and strike new balances between these two poles of separateness and belonging. From one developmental stage to the next, a person has both greater attention and capacity for difference or diversity *and* greater capacity for integration or inclusion. In other words, as consciousness grows and develops, it can both notice more and hold more.

At the same time, at each stage, we exhibit some emphasis on one of these two poles. Leaning towards the pole of difference and diversity, for example, are the **Self-Protective Opportunist**, who seeks singular refuge or advantage, and the **Expert**, who seeks to stand apart from the herd thanks to superior knowledge or skill. In **Redefining**, we stand apart in different ways, by unentangling ourselves from old assumptions holding together our former worldview. Leaning toward the pole of inclusion and embeddedness are the **Conformist**, who finds safe belonging in the social group, and the **Achiever**, whose personal vision provides a safe haven in which to embed. In **Self-Transforming**, we recognize how embedded we are in multiple systems, which continually change us even as we change them.

PART I

CHAPTER 1:

Discovering Queer Superpowers

Growing Into Queer Flourishing

Flourishing expresses aliveness. Queer marks difference. Whatever our sexual orientation or gender identity, we can all benefit from greater aliveness and vitality. By "queer flourishing," I mean to evoke an aliveness that shows up too rarely in ourselves or in the world. Because of specific types of adverse experiences, in order to survive or thrive, LGBTQ+ people have to adapt, even when we do not wish to do so. Yet, while our differences exact a price, queerness also catalyzes many kinds of creativity.

Facing specific obstacles in the world and dilemmas within ourselves, we adapt creatively like ants who suddenly sprout wings to flee a flooded anthill or bears who sleep to survive the scarcity of winter. Queer flourishing is this kind of creatively adaptive aliveness, epitomized by what I call "queer superpowers." Now, I am not arguing for any kind of natural superiority of queer folks over straight people. Indeed, LGBTQ+ folks make exceptional models for adult development not because of any unusual innate capabilities, but rather because of extraordinary solutions to extraordinary challenges that rise up against us over the course of our childhood, adolescence, and adulthood.

Queer flourishing brings alive more of ourselves, including previously deadened parts and new parts waiting to emerge. Whatever our identity or age, we all have parts of ourselves that we subdue and suppress or numb, neglect, and ignore. Indeed, numerous collective practices enable us all to deaden parts of ourselves rather than bring alive more of what we hold within. Pressure to conform to gender norms and expectations amounts to one such collective practice. If we relate differently to love, sex, and the erotic, then mainstream culture resists, and we encounter that resistance when we push against what is normal or expected. The non-standard pathways to flourishing that we must travel because of this resistance present pitfalls and pain different from those typically faced by others.

Are you getting more curious about this notion of "queer flourishing" and what it holds for you?

The most common metaphor for adult development refers to personal "growth." We imagine our increase in personal capacities to be like a body growing in size, strength, or skill. In several ways, the growth metaphor is apt. As we develop, our personal complexity increases—gaining more layers, making more connections, holding more viewpoints, attuning to more nuance.

"Flourishing" implies organic growth, while adding a sense of greater vibrance and vitality. Because of the root it shares with "flower," the word flourishing suggests blooming, whereby a plant's joyful celebration of aliveness in shapes and colors draws bees and others to come enjoy the nectar, spread the pollen, and propagate more life. Flourishing embraces the erotic, the pleasure of increased aliveness in the world. Yet flourishing embraces much more than the sensual. It encompasses holistic thriving and extends to the professional, relational, physical, spiritual, financial, cultural, political, and all other dimensions of life.

"Queer" derives from a root meaning transverse, going against the grain. Once a slur for sexual minorities, "queer" has become an umbrella term used across the diverse identities of lesbian, gay, bisexual, transgender, intersex, asexual, demisexual, non-binary, kink, and others who find themselves outside the bounds of the gender binary and straightlaced heteronormative categories. Given this meaning, it makes sense that queer folk, whose self-understanding puts them outside standard categories of gender and sexuality, would find flourishing in ways different from those of other people.

This book promotes queer flourishing by helping you bring to life more of yourself. The unconventional—yes, queer—structure of this book cuts across genres. Besides my developmental autobiography, especially the still-unfolding story of my gender and sexual orientation, you will at various moments see the scholar in me step forward to explain some bits of research or theory. You will also explore others' queer developmental journeys, depicted in film, stage plays, (auto)fiction, and autobiographies. Friends and advisors from the publishing industry advised me that this queer mix of material surpasses the bounds of what a book is *supposed* to contain. One veteran editor suggested I start over and write a self-help book called *The Ten Superpowers that Every Gay Man Needs to Flourish*. Since, as far as I can tell, there is no clever trick or hack that leads to queer flourishing, I left aside that suggestion. Though I began Flourishing Gays with a focus on gay, bi, and queer men, I have increasingly come to see that these patterns and postures that I call superpowers have profound relevance to many people's developmental journeys, across all gender identities and sexual orientations.

Instead of some slick "how to" manual, I've written this book to be read as if you were on retreat. In these pages, we part from the hustle and bustle. We take time to be more fully present to ourselves and each other. Like a retreat director, I will talk about my personal experience, because it's the truth I'm best suited to tell. In doing so I mean to model vulnerability, self-awareness, and self-compassion so that you can try out these practices for yourself. The questions I pose are intended to nourish and open you to new perspectives on yourself, your life, and your relationships. The queer mix you will find in these pages aims to come at you in different ways and on different levels.

As you read, you will be asked to open your heart and mind, employing your imagination and memory. You will also be asked to attend to specific developmental mindsets. We start with a focus on the **Expert** mind because I expect it to be the easiest for you to notice in yourself. Then we move into the other two conventional stages, the **Conformist** and **Achiever** mindsets before moving onto **Redefining**, the first of the post-conventional stages. Because the shift into later mindsets entails acknowledging our smaller selves and our **shadow** sides, we will then look back at the pre-conventional stage of **Self-Protective Opportunist** before consideration of the post-conventional

> **Shadow:** Those attributes, desires, needs, and other parts of ourselves that we do not want to have and that most of the time we strive to avoid noticing or acknowledging are indeed in us. Pet peeves, that which especially bothers us in other people, typically point to our own shadow material. Instead of recognizing shadow material in ourselves, we tend to see and hate it in other people. See Glossary for further explanation.

Self-Transforming mind. As in life, some twists and turns might surprise you!

I hope this book facilitates this enlivening within you. If you feel disoriented or otherwise challenged by what you encounter, I urge patience, with yourself and with this process. If everything you encountered were already familiar, it might not bring to new life neglected, avoided, or unborn parts of you. Take it as it comes—or skip over and come back. Read it all in one go, or portion out sections for slower digestion. While queer flourishing takes serious work, hold yourself lightly. Indeed, a spirit of play and a sense of humor will serve you well along this journey.

While I trust you to follow the path through this book that best suits you, I do offer two suggestions: First, give yourself space and time to engage with the reflection questions that you find throughout the text. They will help you to grow and develop, rather than to just read *about* personal growth and development. Second, talk about what comes up here with others in your life. Even better, find someone else to read along with you so that you can share with each other the insights, questions, memories, and wonderings that capture your attention. We become ourselves in and through relationships, so solitary exploration of our inner world does not suffice. Connect with someone else as you make this retreat, or even make this retreat in community. Ask yourself: *Have I ever been on retreat? What would it take for me to make space for approaching this book as a retreat experience for the sake of my growth and development?*

Welcome to Queer Flourishing—a place where all the weird and wonderful parts of each of us can come alive!

Reflection Questions to Explore in Quiet or in Community

- *What previous understandings and models of human thriving and flourishing do you bring to your reading of* Queer Flourishing?
- *What previous understandings of "queer" do you bring with you?*
- *What has been your relationship to queerness, queer people, or queer culture up till now?*
- *What were the understandings that younger versions of yourself had for what it would mean for you to flourish? Consider yourself at a few different periods in your life, e.g., just before adolescence, when you were a teenager, and when you were in your early 20s, as well as any later ages or stages of life when your outlook differed significantly from your current one.*

Queer Superpowers of Inner Diversity and Inclusion

The concept of "queer superpowers" puts human development into a gay context as a process of increasing inner diversity and inclusion. To see how, first consider some of the weird and wonderful characters who populate the inner landscapes of gay, bi, and queer men. For example, we have the sissy kid that bullies pick on, the honor roll student with not a wrinkle in his pressed shirt, and some updated version of the gay "clone" who in the 1970s wore Converse, Levi's, and a white T-shirt. Each LGBTQ+ person draws on a collective store of capacities and stratagems to defend their inner landscape, and create safety for the varied parts and versions of themselves who dwell there and show up out in the world. For instance, the now famous power of **Gaydar**, enables us to recognize our queer kin. Carefully compartmentalized **Double Lives**, as a second example, empower some of us to enjoy the pleasures of freedom, while also honoring other values.

I call these capacities and stratagems "queer superpow-

> See Table 2 for an overview of all ten of the queer superpowers. Their names will be boldfaced throughout the book.

ers." They are postures and personality patterns that LGBTQ+ people commonly take on in the search for ever-greater flourishing. When LGBTQ+ people access their individual and collective memories, experiences, and models to support their learning and development, they sometimes grow these specific personal capacities for the purpose of self-nurturing. By consciously building and using a particular queer superpower during a certain period of our lives, we can save ourselves from some harm, gain strength, garner resources, win liberation. Each "queer superpower" amounts to an ingenious strategy for noticing, accepting, expanding, including, and loving ever more diverse and disparate aspects of what we are and what the world is. These postures and personality patterns serve as resources for rest, recovery, nourishment, and support to use along the arduous journey of personal growth. These way stations offer getaway vehicles from captivity, ladders out of holes, wings to soar above war zones.

Gay men and women; cis and transgender children, adolescents, and adults; bisexual, asexual, polyamorous, and other queer people have ingeniously created queer superpowers for themselves and to share with each other. Queer cultures pass on these powers and possibilities, from one generation to the next, with adaptive variations and innovations. While I expect the ten queer superpowers I highlight in this book to have special resonance for gay, bi, and queer men, I also expect that queer and straight readers across all gender identities will find resonance in these patterns and postures. However you identify in terms of your gender and sexuality, the ways your personal psychology and social identities have interacted with the expectations and dynamics in the dominant cultures where you live have evoked in you various ways of *coping*.

The queer superpowers make up a collective store of resources. Any given individual does not necessarily grow into or use all of them. Just as Alpine huts are situated at certain places in the terrain or points along the path, each queer superpower becomes available to us as a possible resource to use at a specific developmental stage. We access and activate queer superpowers as we can and as we need. Though the patterns and possibilities of these superpowers come to us in large part from queer peers, elders, and culture, the process of growing queer superpowers to protect and nurture ourselves occurs mostly subconsciously.

While I may be the first to describe these queer superpowers as such, I did not create them. Queer culture ingeniously evolved them, and queer individuals grew into them to better deal with life. These queer superpowers serve as handholds. Each demonstrates a specific response to adverse circumstances and difficult dynamics we experience at a particular developmental stage. The response accentuates and strengthens certain capacities proper to that stage to generate heroic possibilities and powers that help overcome the challenges at hand.

A metaphor used in the professional community of DEI practitioners regards marginalization as headwinds and privilege as tailwinds. That is to say that disadvantage or marginalization blows like headwinds, pushing against a person's forward movement as they try to advance, slowing the person down. On the other hand, earned and unearned advantages or privileges blow from behind like tailwinds, helping a person move forward faster along their path.

LGBTQ+ folks face particular headwinds and obstacles in life. The adverse conditions of bullying, shaming, gaslighting, and moral castigation—to name just a few examples—burden us with loads to carry and forces to push against. Yet if we can, we sprout tendrils to reach around the obstacles and pull ourselves forward on our paths against the force of the headwinds. This dynamic of responding adaptively to adversity accounts for LGBTQ+ folks finding these special strengths, skills, and abilities, which I am calling queer superpowers.

The limits each superpower imposes can save us from peril at certain times, but also trap us unwittingly. Excessive growth or hypertrophic development in particular capacities naturally creates imbalances that bring their own risks and problems. For example, **Gaydar,** that special power of queer recognition, can serve to help LGBTQ+ people to find our **Pride Tribe,** a group of queer peers with whom we experience belonging. The superpower of the **Pride Tribe** can save us from the dangers of loneliness, self-loathing, despair, and even self-destruction. If overused and overheld, however, **Pride Tribe** can limit us to insular lives, populated entirely by others who share our gender and sexual identity. Like so many superpowers in lore, queer superpowers present pitfalls as well as possibilities. The defenses we create to keep ourselves safe in the heteronormative world shield us so effectively that they help us not only dodge hurts but also, far too often, keep us from intimacy with others.

The powerful allure of these postures and patterns easily overtakes us, grips us, and holds us in place. Our own queer superpowers all too easily *over*power us, and take us in *their* hold instead of us holding them. When this happens, we partly lose sight of ourselves. Our sense of self fuses with the superpower such that we forget who we might be without it.

Extremely useful at certain points of the journey, they hold us back if we stop moving and make any one of these way stations into our primary residence.

Exploring these queer superpowers entails three main steps and numerous benefits. As a first step, just notice these queer superpower patterns and postures in yourself and others. Consider the ways they show up in your own life story. From there, use your new awareness to intentionally activate the superpower when it can help you. In equal measure, allow yourself to let go of these patterns and postures once they have served their purpose. In short, I hope to enable you to notice these patterns so that you can get a grip on them, rather than them having a grip on you. As you gain skill in using the superpower consciously and deliberately, begin to consciously sidestep the pitfalls that superpower presents. In sum, these three steps allow you to hold the superpower rather than be held in its clutches:

1. Notice the queer superpowers
2. Learn to activate and let go of them appropriately
3. Sidestep their pitfalls

Consciousness of the queer superpowers gives us a better sense of direction from one developmental stage to the next. They help us see more clearly the value and the costs of common coping mechanisms. They also give us greater appreciation for the struggles of queer people and for the solutions we come up with to handle our struggles.

The greatest benefit of exploring these queer superpowers, however, lies in gaining irreversible self-awareness. I hope you see aspects of yourself that you cannot unsee. The personal growth work that becomes possible thanks to exploring the queer superpowers starts precisely with this irreversible self-awareness. Once you notice yourself adopting these patterns, they will no longer be able to hold you in their grip without your noticing. The more we can see all the parts and personas, patterns and possibilities within ourselves, the better we can consciously integrate them and become more whole.

What you see about yourself might well generate in you some disconcerting or even profoundly disruptive dissatisfaction with your status quo. I aspire for this process to stir up an unshakeable impulse to reframe your life and begin to live it out differently—more fully, more consciously, more compassionately. I mean for this book to catalyze within you a process that goads you to seek, find, grasp, and hold your heart's desires—and thereby become yourself ever more fully.

Superpowers and Stages of Development

The queer superpowers generate new perspectives on the journey of adult development. In describing these patterns, I mean to enhance the available maps of the territory that we traverse in human development. As we consider how the queer superpowers fit into the sequence of developmental stages, notice the ever-increasing degree of inner diversity and inclusion. *The distinctions and realities that we see determine what we can integrate into ourselves.*

Please keep in mind that there is nothing intrinsic or inevitable about LGBTQ+ people using these characters and capacities. If somebody does use one or another queer superpower, it's a way to survive and increase personal strength. Each queer superpower also has its own cultural history, but those origins will not be our interest here. Instead, we will focus on increasing your awareness of the powers and pitfalls of these patterns to promote your greater human flourishing.

Let's start, for example, with the queer superpower of **Chameleonic Passing**. Imagine a sissy kid who *throws like a girl* and gets beaten up on the playground. Feeling disadvantaged in a world where the bigger kids threaten his basic needs for physical safety, the kid may practice imitating the other boys—how they walk, talk, and throw a ball. He may get so good at mimicking that his peers no longer see him as a sissy. He has accessed the queer superpower of **Chameleonic Passing**. Another kid in the same situation may not be so good at imitating, but might instead become keenly aware of the signs and signals that someone might bully him. He accesses a different superpower, the **Shield of Hypervigilance**. Still another kid might evade the playground altogether, taking refuge in the art studio or the theater or the nurse's office. Or, if his situation at home is as dangerously dire as his situation at school, he may make a **Great Escape** by running away, seeking a gay haven like the Castro or Hell's Kitchen.

These first three queer superpowers arise from a developmental mindset that focuses on meeting basic needs for safety in the face of danger. Threatened by harm, we focus on opportunities to gain advantage or to avoid disadvantage. The "diversity and inclusion" of our inner world, the very structure of our Self, expands to notice and handle power differences, hurts and goodies, tricks and tools for defense or offense. These are the kinds of realities that we start to *differentiate* out there in the world and *include* in how we make sense of it. Hence, these superpowers are associated with the **Self-Protective Opportunist** stage of adult development.

Eventually, our capacities for reading social signals grow into the ability to find our people, the social groups where we can belong and be safe. As the gay or queer kid grows up and the superpower of hypervigilance becomes more nuanced, it becomes **Gaydar**. Like magic glasses that make visible certain signs that straight people miss, **Gaydar** empowers LGBTQ+

people. It allows us to not only to find physical and social safety, but also to meet and select people who will accept, or at least not threaten us.

If we find groups where our queerness is welcomed and affirmed, we access the queer superpower of **Pride Tribe**. While allowing us simply to be ourselves, the **Pride Tribe** may also teach us particular ways to walk, talk, dress, or adorn our bodies. They teach us how to hook up or have sex, channeling our erotic desires and needs for intimacy through the important social groups onto which we have imprinted. They define what kinds of romantic relationships are acceptable and desirable.

By differentiating, noticing, including, and integrating within ourselves the norms and expectations of (certain) social groups, we learn to belong. As our inner diversity and inclusion expand to embrace these social rules and communal values, they reshape our inner landscape. As we become embedded in the social groups that come to matter to us, they change how we make sense of ourselves and our world. You might recognize this as part of the **Conformist** mindset, which is the beginning of **Socialized mind**.

Our keen attention to social groups may lead us to get especially good at embodying their norms, resulting in special affirmation and praise for our competence. This focus on the diversity and inclusion of special skills characterizes the second **Socialized** mindset, the **Expert**. The associated queer superpower is called **The Best Little Kid**, who follows the rules impeccably and excels at meeting expectations to gain status among peers and the authorities who matter most to him. If a boy, **The Best Little Kid** might build his biceps or sculpt his abs. He might perfect a sexual technique to earn a reputation as erotically extraordinary. He might do everything he can to live up to all his parents' dreams for their son.

Table 1: Developmental Mindsets and Queer Superpowers

Queer superpowers become possible in each developmental mindset

	Developmental mindset	Queer superpower
PRE-CONVENTIONAL STAGES	Self-Protective/ Opportunist	• Chameleonic Passing • The Shield of Hypervigilance • The Great Escape
CONVENTIONAL STAGES	Conformist	• Gaydar • Pride Tribe
	Expert	• The Best Little Kid
	Achiever	• The Queen • Double Life
POST-CONVENTIONAL STAGES	Re-defining Self-Transforming	• Second Adolescence • No One Left Behind

Each queer superpower has both strengths and pitfalls

FLOURISHINGGAYS.COM

This superpower might serve us well in junior high or high school, where accolades and recognition come in the form of making the honor roll or a varsity letter for sports performance. However, the **Best Little Kid** character does not automatically fade away with adulthood. Plenty of gay, bi, and queer men who populate corporate offices or do surgery or teach university courses continue to embody this queer superpower long after they have beards and own homes!

The same goes for all the queer superpowers we started to access earlier in life. They stay with us—take a hold of us—if we do not gain awareness and take a hold of them. As an example, remember the sissy kid who employed the queer superpower of **Chameleonic Passing**? Let's imagine that this kid, now a grown man, despises that sissy kid version of himself who used to *throw like a girl* and get beaten up on the playground. As an adult, he still may put a great deal of energy into hiding or suppressing this character that he holds within himself. He pushes his inner sissy down, lest that effeminate kid be seen. Indeed, he keeps this part of himself locked away so tightly that he himself has lost sight of his inner sissy. He hates that kid, but has also mostly forgotten the sissy locked up within himself, in some small inner compartment, a closet of shame and loathing.

By excluding and marginalizing his inner sissy, the man flattens and narrows himself. He might perform a gay version of toxic masculinity that avoids and degrades women, exaggerates his musculature with steroids and tight shirts, and headlines his online dating profile with the tagline "masc for masc." This inner suppression and demonization mirror the marginalization and exclusion of those who are different. **Chameleonic Passing**, the queer superpower that served him so well on the playground, has become a trap. Overholding this queer superpower beyond its time of usefulness, he loses himself, forgetting how to be genuine, authentic, and whole.

Pursuing and acquiring more specialized knowledge and skills while operating principally from the **Expert** mindset, the gay or queer person we are considering as an example gradually comes to formulate his own way of being himself. No longer does he look to his communities of belonging to define his values. No longer do their expectations or norms define him. While those social values and rules stay in him and remain available, he increasingly thinks for himself and acts on the basis of his own vision. You might recall the next stage of human development is called the **Achiever** because here a person's accomplishments become vital to their sense of self. The primary superpower at this stage is the **Queen**.

The **Queen**'s inner diversity sharpens to distinguish and appreciate the values he intentionally chose and defined for himself. Instead of the social group designing and structuring his inner landscape, the **Queen** begins to shape himself as he desires. He builds a honeycomb of internal compartments, wherein to sort and store the parts of life. In this way, he has access to more of himself, including both his feminine and masculine energies. The **Queen** embeds himself into his personal realm, which he rules according to his vision and decree. Compartmentalizing externally as the **Queen** does internally, the queer superpower of the **Double Life** enables some queer people to live out their vision and values by bifurcating how they show up in the world—sometimes straight, sometimes gay, here queer and there unquestionably normal.

As the person's inner diversity and inclusion embrace even more of his inner characters and contradictions, he gains greater appreciation for how context shapes him from moment to moment. He permits his inner child, whether a sissy kid or not, more light and air. No longer occupied so forcefully by his own worldview, he becomes conscious of how his inner landscape is populated with numerous and diverse versions of himself, which step forward in response to various circumstances. Indeed, he cooperates with the systems and contexts in which he finds himself to call forth different characters and resources that he holds within his increasingly complex self. The formerly firm self-definitions increasingly fall away or rise back up, depending on the situation. He experiments by putting himself in queer contexts and takes new risks with how to embody his gayness. He welcomes mistakes and learns from them. This looser, less rigid stance shakes up the meticulously managed realm of the **Queen** and loosens up her sometimes rigid rationality. The gay and queer parts of himself that were forced to stay small for the sake of conformity are now allowed their chance to grow up. As he lets more of himself come forward, he enjoys a **Second Adolescence,** the queer superpower of the **Redefining** stage.

In this more fluid and adaptive stage, he gains new powers and possibilities to shape and change the systems and contexts that in turn shape and change him. The **Redefining** mindset marks a deeper, more radical phase of **Self-Authoring**. In attending to and honoring the cast of inner characters who previously were marginalized, he might go beyond **Second Adolescence**, and access **No One Left Behind**, the last queer superpower we will discuss. This queer superpower goes back in time to perform inner search and rescue missions to the parts deep within the Self that are caught in a war zone or frozen in terror. With **No One Left Behind**, we heal traumas and make peace with the enemies within. This salvific superpower inaugurates the liberation of wounded versions of the Self from the inner closets where they have been imprisoned. The honeycomb of inner closets melts like warm wax. The captives are set free—among them demons and saints, scapegoats and wounded warriors, wise witches, passionate lovers, and cunning tricksters. This exponential expansion of inner diversity and inclusion increasingly peoples the inner landscape with a host of weird and wonderful characters. New learning multiplies and feels infinite. Though the developmental path leading to this stage has already encompassed many twists and turns, this point in the journey can feel like the very beginning of growth and change. Possibilities and powers proliferate more than ever. We gain greater perspective than ever on the developmental process itself, increasing our capacity to appreciate the gifts and limitations of all previous stages and mindsets. This is the beginning of the **Self-Transforming** stage.[23]

In later sections, we will explore each of these ten queer superpowers from various angles and in greater depth. Table 2 below provides an overview that highlights the heroic possibilities and powers as well as the pitfalls and shadow side of each queer superpower, plus the adverse circumstances that prompt its emergence. We will return to Table 2 in each section of the book, highlighting the group of queer superpowers that we focus on that section.

Table 2: The Queer Superpowers

Developmental Stage			Queer Superpower	Adverse Circumstances that prompt superpower's emergence
Self-Sovereign	Self-Protective Opportunist	1	Chameleonic Passing	» Social exclusion » Mocking » Bullying » Shaming » Moral condemnation » Shunning by family / friends » Violent attack
		2	Shield of Hypervigilance	
		3	The Great Escape	
Socialized	Conformist	4	Gaydar	» Cultural values » Gender expectations » Romantic & sexual norms of the straight mainstream » Religious & moral condemnation » Legal persecution
		5	Pride Tribe	
	Expert	6	The Best Little Kid	
Self-Authoring	Achiever	7	The Queen	» Strictures of societal expectations limit creative powers » Socialized cycle of approval-seeking forecloses possibility of greatness
		8	Double Life	
	Redefining	9	Second Adolescence	» Self-imposed limits caused by personal adaptations made earlier in life to survive and thrive » Distressful self-awareness of unintegrated parts of self
Self-Transforming		10	No One Left Behind	

Discovering Queer Superpowers

Description	Heroic Possibilities & Powers	Pitfalls & Shadow
» Adapt to fit wide range of settings	» Shape-shifting » Cloak of invisibility » Avoid unwanted attention » Allow others to imagine you're one of them	» Not being seen or known for who we are » Loneliness » Fusing with our masks and forgetting who we really are
» Early alert system for possible danger	» Prepared to freeze, flee, or fight for safety » Avoid attacks, traps, & ambushes	» Fear & anxiety flood out other emotions » Skittish withdrawal inhibits relationships » Difficulty trusting even the trustworthy
» Depart toxic or abusive life situation to find supportive context	» Muster the courage, creativity, and determination needed for liberation	» Leave behind the good and the bad alike » Change of scenery without inner growth or change – "Running to stand still" » Flee into the clutches of new abusers
» Sense others' queerness	» Tap into intuitive knowing » See people's hidden faces » Empathy for others' shame	» Delusions of queer grandeur, imagining LGBTQ+ folks as superior to straight people » Project own queerness onto others
» Membership in a queer social group	» Strength in solidarity » Self-confidence to cultivate and use atypical gifts	» Gay groupthink papers over personal uniqueness » False sense of superiority
» Meeting and surpassing social standards and expectations	» Achieve excellence » Gain admiration in society » Earn one's way out of shame	» Fitting in to move up, lose sense of self and own unique "weird & wonderful" traits » Trapped by society's definitions of success, e.g., wealth, high position, prestige, luxury, etc.
» Accept and exercise "divine right" to rule one's own realm	» Claim own power » Impervious self-possession » Regal stature and poise » Sharp rationality » Relentlessly strategic in pursuing own vision and goals	» Self-sufficiency limits love – It's lonely at the top » Steamroll over others » Compartmentalization keeps valuable inner resources inaccessible » Haughty overconfidence leaves others impressed but distant
» Bifurcate life into separate domains	» Create space for expression and cultivation of queer self » Honor suite of personal values despite contradicitons	» Split life mirrors splits in the self that limit personal integration » Self-control verges on fraud and deceit
» A controlled coming apart and re-forming of adult self	» Shed conventional version of self in favor of greater authenticity and self-expression » Capacity for experimentation, follwed by rapid iteration, learning, and growth » Creativity and originality, despite societal flak	» Perpetually lost and not found, dissolution of conventional self never resolves into new coherence » Regress back to conventional self
» Return to scenes of wounding, to heal and more fully integrate all parts of self	» Wholeness » Integration of hidden resources and vulnerabilities » Revivification of spiritual scars	» Without sufficient support, re-traumatization can occur

Table 3: Queer Superpowers of Socialized Mind

Developmental Stage			Queer Superpower	Adverse Circumstances that prompt superpower's emergence
Self-Sovereign	Self-Protective Opportunist	1	Chameleonic Passing	» Social exclusion » Mocking » Bullying » Shaming » Moral condemnation » Shunning by family / friends » Violent attack
		2	Shield of Hypervigilance	
		3	The Great Escape	
Socialized	Conformist	4	Gaydar	» Cultural values » Gender expectations » Romantic & sexual norms of the straight mainstream » Religious & moral condemnation » Legal persecution
		5	Pride Tribe	
	Expert	6	The Best Little Kid	
Self-Authoring	Achiever	7	The Queen	» Strictures of societal expectations limit creative powers » Socialized cycle of approval-seeking forecloses possibility of greatness
		8	Double Life	
	Redefining	9	Second Adolescence	» Self-imposed limits caused by personal adaptations made earlier in life to survive and thrive » Distressful self-awareness of unintegrated parts of self
Self-Transforming		10	No One Left Behind	

Discovering Queer Superpowers

Description	Heroic Possibilities & Powers	Pitfalls & Shadow
» Adapt to fit wide range of settings	» Shape-shifting » Cloak of invisibility » Avoid unwanted attention » Allow others to imagine you're one of them	» Not being seen or known for who we are » Loneliness » Fusing with our masks and forgetting who we really are
» Early alert system for possible danger	» Prepared to freeze, flee, or fight for safety » Avoid attacks, traps, & ambushes	» Fear & anxiety flood out other emotions » Skittish withdrawal inhibits relationships » Difficulty trusting even the trustworthy
» Depart toxic or abusive life situation to find supportive context	» Muster the courage, creativity, and determination needed for liberation	» Leave behind the good and the bad alike » Change of scenery without inner growth or change – "Running to stand still" » Flee into the clutches of new abusers
» Sense others' queerness	» Tap into intuitive knowing » See people's hidden faces » Empathy for others' shame	» Delusions of queer grandeur, imagining LGBTQ+ folks as superior to straight people » Project own queerness onto others
» Membership in a queer social group	» Strength in solidarity » Self-confidence to cultivate and use atypical gifts	» Gay groupthink papers over personal uniqueness » False sense of superiority
» Meeting and surpassing social standards and expectations	» Achieve excellence » Gain admiration in society » Earn one's way out of shame	» Fitting in to move up, lose sense of self and own unique "weird & wonderful" traits » Trapped by society's definitions of success, e.g., wealth, high position, prestige, luxury, etc.
» Accept and exercise "divine right" to rule one's own realm	» Claim own power » Impervious self-possession » Regal stature and poise » Sharp rationality » Relentlessly strategic in pursuing own vision and goals	» Self-sufficiency limits love – It's lonely at the top » Steamroll over others » Compartmentalization keeps valuable inner resources inaccessible » Haughty overconfidence leaves others impressed but distant
» Bifurcate life into separate domains	» Create space for expression and cultivation of queer self » Honor suite of personal values despite contradicitons	» Split life mirrors splits in the self that limit personal integration » Self-control verges on fraud and deceit
» A controlled coming apart and re-forming of adult self	» Shed conventional version of self in favor of greater authenticity and self-expression » Capacity for experimentation, follwed by rapid iteration, learning, and growth » Creativity and originality, despite societal flak	» Perpetually lost and not found, dissolution of conventional self never resolves into new coherence » Regress back to conventional self
» Return to scenes of wounding, to heal and more fully integrate all parts of self	» Wholeness » Integration of hidden resources and vulnerabilities » Revivification of spiritual scars	» Without sufficient support, re-traumatization can occur

CHAPTER 2:

Teenage Superpowers

Proud Distinction

- *What "badges of honor" do you remember mattering most to you in your teen years?*
- *Where in your life now do you see remnants of these early sources of proud distinction?*
- *Nowadays, where do you most scrupulously maintain exacting standards for performance or morality?*
- *Whose approval or admiration do you (still) seek through distinguishing yourself by your knowledge, skill, or accomplishment?*

The clients who find their way to me seeking coaching or leadership development have honed their skills for gaining distinction. They have learned how to succeed in a variety of realms—grades and graduations, professional positions and promotions, athletic competitions, and even winning hearts and charming beauties. In particular, the highly accomplished gay, bi, and queer men who come to Flourishing Gays with interest in the Heroes Journey program have typically succeeded in distinguishing themselves by their knowledge, skill, and expertise. Yet, despite so many successes in domains highly esteemed by society, they no longer find themselves jazzed by the accolades and approval they spent so many years to gain. They still know how to win, but these triumphs no longer mean as much to them as before. Achievement no longer satisfies. Recovering overachievers yearn for fulfillment.

Whatever your own saga of triumphs and failures, however you regard your own ranking in society, I wager you know that part of yourself that seeks know-how for the sheer, satisfying pleasure of winning admiring approval. When this part takes the lead in how we see and make sense of the world, we enter a specific developmental stage or mindset. We begin to step back and gain new perspectives on ourselves within our social setting. In other words, our consciousness rises out of our social contexts, and we look back at ourselves from new angles. *How do I measure up to the rest? Where do I stand in the eyes of others?*[24] This perspective can instigate a preoccupation with various kinds of self-comparison—hence, one name for this developmental stage: "**Self-Conscious.**" To gain a sense of self, we primarily look to others. We seek to *distinguish* ourselves from others within the groups to which we belong. The diversity of our inner landscape gains new *distinctions and gradations* by which everyone (especially ourselves!) is ranked in a meritocratic hierarchy.

> **Self-Conscious:** Another term used to refer to the Expert stage of meaning-making. See Glossary for further explanation of this and all other developmental stages.

Adhering scrupulously to the group's norms, we live according to a host of "shoulds" and "oughts" in pursuit of exacting standards for excellence in morality, efficiency, or other kinds of performance. We pay keen attention to how we measure up to our exacting standards. Preoccupied with doing things right, we grow in knowledge and skill. Indeed, know-how becomes our preoccupation. Hence, in addition to the term "**Self-Conscious**," researchers also refer to this stage of development as "**Expert**" mind, because from here we look at reality through the lens of expertise. In the lingo of adult development theory, our sense of self is fused with expertise, and we become "subject" to it.

We desperately need social groups at this stage, but we stand on their peripheries. From the margins, we ask the group's members to commend us for our special knowledge or skill. As a plea for attention, we might threaten to leave the group. We feel good and worthy when we are noticed for our capabilities and knowledge. Whereas just before this moment in our developmental journey we cared most about *belonging in* the group, with **Expert** mind our focus shifts to caring most about *standing out from* the group. In the polarity between diversity and inclusion, the balance tips away from needing inclusion and towards differentiation. Above all, we now value a kind of social diversity based on gradations of skill and knowledge.

This **Expert** mind plays a critical role in helping LGBTQ+ professionals learn to succeed in a world dominated by straight, white men. **Expert** mind gains technical prowess, savvy, and self-confidence that serve us very well in making our way in the world. Thanks to **Expert** mind, we build our character and marshal our resources to fortify and organize ourselves as we forge ahead into new adventures. Before ever embarking on any epic journey, **Expert** mind equips us to stand out even as we fit in. Some of us may even be "overachievers," who win great accolades, honors, and promotions thanks to excellence, diligence, and devotion to our craft.

*So, do you notice this mindset operating in yourself? If so, when did **Expert** mind first emerge in you? What moments epitomize the character of your **Expert** mind?* I think of my own **Expert** mind as "the Golden Boy." Let me describe the time in life when this mindset first emerged in me.

Darling of the Upperclassmen

As a high school freshman, I found myself taken in by a group of upperclassmen at Creighton Prep, the Jesuit boys' high school I attended in Omaha. This group included both boys and the girls they hung out with. They saw something special in me and told me as much in earnest, heartfelt conversations. Some of these exchanges took place during Prep's fabled Freshmen Retreat, which initiated each new class of boys into the Jesuit motto, "Men for Others." At Freshmen Retreat, we learned to practice introspection and vulnerable authenticity. The older boys who led the retreat became my friends and showed me what kind of Prep student I wanted to be.

Looking back from a developmental perspective, I see these upperclassmen as (very!) "important others" for me in those years. I use this phrase in a somewhat technical sense to refer to those whose approval and acceptance we desperately need. Besides holding leadership positions and high grade-point averages, they could dive deeply into emotional, relational, or intellectual topics. They could also get extremely silly. There were skits and choreographed gestures to go along with the songs we performed which inspired raucous laughter— particularly Don McLean's "Leader of the Band." None of us seemed to be having sex with anyone, but we rallied all our verbal aptitude and emotional savvy to parry back and forth with off-color jokes and witticisms. Almost never mean-spirited, our schoolboyish jokes received greater acclaim the dirtier they got!

When I was a freshman at Prep, my sister Carrie was a senior at her all-girls Catholic high school, and she too came separately to befriend these same Prep upperclassmen. For a few brief months before college life swept her up, our social groups merged. I relished these friendships and sharing them with my big sister, three years older. She had always been for me an "important other" on many levels, and for this brief time she became a social peer, which would not happen again until a decade later. Soon she moved out of our house into the dorms at Creighton University, where our parents, both of our grandfathers, and many others in our family had gone to study.

Before she and the Prep upperclassmen graduated, I was chosen to give a speech at an all-school assembly honoring our senior class. I, too, felt honored to stand up before everyone at my school to speak heartfelt words of gratitude and admiration for these older boys who had taken me in and taught me so much. Being asked to give this speech was an acknowledgement of how close I was to these older boys. With tears in my eyes and eloquent words on my lips, that moment at the podium made me feel proud, distinguished, special.

- *Does this story bring up any of your own experiences?*
- *In what social groups have you sought a special place of distinction, whether when younger or even now?*
- *How has this effort to distinguish yourself served you?*

Socializing

- *What communities of belonging and "important others" most influenced your values and worldview as you transitioned into adulthood?*
- *Who plays the role of "important others" in your life today?*

We started with the **Expert** mind, but the developmental stage just before that, called **Conformist** mind, marks the real beginning of a focus on socialization.[25] Often starting in early adolescence, in **Conformist** mind we focus above all on the art of belonging. Like all other stage transitions, the move into this mindset marks a tremendous expansion of our inner diversity and inclusion. We become more fully ourselves and more deeply human through learning from others more profoundly than ever before. For the first time, other people's perspectives come into our inner reality. With **Conformist** mind, we gain the capacity to take in others' points of view. We drop our shields enough, stop disguising enough, and stop escaping enough to at least notice and grasp the feelings, ideas, and expectations of others. As we become increasingly socialized, we plant and prune, shape and shift our inner landscape to *conform* to the values, expectations, and perspectives of society.

Above all we conform to the expectations of those we see as "important others," like those upperclassmen were for me when I was a high school freshman. Their perspectives we internalize. We come to see all else, including ourselves, through the filtering lenses of their external opinions, thoughts, and ways. We adopt their standards for what is good and right and correct. Our "important others" define propriety, desirability, what's cool, what's admirable. We come to belong to them to such an extent that our sense of self is theirs to shape. In the balance between diversity and inclusion, here in early socialization, we lean toward inclusion. Whereas the **Expert** seeks distinction, the **Conformist** learns how not to *make waves* in the groups to which we attach ourselves and our sense of self. Societal norms, especially as conveyed by our "important others," rule over our own needs, such that we become "socialized." We become included as true members of social groups for the first time in our lives. We learn how to operate in society. Through a restructuring of ourselves, we come to know how to think, talk, be, and act so as to fit in.

As noted previously, a feature of the queer **Conformist** mind that enjoys a reputation in mainstream culture is **Gaydar**, that "spidey sense" that LGBTQ+ folks have for sensing each other's shared differences. Among other things, **Gaydar** makes possible the so-called "cruising" in which a passersby's eye contact becomes a double take, then a wink or a flirty *hello*. **Gaydar** notices vague pronouns in casual stories of dates, queer classics on a bookshelf, and the campy irony of carefully curated holiday decorations on a colleague's desk. **Gaydar** *sees* where straight folks fly blind. When developed into a queer superpower, this ability to tune into an unseen dimension goes beyond sussing out other gay or queer folks in a crowd or at the office. The queer superpower of **Gaydar** grows out of the same needs as the **Shield of Hypervigilance** in a still earlier, pre-socialized stage. Our hypervigilance develops as a coping mechanism to deal with the hostility the world has towards our sexual differences. While the **Shield of Hypervigilance** leads us *away* from danger, **Gaydar** leads us *towards* our queer kin. **Gaydar** tunes us in to who might be like us and who might be safe for us. A queer superpower of the **Conformist** stage of development, **Gaydar** only becomes possible with socialization. **Gaydar** relies on a general capacity of the Conformist developmental stage, namely reading social cues.

The **Conformist's** capacity to read social cues creates a serious problem for queer people. The cultural programming that allows us into psychological adulthood conceals a poison pill. Even if we're fortunate enough to have parents who accept and affirm our gender and sexual identity, we cannot completely escape the ambient homophobia and transphobia of dominant society. Hollywood, Disney, the songs our parents and grandparents grew up listening to, and the canon of classic literature all hold up boy-girl, man-woman pairings as the ideal option for all. In becoming genuine members of society, we thus drink in the complex and sometimes subtle aversion, disapproval, and even disgust for gender nonconformity and same-sex love which permeate the societal waters in which we swim. Homophobia and transphobia enter into us along with all of the other social material from our "important others" and generate in us self-doubt and even self-loathing.

Counteracting this pervasive poisoning, the queer superpower of **Pride Tribe** develops in those LGBTQ+ folks whose queer identity finds strong reinforcement and amplification in an LGBTQ+ social group. Using our **Gaydar**, we find our way to others like ourselves. In the **Pride Tribe**, we find a social group that specifically affirms us in our queerness. **Pride Tribe** becomes our important others, who espouse values, expectations, and norms which give room for our gayness to grow. In the **Conformist** practice of selecting "important others" to latch onto, we imprint onto *some* whose gender identity and sexual orientation match our own. Whether we like them or not, admire them or not, or even know them personally or not, certain LGBTQ+ folks in the world get selected by us as important others.

Those upperclassmen who took me into their social group when I was a mere freshman provided a sense of belonging that mattered to me enormously at the time. They let me be one of them.

They taught me to be a certain kind of person. Though I was years younger, they gave me a sense of proud distinction, even superiority over peers my age. When those upperclassmen boys left Creighton Prep for college, I experienced the loss and loneliness of not being seen or known by my classmates as well as I had been by those older boys. I clung to the sense of specialness that they had given me. I sought to deepen friendships with boys my age who could join me in living up to the high standards my older friends had set. I seemed to be ready for and even need the kinds of friendships that I had had with those upperclassmen.

In retrospect, I can see that another affinity had also bound us, at least semi-consciously. Many of these upperclassmen ended up moving to Chicago after college and eventually coming out as gay. Before we even knew it about ourselves, our sexual difference had drawn us to each other. Some inchoate **Gaydar** seems to have brought us together. I see this group as my first **Pride Tribe**.

Jagged Development

- *In what areas have you bounded ahead in your personal growth and development?*
- *In what areas have you lagged behind?*
- *To what degree do you perceive this "**jagged development**" in your life journey?*

The art of fitting in, the essence of the **Conformist** stage of development, requires us to begin observing ourselves in our interactions with others. Before reaching

> **Jagged development:** a personal profile in which some capacities or aspects of the self are highly developed and others much less so. See Glossary for further explanation.

Socialized mind, we could not look at ourselves from a vantage point above the fray. With practice we build this capacity. Comparing living life to dancing on a dance floor, leadership experts Heifetz and Linsky call this perspective "getting on the balcony."[26] When we gain this capacity for taking perspective on ourselves, we become able to dance on the dance floor with our dance partners while simultaneously watching ourselves dance from up on the balcony.

Watching ourselves in this way allows us to learn how to belong and fit into society. Gradually we sharpen our awareness of how we measure up within the group. First, we master the art of belonging and lean into inclusion through conformity with the norms of our important others. Eventually, we start to lean away from inclusion and care most about the ranked diversity within the groups to which we belong. Some in the group measure up better than others. We start to see ourselves and everything else through the lens of social rank as merited by knowledge or skill. We seek to distinguish ourselves within our social groups and in the eyes of our important others. Thus emerges **Expert** mind. As we transition from **Conformist** to **Expert**, we shift our preference in the polarity between diversity and inclusion. We move from a preference for inclusion into a preference for a new kind of diversity—the diversity of social ranking.

Yet different parts of ourselves develop at different paces, some shooting ahead and others lagging behind. Development tends to be jagged. Like anyone else growing through these stages of development, LGBTQ+ kids internalize the social norms, standards, and expectations of the groups where they find belonging. At the same time, they also take into their inner landscape the schemata of sexism, racism, classism, and nationalism—plus transphobia and homophobia, as we have already seen. Keen pupils of social rankings at this **Expert** stage of development, queer kids precisely assess where they stand according to the valuation assigned by each of these social systems.

The result is a kind of "minority stress," a term that refers to the peculiar duress that people go through when their identity is categorically different from the identities of the larger community in which they live. It's context dependent, experienced uniquely by each individual in relation to their community. A Muslim family living in rural Georgia, a Black child adopted into a white family in Montana, or an immigrant from India starting a new life in Sacramento would all experience minority stress very differently. For those of us who discover ourselves to be different by dint of our gender identity and sexual orientation, minority stress plays out with its own particularities. For example, our parents, siblings, or most other relatives are typically straight. They do not share a common queer identity with us. The resulting confusion and alienation that a gay or gender-nonconforming kid might experience can thus differ significantly from experiences of minority stress where a kid shares a marginalized identity in common with their family.

From an **Expert** mindset, an LGBTQ+ person who feels deficient according to sexist and homophobic social structures experiences another type of minority stress. *I'm a girly boy in rural France. What can I do about it?* Or, *I have secret fantasies about both guys and girls. What if they find out?!* Or, *I'm Muslim, South Asian, a first-generation immigrant, and I'm a boy in London who likes other boys. How will I ever succeed and gain rank in this white, Christian-dominated, heterosexual society?* Unable to solve the problems of bigotry and rigid normativity, the queer person finds themselves caught in a bind. Their very sense of self places them low in the power structures and social rankings of society.

One way of handling this impossible situation is to compensate. *If I can't be straight, I'll instead be strong and muscular, or hip and artistic, or socially slick and elegant.* They sidestep the impasse between who they are and what society values by clambering up the social ranks in some other arena. While acquiring knowledge, skill, or expertise in whatever domain they choose in compensation for their perceived failures, they might simultaneously avoid or ignore areas of life related to the parts of their identity which society seems to despise. Maybe they avoid as much as possible all things sexual. Or they instead have plenty of sexual partners, but no substantive dating. Or perhaps they cut a smart figure in social circles, smooth and chic, but maintain an aloof distance. Or they may avoid social scenes altogether, keeping close to family and just a few intimate friends.

This dual dynamic of compensating by intensifying development in certain areas while neglecting or avoiding others makes for jagged development. As LGBTQ+ people, we often find ourselves amazing others with our prowess in some domains, while feeling shamefully inadequate in others. We marshal strengths and systematize ourselves to make up for what's missing. While this dynamic shows up for plenty of straight people, jagged development is particularly characteristic of queer developmental journeys.

I hope that you're beginning to wonder about jagged development in your own life journey. *What arenas of life have you avoided because you felt such a laggard there? What domains did your circumstances and talents lead you into in order to find ways to compensate for what felt inadequate?* To spur further reflection about how this has played out for you, allow me to tell you some of how it worked for me.

I Was Queer Before I Was Gay

The seeds of my own jagged development began to sprout long before I reached the **Expert** stage. As a child growing up in the Catholic and overwhelmingly white community of suburban Omaha, I wasn't sure if I was supposed to be different from the other kids. I had gathered that growing up could be difficult, and we're all trying to figure ourselves out and make sense of the world. *That's what growing up is, right?* I experienced my body with some wonder, especially when puberty began. Being a reader, I sought out books to help me find my bearings amidst the metamorphosis that was underway. It was likely Latin class where I learned that the word adolescence meant "the process of becoming adult." *So that's what was happening to me?* A dusty copy of *Everything You Always Wanted to Know about Sex, But Were Afraid to Ask* (1969) called to me from a shelf at my grandparents' house, in what had been my dad's and uncle's room, where I would sleep when I stayed there. Reading that book late at night, in my early teens in the late 1980s, gave me a 1960s view on topics that were of pressing interest, such as hormones, masturbation, and fancy words like "anilingus."

As near as I could tell, nobody in my family was gay, and I didn't know if I was either. I found girls my age intriguing, like a different species of human. But other boys my age also seemed quite different from me and were at times equally intriguing. There were sides to myself that none of the other boys seemed to have. I really wondered about myself. It wasn't exactly that I felt like anything was wrong with me. I just didn't get it. I was a mystery to myself, and my place in the world wasn't clear. *How do I fit into all this?*

I felt indelibly different, which created a persistent tension in my growing up. My difference pulled and stretched me and caused ever-present discomfort. Sometimes it was beneath the surface and visible only to me, and other times it showed up in ways that other children or adults could see. Some of the most salient aspects of my understory, my inner story, underlie this feeling of difference. My parents divorced when I was three, so for all the years I can remember, I came from a "broken family." That made me different from most kids, but plenty of others had divorced parents. More than divorce, it was my dad's mental illness that epitomized the brokenness that marked me as indelibly different. He suffered greatly throughout his adult life from conditions which modern sensibilities call emotional disturbance and mental illness. Agony and distortion characterized how he experienced himself and the world. His pain and his warped views of his parents, my mother, himself, and God all coated my body and my entire world like a gloppy though invisible paint—heavy, ever-present, irreducible.

In response to so much adult stuff, I retreated to my books. I had inherited this habit from my parents, who were both quite bright, especially when it came to words. I found a refuge from the hard stuff in my family life within the pages of stories of Dr. Doolittle or Encyclopedia Brown, or a volume of the encyclopedia pulled off our kitchen bookshelf. While reading, I could be a boy. I could return to the fantasy land of feckless childhood.

This retreat into my thoughts and imagination proved one of my most effective, even lifesaving, strategies to survive childhood and to thrive the best I could in my given circumstances. I constructed an inner asylum, an ivory tower in my mind, where I could find both safety and self-worth. With time, the precociousness of my intellect became yet another reason for feeling different. I remember this precociousness showing up when my mother was still in law school, before I even reached age 8. Her law school friends would come over to our house to study and socialize. I felt at ease and enjoyed talking with them. They seemed to find me fun and interesting, this little boy who could talk like a much bigger kid. I followed Mom's work life with great interest as she graduated from law school, clerked for a federal judge, and became an associate at a local law firm. I came to know something about lawyering by asking her lots of questions about what she did, and I learned words like "briefs," "torts," "depositions," and "case law." The ways I could use words, ask questions, and understand concepts accentuated my difference from most kids. I seemed to grasp some aspects of the adult world more easily than I did fitting in with classmates, which did not come easy. At the time I didn't know why.

I was "queer" before I was gay. My sexual difference, as I came to understand it later in my teenage years, overlaid these foundational differences, but my childhood queerness had nothing to do with sex, gender, or the erotic. My dad's difference from other parents and my mind's difference from those of other kids marked my entire archive of experience. These differences are what made me queer, at odds with prevailing norms. Branded by these marks that I did not choose for myself, I struggled to find my place, my people, my path.

With my emerging **Expert** mind, I endeavored to compensate for my queerness by distinguishing myself from the herd through accomplishment in academics, sports, and emotional maturity. By the time I got to high school, my precociousness with language and certain kinds of social interactions fit nicely into a newfound excitement for gaining knowledge and skills. Studying languages, leading as class president, and competing in speech and debate captured my attention and whetted my appetite. What flourishing most meant to me at this stage was gaining recognition and distinction for what I could do. Thanks to the holistic approach of Jesuit education, the all-boys college prep school where I studied as a teenager also fostered emotional and interpersonal skills and capacities that had been ungraspable for me earlier in life. Though my mother had always encouraged, even goaded, my older sister and me to talk about our feelings, somehow at Creighton Prep I came to do that in newly meaningful ways.

That's some of the story of jagged development in my life. *How has it shown up in yours?*

The Best Little Kid

- *In what circumstances are you most tempted to try to live up to—or even surpass—everyone else's expectations?*

One particular form of jagged development demands our special attention. We shall refer to this special case as the **Best Little Kid**, the queer superpower of **Expert** mind. The **Best Little Kid** has been a star student of socialization. He strives diligently and with remarkable discipline to surpass societal expectations wherever possible. His gifts, talents, and self-discipline win him ever more accomplishments, which continually impress his peers as he moves through adulthood. He ascends to the highest rank in some domain, a field marshal of social distinction. The **Best Little Kid** so excels at excelling that he deservedly earns the title of queer superhero.

This pattern, this mold that we're calling the **Best Little Kid** undoubtedly emerges in kids of all genders, yet the person's position in the gender hierarchy makes a big difference. Queer superpowers express differently for cisgender boys and men than for girls and women or trans or non-binary folks.

Because of my own identity and experience, I'm best positioned to depict this and the other queer superpowers as they manifest in cisgender boys and men. I hope you can in any case recognize how they show up in you.

This queer superpower serves up success in generous portions. The **Best Little Kid** might excel in any number of arenas, depending on his talent and the opportunities that present themselves. He might become the teacher's pet, following all the school rules and completing every assignment flawlessly. He might absorb all the niceties of pop culture, from the most stylish brands, cuts, and colors of clothing to the intricacies of some music scene's bands, albums, and celebrities. He might find his tribe among the theater kids and win leading roles in the school plays and local theater. He might excel in athletics, earning varsity letters and building the perfect body. Whatever the arena, the **Best Little Kid** relentlessly and religiously pursues merit and distinction. Applying himself with great focus, he might even earn the moniker of "prodigy."

Though the **Best Little Kid** might excel in any social setting, if positioned among important others who value academic and professional achievement, he might get into the best law school, become a summer associate at the swankiest law firm, and then make partner in record time. He might win a Fulbright, a Marshall, a Rhodes, and do his doctorate under the tutelage of the leading experts at one of the poshest universities. Whatever the prestige, wealth, or accomplishment, beneath the mask hides a scared little queer kid, terrified of being found out and then kicked out of the good graces of the world. Always precarious, ever under threat, the **Best Little Kid** endlessly strives to flee his fears.

A niggling realization nags at every turn: *I'm not enough! Damaged goods. Tainted. Irredeemably flawed.* The power of his drive to excel matches the power of his fears. Pointed in opposite directions, one towards merited vaunting and the other towards degraded rejection, these powers create in the **Best Little Kid** a jagged personal development with precipitous summits and deep dark valleys.

This dynamic of striving to get ahead academically, athletically, culturally, financially, or otherwise to make up for lagging in the competition for social merit can continue well beyond young adult years. Some rising gay professionals of Silicon Valley in the Bay Area, for example, or in Hell's Kitchen in Manhattan, epitomize this dynamic. Embodying the "scripts" prescribed by corporate gay culture, they buy their homewares at the right shop, their fine leather tote bags from the right brand, and frequent the right bars and parties, where the *best* people mingle and congratulate each other. They may insatiably create Instagrammable moments that demonstrate over and over just how perfect their abs, or how exotic the waterfall hike, or how impressive the assembled ensemble of fashionable faces.

So many shiny gays perform all the clichés flawlessly, yet are secretly exhausted by the hidden labor involved in desperately evading their fear of not measuring up and constantly struggling to acquire approval. Indeed, desperation tinges the promotions and social media accomplishments, whether tallied in bonus sums or Instagram followers.

I'm accentuating the downside of the dual dynamic of the **Best Little Kid's** jagged development to counterbalance the mainstream approval that this queer superpower wins for those who wield it. Yet, the **Best Little Kid** truly gains much from this particular pathway for coping with homophobia, both internalized and out in the world. Unlike many straight men at this stage, a gay man with the **Best Little Kid** superpower may have developed a more astute capacity to "read the room" and sense interpersonal dynamics among people. Building on earlier practice with the **Shield of Hypervigilance** and the "spidey sense" of **Gaydar** to anticipate imminent danger and find safety, the gay, bi, or queer man at this stage starts to see more layers in the drives, desires, and personalities of those around him. This inchoate awareness stays for now at a relatively unnuanced level, however, since from **Expert** mind a person has rather limited access to interior dynamics, whether his own or other people's.

In the language I use to talk about the Heroes Journey program, I say that it is custom-made leadership development for "highly accomplished" gay, bi, and queer men. I use this phrase to appeal to recovering overachievers who have long acted as **Best Little Boys,** whose self-worth is fused with achievement well into middle age. *I am my work. I am my wealth. I am my posh address. I am my knowledge and expertise.* It can be very hard to let go of this pursuit of approbation and admiration, even when it becomes exhausting. Yet as my clients gradually put their **Best Little Boy** into retirement, they find that greater, more expansive varieties of excellence become available.

A Dutiful Boy

Let me move beyond my own Italian-American, Catholic, Midwestern single-parent family context so that you might more easily locate your own relationship to the **Best Little Kid**. Let's consider how this queer superpower shows up in other times, places, and cultural milieus. In *A Dutiful Boy: A Memoir of a Gay Muslim's Journey to Acceptance* (2020), Mohsin Zaidi tells his story of striving and coping as an immigrant boy growing up in London with brown skin and Pakistani heritage. Zaidi's memoir appeals greatly to me, and not only because he and I became friends years ago when we both lived in Boston. His narrative also reveals the texture of both plight and promise in the developmental journey of someone who at times embodied the **Best Little Kid** queer superpower. For example, having earned a place in a competitive high school, he found himself in "[a]n environment heaving with competition, and with the unwavering focus on getting into a top university."[27] When Mohsin's form tutor asked a group of students which university in "the Russell Group" he would be applying for, Mohsin mumbled in reply that he didn't know, without admitting that he had never heard of this group of the most prestigious research universities in the UK. While in his previous school, Mohsin watched what he said so as not to sound too clever, now at this new school he "feared being ridiculed for saying something stupid."[28] His new peers looked ahead with ambition, by considering how their decisions as teenagers would affect their futures. For Zaidi as a young Muslim, ambition "seemed more important than ever," perhaps as a way to earn the respect and dignity that on some level he always knew he deserved, regardless of accomplishments.

With time, Mohsin learns the ins and outs of elite academics in the UK and studies law at Oxford. As he climbs the ladder of the British class system without the boosts of wealth or white privilege, he develops an ambition, especially by using his legal training in the fight for social justice. Along the way, however, his drive and discipline sometimes waver. In an interview for a prestigious placement at the Supreme Court, his interviewers ask about this:

> "Last question," said one of the two judges on the other side of the desk. . . .
>
> "Why didn't you get a first at university? I'm asking because your CV is strong but this is a competitive process and I want to give you the chance to elaborate."

The question caught me completely off guard, although I should have expected it.²⁹

He responds, "[H]onestly, I think it was a question of attitude rather than ability." While keenly aware of his struggles and experiences of social marginalization as a gay, British, Muslim man of South Asian descent living in London, he finds a way in this interview to refer to these complexities honestly but obliquely, while also claiming his aptitude. He avoids drawing attention to his social identities and family history, which did not confer privilege but rather posed challenges. He hoped the judges would recognize how different and difficult his road to the higher echelons of the British legal system had been, especially compared to white, Christian, upper-class, non-immigrant applicants. "The road had been bumpy, but I didn't say any of that." Beyond his unique talents, personality, and life choices, Mohsin's relative rank in social hierarchies and his multiple social identities affected his way of living out the **Best Little Kid** paradigm.

The Best Little Boy in the World

The name for this queer superpower pays homage to Andrew Tobias's memoir *The Best Little Boy in the World* (which he abbreviates as the BLBITW). Coming a generation or more later, Mohsin Zaidi's *A Dutiful Son* demonstrates the enduring relevance today of the **Best Little Boy**. Though Tobias grew up white in the United States decades earlier, his narrative voice and Zaidi's resonate strongly. In describing his career path, Tobias reveals how the Best Little Boy thought about fitting in through prestige. For example, he applied to Harvard Business School, not out of any desire to become a businessman, but rather. . .

because law school sounded like too much work and medical school was out of the question. I knew a lot of my friends from Yale would be up around Boston, so there would be ample supply of people to idolize. And a Harvard MBA was the kind of thing you would expect the BLBITW to have. What could be straighter than a Harvard MBA? Or more dull, maybe, but we all have to make compromises.[30]

Though accepted into Harvard, the BLBITW also received a job offer from IBM which tempted him greatly. "An office with a view of Manhattan, half a secretary, and lots of money. It sounded like a shortcut in my rat race to remain the best little boy in the world." Besides a shortcut to successfully staying on top, the BLBITW liked how safe the corporate job seemed. He got a jump on his peers by ascending the corporate ladder while they did grad school. "The BLBITW was indeed the youngest to rise the fastest to the mostest ever."

The secret to his success? It was "sublimating my sexual energy into my work," as he had long been doing before then. Tobias writes more ironically, with tongue in cheek, compared to Zaidi's more sincere and heartfelt tone. Yet, both similarly seek and find pathways to "remain" *the best little boy in the world*, a role the narrator here had apparently been playing already for years. Both find safety in seeming normal and earning accolades: "What could be straighter than a Harvard MBA?"

Both Zaidi and Tobias also reveal their fears and insecurities. In one passage, Tobias directly confesses his sense of himself as an imposter. With all of his "shining performances," he never really felt adequate. The feeling went far beyond embarrassment.

"It was the basic understanding—that sick, guilty feeling in the deepest recesses of my psyche—that I was a phony. I was *not* the best little boy in the world as my parents thought." Acting polite fit into the BLBITW's persona. However, ...

> it was for the wrong reasons. I was not polite because I loved other people or was considerate or believed in the Golden Rule, or any of that other crap. I was a goody-goody because it was the proven road to reward. It was the way to play the game. . . . And deep down, I knew I wasn't "good" at all—just selfish, just out for myself.[31]

Written almost 50 years before *A Dutiful Boy*, Tobias's account has less texture of intersectional identities than Zaidi's, but includes more humor, which serves to keep things light.

But in the final sections of *The Best Little Boy in the World*, Tobias drops the defensive humor in favor of a sober and almost sentimental confession. When he first published the book, Tobias did so pseudonymously, with the pen name John Reid. In an epigraph, he recognizes a contradiction in doing so. The book, by his account, is all about "owning up to one's true identity." However, he says using the fake pen name "is the least I can do for my parents, who have done a great deal for me." In an ideal world, a pen name wouldn't be necessary. "But, then again, ideally there would be no reason to write a book like this at all."[32] Not yet out to his parents for almost the entire narrative, Tobias chronicles his awkward odyssey of coming out and coming into his own. The very last chapter of the book consists of two sentences: "I told them. They said that so far as they were concerned, I was still the best little boy in the world."[33]

The account throughout Tobias's memoir of how he played straight and earned respect through accomplishments follows his awkward, endearing, and often confused attempts to come into his own as a gay man. Running away and running towards his sexual identity simultaneously, this Best Little Boy in the World fears what shame or calumny his gayness might bring upon his parents, "who have done a great deal for [him]." This final chapter in which he reveals their enduring love for and even pride in him moves me. I confess that Tobias's account of how his parents still consider him the best little boy in the world brings tears to my eyes every time I read it or tell someone else about it. The poignancy comes not only from the resonance with my own efforts to be the **Best Little Kid** but from the apparent needlessness of the narrator's running away from himself, with his years-long pseudonymity.

The pseudonymous narrator of Andrew Tobias as John Reid in *The Best Little Boy in the World* (1973) and Mohsin Zaidi in *A Dutiful Son* (2020), both portray themselves with humility and vulnerability. These two memoirs bring to life this queer superpower of the **Expert** stage and illustrate how the **Best Little Kid** shows up in two different cultural and historical contexts. The compassionate distance from which both authors describe their younger selves bespeaks a more mature, later stage perspective, no longer operating from an **Expert** mindset. *As you make your way from their examples to mine to your own, how easy or hard is it for you to regard your own* **Best Little Kid** *with compassionate distance?*

Naming the Golden Boy

My **Best Little Kid** began to emerge when I started high school. On the first day of class at Prep, each teacher read out my name from their class roster as "Fred Longo." Outed as "Fred," I felt mortified! Besides all of my Dad's weirdness, which no one in the class knew about, that name sounded so old-fashioned! "Nick," I insisted, "not Fred." In French class that day, Fr. Brennan negotiated with each student to choose a French name. Thinking my nickname came from "Nicholas," Fr. Brennan offered that in a French pronunciation as a name for me. "But no, I'm Fred Dominic," I objected. "*Dominique, alors!*" he exclaimed. From then on, in French class, my teachers and classmates called me Dominique.

I soon found my way to the secretaries at the school's front office and announced that I needed to change my name on school records. They directed me to the assistant principal, who was bemused by my consternation at being called by my legal first name. He ended up changing the school records so that what teachers would see on their class rosters was "F. Dominic 'Nick' Longo," rather than "Fred D. Longo." I felt relieved at this administrative accomplishment, even if the result seemed a bit stilted and technical. A symbolically significant step in the direction of becoming my own person, this renaming christened the golden boy version of myself, my own **Best Little Kid**. Soon enough, teachers would know me without needing to rely on the class roster.

A Developmental Companion

At Prep, neither my smarts nor my single-parent family structure seemed so queer as before. I left behind the parochial life of St. James/Seton, the parish school where I had spent first through eighth grades. My father's eccentricity faded from view, as years passed without my seeing him at all. Among the teachers and Jesuits at Creighton Prep, I found many of the father figures that Mom had always wanted me to have. Among my classmates in this all-boys, college preparatory school that drew students from all over the city, I found peers with smarts and one-parent families like mine.

Most important of these, my friend Rob companioned me in high school and college, and still to this day remains a close friend. Without any doubt, he became an "important other" who influenced my values, my outlook, and my sense of what life could be. Like me, Rob's parents were divorced, and he grew up living with his mom and his older sister. Thanks to the practice we each got at home, both of us appreciated and befriended girls easily. We enjoyed talking with them about subjects we found meaningful, such as drinking (Rob and I didn't drink while in high school, though the cool kids did), the Catholic Church (he respected it, while I was part of it), and sex (he was having it, while I was waiting).

We also both possessed a certain facility with emotional expression, a capacity that Prep cultivated in us, especially through the spiritual retreats that Rob and I took part in and led throughout our high school years. This facility with emotion may well have been the most feminine quality that Rob and I shared. Supporting each other's growth into the kind of man we each hoped to be, we confided in each other about experiences of delight, overwhelm, disappointment, frustration, confusion, and yearning. We heard and amplified each other's dreams and aspirations. We created safe and tender space for each other's tears and hurts.

Joe Prep

Rob and I, and other friends, adopted an orientation towards service and made expressing our emotions an integral part of our masculinity. We earnestly embodied the Jesuit motto "Men for Others," in part by mentoring younger Prep students, as those upperclassmen who had taken me into their social group had done for me. Some of us played sports, others did theater, all of us took part in campus ministry. We led retreats and sang in the liturgical choir. Alongside overloading my schedule with advanced placement courses, I became involved in so many extracurriculars that listing them all now feels too laborious to undertake. My friends and I strived to earn the highest grades possible and gloried in the approbation we received from both parents and teachers for our academic successes.

The achievement that went most to my head was not the high grades or varsity letters, but being elected class president sophomore and junior years. I was also secretly proud of how trusted I was by teachers and Jesuits. I could show up in the evening and ring the room of the Jesuit brother who was dean of students and lived in the residence adjacent to the school building. He would give me the keys to let myself into the physics lab where I would use the Macintosh computers for homework as late as I needed. The trust of the Jesuits and the election by my classmates meant so much to me because they reinforced my sense of self as special.

Seeing myself as particularly smart, particularly mature, particularly athletic, and particularly known for being a "good boy," I enjoyed a (not so) secretly smug sense of superiority. I didn't want or need to fit in so much as I wanted to lean into shining bright. To a large extent, my friends and I defined ourselves over against the more mainstream kids.

We congratulated ourselves on our academic achievements, the depth of our conversations and relationships, and our moral virtue. We fit in with each other by not needing to fit in with the more popular kids who seemed to us much less self-aware. We especially looked down on them for drinking, which we rejected on moral grounds and with highly judgmental accounts of how and why it was better not to drink as teenagers. I prided myself on my positive contributions to these conversations and to the moral fiber of our friend group. I knew what was right, and I lived up to it. The praise and grades and prizes that came to me from the world in which I lived reinforced this superior self-image.

In these high school years, I was developing my **Expert** form of mind and accessing the **Best Little Kid** queer superpower. Indeed, being a **Best Little Boy** gave me a sense of self in these years. It covered over the strangeness, the queerness, that lay beneath the surface. I spent a great deal of energy in those years fitting in as a stand-out, a superlative Prep boy, epitomizing all the school's stated and unstated values as best I could. In this effort, which kept me up studying late even after hours of practice with the track or gymnastics team, I tried to draw attention away from the misfit inside me, the parts of me that felt socially sluggish, awkward, and off-balance. It's not that the golden boy role that I played so well was a false ruse. Rather, as a golden boy, as the **Best Little Boy**, I played up certain parts of myself so as to downplay other parts.

By no means am I claiming to have "graduated" from the **Expert** form of mind when I got my high school diploma! Rather, in these years I first felt the pleasure of receiving approval from "important others" for my prowess, standing out from the crowd through my scholastic and other accomplishments. I constructed a version of myself in the **Best Little Kid** mold naturally and rather unwittingly. While inhabiting this version of myself, I had very limited capacity to see that I was so fully relying on my abilities, knowledge, and skills to construct a sense of self.

- *How about you? In what parts of your life have you found your sense of self fused with your knowledge or skillfulness?*

School Mind

- *What is your mental model of personal growth?*
- *How do you envision the process of personal development proceeding?*

Our years in formal education teach us much more than reading, writing, and arithmetic. School teaches us how to behave, how to be, even who to be. For anyone who spends years studying in educational institutions—most likely anyone who has this book in their hands—school shapes our conception of the very nature of personal growth and development. This understanding stays with us long after graduation. Let's call this attitude "school mind." Societies design schooling to initiate us into society, in other words, to cultivate **Socialized** mind in us, and school mind makes part of that **Socialized** form of consciousness. The stories I have been sharing of my high school experience illustrate how this process played out in me.

Let's take a step back now and recognize that the way we conceptualize personal growth and development depends on which developmental mindset we are using at the time. School mind shows up for some business owners and other organizational leaders who come to me for help with leadership development or diversity, equity, inclusion, and belonging initiatives.

When school mind predominates, they approach me as a trainer. In other words, they regard me as someone who will impart knowledge and skills to them and their colleagues. Similarly, the straight and gay folks who come to me for executive coaching, and the gay, bi, and queer men who express interest in the Heroes Journey program often bring a scholastic mental model for the learning and growth that they seek.

It's no surprise that so many show up with this understanding of personal growth and development, since the skill-oriented **Expert** mindset appears as the most common developmental stage among adults. According to a study by researcher Susanne Cook-Greuter (reflected in the last column of the following table), 37 percent of a group of more than 4,500 participants aged 18–82 predominantly operate from an **Expert** form of mind.

Table 4: Developmental Stages as Named by Researchers[34]

Stage Number	Names of Developmental Stages, by researcher					Portion of population aged 18-82, n=4510 (Cook-Greuter, 1999)
	Global Leadership Associates (2020) *Levels of Leadership Development*	Susanne Cook-Greuter (2013) *Ego Development Stage*	William Torbert (2005) *Action Logic*	Jennifer Garvey Berger (2012) *Stage of Mind*	Robert Kegan (1982) *Order of Consciousness*	
2	N/A	Impulsive	Impulsive	Self-Sovereign	Imperial Self	4%
2/3	Opportunist	Self-Defensive or Self-Protective	Opportunist			
3	Diplomat	Conformist	Diplomat	Socialized	Interpersonal Self	11%
3/4	Expert	Self-Conscious	Expert/ Technician			37%
4	Achiever	Conscientious	Achiever	Self-Authored	Institutional Self	30%
4/5	Redefining	Individualist	Individualist			11%
5	Transforming	Autonomous	Strategist	Self-Transforming	Inter-Individual Self	5%
5/6	Alchemical	Construct-Aware/ Ego-Aware	Alchemist			2%

Based on these data, for most people, adult development pertains to moving towards and into the **Achiever** (4) stage, at which Cook-Greuter's research puts another 30 percent of adults. These figures help explain why, when we look around the LGBTQ+ community, we see so many **Best Little Kids**.

How We See Adult Development Depends on Our Mindset

The prevalence of the **Expert** form of mind might also play into your own most conscious motivations for picking up this book. You might be looking to grow as a leader and flourish as a human being, so you delve into reading a book by an author who claims expertise in such endeavors. Perhaps as you have been reading and as you now take in the data in Table 4, you have noticed yourself wondering what stage you are in. Indeed, I present this information in this form in order to activate your **Expert** mind. Is it working?

Try to stand back and locate that part of yourself which sees the stages as a hierarchy. *Do you wonder where you stack up in the rankings or how quickly you can move up the scale?* Notice how on some level you may have been comparing yourself to other people in your life. Maybe you've been wondering about the developmental stage of your partner or your parents or that colleague who got the promotion that really should have been yours!

Perhaps you find yourself thinking of personal growth and development as like an academic degree program. Adult development theory can admittedly give the impression that stages are indeed like educational grade levels. After all, this theory relates to capability building, maturation, and growing up. The sequence of stages is most easily represented and summarized in a progressive linear series or a table with columns and rows demarcated by clean lines (as in Table 4). We might even imagine that stages take equal portions of time (like semesters) during which we work on growing in different areas (like studying various subjects). *Each area probably comprises daily lessons and skills practice, punctuated by tests, which we can pass or fail, right?* School, after all, progresses in a linear fashion (onwards and upwards!) towards a goal (graduation) through a set of modular units. While some exceptional students do skip or repeat grade levels, most students spend the same single calendar year in a grade before moving on. Each student receives higher or lower marks to assess their mastery of curricular material, but so long as they are good enough, they advance in the educational system. In human development, *we should aim towards making it to the end, or at least go as far as possible, right? Later stages must be better than earlier stages, right?*

These ways of looking at personal development come from an **Expert** form of mind. Nothing wrong with these perspectives! Indeed, the theory lends itself to attending to rankings and comparisons. The notion of a sequence of stages can naturally instigate a desire to progress. At the same time, these perspectives have limitations that obscure important aspects of our own and other people's development journeys. By offering a few alternatives to these **Expert**-mind perspectives on human development, I mean to help you more clearly locate the **Expert** mind within yourself and better understand adult development theory more broadly.

Most crucially, let's remember that *developmental stages describe theoretical paradigms, not anyone's actual meaning-making.* As mentioned previously, in order to match the range of terms used by researchers, throughout this book I use the phrase "developmental stage" more or less synonymously with "mind," "form of mind," "structure of mind," and at times "mindset" and "self." Other terms used in the research literature for paradigmatic ways of making meaning include "action logic" (especially by Torbert) and "order of consciousness" (especially by Kegan).[35] The stages are numbered by convention used by researchers and theorists in this field, who apply their own various labels to each stage. (Aside from this section, we will omit the numbers in favor of the stage names.) For example, Kegan in his later work labels them **Self-Sovereign** (2), **Socialized** (3), **Self-Authoring** (4), **and Self-Transforming** (5). Cook-Greuter and others describe an additional stage after Kegan's sequence, which they label as Post-Autonomous or Unitive (6). The use of larger numbers for later stages conveys that these paradigmatic "stages" of human development map increasingly expansive levels of consciousness. In other words, at each later developmental stage, our capacities for perceiving reality and making sense of its complexity grow larger.

Each paradigmatic stage also marks some preference between the poles of autonomy and belonging, differentiation and integration, diversity and inclusion. While growth demands both independence *and* connectedness, diversity *and* inclusion, at various times we seem to favor one pole over the other. In other words, our main developmental work always seems to lie on one side or the other of this polarity, and we are ever creating what Kegan calls a new "evolutionary truce" between the two poles.[36] In the table below, those forms of mind numbered using a front slash between two numbers favor the pole of greater differentiation and separateness. In those stages represented by whole numbers, we favor the pole of greater embeddedness, integration, and inclusion.[37] For example, the **Self-Protective Opportunist** form of mind occurs between early **Self-Sovereign mind**, which we shall refer to as **Impulsive** (2) and early **Socialized mind**, which we shall call **Conformist** (3), so is referred to numerically as (2/3). Similarly, the **Expert** stage is located between **Conformist** (3) and early **Self-Authoring**, which we shall call **Achiever** (4), is referred to numerically as (3/4). Table 5 shows the stages in terms of preference on the diversity and inclusion polarity, using the stage names that we will primarily use throughout the rest of the book.

Kegan does not recognize as separate developmental stages these forms of mind demarcated with a slash. For him and certain other researchers, **"Socialized Mind"** encompasses what another school of researchers regard as two stages, which can be called **Conformist** (3) and **Expert** (3/4). Differences in theorists' approaches will generally not concern us, but I find value in both Kegan's way of regarding the stages and the alternative approach which elevates the forms of mind demarcated with a slash to stage status, each with its own name. Because our focus in this book is on *adult* development, we will not address the developmental stages before the **Self-Sovereign** stage (2). We will also not address the latest stages in this sequence, 5/6 and 6, as they deserve a different kind of treatment.

In numbered form, adult development stages come in this sequence: 2, 2/3, 3, 3/4, 4, 4/5, 5, 5/6, 6. In the course of our development, the sequence of the emergence of these forms of mind in us does not vary from person to person. As already noted, we do not skip over any stage. We also retain all earlier forms of mind, which always continue to exist and operate within us.

Table 5: Developmental Stages of Diversity and Inclusion

Stage Number	Names of Developmental Stages, as used in this book		Preferred Pole on Diversity & Inclusion Polarity
2	Self-Sovereign		
2/3		Self-Protective Opportunist	Diversity
3	Socialized	Conformist	Inclusion
3/4		Expert	Diversity
4	Self-Authored	Achiever	Inclusion
4/5		Redefining	Diversity
5	Self-Transforming		Diversity & Inclusion
5/6			
6	Unitive		Neither

Theorists describe as our developmental "center of gravity" the kind of meaning-making that most often characterizes our way in the world at a certain time of life. *But real-life human beings dynamically shift their meaning-making in daily life from one stage to another.* In other words, each person makes meaning across a "developmental range" of mindsets or stages.[38] We might understand these developmental stages as internal operating systems that we switch between, just as our bodies switch between ketosis and glycolysis depending on the food available in our digestive systems or stored fat. Or think of how a jet plane uses one engine for taxiing on the tarmac and another for flying in the air.

We operate primarily from a certain developmental stage as our "center of gravity," but in certain situations, we adaptively switch to the mindset of an earlier stage, because it matches the demands facing us. When jostled in a violent mob, for example, or threatened by a scared animal, we need to devise defensive and offensive measures to protect our physical safety. We switch to the mode or mindset best suited to enable us to survive the violent threats of such a situation. Yet, switching internal operating systems can sometimes be *maladaptive*. For example, in a work setting where colleagues are giving us feedback, we might interpret criticism as if it were violence, and switch into survival mode to safeguard our safety and well-being. We devise defensive and offensive measures in response to the feedback, rather than open ourselves to learning and changing from our colleagues' observations and suggestions. These moments of **"fallback"**

> **Fallback:** The experience of a temporary and involuntary shift to an earlier and thus more limited form of meaning-making. Fallback can be triggered by threats, stress, and social context, such as an adult's holiday visit back their parents' home. See Glossary for further explanation.

are utterly normal and part of every person's life. In fact, we might unconsciously abide in fallback most of the time. Operating from an earlier mindset than the most capacious one we have reached describes normal life for some people. In any case, with increasing self-awareness and reflection, moments of fallback can serve as invaluable sources of insight, self-understanding, and further development.[39]

As noted in Part I, these first sections of this book focus largely on **Expert** mind, based on my assumption that virtually all readers will, without too much difficulty, be able to get in touch with this part of themselves. Whatever your developmental center of gravity, personal growth requires working across your entire developmental range. Given the prevalence of **Expert** mind and how commonly people approach personal growth from an **Expert** form of mind, we have started this journey into greater flourishing primarily by exploring this developmental stage. However, the path forward is not linear—neither in this book nor in our developmental journeys!

After the preliminaries in Part I, now in Part II we are delving into the two stages of **Socialized** mind. In Part III we will turn our attention to the **Achiever** mindset of early **Self-Authoring**, and in Part IV to later **Self-Authoring**, as well as the shift into **Self-Transforming** mind. More on those stages in due time!

"The map is not the territory"

If you find this discussion of movement back and forth between developmental stages and the difference between developmental theory and real-life human beings confusing, you might try recalling the map metaphor I introduced in Part I. In his elaboration of a body of thought that he called "general semantics," the Polish-American scholar Alfred Korzybski (d. 1950) uttered the famous sentence: "The map is not the territory." Korzybski highlighted a common confusion that results from regarding words as if they were that to which they refer. In the context of development theory, Korzybski's epigram underscores how descriptions of developmental stages merely offer paradigms, nothing more. Like geographical maps, these paradigmatic stages can help us move through the actual territory of living, growing, learning, and developing as conscious beings.

Besides this reminder that theory provides only imperfect representations, the map-territory metaphor might help us see growing and developing as a journey, stages as different territories, and adult development theory as a map. Indeed, we might playfully compare adult development theory to J. R. R. Tolkien's map of Middle-earth, used by the hobbit Frodo Baggins and his companions to find their way to the land of Mordor.[40] Each stage becomes a land with its own culture, creatures, perils, monsters, treasures, and pathways. The topography and expanse of each land varies tremendously. What it feels like to be in each land, how things operate, and what you would find there vary greatly.

If the stages are the different lands of Tolkien's world, the conventional stages of human development (3, 3/4, and 4) are the Shire, the homeland of the hobbits. There Bilbo and Frodo's close and distant relations live out their lives more or less following shared expectations. Most hobbits never leave the Shire, just as most people never leave the conventional stages. Others might live on the borderland, crossing back and forth between two territories in a seesawing loop before choosing one or the other. But different individuals have different experiences, and their journeys are not the same.

Gandalf the Grey lives as a wizard in a wider realm and operates by different principles. He abides beyond convention.

This post-conventional character possesses knowledge and powers far beyond anything of the hobbits. While Gandalf understands the hobbits, to them his world looks mysterious, wonderful, and scary. Yet, Gandalf visits the Shire from time to time and enjoys close friendship with Frodo and his uncle Bilbo. This jibes with the principle from adult development theory that a person at an earlier stage cannot fully grasp a later form of mind, though someone at a later stage not only can understand all the earlier stages but also still holds and can access them when needed or desired.[41] Indeed, like Russian dolls, each later form of mind includes—and transcends—the previous ones.

The fact that someone operates from a later stage of development does not mean they are morally superior. Later-stage characters can embrace evil just as earlier-stage ones. Saruman the White, for example, the greatest of Gandalf's order of wizards, illustrates how terrible later-stage powers might be when turned to evil purposes. In contrast, Frodo's simple companions from the Shire, especially Samwise Gamgee, illustrate how people in earlier stages might do great good from within the constraints of their current capacities.

This section has aimed to engage your **Expert** mind, by taking a somewhat technical approach and introducing research and other material about stages of adult development.

I hope that reframing adult development as an adventurous journey has helped you adjust and expand your perspective toward development while also deepening your understanding of the **Expert** stage. The temptation to measure ourselves or others against the stage descriptions as standards can yield unhelpful energies such as competitiveness or a sense of insufficiency. Developmentalist and master coach Jan Rybeck counters this kind of thinking with the pragmatic wisdom to use the stages as a map, not a yardstick.

- *What do you notice happening in yourself as you have read this section?*
- *Have you noticed a tendency to use an **Expert** mindset when making sense of adult development theory?*
- *What do you notice about your mental model of personal growth and development? Does some part of you think of it like a contest or competition with others? An obstacle course with trophies and rewards waiting if you complete it? A recipe that you need to follow in order to succeed? A video game with levels that you can complete (if you learn how)?*
- *How has what you've read so far affected your thinking regarding your motivations for reading this book?*

Teen Cool

- *What principles, assumptions, beliefs, and expectations did you inherit from your family?*
- *What communities of belonging did you find along the way that similarly influenced your worldview?*

I notice that when new clients tell me the story of their development and how they got to where they currently find themselves, they most often tell that story in terms of decisions they made and the consequences of those decisions. This tendency shows up among almost all the different kinds of clients I work with—across the entire gender spectrum, whether identifying as straight, gay, bi, or something else, whether in their 30s or their 60s, whether originally from North America, Europe, or Latin America, and whether they are coming for 1-on-1 coaching or a group program of some kind. *Leaders are* supposed *to direct the course of their own lives, right?*

> *I got married the first time, because I thought that's what love was. S/He was the person in my life that I thought could be my partner for making the life that I thought I wanted and was destined to have . . .*
>
> *I left the little town where I grew up and set out to find somewhere more exciting. Or somewhere where I could be myself. Or anywhere to escape my parents' small-mindedness or bigotry or despair or alcoholism.*

While the content of life stories varies wildly, almost everyone seems to tell their story with emphasis on *my decisions* and what happened as a result.

Exceptions to this pattern show up among people of all identities and backgrounds, but I especially notice a different emphasis in the stories told by new clients who highlight the importance of religion or cultural tradition in their family of origin.

> *I married a woman, although I knew I was gay, because that's what I knew I was supposed to do as a Catholic (or Evangelical Christian or Muslim).*
>
> *I stayed in my hometown and spent most of my weekends with my family because that's what good Mormons (or Jews or Filipinos) do.*

I regard this general tendency of emphasizing *my own decisions* when people tell the story of their life as connected to the cultural impact of the Enlightenment, with its heady celebration of the power of reason, as exercised by the individual. Especially since that era, emphasis on individual autonomy and freedom has been a hallmark of the West. My clients who come from the Middle East or Asia, or whose families are most deeply rooted in religious or cultural traditions, tend to see the story of their own lives a bit differently, with greater emphasis on the influence of their home community.

Depending on where your own emphasis lies in the polarity between the importance of the individual and the importance of the community, you might find greater or lesser difficulty in noticing and appreciating the prevalence of the **Conformist** mindset within yourself. I find that clients who come with a desire to grow and develop as human beings and as leaders can locate their **Expert** mind much more easily than their **Conformist** mind. Since you have picked up this book which promises to help you grow and learn, I'm supposing the same might be the case for you.

This section aims to help you locate your **Conformist** mind, the part of yourself that embeds in social groups, in communities of belonging. We need this part of ourselves to know how to belong, how to be a member of a group, and how to absorb the spoken and unspoken rules and values of a community. Reflecting on experiences of social belonging in our preteen and teen years can help us gain increased awareness of this part of our **Socialized** mind. Looking back on this part of my life, one aspect I especially notice is how peer groups offered some sense of belonging and a measure of protection from the general discomfort I felt, my queer sense of strangeness.

Around fifth grade, I discovered girls and they discovered me. I was good at talking and liked doing it, just like the girls I knew. We talked a lot! On the phone, walking around the neighborhood, at Roanoke Pool, at recess—talking was what we did. They were much more fun to talk to and had much more to say than the boys my age. They also taught me about hair spray and bangs and how cool I could be if I wore sunglasses. I spent a lot of time performing *teen cool* with a particular group of four girls, walking the suburban streets of Sunny Slope and Roanoke, our neighborhood subdivisions. *Oh, how cool we were!*

In those years of middle school and junior high, I also played on the dark side. After midnight, while our parents slumbered, I would climb out my bedroom window and scamper down the roof to our garden wall. Out into the dark, at the park or behind someone's house, I would meet with a few boys who were my neighborhood friends. We would go gallivanting, acting naughty and *teen cool* in all kinds of boyish, Tom Sawyer ways. We stole flags from the golf courses, we tore hood ornaments off Cadillacs, we hurled firebombs fueled by hair spray into the tennis courts and watched the flames on the concrete. We smoked cigarettes, met up with girls, and tried to kiss them. *Hellions, we were!*

I felt a certain degree of moral muddle about some of these boyish antics, but not about sneaking out. Leaving home for a few hours late at night gave me the freedom to be a boy. Flouting decorum and responsibility, I broke free on those summer nights. *Rebelling felt good!* The job lists Mom left every day burdened my sister and me with cleaning, cooking, and laundry duties, whether during the school year or the summer months. I had too little levity and too few carefree hours when I could be *a real boy*. In certain domains, I had been required to become an adult long before I was ready.

The demand of taking on heavy burdens early in life went beyond the yellow legal pad on the kitchen table with our daily job list. Divorce, mental illness, domestic violence, alcoholism, drug use, visitation rights, and child support all seeped from my parents' lives like ink blots on our benign suburban Omaha life, and I was forced to make sense of them, like dark and menacing forms of a life-sized Rorschach test. My grandparents, parents, sister, and I each struggled in our own way with these challenges. Heartache, confusion, anger, shame, and sadness permeated our family culture, along with ever-present affection, appreciation, and love.

Teen cool gave me relief from these adult concerns. Whether sneaking out late at night to play the bad boy or tromping around and tanning by the pool wearing sunglasses and coiffed bangs with the girls, I found ways to be a kid when I could. In performing *teen cool*, I found age- and stage-appropriate outlets for my early **Socialized** mind, the **Conformist**.

A symbolic culmination of my reaching for *teen cool* took place at the junior high talent show at St. James/Seton School, which had held so much of my world in the previous eight years, as the container for my experiences of school, church, and friends. Three girls and I danced and triumphantly sang "We Are Family" by Sister Sledge. We were hot stuff, and we flaunted it before the younger St. James kids. *We showed them how it's done!* Besides chosen family, disco tunes, and 1980s cool, this stage performance epitomized the awkward group mimicry of *teen cool*. In front of our peers, we showed off how well we were reaching beyond what we had received from our families and the Catholic school where we had been students all those years.

- *How about your first experiences of finding cliques or social groups where you could belong?*

- *What values did these groups instill in you that most differed from those of your family of origin?*
- *How does reflecting on your early experiences of socialization help you to locate that part of yourself now?*
- *What different preferences have you held at various phases of your life in the polarity between importance of the individual and importance of the community?*

Growing Up and Growing into Gender

- *In your early years, to what extent did your personal style or behavior fit with the gender norms and expectations that your environment put on you?*
- *Who in your life back then most clearly served as models for your way of living out your gender?*

Of all the dimensions of our socialization, gender tends to most elude notice. We are so deeply embedded in it that we look at ourselves and others through the lens of gender, rather than look at gender itself. Gender norms vary profoundly from one culture to another and one historical moment to the next. Yet, mainstream perspectives in virtually any racial, cultural, religious, or historical context tend to regard their gender norms—whatever they might be—as natural, even inevitable. *That's just how boys are.* Or, *that's just what women are like.* Queer lives run up against such assumptions.

I see gender exerting powerful forces onto every client and colleague I have worked with, whether they identify as men, women, non-binary, or gender fluid. Gender imposes force onto individuals to conform to norms they did not choose for themselves. Patriarchy binds and limits everyone involved. Making gender object and seeing it as a component of socialization can empower us. Recognizing gender as a force that works on us and as a system within which we live expands our agency and freedom to choose which norms to honor, when, and how. Through reflection and exploration in our work together, my clients grow greater capacity to write the story of their lives, rather than let so much of it be written for them by gender. Through experiments with supposedly masculine or feminine characteristics, markers, or behaviors, we discover new ways to express ourselves creatively and live vibrant lives joyfully.

One kind of reflection that especially helps illuminate the power of gender on us looks back to our early life to inquire into who gendered us and how, especially before and during adolescence. In this section, I offer a model for this kind of exploration, a partial account of my growing up and into gender, within the cultural and historical context of my early life, in the hopes that it will spur you to similar reflection.

I received a great many invaluable gifts from my mother, who raised my sister Carrie and me with only occasional and sporadic involvement from our father. Among those gifts, Mom instilled in me a great many characteristics that our culture regarded as feminine. For example, she put great emphasis on emotional expression. She would beg and coax us to express our feelings throughout the divorce, as well as the confusion and difficulties we experienced having her as effectively our only parent. This practice of expressing feelings took place most often during the evening prayer ritual the three of us kept. Since as the youngest I had the earliest bedtime, we would gather on my bed, sing some songs, and pray. We would offer petitions, talk about our feelings, and describe how we were doing. We would ask God for what we needed and wanted, given the difficulties we were going through. We would hear each other, share hugs and kisses, and Mom would lull me to sleep. This sacred family ritual brought us healing and fostered mutual support.

In my grade school years, I had no particular awareness of difference from other kids in terms of my sexuality, but I knew I was different in terms of gender roles at home. Unlike everyone else I knew, I grew up in a feminine household, just myself with Carrie and Mom. I knew from a relatively early age that my mother was playing the role of breadwinner, and my sister and I were playing the role of homemakers. My mother went to the office every day, she had a secretary, and took business trips. We did the laundry, the dusting, and the vacuuming. I was aware that, in this arrangement, the three of us played reassigned versions of so-called traditional gender roles, as previously understood for many decades in American society before the 1980s of my childhood.

By the time I got my driver's license at age 16, I did most of the grocery shopping and cooking for our family. Mom would give me a blank check made out to Albertson's supermarket, and I would choose what I wanted to cook. Though she was a good cook, she stopped doing it, except on special occasions. When I needed coaching through a new recipe, I would call her at the office and ask how to do this or that. Though I was playing the homemaker role in a certain way, I didn't feel at all girlish—perhaps because the men in my Italian family all cooked. Cooking is part of the Italian-American way of doing manhood.

Feminine hygiene products were routine shopping needs. I knew exactly what kind of pad and tampon my mom and sister each used, so there I was, a 16-year-old boy buying big boxes of maxi pads and such! I didn't exactly want to run into my friends from school at that moment, but I also didn't feel ashamed. I knew that menstruation was just part of having a female body. When I first heard the definition of feminism as holding the radical idea that women are fully human beings, I realized how natural and how obvious such a proposition had always felt to me. Indeed, I felt proud that already as a teenager I saw myself as a feminist.

Nonetheless, our family was always a comfortable place for me to be in my boyishness and to be 'the boy of the house.' I knew I was not 'the man of the house,' though as I became physically bigger and stronger as a teenager, that changed to some degree. But at first, I was just a boy. As I see it today, my gender performance as a boy was unremarkable. I was unselfconscious in performing normative male gender. I fit easily and comfortably into many of the gender norms of my culture and my society for what boys do. I played in the dirt. I was good at sports. On the other hand, I didn't like fighting. I would even refuse to fight, but I could be aggressive on the basketball court or the soccer field, where I played fullback and relished slide-tackling. I was strong and adept, not timid.

I was also very comfortable with girly things like dolls or dresses, even if I had no particular interest in them. I didn't sneer at them. They were what my sister played with, and that was fine by me. There were times I would play with her and the girls in the neighborhood, all three years older than me. I remember, around the age of eight or nine, dressing up at least once with them in dresses and such, but it just felt like silly play, nothing of any particular significance. None of this posed any threat to my boyishness or my understanding of myself as a boy. Had I been a sissy boy, I imagine my mom would have been deeply uncomfortable, even horrified. Yet, I don't recall any specific pressure to conform to boyish norms or eschew girly ways. Still, beyond her progressive bent to imbue me with traditionally feminine gifts like emotional self-expression (as well as traditionally masculine gifts like powerful advocacy for justice), the power of gender to limit and stifle also came at me through her.

Longo Machismo

My dad's father, Grandpa Longo, played an enormous role in my life until the day he died. Born in Omaha in 1914, the first-born of immigrant parents, he brought into my life a great deal from earlier eras. In his way of being a man in the world, he held within himself a host of intriguing characters. Among these sides of Dr. Joseph A. Longo, Sr., were the virile young buck who dreamt of prize fighting like his older Sicilian friend, Milio Milliti; the prodigious student who bounded through college and medical school before he was 22; the officer in the Army running a 2,000-bed hospital in Europe during World War II; the silent partner in the Studio Inn, a dazzling nightclub where famous performers would sing in the 1960s; and the real estate developer who lost his first fortune building the Longo Apartments in downtown Omaha, fashionably furnished condominiums for which there was not sufficient demand. Grandpa was all these things.

He told many stories of his life, very often repeating the same tales. He would drive us around the city taking all kinds of detours to see homes and hospitals that held nostalgia for him. "My Daddy built that wall and made that curb! Look, Nick! I helped him on the job and to get the contract from the City of Omaha." Excited to hear a new story and nonetheless a little incredulous, I asked how, as a child of nine or ten years old, he would have helped my great-grandfather, whom we called "Nanu Longo" get work.

"I would translate for him with the city officials, so he could bid for jobs like this." My eyes would widen as I wondered what being bilingual would feel like. I would imagine my Nanu, Alfio Longo, an immigrant from "the old country," illiterate and proud, possessing strong arms and some version of the American dream, whereby his children would advance into affluence and ease that he would never know.

Beyond these earlier versions of himself, whom I found to be such intriguing characters, Grandpa showed up in my world as a family doctor who delivered so many babies that everywhere we went mothers would come up to grasp his hand, saying things like, "Oh, Doctor Longo, you delivered me, and you delivered my three children!" He would be gracious and charming in receiving this affection and celebrity, calling most of these former patients "Sweetheart," because—as he would tell us after the encounter—he couldn't remember their names.

When Grandpa would come home, I would often be with Grandma in the kitchen, helping her prepare dinner, learning to cook, and talking. On his way in from the garage, he might put some groceries in the basement refrigerator or storage freezer down. Coming upstairs into the kitchen, he would sometimes bring a paper bag or even a crate full of peppers, eggplants, or tomatoes. Grandma would ask where the produce was from, and Grandpa would say that one of the "little old people" he cared for in their old neighborhood, Omaha's Little Italy, was in difficult circumstances and had given the vegetables as payment. Depending on the patient and their story, Grandma might give him a little flak for being such a pushover.

On weekends we might go to their country club, Happy Hallow, where I would see other sides of Grandpa and his ways of being a man in the world. When I would golf with him, I would take in the roostering among his peers in the men's locker room, which was bedecked in fancy carpeting. Since our time together was usually at his home rather than at Happy Hallow, I came to understand something about his domestic morning ritual of preening for seemingly hours nude in front of the mirror, meticulously shaving and trimming his face. He would slap on emerald-green Skin Bracer aftershave, swish and gargle with Listerine in virtually the same hue of green—and run a black plastic comb through his hair after pulling it out of a bright blue Barbicide jar. When he emerged from what Grandma would call his *boudoir*, she would exclaim with a touch of teasing:

"There's Beau Brummel!"

Grandpa would whistle and impishly make one of his stock jokes about himself: "Dressed like a high-class pimp!"

In the Happy Hallow locker room, I could see Grandpa as one among many "high-class pimps," each man preening and performing a style of masculine classiness to impress each other. Something about class feels important in understanding my grandfather's masculinity. Living his life as Joseph—not as Giuseppe—my grandfather realized the American dream that his father Alfio and his mother Antonia had for him. "Social mobility" describes a crucial feature of my grandfather's life journey. He golfed and dined with other wealthy Omahans, even billionaire Warren Buffett, whom we would see occasionally in the Happy Hallow dining room. As a charming and outgoing physician and surgeon, he seemed to claim his place in high society.

Looking back at my grandfather's life and his sense of self, as far as I can tell, Grandpa fundamentally understood himself as what today we would call "a person of color." By this, I don't mean that he thought of himself as Black or even like Black folks. Indeed, he exuded both superiority and pity towards his Black patients. He would regularly make racist jokes and comments, especially in response to scenes on television shows we would watch together. Carrie and I would scold him, saying "That's racist, Grandpa!" to which he would respond with feigned repentance.

But Grandpa recognized that his social position in his world, the world of Omaha, was pegged to his ethnicity. In his formative years, he had been racialized and degraded as a "wop" or a "dego." Pronounced like "day-go," this slur derives from the Spanish and Portuguese given name Diego and became attached to Italians by the late nineteenth century. He understood himself to exist in what scholar Isabel Wilkerson has put forward as the "middle caste" to capture the status of Latinos and Asians in America.[42] Italians like my grandfather in the early and mid-twentieth century knew they were similarly relegated to intermediary status in the American racial hierarchy. In fact, they could not *un*know it. "Dego" indelibly marked my grandfather's sense of self.

He found himself in a world that knew him as Italian, not white; as ethnic, not regular. Grandpa spoke the Sicilian dialect as his mother tongue, and he never forgot it. In Omaha's Little Italy around South 10th Street where he and Grandma were born and raised, they grew up speaking the language of nineteenth-century Carlentini, the Sicilian town whose young men and women emigrated to Omaha around the turn of the twentieth century for the sake of economic opportunity and social mobility—their American dream.

As I write this, I have in front of me an image of his birth certificate, where his full name is registered as *Giuseppe Longo*. Besides also recording the birthplace of his parents as "Italy," their respective occupations as "Day Laborer" and "Housewife," that document also specifies their color as "White." Despite this racial categorization officially recorded on his birth certificate, no matter the prestige of his work, reputation, home address, or country club membership, my sense of my grandfather is that he never actually gained entry into the club of whiteness and always saw himself as other than white.

During his lifetime, it did seem that Italian-Americans were allowed or subsumed into the club of whiteness. We were deracialized, that is, granted an undifferentiated status as white. Understanding something of my grandfather's and my father's experiences being racialized, I've come to describe myself as *recently* white. Discrimination against Italians in the United States today does still occur, but it seems as outdated as the epithet "dego," which for Grandpa and his generation had been the damning and identifying slur. Nowadays, few Americans of my generation or younger seem to even know the word, much less use it. More important than slurs, the structures of racism against Italians in America seem now to have been dismantled or repurposed.

This racial and ethnic reality casts light on exactly how Grandpa's way of being a man ran counter to the white Midwest masculinities that otherwise surrounded me. Considering solely his body and what we might call his "bodily practices," he held himself and lived in his body very differently from the white men I knew, the neighbors and priests and other kids' fathers who seemed to have no particular ethnicity, at least not one that made them at all different. Most men withheld their affection. Grandpa kissed his children, grandchildren, siblings, cousins, and friends when saying hello or goodbye. "Boys don't cry," that first commandment of modern American masculinity, applied to all the boys and men I knew outside our family, but not to Grandpa. He cried daily, mostly about my Dad. The sufferings of his beloved son Fred broke Grandpa's heart. But Grandpa cried lots of other times too, such as when telling stories about his parents, though he left unsaid whatever regrets and hurts he still harbored, decades after their deaths. He also wept piously and sincerely when talking of his faith in God, who loved and forgave him, "though I've been a bastard many times."

Besides the kissing and the crying, Grandpa dressed and undressed his body in ways different from the other men I knew. I've already mentioned his vain preening as he dressed up in a suit and tie every day for work and on Sundays for church. On the flip side of this formality out in the world, at home, he would wear a zip-up one-piece leisure suit, unless guests were coming over.

Most at odds with what I knew from my friends and their homes, no taboo against nudity operated at Grandma and Grandpa's house. While we gently held some lines of discretion between undressed male and female bodies, no awkwardness or strangeness whatsoever was put onto boys or men sharing space when nude. Grandpa held his aging, sagging, and somewhat overweight body with total ease and normalcy. Never traipsing around or flaunting his nudity, he stood unperturbed in his *boudoir* in the morning, no matter who else from the family came around.

His penis looked different from the few other penises I saw in my youth, those of my dad, uncle, or other boys my age. I didn't know how to make sense of this difference at the time, except that his penis seemed saggy, like the rest of his elderly body. Like most Italians—and most men around the world—Grandpa's penis was fully intact. His foreskin had not been cut off when he was an infant or boy. Reflecting back on it now, this seems like another signifier of Grandpa's racial and ethnic identity as Italian, unlike his children, who earlier in their lives were subsumed into the club of American whiteness, where male genital cutting became a norm under pressure from the temperance movement in the early 20th century.

Reading this account of my experience finding my way in gender, what do you notice about your own?

- *When you were a child, to what various class-specific, culture-specific, and generation-specific gender performances were you regularly exposed?*
- *In the years just before your adolescence, how do you remember making sense of racism and racialized norms for women and men?*
- *What influence on your gender do you see your cultural heritage having had?*
- *What kinds of bodies did you see as a child?*
- *How were those bodies marked culturally and racially differently from your own?*

CHAPTER 3:

Dark Sides

Powers and Pitfalls

- *What "superpowers" do you recognize in yourself? What's queer about them?*
- *When have you experienced some version of **Gaydar**, **Pride Tribe**, or the **Best Little Kid** in your own life?*

Each queer superpower accentuates and strengthens capacities of a certain developmental stage to generate heroic possibilities and powers needed to overcome adverse circumstances and difficult dynamics that LGBTQ+ people experience at that particular stage.[43] However, excessive growth or hypertrophic development in these particular capacities naturally creates imbalances that bring their own risks and problems. Because the pitfalls of queer superpowers stem precisely from stage-specific strengths, we tend to avoid seeing these downside possibilities in favor of instead embracing all the benefits of the superpower. In this section, we shall look closely at this correlation between powers and pitfalls to counteract the natural tendency to overlook the risks and problems resulting from overdeveloped strengths.

When operating from **Socialized** mind—whether **Conformist** or **Expert**—the adverse circumstances that exact an especially painful toll pertain to social pressures. Gender expectations and sexual norms of the straight mainstream can all create tensions that we find especially difficult to manage. These norms exert power in many forms, including family lore, cultural values, religious and moral frameworks, and discrimination or persecution supported by laws and organizational policies.

In this context of social pressures, the **Best Little Kid,** in order to make up for the shameful parts of himself that he hopes to hide, supercharges the capacity of **Expert** mind to gain distinction and rank through building knowledge and skills that garner admiration. The **Best Little Kid** builds real strength and achieves actual accomplishments through his efforts, yet the superpower also takes its toll. The **Best Little Kid** suffers from a specific variety of Imposter Syndrome. However explicitly or implicitly, some inner voice insidiously suggests something along the lines of: *"I look like a real man, but I'm actually just a faggot."* Drawing attention to his prestigious accomplishments, he works to avoid being found out for who he really is. In some areas a star, while in other developmental areas a laggard, the **Best Little Kid** seesaws between boasting and cringing. Closeting, covering, and passing enhance his charade. *If I'm not the best little boy in the whole world, I'll be found out! They'll know I'm just an imposter!* Fear drives this pursuit.

Resolving to put his best foot forward, the **Best Little Boy** strives to earn his way out of his shame. Acutely aware of gender expectations in his society, he says to himself, *My manliness doesn't measure up, so I'll achieve perfection in every other way* *possible.* Stepping into this role of the **Best Little Boy**, he excels exceedingly, drives himself relentlessly, and shifts his talents into overdrive. *I shall move up the ladder the fastest to the mostest ever!* Every detail deserves attention, and each scenario its due consideration. Sometimes a persnickety embodiment of perfect faggotry arises out of this mode that says: *I must deliver with panache!*

Gaydar, for its part, emerges when, in response to disapproving social forces, a queer person in **Conformist** mind supercharges their newly gained capacity to tune into social cues and see the social identities of other people. Thanks to **Gaydar**, they can sense the otherwise invisible identities of other queer people. **Gaydar** thus makes possible solidarity and (hopefully) safety. Yet, like any queer superpower, when overused, **Gaydar** presents pitfalls. Spending so much time and energy scanning the crowd for other queer souls, we might find ourselves overvaluing LGBTQ+ people as superior to *regular ole boring straight people.* **Gaydar** might also turn into a kind of wishful thinking that distorts our keen perception of social cues so that we end up projecting our gayness onto others who do not identify as gay or queer.

The other queer superpower of the **Socialized** stages, **Pride Tribe,** supercharges the **Conformist** mind's capacity to gain true belonging in a social group. Faced with difficult and disapproving social pressures, the LGBTQ+ person, if lucky or wise, finds a queer peer group who affirms and upholds them. Moving beyond family of origin, they find *chosen family.*

The opinions and expectations of this tribe then take root within and remake us. We overcome a perpetual sense of insecurity from the "me versus the world" mindset in the **Self-Protective Opportunist** form of mind and find a comforting embrace of "safety in numbers" through a **Socialized** "us versus them" perspective. Like a bee finding a hive, upon reaching **Socialized** mind, we gain a role, learn our place, and fit into an organized group. We attach to one or more Queen Bees, important others whose implicit and explicit direction guides us and defines the right way to be, behave, and operate in the world.

But because we see the **Pride Tribe** and its ways as unquestionable norms, we may come to blindly reject any deviation from what we now know to be *the right way* of being or behaving. Straight people, so often *oblivious* to sexual orientation and its very range and possibilities, are *square, boring, cookie-cutter figures, programmed by Hollywood and dead white men and holy books*. We in the **Pride Tribe** *are enlightened, liberated, dazzlingly delightful, the very pizzazz of humanity*.

In gay men's version of **Pride Tribe**, *it is we who create all that is fabulous in the arts and fashion and parties*. We might deign to bring our "queer eye for the straight guy" and *spruce up the sadly baggy suits of the straight and narrow men or the gauche style sense of unsophisticated suburban women*. Indeed, reacting against stigma and projecting our **Gaydar**, we might form a collectively held belief that *most straight guys (or at least the hot and smart or cool ones!) are actually gay, but just don't know it because they lack self-awareness. They just don't yet know how good it is to be gay!*

In this reactive mode of **Pride Tribe**, we swarm together in an ever-narrowing array of distinctive subgroups and communities—bears, twinks, leathermen, pigs, otters, Radical Faeries, shiny corporate gays, artsy queers, gym bunnies, bottoms and tops, femme and butch, pocket gays, muscle queens, Preppie gays, Broadway queens, and more. Life for gay men operating out of **Socialized** mind, which finds identity outside of themselves, can become all about getting invited to that exclusive club or having stories about the White Party. Our Fire Island share defines who we are, or the theme of the week we spend in Provincetown, or the queer activist group that fills our Instagram feed and with whom we protest and fundraise. We might adamantly insist that everyone give their pronouns at the start of every meeting, because that is *the right way* to behave. We might live in a certain neighborhood (Williamsburg? Bushwick? Chelsea? WeHo? The Castro? Boys Town? Kreuz-kölln?), because that is *the best neighborhood*, as defined by the important others with whom we are aligned.

Table 6: Focus on Queer Superpowers of Socialized Mind

Developmental Stage	Queer Superpower	Adverse Circumstances that prompt superpower's emergence	Description	Heroic Possibilities & Powers	Pitfalls & Shadow
Socialized	Gaydar	» Cultural values » Gender expectations » Romantic & sexual norms of the straight mainstream » Religious & moral condemnation » Legal persecution	» Sense others' queerness	» Tap into intuitive knowing » See people's hidden faces » Empathy for others' shame	» Delusions of queer grandeur, imagining LGBTQ+ folks as superior to straight people » Project own queerness onto others
	Pride Tribe		» Membership in a queer social group	» Strength in solidarity » Self-confidence to cultivate and use atypical gifts	» Gay groupthink papers over personal uniqueness » False sense of superiority
	The Best Little Kid		» Meeting and surpassing social standards and expectations	» Achieve excellence » Gain admiration in society » Earn one's way out of shame	» Fitting in to move up, lose sense of self and own unique "weird & wonderful" traits » Trapped by society's definitions of success, e.g., wealth, high position, prestige, luxury, etc.

Conformist appears with Gaydar; Expert appears with The Best Little Kid.

Gay groupthink empowers not only our feelings of security, but of self-esteem. In harmony with the expectations of our tribe, we feel good about ourselves. We know that we matter. **Socialized** mind gives coherence to the self from the outside in. The power of **Pride Tribe** affirms our difference from the straight majority as not just setting us apart but as distinguishing us as *better, right, fabulous*.

At the same time, seeking ongoing approval from those others whom we have deemed "ours" takes energy and attention. The **Pride Tribe** and **Best Little Boy** superpowers combine as we chase material possessions and other status symbols, which could be "likes" or followers on Facebook or Instagram as readily as a certain job title in a certain kind of company or a certain kind of hipster mustache or beard. We are secretly dogged by the grip of an existential threat: the shame of exclusion from our tribe. Belonging or not puts at stake our very sense of self. Any disapproval from the group feels like a threat of being shunned, excommunicated, cast out. Were that to happen, we would not know who we are. It would feel like death.

All queer superpowers thus have shadows, the dark downsides that we tend to avoid seeing. The shadow side of the **Pride Tribe** superpower makes us into a cliché without us even noticing. LGBTQ+ folks are prone to pre-packaged and prefabricated molds, scripts, and tropes just as straight people are. Gay clichés might be different from *ho-hum straight lives*, but they are no less limiting when adopted out of a sense of inevitability. Parroting groupthink, we look outside of ourselves for a North Star to guide our trajectory through life. Our skies, moreover, are filled with arrays of bright stars leading us in different directions. We judge others by how they dress and talk, hurling easy condemnations for whatever falls outside of the norms that inhabit us. "Shoulds" hang over our every move, and we project those omnipresent obligations onto everyone else.

Straight, Not Just Acting

Teen cool only gave me temporary and partial relief from the feeling of queerness that gloppily stuck to my sense of self. Early exposure to so many weighty adult issues exacerbated the struggles of adolescence in ways that I could not easily escape. Indeed, "straight-acting" versions of the queer superpowers of **Gaydar, Pride Tribe**, and the **Best Little Kid** helped me make it through my high school years.

Admittedly, my use of these superpowers did not appear especially queer. My "golden boy" version of the **Best Little Kid** did not at all think of himself as gay. In fact, I would say that he was not gay. Rather he was a teenage version of a person who eventually became a gay man. I knew I was different, and queer in several non-sexual senses. The **Best Little Boy** gave me a way to attempt to earn my way out of the shame I felt for being so queer. That golden boy, Joe Prep, served me well for a few years, especially in high school. He helped me *do the work of becoming myself*—until he didn't help anymore.

- *What use have you made of these three queer superpowers at different times of your life?*

The Boys in the Band

- *What plays, films, short stories, or novels set in another historical period or cultural context have most usefully shed light on aspects of yourself that you previously had not noticed?*

Mart Crowley's stage play *The Boys in the Band* dramatizes the dynamics of a group of gay friends in New York City who come together to celebrate a birthday. A 1968 Broadway hit, it was made into a 1970 film, revived on Broadway for its 50th anniversary (2018), and recently remade into a new film version (2020) with the same all-gay cast, including Zachary Quinto, Andrew Rannells, and Jim Parsons. If you haven't already seen *The Boys in the Band*, go out and do so now! Either way, I hope this account of the classic gay drama prompts new insights for you about the queer superpowers of **Socialized** mind.

The Boys in the Band captures and conveys the power of **Pride Tribe**, the pitfalls of **Gaydar**, and the shadow side of the

Best Little Kid. Though originally set in the 1960s, its portrayal of gay male culture remains resonant. Though the story is set in a New York City apartment back in the 1960s, I find the gay men in the drama and the dynamics between them to be exceedingly familiar, and the dated lingo and cultural references allow me to stand outside my own contemporary gay cultural context and see with fresh eyes personal dynamics familiar from my lived experience.

If you're not up for delving into this drama, feel free to skip over this section and come back to it some other time.

Michael, the host of the party and the protagonist of the drama, is carrying a bottle of scotch when he first appears, crossing the stage to sit down on the couch and put ribbons on a present for his friend Harold, whose birthday party provides the occasion for the friends to assemble.

His friend Donald arrives at Michael's early after having "the doctor" (a psychiatrist, we learn) cancel on him for a date. Donald and Michael banter about shopping, drinking, depression, balding, the "Butch Assurance" provided by the firm hold of a men's hairspray brand, and the intimacy of sharing toothbrushes when Donald comes in from the Hamptons of Long Island to stay at Michael's in the city. The "five screaming queens" who are coming for the party are "really all Harold's friends," Michael explains.[44] "It's *his* birthday, and I want everything to be just the way he'd want it." Giving Donald the lay of the land, Michael reassures him: "I think you know everybody anyway—they're the same old tired fairies you've seen around since the day one. Actually, there'll be seven, counting Harold and you and me."

> **DONALD**. Are you calling me a screaming queen or a tired fairy?
>
> **MICHAEL**. Oh, I beg your pardon—six tired, screaming fairy queens and one anxious queer.

Two surprise entrants to the party—one stripper plus Michael's college roommate—complete the cast of characters.

Michael's apartment provides a gay refuge of safety, where the boys will be boys, gaily. They trade sexual innuendo, speak in code (e.g., using feminine pronouns for men, calling each other Mary and Nellie), appropriate homophobic slurs (faggot, fruit, fairy, queen), and speak of institutions that comprise the gay male culture of the day (e.g., gay bathhouses, Fire Island, gay bars). Trying to get dour Donald into a party mood, Michael himself queens out and plays a diva before the others arrive with a Judy Garland imitation.

> **MICHAEL**. Oh, Donald, you're so serious tonight!
>
> "FORGET YOUR TROUBLES, C'MON GET HAPPY!"[45]

These men rely on each other to be themselves. It is mostly (only?) here, in the band, that the boys can be (gay) boys. They speak each other's language, trading the winks and code words of insiders. This is **Pride Tribe**!

The references and winks of the band's insider language proliferate as the other boys in the band arrive. The differences of their Jewish, Puerto Rican, Black, and Catholic experiences of gayness appear in their bodies and distinctive manners. Among them are runts and jocks, sissy boys, and those whose beefy bodies or butch manners let them pass as straight. As becomes apparent, character by character, the boys in the band are bound together not only by affection but also by their common experience of queer trauma—rejection, loss, betrayal, and misdirected affections, such as that fooling around which was just play for the straight boy but a disclosure of profound passion for the gay boy. Their coping mechanisms range from getting high and hoarding barbiturates to heavy drinking and compulsive shopping (on credit). Some of them reveal their version of the **Great Escape**, which preceded their finding this **Pride Tribe** with whom they celebrate on this night.

The impending intrusion of someone from outside the **Pride Tribe**, however, disturbs the comfortable safety of the group. Having received a call from Alan McCarthy, a lawyer from DC who had been Michael's college roommate at Georgetown, Michael prepares his gay guests for Alan's arrival. "Listen, everybody, this old college friend of mine is in town and he's stopping by for a fast drink on his way to dinner somewhere. But, listen, he's *straight*, so . . ."[46] Michael describes to his friends where he puts himself on the **closeting–coming out continuum** when with his old pal Alan:

Closeting–coming out continuum: A fluid array of social positions for LGBTQ+ people in their self-disclosure of sexual orientation or gender identity. Because LGBTQ+ people are often an invisible minority in the sense that their non-normative sexual orientation or gender identity is not, in many cases, apparent, coming out is an ongoing experience. Whenever an LGBTQ+ person faces someone else for the first time, the choice whether and how much to conceal or disclose arises. See Glossary for further explanation.

MICHAEL. It's not that I care what he would think of me, really—it's just that *he's* not ready for it. And he never will be.[47]

The others are surprised. Can Michael be sure Alan doesn't know he's gay?

MICHAEL. If there's the slightest suspicion, he's never let on one bit.

EMORY. What's he had, a lobotomy?

As Michael goes on describing his history in the closet, we see not only more of his reasoning but also more of his fears. "I was super-careful when I was in college, and I still am whenever I see him. I don't know why, but I am." Michael gets defensive and justifies his actions. "You may think it was a crock of shit, Donald, but to him I'm sure we were close friends. The closest. To pop that balloon now just wouldn't be fair to him. And if that's phony of me, Donald, then that's phony of me . . ." Closeting works, according to Michael, because "it's much simpler to deal with the world according to its rules and then go right ahead and do what you damn well please." So, when in college Michael "butched it up quite a bit. And I didn't think I was lying to myself. I really thought I was straight." Preparing his gay guests for a visit by his straight college friend, Michael asks them to protect and preserve the duplicity he employs in continuing a valued friendship from an earlier era of his life. Shortly thereafter, Alan calls back to say he is not coming that evening after all—but then he shows up anyway.

When Alan makes his unexpected appearance at the apartment, Michael and most of the other characters are dancing a "precision routine" that they used to do together on Fire Island. The stage directions describe the dancers as *"turning and slapping their knees and heels and laughing with abandon."*[48] Outsiders to mainstream American society, the boys in the band form a sacrosanct inside place, where the presence of straight Alan soon presents threatened and actual violence, just as the wide heteronormative world outside always threatens the safe sanctuary of the fairies.

Socialized Mind Imprints on "Important Others"

Reflecting on *The Boys in the Band* and the way queer superpowers operate in the play helps us understand adult development and illustrates what distinguishes queer developmental journeys. These gay characters have learned how to be, think, talk, and act so as to fit in with each other and how to operate in the wider society, which Alan represents. Michael's friend Donald has not embraced **Pride Tribe** the way the other characters have, but he speaks gay fluently and joins smoothly in their banter.

From a developmental viewpoint, becoming subject to the norms of society and specific social groups marks a great feat for the adolescent. **Socialized** mind allows us into the adult world as societal rules and the specific expectations of individuals and groups whom we emulate become structurally constitutive of our outlooks on reality, including ourselves. Yet Michael, Donald, and the other boys in this gay band are no teenagers. These fictional characters display how the **Conformist** or **Socialized** mind (like all other developmental stages) does not necessarily track with our physical maturation or aging. As we shall see when we return to these characters, they too have other layers of complexity beyond their enmeshment in **Pride Tribe**.

In what we have seen so far of them, they seem to be operating out of a **Conformist** mindset. The dance number they are performing when Alan shows up symbolizes this way of operating. They know the moves, the gestures, the timing, and the spirit of the "precision routine." They move as one, in sync with each other, and revel in their performance. It feels so good to fly as a flock, to know how to move, to fulfill the group's expectations by playing your role just as rehearsed!

Gaydar, **Pride Tribe**, and all aspects of this or any developmental stage operate out of a certain mindset or consciousness, which determines what we perceive, where we direct our attention, and how we make sense of what we notice. We can understand these developmental stages of consciousness according to their structure and their contents. In terms of structure, consciousness is like the lens through which we see ourselves, others, and the world. But this lens shapes our reality both inside and out. It not only forms eyeglasses through which we see the world, but becomes the lens of a projector we use to project an overlay and backdrop of meaning onto everything around us. In other words, our consciousness projects a context in which we understand all of reality.

In the **Conformist** mindset, what structures our consciousness and the reality that we see are the expectations of those "important others" upon whom we imprint. In this developmental stage, our very self exists in the reality we share with them. When operating out of this **Socialized** mindset, they ultimately set our priorities and shape our views. For knowledge or truth, we look to those whom we regard as worthy authorities or experts. Like spiders who weave the webs on which they live and move, we humans weave webs of meaning to structure the world we inhabit. Indeed, by weaving webs of meaning, we structure our very selves. When operating from **Conformist** mind, we weave those webs of material supplied by our "important others."

Michael and the other boys have elected each other as "important others." They have fused part of themselves with the norms, rules, and expectations of this **Pride Tribe**.

The Shadow Side of *The Boys in the Band*

Compared to autobiography or memoirs like *The Best Little Boy in the World* or *A Dutiful Boy*, the dramatic genre of *The Boys in the Band* brings characters to life more vividly and offers alternative perspectives on the human condition. *The Boys in the Band* thus provides additional insights into the **Best Little Kid** as a queer superpower of the **Expert** stage of development. The play's protagonist, Michael, epitomizes the **Best Little Kid**, especially in its shadow sides.

These shadow sides include the inevitable and dogged self-doubt that comes from fusing our self-image with others' approval and their acknowledgement of our knowledge or accomplishments. We have already seen how the existential insecurity of the **Self-Protective Opportunist** "me vs. the world" transformed into the social insecurity of "us vs. them" of the **Conformist** mindset, where shunning is the equivalent of death. The focus of anxiety in this **Expert** stage, in contrast, focuses on the terrible prospect of "losing this sense of specialness."[49] We "fear being reabsorbed and getting drawn back into the fold, into the mass of others."

The **Best Little Kid** can turn his desperate self-doubt viciously onto others. With a sharp eye for violations of collectively defined standards, he sees others' vulnerabilities and weaknesses. Redirecting his usually inwardly directed hatred of his own less-than places, his loathing of weakness and inferiority can become a cruelly insightful attack weapon, piercing other peoples' shields and defenses. Along these lines, we see Michael expose and attack the vulnerabilities of the other boys in the band, and then go after his college roommate, Alan. But before that viciousness, we see Michael in the precarious balancing act of someone in recovery. The piercing gazes of Donald and Harold allow us to see Michael trying hard to leave behind bad habits.

Interested in more exploration of how the shadow side of the **Best Little Kid** comes out in *The Boys in the Band*? On the book website, QueerFlourishing.com, you'll find bonus material with further discussion of Michael's dark side flaring up as he manipulates the party into a vicious game of truth-telling.

Creature of the Night

- *In your teen years, what places or practices gave you access to "the dark side" of life and yourself?*

In my teen years, I gave little attention to what Carl Jung calls *the shadow*, those parts of ourselves that we reject and work to avoid seeing. Like Michael in *The Boys in the Band*, I found my own ways of averting my attention from those shadowy reflections of myself that hounded me. Besides reveling in my academic, athletic, and other extracurricular achievements, over-intellectualization also served my avoidance of the shadow. Being a "know-it-all" and exerting a sense of superiority supported a certain sense of self that kept me comfortably apart from shadows cast by my family—mental illness, alcoholism, divorce, and domestic violence. With straight A's and loads of AP classes, I created safety and security far away from dark depths, including the impacts these overwhelming experiences in my family had had on me. I ran through my adolescent years at a victorious pace, blithely ignoring the shadow darting right below my feet.

In early adolescence, I would sneak out late at night with my neighborhood friends into the darkness to romp and revel in rule-breaking. In later adolescence, the shadow flirted with me in other ways. The AMC Theater at Westroads Mall on certain late Friday and Saturday nights provided one significant stage for such teasing, flirting, fantasizing, and play-acting. On those nights the movie theater became a stage where we, the audience, followed the characters on screen in becoming weirdos, aliens, and transgressors—creatures of the night.

The *Rocky Horror Picture Show* brought my friends and me into an alternative reality, where gender norms and sexual rules got wacky. Like Brad and Janet arriving at that castle after getting a flat tire in a late-night rainstorm, we Catholic school teens showed up for a titillating and scandalizing (but harmless) encounter with high-heeled mad scientist Frank N. Furter, his boy toy and laboratory creation Rocky, tapdancing Magenta, and the rest of the cast of fantastical characters. Singing *"By the light of the night, it'll all be alright,"* Frank N. Furter blessed our cavorting in the shadow, as he did for Brad and Janet in the film.

The first time Rob and I and our other friends showed up as Rocky "virgins," we couldn't have known what we were in for. Honors students from all-boys Creighton Prep and its Catholic all-girls sister schools, Marian, Mercy, and Duchesne, we got special permission to stay out past curfew (or at least I had to!) to go to this 1975 interactive cult movie about which our parents had at most vague impressions of throwing rice and toast in bawdy (but harmless) play. And play it was, though more transgressive play than my mother would have wanted for me at that age!

Bedecked in platform heels, a Dracula cape, and the finery of fishnet hose strapped with garter belts to bikini bottoms that revealed as much as they held in, Frank N. Furter descended by elevator [*I want, I need, gotta have high heels*] behind Brad and Janet's backs after they were shocked by the "Time Warp" song and dance [*It's just a jump to the left*....] performed by the cast of weirdos under the banner of the Annual Transylvanian Convention.

Frank embodies *Rocky Horror*. He follows his lurid desires. Sensual, transgressive, and seductive, this "sweet transvestite" introduces himself to Brad and Janet with a string of claims and caveats:

> Don't get strung out [A *beat.*] by the way I look [A *beat.*]
>
> Don't judge a book by its cover-er-er
>
> I'm not much of a man by the light of day
>
> But by night I'm one hell of a lover-er-er
>
> I'm just a sweet transvestite [*Boom-chicka, boom-chicka, boom-chicka, boom!*]
>
> From Tra-a-a-a-ansexual, [A *beat.*] Transylvania-a-a-a-a

Flinging off his satin cape to reveal *a pearl necklace* and the rest of his regalia, Frank beckons to Brad and Janet: "*Why don't you stay for the night [Night!] Or maybe a bite [Bite!] I could show you my* [A *beat.*] *favorite obsession/ I've been making a man/ With blonde hair and a tan/ And he's good for relieving my* ["sexual!"] *tension.*" Like Mary Shelley's Dr. Frankenstein, this Frank also brings a man to life in his laboratory. Indeed, he creates the man of his dreams a hunk he names "Rocky." Eventually, Frank pretends he's Janet and climbs into Brad's bed to seduce him and then plays Brad climbing into Janet's bed to seduce her. He murders his former lover Eddie (played by singer Meat Loaf) and then serves up the cadaver (in meatloaf form?) to Brad, Janet, and the gang for a cannibalistic feast. The plot gets even weirder from there, with laser guns, spaceships, and Dr. Scott (Brad and Janet's high school science teacher), not to mention the serious and scholarly narrator—apparently a criminologist—who tells the tale from his library, like Sherlock Holmes reviewing a case he has untangled.

Going to these interactive screenings of *Rocky Horror* some 20 or 30 times in my high school years—plus renting it at Blockbuster and watching it sometimes at home on the little screen (a practice that *Rocky* groupies like us dubbed "masturbation")—I gradually became an insider who knew the "precision routine" of gestures and jokes and their intricate timing to interact with the film's dialogue and visuals. I reveled in coaching newcomers to "transexual Transylvania" in these scripts and in learning new parts from the theater kids in my group of friends who knew more of the lines than I did. In between our late-night jaunts to this queer cinematic experience, my friends and I would make up new quips for *Rocky*, imagining we could contribute to the repertoire of audience participation parts.

Rocky gave us practice unlearning the rigid rules about sex and gender instilled in us by parents, teachers, and priests. At *Rocky*, we could hold more lightly the Catholic sex ed curriculum about chastity, whose definition we learned to be "appropriate sexual control and direction for one's place in life." Technical terms from the catechism like "procreation"—the only morally upstanding reason for sexual intercourse between husband and wife—lost some of their grim power and dire tone when juxtaposed with ribald shadow puppets and aliens in drag. With a "jump to the left" and "a step to the right," on those *Rocky* nights, we mimed and play-acted a queer counterculture, worlds away from the Catholic suburban life in which we spent our days. This play-acting left our straight and somewhat narrow lives unperturbed. It made for a discreet and compartmentalized place of silly fun and naughty joking. We played at sluttiness; we lip-synced cross-dressing; we mimed BDSM and other kinks. The queer culture of Rocky Horror allowed us to play on the dark side.

Coming home from *Rocky* one Saturday night, I found my mom still up and waiting at the front door to say hi to my friends. Our friends, the girls from Marian, had had the bright idea and the bright red lipstick to write "HOT" on my left cheek and "SEX" on my right. When she saw me, my mother stood aghast. *"What do you have written on your face?! Get that off of you, right now!"* For my part, I thought it added to my cachet of coolness. Playing dress-up and taking part in imagining ourselves as queer aliens from transsexual Transylvania in no way destabilized the **Best Little Boy** role that I had cast myself in for those high school years.

Rocky Horror made space for transgressive gender play that I found very comfortable, even if my mother didn't. My boyishness, my adolescent maleness, felt so apparent and unimpeachable that wearing lipstick or mimicking transvestites in fishnets posed no threat to my sense of self. While I did feel uncertain about my sexual interests and what that uncertainty might mean about my sexual identity, I never felt uncertain about my place in the gender binary.

- *How about in your youth? What flirtations with your shadow flickered back then?*

GRIEF and Alejandro

- *What watershed events ended your innocence?*

Through my cinematic flirts with the shadow at *Rocky Horror* and other liberating experiences, by senior year, the golden boy role of "Joe Prep" that I had been playing was beginning to slip away. A series of losses and blows further pummeled this golden boy version of myself, until his sunny disposition could no longer plausibly hold me in his grip.

At the end of junior year, I ran for student body president but lost. My girlfriend of junior year and her whole group of friends were a year ahead of me, so they graduated and went off to college. I came into senior year feeling like an outsider in a world where I had previously enjoyed high position and much social capital. Those close friends who were classmates of mine at Prep all seemed to have someone they were closer to than to me. Tom had Carl and Matt; Paul had Nick; Rob had Mike. I knew they all liked and cared about me, but I felt left out. I wanted a best friend and somehow never seemed to find one.

Creighton Prep afforded me numerous supports to help me find my way through travails of adolescent life such as these. One of them was a fellowship group led by Greg, the teacher who orchestrated my high school's Freshman Retreat, whom we called by his first name. Each year Greg would invite to this group select sophomores in whom he saw something special, such as depth, maturity, and distinctive perspectives. He might invite the football star, the class president, the rock guitarist—all bright, shiny, good-natured, and admirable in their own ways. In our Junior and Senior years, we would come together every week or two for open sharing about personal challenges and questions we were facing. We spoke of girls, faith, parents, deaths, loves, drinking, morals, racism, growing up, cliques, fights, hurts, mistakes—the entire panoply of teenage issues.

Senior year, I entered into a social group of exchange students from all over Europe and Latin America, and became especially close with a boy my age from Venezuela named Moises Alejandro Salazar Gonzalez, whom we called Alex. I loved hearing Alex's stories of the very different life he lived in his home country. His darker skin and hair, his ease with his body and emotions, and the warmth of his personality all felt so comfortable and familiar to me. He felt like family. Through Alex, I befriended Kasia from Poland, Silke from Germany, Cecilia from Colombia, and Ana Maria, like Alex, from Venezuela. These Latin American and European teenagers expanded my world and opened my eyes to what other ways life could be, beyond the world in which up till then I had always lived. Alex eventually left his original host family for some reason and moved in with my friend Mike's family. They had already planned a family trip for spring break, so Alex came and stayed at my house for those ten days. My mom enjoyed Alex as much as I did, and for the first time in my life, I got to relish having a brother.

In the spring of this year, a horrific event ended my remaining reliance on the golden boy role. In making sense of this experience today, I am grateful to be able to share with you a reflective piece that I wrote just seven years after high school, in my mid-20s. From that closer vantage point, the details and texture of this shattering experience are more available than they are to my memory now. (If you wish to avoid graphic description of harm, please skip to the next section.)

March 25, 1993. The first night of GRIEF Senior retreat.
We had only just completed the settling-in phase of our retreat weekend. Two years of getting to know each

other preceded this weekend. We had trusted each other enough to talk about hard issues, fun issues—parents, divorce, girlfriends, ambitions, God, values, our gifts, our weaknesses. GRIEF: "Greater Respect in Every Friend" was a group of some of the most interesting Prepsters, who were also usually popular, good-looking, and a leader in some arena. This retreat was to be a culmination of sorts of our commitment to one another. Bags had been put in rooms, a quick dinner was consumed with laughter, and we were all settling down from the studies of the week, for a break from the stresses of senior year of high school—college applications, growing out of Prep, all of us already heading for disparate adult trajectories.

Greg, as usual, was in his slightly odd retreat mode, bracing for emotionality and relational dynamics that he relished. We were now beginning our first session, when the phone rang. Greg answered, and it very quickly changed his demeanor. Retreat mode left for something more serious and more real. Greg changed out of the man who was so caught up with the emotional life of his students to a strong adult and educator who was suddenly responsible for breaking tragic news to a group of teenagers. "Alex Salazar and Matt R. were involved in an accident. Alex was shot. He didn't make it."

My inner landscape suddenly transformed: Dissipated were the slight aloofness and heavy-handed judgmentalism toward Greg that I used to cope with somehow having fallen out of his favor; gone was any thought of retreat or the anticipation of growth and deepened relationships from it. Instead, death slammed its reality into me. As my emotions caught up with this reality, my spirit felt first like an ankle twisted hard and suddenly against an unforeseen obstacle. Then, the tendons and muscles and skin of my soul which loved Alex like a brother were twisted further, and ripped, as he was torn from me, crudely and abruptly. I erupted in pain.

Wailing and hot, tense and trembling, the tingle of new places of hurt and loss rapidly took form within me, right next to the husk of my father. Two tattered figures now. Statues, shadows, nuclear-blast images of real people once there now burned into the walls of my home. First a father long gone, his image cold; now a brother from Venezuela adopted into my family, his image smoldering hot, his imprint on my soul right fresh from the red-hot brand. I bit hard into my hand to mark that moment of loss. The other boys had gathered around me and held me and tried to soothe my grief. Tom and Carl, Jeff and Scott, Matt and Robb. There were more than a dozen of us in that group. Though part of me was oblivious, I could have been in no better place to receive the news of Alex's death than among that group of peers who were ready and able to stand around me, their arms around me and hands grasping me in support and love, as if to say, though you have lost one brother, you have many more, Nick.

Alex's tragic death seared me. Like a white-hot flash of senseless, needless violence, the accidental gunshot that blew his head off left a mushroom cloud of traumatic reverberations. My primordial traumas, all related to my Dad, were now matched by a fresh wound. Alex's shadow got burned onto my psyche right next to the shadow of my father, who though still alive had long lived as a phantom in my life.

After spending all the days of high school running into the brightness of the golden boy persona as "Joe Prep"—class president, varsity athlete, and pious prodigy—Alex's sudden death brought my awareness back to the dark depths of loss, pain, and grief that had clouded and confused my childhood, marking me as indelibly different, queer. As I painfully envisioned again and again that gun discharging and blowing his head apart, another layer of constructed naiveté and sunny disposition peeled off of me, dropping to the ground like flakes of old paint.

Before this shocking loss, I had long exuded a sunny disposition, rooted in a rational optimism and encouraged by my family and teachers. My Uncle Chuck would say, "You have a big brain, Nick. You can do anything you want. Just put your mind to it and work hard. You can be anything." I solemnly took in his words. *He knows something about me and about life*, I thought to myself. *Pay heed. Listen up!*

Based on this explicit guidance from Uncle Chuck and less obvious encouragement from myriad other sources, I came to hold a foundational belief that with hard work I could develop my talents, knowledge, and skills to become whatever kind of success I desired. This belief fueled late nights of studying throughout high school. *God gave me a "big brain." It was on me to use it, train it, apply it.* Therein lay success and happiness, whose contours and features the American dream and the dreams of my family and larger community defined and delimited.

Alejandro's accidental death shattered this bright outlook. Life wasn't so simple now that the shadow of death could no longer be ignored. While I wasn't ready to delve into the shadow sides of myself, Alex's death nonetheless shook loose the golden boy's hold on me. I became quieter. Tears came often and easily. For months on end, every morning, as I awoke my very first thought arrived like a blaring alarm: Alex is dead! This daily alert startled and shook me into waking consciousness. The shaking and shock of Alex's violent death blew apart my sunny disposition and gave me perspective on my Joe Prep persona, the golden boy, the **Best Little Boy**. From then on, no longer did I blithely run the circuit of learning, exceling, and gaining praise without noticing what I was up to. I saw this shiny happy version of myself and now I knew what he was up to. I came to recognize the golden boy as a pattern or habit that I was starting to outgrow.

That summer after high school graduation felt like a quiet waiting period, an in-between time. One version of me died with Alex, and the next version of myself hadn't yet been born. Joe Prep no longer, I was on my way to becoming some other, fuller version of myself, but did not yet know who.

- *What new difficulties did you face after the end of your innocence?*

Rise and Fall of the Golden Boy

- *What childhood names or nicknames did you shed or take on during your adolescence?*
- *What did these name changes mean to you back then?*
- *What meaning do you now put onto these name changes?*

Nick, the name I grew up with, resulted from a tussle between my parents. My dad, Fred Charles, wanted me to have his name and be Fred Charles, Junior. Fred was an Americanized version of Alfio, his father's father's name, and he wanted to continue the tradition. Mom refused, preferring something more up-to-date. I suppose that, even before she had seen the depths of his problems, she also wanted more space for me to be my own person rather than to dwell in the shadow of my dad. After some apparently heated exchanges, they named me Fred Dominic, choosing an alternative middle name with no precedents in the family but that signaled my Italian heritage without being too "ethnic." In this compromise, they also decided to call me "Nick," a diminutive from my middle name that also expressed their affection.

My name thus left me with a layered legacy. "Fred Dominic Longo" signals to others my Italian ethnicity, especially in the final vowel of my family name. But through anglicizing Alfio, not even to Alfred, but to Fred, my name also partially obscures my ethnic origins. Still, because I inherited "Alfio" from my illiterate great-grandfather, *Nanu Longo*, my name always reminds me of the Sicilian heritage brought to Omaha by his and *Nana's* voyage across the ocean. Most of all, my name always reminds me of my father and then of the strife between him and my mother.

Sometime during my last year of junior high, in 1988–89, I learned the word "eponymous" thanks to the *Eponymous* album by the band R.E.M. Learning the word brought my attention to the significance of the name imposed by my parents seemingly indelibly onto my person. Around this time, I gained awareness of the residue of shame that stuck to me uncomfortably on account of my name. Because so much of my queerness connected to my dad's eccentricity, his mental illness, his violence, and his rage, the form of my name has always felt like it both partially reveals and partially obscures what set me apart from the herd.

Boy to Man, Man to Boy

Before I went off to college far beyond the Omaha of my childhood, I yearned to know my father once again. Reminders of him abounded, of course, especially at my grandparents' home, but I hadn't seen him since I was 13. Reconnecting with him felt like necessary preparation for leaving home. I needed to know the man whose legacy had made me so "queer," before embarking on the transition into becoming my own man.

I saw him a great deal that summer, spending maybe seven hours at a time at his home making a single meal together, eating and talking, digesting and crying, and laughing while trading stories. Having missed out on sharing so much, we both knew how special this time together was. I relished the great quantities of food and family lore. We feasted on these rare and irreplaceable shared moments, for which we had both long yearned. We also both knew that they did not make up for lost time. I had long reached out grasping for him, but he had eluded me like a phantom. Except during some of these exquisite moments, he would never be for me the kind of father he might once have dreamed to be, or for which I had so fervently wished. Still, he appreciated my interest in and attention to him, and I got to know this man whose strangeness had so indelibly marked my identity.

Because Creighton Prep had given me many models worth imitating, I was no longer wondering how to be a man. But getting to know my dad again when I was eighteen years old filled in gaps in my sense of what it meant to be a Longo, what it meant to be Fred's son, what it meant to be me in my family. So that I could leave home and become myself more fully, the boy in me needed to meet the man my dad was. In turn, the emerging man in me also encountered the boy in him as I took in his tender stories of adventure and grievance.

Charting a Course to College

The college search had seemed to channel into a single high-stakes decision all my teenage dreams for the life I wanted to live and the person I wanted to become. I knew I had pretty good grades and ranked high in my class at Creighton Prep, but I really had no idea what kind of school I could get into, nor what we would be able to afford. We were no longer in a land of scarcity and financial stress as we had been during Mom's law school years right after the divorce, but tuition fees seemed insuperably high. My grandparents, my parents, and their siblings had all gone to the University of Nebraska or to Creighton, the Jesuit university in Omaha, where my sister was already studying. I dreamt of elsewhere.

The summer before my senior year, we combined our family vacation with college visits to Notre Dame, Cornell, Holy Cross, Harvard, Boston College, Princeton, and Georgetown. Imagining myself in these different places excited me. I wondered how I would find my place amidst the posh "eating clubs" at Princeton or the political energy around Georgetown in Washington, DC. The right-leaning Catholic piety of Notre Dame, with its Marian grotto and "parietals" keeping out opposite-sex visitors from the dorms at certain hours, felt both familiar and uncomfortable. I felt ready to spread my wings and exercise my autonomy, not find a new kind of parental force to impose curfews or the rosary onto me!

Stretching beyond the religious subculture in which I had lived up till then, I applied to a dozen schools total. Only three were Catholic, one of which ended up feeling like the right balance between comfort and challenge. By spring, both Rob and I decided on Boston College.

Call Me by My Name

Following Alex's death, the ambitions I hatched for college centered on spreading my wings, exploring the wider world, and investigating my homoerotic stirrings. All of these would require paring back the high intensity of sports and other extracurriculars which had filled my high school years. I was looking for space and time for myself and my explorations, principally in books and in the city of Boston. I also had a vague inclination to start going by Dominic rather than Nick. I always liked this full version of my middle name. Changing what people would call me seemed like a fitting way to mark my move out of childhood, out of Omaha, and out of the family nest.

Asking Rob to call me by a new name, however, felt entirely different from using it in introducing myself to strangers. We had agreed to be roommates. Rob assured me he would be fine switching up what he called me, but I had hang-ups. Changing my name started to seem to me pretentious and affected. The musician Prince had just changed his name to an unpronounceable symbol. I was not about to be "the [affected, pretentious, queer] guy formerly known as Nick"! On some level, I knew that many gay men insisted on the long versions of their names. *I'm no longer "Billy"—call me "William."* Or *Not "Bobby," but "Robert"!* I remained "Nick," as I had been called my whole life up to the time Rob and I moved into Duchesne Hall on Boston College's Newton campus for our freshman year, even if a new version of myself was in the process of being born. I had imagined a fuller transition from the version of me embedded in Omaha into someone who was more self-possessed—but I wasn't quite ready for that move. In terms of developmental stages, this name change seems to have been my **Socialized** mind looking forward to the option of establishing a **Self-Authoring** self but then realizing that I was not there yet. More work would be required to become myself that fully.

PART II

Table 7: Queer Superpowers of Early Self-Authoring

Developmental Stage			Queer Superpower	Adverse Circumstances that prompt superpower's emergence
Self-Sovereign	Self-Protective Opportunist	1	Chameleonic Passing	» Social exclusion » Mocking » Bullying » Shaming » Moral condemnation » Shunning by family / friends » Violent attack
		2	Shield of Hypervigilance	
		3	The Great Escape	
Socialized	Conformist	4	Gaydar	» Cultural values » Gender expectations » Romantic & sexual norms of the straight mainstream » Religious & moral condemnation » Legal persecution
		5	Pride Tribe	
	Expert	6	The Best Little Kid	
Self-Authoring	Achiever	7	The Queen	» Strictures of societal expectations limit creative powers » Socialized cycle of approval-seeking forecloses possibility of greatness
		8	Double Life	
	Redefining	9	Second Adolescence	» Self-imposed limits caused by personal adaptations made earlier in life to survive and thrive » Distressful self-awareness of unintegrated parts of self
Self-Transforming		10	No One Left Behind	

Queer Flourishing

Description	Heroic Possibilities & Powers	Pitfalls & Shadow
» Adapt to fit wide range of settings	» Shape-shifting » Cloak of invisibility » Avoid unwanted attention » Allow others to imagine you're one of them	» Not being seen or known for who we are » Loneliness » Fusing with our masks and forgetting who we really are
» Early alert system for possible danger	» Prepared to freeze, flee, or fight for safety » Avoid attacks, traps, & ambushes	» Fear & anxiety flood out other emotions » Skittish withdrawal inhibits relationships » Difficulty trusting even the trustworthy
» Depart toxic or abusive life situation to find supportive context	» Muster the courage, creativity, and determination needed for liberation	» Leave behind the good and the bad alike » Change of scenery without inner growth or change – "Running to stand still" » Flee into the clutches of new abusers
» Sense others' queerness	» Tap into intuitive knowing » See people's hidden faces » Empathy for others' shame	» Delusions of queer grandeur, imagining LGBTQ+ folks as superior to straight people » Project own queerness onto others
» Membership in a queer social group	» Strength in solidarity » Self-confidence to cultivate and use atypical gifts	» Gay groupthink papers over personal uniqueness » False sense of superiority
» Meeting and surpassing social standards and expectations	» Achieve excellence » Gain admiration in society » Earn one's way out of shame	» Fitting in to move up, lose sense of self and own unique "weird & wonderful" traits » Trapped by society's definitions of success, e.g., wealth, high position, prestige, luxury, etc.
» Accept and exercise "divine right" to rule one's own realm	» Claim own power » Impervious self-possession » Regal stature and poise » Sharp rationality » Relentlessly strategic in pursuing own vision and goals	» Self-sufficiency limits love – It's lonely at the top » Steamroll over others » Compartmentalization keeps valuable inner resources inaccessible » Haughty overconfidence leaves others impressed but distant
» Bifurcate life into separate domains	» Create space for expression and cultivation of queer self » Honor suite of personal values despite contradicitons	» Split life mirrors splits in the self that limit personal integration » Self-control verges on fraud and deceit
» A controlled coming apart and re-forming of adult self	» Shed conventional version of self in favor of greater authenticity and self-expression » Capacity for experimentation, follwed by rapid iteration, learning, and growth » Creativity and originality, despite societal flak	» Perpetually lost and not found, dissolution of conventional self never resolves into new coherence » Regress back to conventional self
» Return to scenes of wounding, to heal and more fully integrate all parts of self	» Wholeness » Integration of hidden resources and vulnerabilities » Revivification of spiritual scars	» Without sufficient support, re-traumatization can occur

CHAPTER 4:

Queen Rising

My Great Sending Off

Four years later, I had my regal moment. Chosen to be Chief Marshall of the Order of the Cross and Crown by merit of my outstanding scholarship and service as an undergraduate, I stood in medieval academic regalia and delivered the Commencement address before thousands. The audience was made up of fellow graduates, their families, and the faculty and staff who had shepherded us through Boston College. "This Ignatian Village . . ." were the first words of my valedictory address, which I had composed and practiced in quiet pre-dawn hours of private reflection and study for months after learning that the University was bestowing this honor upon me.

I compared the four years of undergraduate life the Class of 1997 had gone through together to the "long retreat" in which Jesuits in formation undertake the Spiritual Exercises of Saint Ignatius of Loyola. We had lived, learned, and toiled together in ways inspired by Ignatius. This seemed to me the heart of Jesuit education. I framed our graduation as a sending forth to go "light the world on fire," a saying important to Jesuits and often attributed to Ignatius when he sent his *compañero* Francis

Xavier off to Asia to share with those he encountered there the love of God so that it burned brightly in all their hearts.

I reminded those gathered of the depiction of Pentecost as a euphoric reversal of Babel through the sending of the Spirit onto the community of followers of Christ (Acts 2.13). In that New Testament scene, the preaching of the apostles in Greek was understood by people from different lands and nationalities could understand as if hearing the preaching in their various native tongues. Invoking the irony of that text, I noted how that graduation morning some might see us graduates and exclaim, like those onlookers of the earliest Christian community who were lit with the Spirit, "They have had too much wine!" I—and many of my classmates—had indeed had too much to drink the night before! However euphoric we might have been, many of us were also hungover—I know I was.

I had spent the night before Commencement with my girlfriend Carly and my friend Jeremy in the off-campus Cleveland Circle apartment I had already moved into for my post-graduation summer.[50] We had been drinking vodka borrowed from my flatmate, and when that ran out, we moved onto a bottle of ouzo that as a resident assistant I had confiscated from a Greek-American underage student and illicitly kept. In my inebriation that night, I held out my hand and touched Jeremy while making out with Carly. I wanted them both. While by then I could admit at least to myself that wanting, to them I could only drunkenly gesture towards my desires. He was the forbidden fruit, she the licit consort. Nothing more happened, but I brought to the academic festivities of the next morning blurry memories of the fantasies that formed in that trio.

In my role as Chief Marshall, I had the honor of meeting our celebrity Commencement speaker, Janet Reno, the first woman to hold the position of US Attorney General. Sharing the dais with her held special significance for me, given the prominence of another woman attorney in my life, namely, my mother.

This regal moment rapidly gave way to anticlimax. Almost immediately following my college graduation, the rise of my inner **Queen** slumped into feelings of deflated disappointment. Before going into how that happened, how did this **Queen** rise within me? Allow me to go back and chronicle her rise to power, how she increasingly ruled the roost of my life during my four years of college. As ever, my hope in telling my story aims toward you reflecting on yours.

- *What regal moments have placed you on some dais, at some pinnacle?*
- *What significance do these moments have for you as you make sense of yourself and your life?*

Queenly Self-Authoring

- *What character traits, capabilities, and social energies do you associate with the moniker "queen" as referring to gay or queer men?*

The term "queen" in gay culture today is used quite loosely. Sometimes merely playful, "queen" often comes with a dollop of snark. *What are those queens doing here?* These days among the gays, "queen" seems to mean flamboyant and effeminate, plus haughty, persnickety, and tempestuous. *John queened out last night—he had such a hissy fit!* Attitudes towards queens or being queeny range from affectionate teasing to disparaging put-downs. *He's so queeny!* Someone might talk matter-of-factly about oneself or friends as queens. *There were about fifteen queens at the pool party where I first met my fiancé.* Or we might use it to express exasperation. *What a queen!* Or a profile on Grindr or Scruff might spout internalized homophobia and misogyny directed against more effeminate gay men by declaring, *No queens!* Afraid of their own gayness or even self-hating, those who disparage queens strive to distance themselves from flamboyance. They dread being seen as *a flamer.*

Though "queen" holds these layers of meaning today, until the 1960s the term was reserved in the gay community for queer men in positions of "leadership and honor," according to Channing Gerard Joseph, whose research aims to recover Black queer cultural history.[51] His forthcoming book, *The House of Swann*, profiles an almost forgotten pioneer of queer activism, William Charles Swann, whom Joseph credits with coining the term "drag queen." In April 1888, Swann, a former slave, was hosting a gathering at his home in Washington, DC, to celebrate his 30th birthday. The party was raided by the police, who dispersed a group of men dressed in women's finery. Unlike many of his guests, according to a contemporary newspaper article, Swann did not run from the police, but rather positioned himself and his elegant gown at the door of his apartment to try to bar their entry into his home. After the confrontation, this queen went on to lead a life of mentoring, advocating, speaking up, speaking out, and protesting for the queer community. Joseph calls this birthday celebration one of the earliest known "drag balls" and William Charles Swann its queen, who held a position of leadership and honor in her community.

Queens bear a noble history in queer culture. In raising up this regal title to name one of the queer superpowers, I mean to do honor to that history. Black queer culture, in particular, seems to have led the way in creating the kind of **Queen** to which I refer. Today, the American drag queen and impresario RuPaul epitomizes the arch wit, self-possession, and incisive, interpersonal intelligence of the **Queen** superpower at her height. While I leave it to Channing Gerard Joseph and other cultural historians to illuminate how much the term queen has previously been applied to powerful and independent gay and queer men who demonstrate access to both feminine and masculine energies, that is indeed how I am using the term here.

As a queer superpower, the **Queen** has assumed her rightful authority and power. Her intellect towers. She knows that her greatness lies in her independence and lucid thinking. The **Queen** finds her North Star within herself, guiding her path and measuring her progress. She sets her own goals and chooses the criteria and standards by which to evaluate herself (and others). She has wrested back control of her life from even the most important others. She now presides as Chair of her internal Board of Directors. Rather than abiding primarily in her interpersonal relationships, she has become *her own person* in the truest sense.

The **Queen** can be highly rational and analytical. She gets to the root causes and reasons for things, whether in a work situation or in someone's personality (including her own). At this stage, "people have enough of a perspective on themselves as objects and on their life as changing over time to become truly introspective."[52] Between her adept interpersonal skills and complex cognitive function, the **Queen** is an institution. Her prescience glitters with potency and charge.

The confidence of the Queen is so convincing that she can give others the impression that she is more mature and perspicacious than she actually is. Her decisive determination projects an aura of high self-esteem. She knows her plans and priorities. Whereas in the **Expert** stage, the focus was squarely on *doing things right*, now the focus is on *doing the right things*—and doing them efficiently and effectively.[53] While the **Queen** does look back in time to reflect on her past feelings and dreams, she tends to be more oriented towards the future. She has her five-year plan set. So much is yet to be accomplished! The **Achiever** mindset finds its meaning and self-worth in *goals*—first formulating them, then working towards them, and finally reaching them.

The **Queen** represents a particularly gay way of inhabiting the early **Self-Authoring**, **Achiever** stage of human development. At times bitchy, ironic and witty, or dressed with a flair, even panache, expressing a studied aesthetic, she has tapped into at least some of the feminine energy available in gay male culture. She has come to own her gayness enough to enjoy topping or bottoming or whatever her sexual preference is without serious hang-up or hesitation. Her self-referential usage of masculine and feminine pronouns interchangeably, ironically, playfully expresses her comfort with her place in the gender binary and with her gayness. Accordingly, we take on this use of *both* he/him/his *and* she/her/hers pronouns to refer to the **Queen** in this book.

The truce the **Queen** has with her gayness comes from a dual dynamic of exploration and compartmentalization. She has sampled many of the possibilities that she holds within her inner realm and those additional possibilities that lie outside herself, in the world, just awaiting a claimant or conqueror. Along her path to the throne of self-possession and success, she has selected what to claim and has delimited careful boundaries for those selections. Like a queen bee, she has assigned compartments in the honeycomb over which she reigns. *A place for each and everything, and each and everything in its place.* She has instituted a regime, thoughtfully planned out and carefully guarded. The **Queen**'s logical embrace of what Descartes called "clear and distinct ideas" makes possible the realization of her plans and ambitions. When feelings arise, they present a problem to be handled, a potential disruption to the royal administration. She deals with them, puts them in their proper compartment, and gets back to the work of ruling the realm.

This **Achiever** form of mind grows out of **Expert** mindset, in which we attend carefully to rules and external standards, such that we gradually come to know ourselves better and better, including our talents, potential, shortcomings, and pitfalls. We come to act and be in the world with what specifically and who distinctively we are. Eventually, we may arrive at a place where we set our own standards and legislate our own laws. Rather than internalizing other people's priorities and perspectives, we select and define values for ourselves. We construct an inner realm and rule over it, even as we continue to navigate with even greater skill the rules, customs, and values of the cultures in which we live. Here, we become our own person, instead of being determined essentially by other people. We finally create a Self, "an 'I' that has, rather than is, its relationships."[54] For the first time, we truly have "autonomy," meaning etymologically "a law unto ourselves." How marvelous!

Our individuation at this stage involves differentiating ourselves within society through crafting and pursuing a personal vision for ourselves and our lives. We still hold some version of the dreams offered to us by our culture, family, religion, or other community, but now we customize that dream for ourselves. Still retaining access to our **Conformist** self, we remain aware of others' perspectives and societal expectations. We even seek out others to gather material to fortify our outlook. Nevertheless, we prioritize our own values, vision, and sense of purpose in choosing how to be and what to do. We set goals for success and seek effectiveness, rather than caring most about efficiency.

Increasingly, we come to discover structures, recurring patterns, and the rules and measures which explain how the world works, including ourselves and other beings. These discoveries empower and enable us to connect dots, both backwards and forwards in time. Becoming our own person in the world thus involves our coming to grasp causality and formulate goals.

We become our own highest authority for our life. We embed ourselves in an ideology of our own making. We grind and polish our distinctive lenses through which to see the world. We begin authoring our life story, rather than ceding the pen to important or expert others. This kind of competent independence and personal agency embodies the kind of person that educational, job training, professional development, and leadership programs typically strive to cultivate.

The Heroes Journey program at the heart of Flourishing Gays is designed especially for gay, bi, and queer men who are moving out of the **Achiever** form of mind. I often encounter the **Queen** in my clients. Descriptions of the program describe it as targeting highly accomplished gay, bi, and queer men, in the hopes of attracting recovering overachievers—those who have long used achievement to try to earn their way out of shame, and who are ready to let go of this pattern in their lives. When coaching a **Queen**, I stand in my own power and meet their regal self-possession and their rigor with my own. Scientifically validated psychometric assessments developed by experts in leadership and human development, as well as intercultural development, provide my clients with objective data about where they are in their developmental journeys.

Yet, alongside these moves to meet the **Queen**'s power with my own, I also bring deep wells of compassion to a client who shows up in the full regalia of the **Queen**. I look to their suffering and their yearnings that go beyond their unmet goals and five-year plans. Through powerful questions and reflecting back all that I see in them, I point the **Queen** beyond achievement toward her potential fulfillment. When I become aware of her locked-up compartments of feelings and parts of herself that she keeps hidden away, I gently let on that I see those compartments. Queens bear great burdens—all the responsibilities that come along with ruling the realm. That tremendous weight can become oppressive. The fervent commitment and dogged dedication to these responsibilities can effectively fuse a **Queen**'s sense of self with the burdens she bears. *Who might you be if you unhook yourself from that yoke? Where might you go and what might you do, if you dropped those burdens, your Majesty?*

- *What in the account of the **Queen** superpower differs from the associations that you had previously to "the Queen" as a gay male character in popular culture?*
- *Who in your social world most fully embodies the **Queen** superpower?*
- *What about that person do you find most compelling and admirable?*
- *What about them most turns you off? What about them do you dislike or even disdain?*

Climbing the Ivory Tower to Straight Self-Authoring

- *What developmental companions have most helped you to become yourself?*

Over my college years, I was like a bee becoming a **Queen**. Moving beyond the groupthink my world had imposed, I was changing according to designs I found deep within myself.

The transition from Creighton Prep to Boston College had replaced one set of "important others" with another and one set of standards for being the **Best Little Kid** with another. I started to step away from the powerful pull of others' approval and move closer to self-governance. I congratulated myself for my independence of mind and self-sufficiency. *I'm marching to the beat of my own drum.*

Early in life, I had begun carving out a heady realm and retreating to the ivory tower of my intellect through reading. Favorites included *Encyclopedia Brown, Dr. Doolittle,* Isaac Asimov, Robert Heinlein, and one teen summer as much Ernest Hemmingway as I could find in the basement among my parents' college texts. Back then I was finding respite from the all-too-adult complexities that my life presented while proving myself to my mom, teachers, and to certain Jesuits. In college, I came to care more for what I thought of myself. Careful yet voluminous reading of great literature fed this turn inward. Humanities professors guided and encouraged me to come to know myself more deeply through engaging in the "Great Conversation" of the Western cultural tradition. As a child, literature had transported me away from Omaha through imaginative forays across the real and fictional universes. Now literature nourished a process of growing the universe within myself.

Later in life, in a graduate seminar on queer theology taught by Mark Jordan—a teacher, writer, and mentor, whom I came to admire greatly—I encountered the phrase "a honeycomb of closets" in his book *The Silence of Sodom*.[55] Jordan uses the phrase to describe the Catholic Church, with its many gay priests, who often feel isolated from one another. I see now how this queer metaphor aptly describes the form of mind and the structure of life that I was constructing in my college years. In this way, I defensively limited the threats of my non-standard erotic impulses and fantasies by carefully demarcating boundaries for my respectable self. *Here he works, here he excels, here he prays, here he becomes his own person.* The compartments I constructed for my life comprised a honeycomb of spaces in which I worked and played, grew and learned. I was busy as a bee building "a honeycomb of closets" within myself for me to inhabit. I had not yet fully formed a **Double Life**; I had not yet become a **Queen**. But, boy, was I on my way!

On the way to becoming a closet **Queen** and constructing a **Double Life**, certain aspects of my cognitive and emotional intelligence bounded ahead, while other parts of myself stayed stunted and unexplored. I don't look at the straight life I lived in these years as "false consciousness," but rather as the best steps I could muster on the journey to becoming myself. Romantic or sexual experiences with other guys did not seem like legitimate options for me at Boston College any more than at Creighton Prep. Though I knew a few gay undergraduates, I did not have enough social support or role models to learn how to put together a coherent sense of self that included gayness.

In my college years, "Dominic" begins to emerge, choosing and assembling values and social identities to construct a worldview and a Self. With the **Achiever** mindset I began to try on in these years, I perceived this sense of Self that I was then creating to be much fuller and more carefully constructed than it looks to me now. My college years leading up to that regal moment on the dais at graduation tell the story of the birth of "Dominic."

My use of the "queer superpowers" in my high school and college years did not appear especially queer. The version of the **Queen** I created did not look very gay at all. Indeed, he had a serious girlfriend! In high school, I had noticed a desire to explore my gay side, but didn't know how. The "secret pledge" I made to myself to explore this in college functioned as a placeholder for this work, which I postponed. Though inhabiting a straight social identity in high school and college limited me in certain ways, to a large degree it served my personal development. When there were parts of me that were ready to grow that did not fit into the straight mold, those parts found their way out. I pursued my exploration and experimentation in roundabout ways around the edges of my life—sideways, not straight-on. Had looser, less constrained models for living as a straight young man been available to me, my developmental journey might have been easier, with less confusion, shame, or inner conflict. Had there been models for a bisexual identity that felt within reach, I might have happily inhabited such an identity. Given what options I did see as viable, I did the best I could to keep up the work of growing into myself.

Rob and I delighted in accompanying each other in life. By going together to Boston College, we brought with us there the best of our Creighton Prep experience. As roommates in our freshman and sophomore years, we encouraged each other to pursue our respective interests. Without any competitive energy, we admired one another's intellectual accomplishments and expanding range of knowledge and skills. He got into geology and geoscience and advocated for a better recycling program on campus. I kept adding languages and delved into comparative literature, while singing in liturgical and orchestral choirs on campus. We gradually cared less and less for anyone's approval, even each other's. The support we gave each other helped us each increasingly become our own person, to chart our course, to choose our goals, and decide what path to take to achieve them.

We egged each other on to approach our many growth edges in ways that especially helped me to become myself as a loving and sexual man. In wide-ranging conversations, we would as easily exchange sexual banter in great levity as we would delve deep into moral or spiritual matters of great gravity. Both the playfulness and the earnest soul-searching helped us each to become more fully ourselves.

Because I lived such a straight life in college, one experience of gender play especially deserves mention. Halloween our freshman year, Rob and I found our way to a midnight showing of *Rocky Horror* in Harvard Square. Some girls we knew through the BC Honors Program joined in the fun, and we all got dressed up in *Rocky*-themed costumes. One of them lent me a "house dress," another some fishnet stockings. They offered to use Aquanet hairspray to "rat" my bangs, which were so long at that time they could reach past my chin. I was unfamiliar with the term, but they assured me it would make me look sexy and wild like a rockstar. With their deft ministrations, my bangs reached quite a few inches above my head, probably more like a rat's nest than I would have liked to admit!

That Halloween night remains one of the few times in my life (so far!) when I dressed in drag. Besides the bangs, the dress, and the fishnets, the girls put frosted lipstick and eye shadow on me, along with rouge and eyeliner. Because no one had heels big enough for my feet (nor could I have walked in them!), for ironic effect I wore my black Teva sandals. I was ravishing as a "sweet transvestite," I'm sure.

The event organizers must have thought so too because I won the prize for "best virgin costume." In *Rocky Horror* groupie lingo, "virgin" referred to someone who had never seen the show before. I don't recall whether I had stretched the truth about my "virgin" status or just told them that was my first time seeing *Rocky* in Boston. In any case, the inflatable cherry sucker the size of a tennis racket they awarded as my trophy sat in our dorm room for the rest of the year, a memento of a night of queer gender play on the edge of respectability!

The version of masculinity that Rob and I shared had long included ease and comfort with the feminine, but aside from romps like that night at *Rocky Horror*, I didn't feel at ease stepping out of the straight and narrow of heterosexual expectations. I was on my way to becoming what Michael in *The Boys in the Band* might call a "closet **Queen**," the kind of husband who tells his wife he's running to Home Depot only to drop by some shady park to cruise for furtive sex with another man. Though on the path to one day embracing a **Double Life**, I never quite got there.

My inner **Queen** was carving out spaces and erecting walls, a honeycomb of compartments to keep my diverse parts penned in. I was increasingly reflective and introspective, but I avoided looking too intently into some of those cells. I was, for example, building rigid barriers between my solitary study and my socializing, my homoerotic exchanges and my straight romance. Though I would hardly have admitted it to myself at the time, I kept my inner life tidy through the careful use of compartmentalization. My approach to internal "home economics" could have been described by the proverb in *Mrs. Beeton's Book of Household Management*, a Victorian guide to ruling the roost: "A place for everything, and everything in its place."

Increasingly, I lived from the inside out. Finding new role models among Jesuits and professors at Boston College, I was inspired to look inward for my answers and for the questions that felt most worth asking. Living life primarily through my intellect, I spent much more time quiet, alone, and reflective. Still gregarious in certain moments, I focused more on cultivating my inner life and constructing various visions for what kind of person I thought I wanted to be.

Through solitary concentration and thoughtful responses to prods and challenges from the "important others" in my life, I increasingly crafted my values, religious and spiritual commitments, and how I inhabited my body. The outside-in version of me, for whom others' expectations and views ultimately defined me, diminished in strength and no longer held primacy of place in my interior realm. My liberal arts education and all that came with it empowered me to pick up the pen and author more of the book of my life.

- *What queer gender play shows up in your life story, and what did it mean for you at the time?*
- *What experiments or habits fed the transition that you have gone through from living from the "outside in" to living from the "inside out"?*

Life as a Queen

- *What traits of the **Queen** superpower do you most embody?*
- *When does your inner **Queen** especially come out to "rule the roost"?*

In the contemporary West, one version of the **Queen** sits on a corporate throne. Whether or not born into royalty, this queer **Queen** has ascended the ranks by his own hard work, determination, and strategy. He has learned a great deal, taken to heart some hard lessons, and persevered despite significant challenges. The corporate **Queen** feels safe (emotionally and otherwise), secure (financially and otherwise), and successful (professionally and otherwise). Because of his developmental journey, which he sees as a great success, the **Queen** and many others in Self-Authoring, Achiever mind "generally believe in the *perfectibility of humankind*."[56] The corporate **Queen** enjoys high position and status in his chosen field, whether industry, government, or non-profit. His title, prestige, and earnings demonstrate his worth and value. The **Best Little Kid** has now won the game, shown he matters, and maybe, just maybe, earned his way out of his shame. This transition, from **Best Little Kid** to **Queen**, marks a vital personal expansion. For some, the process of making this developmental shift fills many years of adult life.

The corporate **Queen** has for a long time demonstrated ever more creativity and courage in being his own person, constructing his life, and choosing who to make his family and where to make his home. Each of these areas of creativity and courage grows out of a distinctive hurt that LGBTQ+ folks commonly experience. Having been told by family, religion, and society that he is intrinsically disordered, broken, and bad, the **Queen** has become his own person to such a degree that he has demonstrated his own worth—first to himself and also to others. Having learned that so many of the molds and pathways offered by mainstream society are not available to him, he has constructed his own life path and form, which remain recognizably admirable to the straight majority. In many cases, having been rejected by family—whether violently thrown out of his parents' home or merely despised in certain arguments with certain relatives—the **Queen** has found a **Pride Tribe**, a chosen family to substitute for or complement the family into which he was born.

Because of his truce with his gayness, the corporate **Queen** may be publicly partnered or officially married. He may publicly play gay leadership roles. Wealthier **Queens** might sit on the board of gay charities or other organizations, or at least donate to them and attend their high-profile galas. On the other hand, he may be quiet about his sexual proclivities and romantic inclinations. He may be so buried in work and responsibility that he hardly ever dates. Finding affective outlets in friendships, family relationships, and furtive sex, he might close himself off from the deeper sexual intimacy that comes from emotional vulnerability and relational commitment.

The Culmination of Convention

In his early work, before using the term "**Self-Authoring**," adult development expert Robert Kegan called this stage the Institutional Self, because at this point in development a person *institutes* or "sets up" the "statutes" for their realm.[57] This **Self-Authoring** step of self-definition represents a high point in the process of greater and greater differentiation, that is, constructing a separate self-identity, a process which has been underway since separating from the original symbiotic fusion with the mother. In **Self-Authoring** mind, we truly become our own person in the world. The **Queen** thus embodies a particularly gay way of being one's own person.[58]

Western cultures celebrate "the acquisition of this scientific, rational frame of mind . . . as the goal of socialization and schooling." Indeed, in many contemporary cultures, this early **Self-Authoring**, **Achiever** mind "defines what it means to be seen as a fully grown adult."[59] For this reason, theorists regard this stage as the culmination of the so-called **conventional** stages. Though we come into our own in this form of mind, the conventions of the cultural milieu in which we live still condition our notion of self-definition. Indeed, compared to a child at the beginning of the developmental journey, someone at this **Achiever** stage is much more "normal," because of being so powerfully shaped by the ambient culture, society, and historical moment in which they live. At the same time, a person operating from **Achiever** mind is also more influenced and shaped by their cultural milieu than someone in the later stages of development. After all, both young children and people far into the post-conventional stages stand apart from the pressures and expectations of their environment, though for different reasons. Moving from **Self-Sovereign** into **Socialized** mind entails joining into the conventions, expectations, and rules of society, while moving beyond **Achiever** mind involves transcending convention and the limits of scientific objectivity and linear rationality.

Thanks to the marginalized position that queer people inhabit due to heterosexist, homophobic, and transphobic attitudes and structures, we gain some advantage in the process of transcending societal conventions and expectations. While queer people cannot and do not skip over the conventional stages of human development, our social situation outside of sexual and gender norms allows us more easily to notice the limits of convention. Even though we get socialized into our own sets of queer conventions, our marginalized position in society at large serves as a resource for gaining perspective on all social conventions, even those dear to other gay men, for example. Queer developmental journeys thus hold a certain momentum that drives us towards making sense of reality in post-conventional ways.

Compartmentalizing into a Double Life

The masterful compartmentalization of the **Queen** gives rise to a second queer superpower, the **Double Life**. Navigating the mines and pitfalls that heteronormative society lays out to mark the legitimate territory for citizens to explore, claim, and inhabit prods some queer people to split their lives and their personas into at least two versions. Accessing this queer superpower, they create one life in the straight world and another among the underworlds and dark forests of condemned edge dwellers.

In the American context of gay, bi, and queer men's lives, the phrase "double life" conjures up the man married to a woman, living a conventional life, perhaps with several kids in the suburbs, while also having gay lovers and social circles. He has employed his power of compartmentalization to split himself in two—a straight self and a gay self. One self receives societal approbation, the other fulfills desires that come from deep within. He learns to code-switch, speaking gay here and speaking straight there. He has mastered the conventions of the straight culture in which he grew up, and he has also come to know the ways of queer culture. He is bi-cultural.

Without diminishing the potential damage that men in such situations do, especially to their wives and children, I mean to reappropriate the **Double Life** as a queer superpower by placing it in a larger context beyond the example of gay men who cheat on their wives through sex with men. Rather, as a queer superpower, the **Double Life** points to a complex of formidable capacities. Significant self-awareness and self-control are needed to monitor oneself so that one side of life does not spill into the other. The earlier queer superpower of **Chameleonic Passing** now grows into two full-fledged personas that match the two different worlds. The **Double Life** builds on other earlier superpowers as well. Like a **Great Escape**, it is a secret passage built into one's normal life, so that by traveling back and forth, two worlds remain easy and always accessible. On one side of that passage lives a **Pride Tribe**, who provides support, affirmation, and joy to the queer side of the self. **Gaydar** might operate on both sides of the **Double Life**, letting the split self find allies and lovers wherever they might be.

As an insight into the **Queen**'s compartmentalization and the **Double Life**, consider how Human Resource departments and Employee Resource Groups often herald the motto of "Bring your whole self to work!" Explaining this motto, they commonly describe a desired work environment where team members can be forthcoming and open about their racial, cultural, sexual, and gender identities as well as hobbies and personal interests. Advocates of this approach might highlight the downsides of closeting and covering, such as the extra energy needed to strive to fit in with white or straight culture, for example. Though adult development theory might still be unfamiliar in many corporate contexts, I suppose that campaigns to encourage people to "bring their whole self to work" aim to create space for people's inner voice, personal authority, and their sense of self apart from groupthink or group membership. In other words, "Bring your whole self to work!" makes part of the corporate apparatus that cultivates **Self-Authoring** mind.

Among the professionals I have worked with who seem primarily to operate from **Self-Authoring** mind, I've noticed a common adjustment or even resistance to "Bring your whole self to work!" They talk instead about bringing one's *best* self to work. The **Queen** enjoys a degree of self-awareness that allows her to notice her shadow. She knows she holds within herself many dark places, including wounds and shame and hostility towards others—shadowy aspects that warrant no welcome in the workplace. "Bring your *best* self to work (not your whole self)!" thus demonstrates the **Queen**'s characteristic combination of keen self-awareness, successful self-management, and useful compartmentalization. The politics of respectability govern office spaces, and since she is deft at politics, the **Queen** adapts to her surroundings. Living a **Double Life** allows the **Queen** to wield her formidable powers at work while retaining license to flip into fabulous faggotry at other times and in other spaces.

- *What realms of your own life do you most wall off to keep one part of your world from another?*

The Queen's Dilemmas and Defenses

- *What workaholics inhabit your world?*
- *What is your relationship to overwork?*

Though the **Queen** looms large, she casts a long shadow, wherein many demons dwell. She can be desperately lonely deep down because of the lack of intimacy in her life. The **Queen** may face a sense of ultimate meaninglessness, having achieved all her dreams but left wondering what else life might possibly be. Because of an exaggerated sense of responsibility for how things turn out in any given situation, she can feel guilty and inadequate. In the face of setbacks or failures, "not being successful is taken as a sign one has not done one's best or betrayed one deepest potential."[60]

The **Queen**'s sense of self-sufficiency limits her joy and fulfillment. Unlike someone in the **Self-Sovereign** stage, who rules his petite realm like a petty tyrant, the **Queen,** with a **Self-Authoring** form of mind, retains a certain openness to the views and feelings of other people. She learned to be permeable to others earlier in life, when she dwelled primarily in **Socialized** mind. Though she has taken back her sense of self and zipped up the seams of her identity to secure herself, she knows how to attend to others. Indeed, they can make significant contributions to her agenda offering opinions and arguments that shore up her views. Other people are useful. Those who have agendas that align with the **Queen**'s can be allies.

Yet allies are not intimates. When she slows down to take notice, the **Queen** sees that she lives on an island, unto herself. She thus holds within herself both a proud strength of mind and a clutching, headstrong isolation. In the shadow of her self-sufficiency dwells the **Ice Queen**. Impervious and impenetrable, the **Ice Queen** manages herself meticulously—especially her emotions. She reigns with irony and wit, keeping her distance while having her way.

An office or bureaucracy typically offers no explicitly developmental support for colleagues in this **Achiever** mindset to grow beyond their current stage. To make partner or be promoted to senior management, an organization might put developmental demands on rising professionals and offer them developmental support to reach an **Achiever** mindset. Once there, however, the rising professional is expected to mentor more junior people who aspire to similar success. They see themselves as a leader and a guide for others more than as a work in progress.

At first, the corporate **Queen** may seem never to tire of congratulating herself or doling out guidance to her juniors. Challenges to her sublime self-governance, such as some strong emotions, do sometimes arise. Bitter disappointment at being passed over for a promotion, heartsickness at being left by a lover, grief at the death of a parent or sibling, or other confrontations with mortality, such as a milestone birthday, might shake the foundations of her well-governed realm such that she cannot easily maintain a serene posture of regal splendor. Such challenges to her carefully regulated system might disrupt her current way of making sense of herself and the world. They could spur so-called "vertical development" by prompting the beginnings of a transition to a new developmental stage.

However, the **Queen** most often avoids or at least postpones this kind of growth and change, preferring instead to take one of two paths. One option is to learn some new knowledge or skill that allows her to deal with the disruption of whatever discrepant data or overwhelming experience has threatened her equanimity. This adaptation of learning new skills and knowledge is what adult development theory calls "horizontal development." The second option is for her to adopt defense mechanisms to stave off the threat. We've already noted how some other defenses commonly feature in the **Queen**'s workings, such as compartmentalization that keeps the aspects of life in separated silos and intellectualization that strains to remove all emotion from oneself. Depending on her style, the **Queen** might also defend her current sense of self with rationalizations that explain away the challenge, or with displacement that directs strong emotions such as anger at someone who does not actually pose a threat.

Over time, the corporate **Queen** might become increasingly effective at this unconscious defensive strategy. Yet, the strategy of learning new knowledge and skills becomes less and less sufficient to handle the complex challenges she faces. Meanwhile, the corporate bureaucracy "collude[s] with the defensive side of personality seeking to resist the upheavals of evolution. The traditional workplace overholds ideological adulthood [i.e., the Self-Authoring stage]."[61] The corporate **Queen** thus often succeeds at staving off vertical development, that reconfiguration and expansion of one's way of making sense of oneself and the world. Freezing herself developmentally, the **Queen** prevents herself from daring to upend the carefully regulated administration of her self-governance. She siphons off her dark and dynamic energies into queer compartments. She becomes the **Ice Queen**.

Prone to depression, the **Ice Queen** denies, represses, and avoids. Leaning into her strength and prowess at achieving and accomplishing, the **Ice Queen** works overtime to hold herself together and resist personal evolution. Kegan describes workaholism as a hypermasculine "depressive equivalent."

Forceful developmental inertia keeps **Achievers** in their current stage. **Queens** possesses the kind of maturity that mainstream society wants leaders to embody. To preserve their respectability and keep them contributing to the corporate mission, the heteronormative social system willingly turns a blind eye to the **Double Life** that some **Queens** live. Indeed, most of the leadership development industry aims to grow people into an early **Self-Authoring, Achiever** form of mind. The **Queen** sees herself as having arrived, and this belief is reinforced by employers, families, and civil society. The **Queen** may well meet her first introduction to adult human development theory with incredulity, at least when she gets to the part about well-documented stages of development beyond what she knows herself to have reached. The **Queen** sees herself as *a winner* in the maturity game. She is no child, and she knows it.

Adult human development theory thus challenges the **Queen**. It threatens her self-image. While she is ready to learn new things, work on or compensate for her weaknesses, and build on her strengths, the prospect of questioning the very foundations of her worldview is daunting. The cost of moving beyond a **Self-Authoring, Achiever** form of mind is high, and the losses sizable—yet the gains are extraordinary.

Fascinating complexity proliferates in the systems found in nature, organizations, and the human personality. Every tiny system—the atom itself—holds mysteries beyond the reach of linear causality and non-permeable borders. Like fractals, the tiny and the cosmic, the personal and the societal mirror each other in their complexity. This systems-view of reality eludes the **Queen**, though whatever of its intimations she senses become a doorway into a new way for her.

When we encounter the **Queen** in ourselves and others, we do well to stand in our power *and* be vulnerable. This polarity between power and vulnerability for her feels impossible. Yet she might be intrigued and enticed into allowing herself to see something real beyond the bounds of her worldview—whether it is most informed by Newtonian physics, Cartesian logic, Kantian moral imperatives, or something else. We can appreciate the great power of her self-discipline and strength of character, while coaxing tenderness around her limitations.

Likewise, the **Queen**'s capacity for introspection, looking back at herself in the past and the present, noticing feelings and thoughts and their development along with her own, becomes a tremendous resource to the **Queen**. Introspection can heighten her current powers and illuminate inner potential still waiting to be realized. When we encounter the **Queen**, we can encourage her to slow down, step back, and be with herself more fully. A couple of specific areas especially worth her attention are her certainty and assumptions. Thanks to her belief in human perfectibility, her curiosity, interest in learning and self-improvement, and her commitment to right thinking, with proper care and prodding she can be coaxed into noticing the discrepancies and drawbacks of her firmly held beliefs. Powerful questions can prompt her to practice more profound self-examination. When this inner work does not shore up her carefully constructed worldview but rather plunges her into the rift valleys of her oceanic depths, the very foundations of her self-governance and self-regulation will shake.

Sex with the **Queen** can be adventurous and affirming. She attends to her partners' needs. She makes love with consideration and awareness, both of her own experience and that of her intimate partners. Unlike those in **Socialized** mind, the **Queen** is capable of truly seeing the other person as a person, with their own wants, needs, and perspectives. However capable of consideration and even empathy, the **Queen** does not lose her Self in lovemaking. Sex and the erotic can feel to the **Queen** like problems to be solved, demands that must be dealt with. The fires of desire and the impulse to connect with others threaten her self-regulated stability. Sex upsets self-governance. The ecstatic pleasure of profound vulnerability risks the loss of self-control and autonomy, her everything.

- *In what circumstances do you notice yourself relying on rationalization or intellectualization to avoid dealing with difficult feelings or realizations?*

Carly

- *In what ways have experiences of falling in love helped or hindered your growth and maturation?*
- *What shifts in your understanding of your ethnic, racial, socioeconomic, and religious identity took place during your transition into early adulthood?*
- *In what ways did developmental companions serve as sounding boards for you during that transitional period?*

Besides my close friend Rob, my girlfriend Carly was another vitally important developmental companion in my college years. Our relationship created a nurturing and challenging space in which to form my own identity. Our exploration of our similarities and differences helped me to decide which values to live by and to reflect on the influences of my social class, ethnicity, religious background, and family history. I learned to disagree and differ in values while holding her with respect and admiration. With Carly, I tried on living a conventional life as a straight man in America.

We met at Casino Night, an orientation event just before classes started our first week at Boston College—me a fresh-faced first year and Carly a sophomore, who transferred from another school. Carly came from a small Midwestern town with about as many inhabitants as Creighton Prep had students. I brought an Omahan's sense of superiority to her small-town roots. *What of interest could possibly happen in rural America?!* Nonetheless, amidst crowds of kids from Long Island, New Jersey, and New England, Carly and I shared a common culture as fellow Midwesterners. Still, I had scarcely any sense of what her life growing up in a Protestant farm family living in a small town might have been like.

We quickly discovered we had both registered for the same Microeconomics course, so we sat together twice a week and often had lunch afterward. She was fun, kind, good-natured, and easy to talk to. Whip-smart and curious, she loved learning and wanted to explore more of Boston and the Northeast, as I did. We also shared humility about coming from the Midwest while rolling our eyes at how provincial our classmates from New Jersey or Long Island seemed, with their apparent beliefs that their home states were the center of the universe!

Like many Midwesterners, Carly exuded a frank and sincere friendliness. We encouraged each other's unpretentious, yet disciplined and high-achieving way of moving through college. I marveled at and learned from her way of organizing herself with task lists. I also admired her commitment to early morning exercise, which she professed not to enjoy but did anyway, motivating herself with mantras like *Gotta be thin to be beautiful!*

For me, a day well spent was sitting with the original Latin of Ovid's *Metamorphoses* or some other classic text and luxuriating in its turns of phrase and cultural references. For Carly, a day well spent was completing and checking off tasks. She set out in her daily planner a succinct and comprehensive list of the work she needed to get done for each class and by when. Crossing items off one by one, she progressed towards accomplishment and rewarded herself with treats along the way. She would gently chide me for my daydreaming, absent-minded professor approach to study, and I would chide her for turning education into a checklist. Still, we admired each other, enriched by our exchanges.

In those first months, Carly felt like a long-lost cousin. Being together felt easy and fun. We teased each other affectionately, helped each other out, and kept discovering common interests. Our differences presented opportunities for conversation—something we both excelled at!

Romantic Explorations

Our relationship gradually shifted from friendship to romance. Upperclassmen would invite us to parties in the Mods, the epicenter of campus social life. According to student lore, these two-story modular housing units (replete with yards) were built in the 1970s after the Vietnam War for older students who were already married and had children. To be invited to the Mods as a freshman, where the best BC parties happened, gave me some cool points! Late in the night at a couple of those parties, I sensed some amorous vibes from Carly and began suspecting that she was interested in me for more than mere friendship.

As Spring Break approached, I bided my time and played coy, unsure of what I wanted. We decided to spend the week together, exploring the Northeast. When a kid in my biology class named Dave told me he was just going home to New York for Spring Break, I asked whether Carly and I could crash with him for a few days while we explored the city. He checked with his parents and told me we would be welcome, though he clarified that they lived in Long Island, not the City. Shrugging, I assured him that it would be close enough.

Carly and I spent two nights at Dave's. We got up both mornings before 7 a.m., took the Long Island Railroad into Manhattan, toured the Statue of Liberty, Central Park, the Guggenheim and Metropolitan Museums, Fifth Avenue, the Village, Chinatown, Little Italy, and more. One night we went to a Broadway show, the next a jazz club. We were fascinated to hear Dave's mom share she had visited the shops on Fifth Avenue just once as a girl and had never been to the Met or Statue of Liberty, despite living on Long Island her whole life.

Besides NYC, we also visited a high school friend of mine in Providence, Rhode Island, who one night borrowed a fake ID from someone for me to use, so we could all go to some dive bar owned by local police officers. He explained to us that organized crime and the police were overlapping institutions in Rhode Island, cooperating to make money from underage drinking. The intrigue made for quite a shock to our Midwestern sensibilities!

Between our visits to NYC and Providence, Carly and I kissed for the first time. Travelling together and having loads of new experiences while exploring new places, our relationship turned squarely to romance. We were now dating!

As with my friend Rob, telling the story of my relationship with Carly feels important because in loving her as best as I could over the following years, I grew into myself more fully as a loving, sexual man. When dating her, I did not know myself to be gay and hide or ignore it. In our relationship, I did what I was ready to do to move towards becoming more fully myself. Had I met a boy early in college who was open to sexual experimentation and who seemed as promising a developmental companion as Carly or Rob, I might have found myself coming out many years earlier than I did. But that's not how it went. Carly was that person for me, and our falling in love helped us both flourish.

We practiced paying attention to how the other seemed to be feeling and tried to find thoughtful and caring ways of responding. When she felt frustrated with her sisters and brother, I would ask questions and listen. When I struggled to see who I hoped to become through my intensive studies, she would ask questions, listen, and help me see new perspectives.

We challenged each other as a matter of course. We practiced compromise and found ways to take into account our differing habits and mindsets. For example, come Tuesday or Wednesday each week, she wanted clear plans for the weekend. I preferred to focus on whatever I was reading and put off such planning till Thursday night or even Friday. We compromised by deciding early in the week which weekend night we would go out, but we waited to determine what flavors of fun we would have until I found the space of mind to consider what I would be up for. Studies filled my consciousness, and social plans fit in around the edges.

Over time, we learned how to express frustration with each other, argue lovingly, apologize responsibly, and make up after hurt feelings. We talked explicitly about how we were practicing for marriage, whether we would one day be marrying each other or someone else. In short, we practiced loving each other, and we became bigger people through the process.

As our relationship lengthened and became more adult-like throughout our college years, I noticed how much approval I received from older adults for being in the kind of man-woman relationship everyone seemed to expect for me. Aunts, uncles, my parents, and others' parents would share tender memories from their romantic lives. *What could be better than being young and in love?* Even hosts at restaurants, clerks at stores, and front desk clerks at hotels would express their approval to me for being a young man with a young woman on his arm. This is what the whole world wanted for me, or so it seemed.

Crossing Our Intersectionalities

I'm not sure I had even heard of a WASP before Carly told me she identified as a White Anglo-Saxon Protestant. Beyond that, her roots seemed vague and diffuse—maybe English, French, or German. As we learned more about each other and more about American history through living in Boston—where memories of the colonial and revolutionary periods remain brightly alive—Carly and I came to know something about our differing places in the American story. She associated more with the Daughters of Liberty who had fought for independence, while I associated more with the Irish who fled to Boston from their Hibernian homeland to escape starvation in the mid-nineteenth century.

I understood myself simply as white and assumed that next to Carly I just looked like a well-tanned white guy. The darker side of my ethnic identity as Sicilian, however, felt further afield from the Waspy world from which Carly originated. We would visit the North End of Boston for the pleasure of its small streets, Italian restaurants, and quaint feel. I came to see myself as an insider-outsider there. I would see men who looked like my grandfather's friends smoking in the cafes and women picking up fresh vegetables from Quincy Market. Visiting the North End would prompt me to tell Carly stories of my family, through which we both came to see new things about ourselves and each other.

I came to see more fully how social class and ethnicity were implicated. My grandparents had all gone to college, a relative rarity for Americans back in the 1930s and '40s. Through attending local non-elite universities in Omaha and Lincoln, my Sicilian grandparents climbed into affluence, while their parents had been illiterate and poor for most of their lives. The social mobility of what journalist Tom Brokaw called "the greatest generation" seemed to me both admirable and entirely normal. This rags-to-riches journey of my grandparents shaped how my parents and I related to money, wealth, and *the rich* in America.

This was when I began to realize on some level that, as Irish- and Italian-American, I'm not simply white, but *recently white*. Only recently had my family been admitted to the racial club of whiteness in America. Our privilege as white and middle-class was newly received and thus revocable, though we avoided admitting this, even to ourselves. While my family might not have seen our racial, ethnic, and class privilege as precarious, we could not take it for granted. My mom's own experience of relative poverty following her divorce and the subsidized school lunches we received early in grade school made clear that I could not assume affluence or material comfort would always be my lot in life.

Drinking

The place of alcohol in our lives marked a difference between Carly and me of special significance. Like seemingly everyone at Boston College, Carly drank. Cheap beer (Busch Light being her flavor of choice) filled her weekend nights and gave reason for her frequent workouts. *Gotta work off those empty calories!* When she drank to excess, she took the crummy feeling of hangover as a well-deserved punishment, or at times denied that she had any hangover as part of a story about herself as disciplined, responsible, and mature.

While Carly told fun high school stories of kegs in farm fields and running away from police who broke up teen parties, to me alcohol represented mental illness or moral failing. I didn't drink at all when I entered college. In the story I had constructed about alcohol, adults leaned on it like a crutch because of the difficulty of bearing the stresses and problems of their lives. Talking with Carly about drinking led to sharing more of my family history. I gained new perspectives on the origins of my attitude towards alcohol, an aspect of adult life that I feared. She listened open-heartedly as I got vulnerable about this tender part of myself, though I sensed that deep conversations like that one had taken place more often in my home growing up than in hers. Recounting some of what I told Carly feels valuable here as an example of how our relationship helped me to work through what I had received from my family. Telling her these stories freed me from them to a certain extent. Instead of staying embedded in beliefs and assumptions from my childhood, I became able to rewrite the story of alcohol in my life.

Mom often spoke of the stress of her work while holding a full-to-the-brim glass of chardonnay for "relaxation" as she read the *Omaha World-Herald*. Dad would drink whiskey before dinner, sipping on a couple of shots of Jack Daniels, explicitly delighting in the "buzz" he would get. Somewhere in late childhood, Carrie and I got the idea that Dad was an alcoholic, an identity that came to be intertwined with his peculiar and distorted manner of talking and acting. It was probably Uncle Chuck, who corrected this impression by telling us that Dad's drinking was more likely a way of self-medicating or dimming the drone of his demons.

Our grandfathers, on the other hand, really were alcoholics. One got sober before I was born, and the other drank problematically until he died. The story Mom told about her father was that he had a compulsive personality. Whether drinking, playing cards, or golfing, he became fixated on his pleasures, pursuing them with intensity and drive. His drinking and his divorce from my grandmother preceded my birth, so when he would come to town or we would visit him in North Carolina, Florida, or Georgia, I met teetotaler versions of my Grandpa Quinn. Gruff yet kind, he kept to a limited emotional range, as far as I ever saw. He seemed like a character from some TV show in the 1950s or 1960s. Hard-charging, womanizing, boastful, and competitive, he made and lost several fortunes—or at least that was the idea of him I received. He took me hunting once or twice when I was ten or eleven and taught me how to clean the guts out of the ducks and pheasants he would shoot out of the sky. Besides Grandpa's gruff affection, what I mostly remember from those hunting trips was adoring his hunting dog, Daisy. A strong Black Labrador, gentle and eager, she would frolic with me and cower when Grandpa would bellow at her. He had trained her well, yet severely, it seemed.

In contrast to this emotionally constrained model of a recovering alcoholic who put drinking behind him years ago, my other grandfather poured alcohol into his broken heart all the years of my life. When Grandpa Longo was drinking, the atmosphere in the house felt charged, the air polluted with shame, pain, and sorrow. Some of my worst encounters with Grandpa's addiction took place when Grandma was out of town. She would go to California for the holidays weeks before he would, so she could spend time with her children there while he continued seeing patients in Omaha. Grandpa would get lonely in those wintery weeks and off-kilter. Separately, both he and Grandma would ask Carrie and me to make a special effort to visit him. Sensitive to his need for company, we would, but those visits seldom went well.

Grandma and Grandpa's basement housed many of our family's shadows, its musty mysteries dispersed in multiple rooms. As kids we loved exploring that basement, finding things like the army trunk where Grandpa kept his uniform, belt, and satchel from World War II. One room had a dart board on the wall, two punching bags hanging in a corner, and a pool table where Dad taught us to measure angles and foresee ricochets. At some point after the divorce from my mom, he lived in the finished bedroom in that basement, a boomerang child back in his parents' house. I have many memories of him from those years in my grandparents' grand home. In one that stands out, he is in front of that hanging speed bag, poised in a fighter's stance, practicing the timing of his punches, working up a sweat as he concentrated his eyes on the bag and flew his fists in the right rhythm.

That basement also had what we called a "cold room," with a special door, shelves, and a concrete floor. Kept inside were preserved olives, pickled peppers, canned goods, pasta, homemade wine, and crates of home-grown vegetables that some patients would give Grandpa when they lacked the money to pay for the healthcare he provided them. I don't remember ever hearing our cold room referred to by its Italian name, *cantina*, but I later learned that the *cantina* or cold room was one of several features common in Italian immigrants' homes in America. Another was the vegetable garden, like the one at Grandma and Grandpa's house where we grew tomatoes, basil, mint, and hot peppers.

The cold room was also one of the places Grandpa stashed bottles of booze. He would go down, purportedly to take vegetables out of the extra refrigerator or steaks from the seven-foot-long white commercial freezer. While he putzed around down there, he would find his stash and take swigs. Lucid and cheerful when we would first arrive for our early December visits, Grandpa would come back up from the basement glassy-eyed and hazy, not quite sharp enough to engage in conversation beyond predictable tropes. In just a few minutes he would turn from cogent to loopy.

Depending on how bad his state was and how late in the evening, I would quietly go into the other room, and let him fall asleep on the couch, or sometimes even drive home before we would eat dinner. Other times, I would tell him ahead of time that I would come over so long as he promised not to drink while I was there. When he agreed to this, he would keep his promise.

When we were little, he would routinely ask me or Carrie to get him another beer from the fridge. We would comply, but eventually decided not to enable him in this way. By the time we were both adolescents, we would refuse these requests boldly. "No, Grandpa!" Sometimes he would forego drinking that next beer, but sometimes he would get up and get it himself.

When Grandma was at home and we would all eat together, he drank less often. Even when he did, he would usually stay more cogent and emotionally balanced. Still, sometimes he would go off on a rant—turning red in the face, bugging out his eyes, pointing his finger up, and shaking his arm for emphasis. Grandma was skilled at calming him and redirecting his focus, though at times she would express her frustration. "Attorna, attorna!" she would exclaim in their Sicilian dialect, meaning "Again, again!" when he would repeat himself on some loop. "Testa dura!" [Hard-headed!] she would call him when he clung too stubbornly to some topic.

These outbursts, which almost always came at dinner, our time for conversation and the delights of food, upset me greatly and left me on edge. I would sweat, getting sticky and hot under my arms and shirt collar. My eyes, like his, would widen. Muscles inside my lower abdomen would tighten and flutter. Though I never felt threatened by Grandpa, a feeling of fright and fluster would come over me in these moments, layered onto deeper tremors of dread that seemed like foreboding. I believe now these were reactivated memories of my father's violence and rage from early childhood, fanned embers of remembered pain.

Against this fraught background, I rejected the American teenage drinking culture embraced by some of the kids at Prep and our sister schools. The popular kids I knew seemed to be divided into those who drank and those who didn't. Many of my close friends at Prep also heartily rejected drinking. We would have impassioned conversations enumerating the reasons why our way was the right way and complimenting ourselves for choosing this moral high road.

The fear of being or becoming an alcoholic terrified me. Carrie and I shared a concern that we would inherit this trait, just as we had our dad's nose or skin color. His alcoholism felt like a close second to his mental illness, which we feared even more we would inherit—though the two largely merged in my mind. We very seldom admitted these fears to anyone but each other and Mom. Indeed, I'm now aware of how much I worked during my grade school, high school, and college years to avoid admitting these fears even to myself. Like a shadow, these fearsome possibilities hounded me. The prospect of drinking seemed to promise a catastrophic intensification of the off-kilter strangeness that already dogged me.

At one family feast when I was thirteen, these fears went to the wayside, and I tried out what drinking alcohol could be. My cousin Gina's wedding in San Francisco brought great excitement to the family. She and her fiancé were smart, fun, and beautiful. When they were dating while in college at Creighton in Omaha, they would pick me up for evenings together at their downtown apartment. We would rent a movie from Blockbuster to watch on their VCR, order pizza, and make popcorn. Eight years older than me, they seemed already like adults as I just was beginning adolescence.

The prenuptial dinner was in Aunt Marilyn's backyard, with the reception the following night at the Presidio. She and Uncle Matt had renovated a gorgeous Victorian home on Scott Street, next to Alamo Square, with a magical garden where we would eat, drink, and dance the night away. The wedding Mass would be the next morning in North Beach at Saints Peter and Paul Church, the spiritual home of the local Italian-American Catholic community. Family friends who ran a Japanese restaurant provided an open sushi bar all night, besides the more traditional Italian meal of chicken alfredo and pasta with white clam or pesto sauce.

Gina's brother, my cousin Gary, offered an effusively affectionate toast to his beloved sister, culminating in a racy Italian wedding *brindisi*:

Aqua fina
Vino puro
Minchia dura
Sticchio caldo

Those of us who didn't know any Italian looked to other relatives during the toast for a translation, which I heard from my cousin Joe: *Clear water, pure wine, hard dick, hot pussy*! For me as a thirteen-year-old, Gary's toast felt both titillating and nostalgic. It seemed to hearken back to weddings in what Grandma and Grandpa called "the old country," meaning Sicily, and the generations of our ancestors who lived their lives there. The very occasion of a wedding, a public celebration of the romantic and sexual love between a man and a woman, seemed to connect our feast in the summer of 1988 with countless other Sicilian wedding feasts across the generations before us. The vibrance of family tradition charged the air with hope, love, and joy. That energy inebriated me, even before taking any drink that night.

But drink I did indeed. My sister Carrie and I had two cousins from Phoenix who matched us in age, Tony and Susie. The wedding gave us a chance to get reacquainted with them and their seven siblings, as well as so many other relatives and family friends who, though not actually related, we still called our "Aunts" and "Uncles." Standing at the bar set up for the fancy backyard affair, Tony, Susie, Carrie, and I learned from our (actual) Uncle Chuck what a "tequila shooter" was. The very directions for how to shoot tequila added to the racy, adult sexiness of the feast. "Lick, drink, suck!" Licking the corner of our hand between thumb and index finger, we first sprinkled salt to stick to our moistened skin and held with the same hand a lemon wedge. Holding in the other hand a shot of José Cuervo, we licked off the salt, drank down the tequila, and then sucked on the lemon. This choreographed group drinking routine was fun! Enacting and re-enacting this new "precision routine" felt like a step into adulthood, with the California pizzazz that seemed to make my relatives who lived there sparkle with a vitality and glamour unknown to me in my Omaha life.

I drank eight tequila shooters that night, plus a wine cooler with my pasta. I felt very grown up! Of course, Mom was appalled when she found out I was drinking, especially so much. She expressed anger at Chuck, her former brother-in-law, for encouraging us kids in this way. Carrie had fewer shots, yet her face and neck were flushed, and she was swaying slightly as Mom chastised and cautioned us. I, on the other hand, was not showing signs of drunkenness, which worried Mom even more. When we woke up the next morning, I had no headache, upset stomach, or other hangover symptoms. Mom explained her worries that my apparently high tolerance signaled a risk factor for becoming an alcoholic like so many other men in the family.

All of this family history swirled in my memory, as I observed how effective a person Carly was even with alcohol playing a prominent and regular part in her life. Gradually, the old stories I used to tell myself about drinking alcohol as a great moral failing began to come apart and dissolve. I began to experiment with letting alcohol into my life and rewriting (on my own terms) how to be with all that I had received from my family of origin. My relationship to alcohol represents an especially significant example illustrating my increasingly **Self-Authoring** mindset in these years.

- *What beliefs and formative experiences about alcohol have influenced the role you have given it to play in your life?*

Transgressive Titillations of a Young Catholic Intellectual

- *What hopes and dreams, what vision for your life did you have for yourself as you left adolescence and embarked on adulthood?*

- *What interrelationships have you experienced between your sexual life and your spiritual life?*

Aside from Rob and Carly, peers in college mattered to me much less, or much differently, than they had when I was in high school. From a developmental perspective, this change looks like a shift in how I was relating to "important others." During my "golden boy" high school years, distinguishing myself amongst my peers, for example, by being elected class president, had meant everything to me. Now Boston College had plenty of remarkably kind, loving, mature, and smart undergraduates, and when I would meet ones who impressed me with their wisdom, maturity, or brains, I paid attention and struck up a friendship in many cases. Belonging to peer groups, however, felt much less important to me. As I relied less on **Socialized** sense-making and moved towards the **Achiever** form of mind, I relied much less on my peers for approval or praise and often suffered from a sense of superiority over them, especially intellectually and morally.

From another angle, I was exercising more discernment in selecting whose praise or influence to seek. For example, professors and priests from whom I sensed I could especially learn were high on that list. Jesuits had functioned as an important reference group for me at Creighton Prep, where some felt like uncles, and others like grandfathers. When I came to know Jesuits at BC, I expected we might similarly drop formality and become familiar in our interactions. Though I was projecting Midwestern openness onto these New England Province Jesuits, they generally welcomed my friendliness and seemed at ease with my familiarity. Not only Jesuits, but many of the laypeople who taught or otherwise worked at Prep and BC seemed wise and admirable, and I put credence in how they saw the world.

I began to glean from these various influences elements to use in constructing my own vision of the world, my faith, and my life. From one professor in particular, Mark O'Connor, I heard a great deal about a kind of person called a "Catholic intellectual." I felt like I already knew what a Catholic was, but from Professor O'Connor (whom we generally called "Mark"), I came to understand an "intellectual" as someone committed to "the life of the mind." Over the course of sophomore year, I started taking on "Catholic intellectual" as a new way to understand myself. This shift in self-understanding took place mostly over the course of many early morning sessions of quiet study and reflection. The Western Cultural Traditions seminar I took that year as part of the undergraduate Honors Program started with Shakespeare and ended with Marx, Freud, and Nietzsche. It was a "great books" course, meaning we read no secondary sources, only the classic texts themselves. We practiced close reading, attending carefully to wordplay, nuance, poetic devices, and intertextual references. Few of these texts had been written in English, so we read them in translation, and Mark would highlight certain elements apparent only in the original to save crucial *leitmotiv*s, or recurring themes, and other nuances from being "lost in translation" for us as we read the English versions.

I found this kind of reading enormously stimulating and satisfying. It gave me access to the "Great Conversation" of sages across the ages. In conversation with Sophocles, Homer, the biblical authors Montaigne, Cervantes, Rousseau, Joseph Conrad, Dostoevsky, and so many others, I strove to make sense of myself and reality as far as I could grasp. Developing the technical prowess to do this kind of study felt daunting but within reach. Gaining unmediated access to the actual words written by extraordinarily imaginative, incisive, and perspicacious authors deserved all the attention I could give. Besides majoring in French language and literature and continuing to read literature in Latin, I started studying German, then ancient Greek, and then Hebrew.

I became extremely planful about my academic pathways and created detailed scenarios of courses, majors, and languages. I sought the counsel of my new reference group—the professors of Boston College—and ultimately made my own decisions about which pathways to select. Among other decisions, one notable choice was to skip the Junior Year Abroad experience and instead make my third year at university the academic culmination of my intellectual achievements in college. I didn't need this overly structured and extremely safe container to encounter the world outside the USA. I just knew I would be spending significant time after college in foreign lands, speaking their languages and learning their cultures by living in them.

I'm pretty sure neither Carly nor I knew the term "sapiosexual" back in those days, but she knew she was smart and attracted to guys who were smart. As a Human Resources major, she spent much less time than I did doing extremely close readings of classic texts from centuries past or undertaking philosophical reflection. Yet, she admired and supported me and my passion for these pursuits, as I admired and supported her and her pursuits.

Spiritual Development

Religion made for another area where differences between Carly and me helped me to construct my identity and form my sense of self. At Boston College, I was definitely an insider to the Catholic culture of the place. As a graduate of a Jesuit institution, I was an insider to the particular community of Catholics especially influenced by St. Ignatius of Loyola, the spiritual charism that he created, and the community of vowed religious men that he founded, called the Jesuits or, more formally, the Society of Jesus. Though only three of the twelve universities I had applied to were Catholic, by choosing BC I was continuing my time in Catholic schools, which had started in first grade at my parochial grade school.

In contrast, Carly had a loose affiliation with Lutheran Christianity, but it didn't seem to be a significant part of her life or something she reflected much on. When we ate together at her place or mine, she and I would sometimes say grace before meals, as my family back home always did. She would fold her hands; I would make the sign of the cross. She would start her prayer by addressing "Heavenly Father," a phrase I had not heard used before in prayer. She liked Christmas and Easter and the nice things people did for those holidays.

Carly would sometimes come with me to Mass on campus, and we would talk about it afterward. She would ask about certain things that happened, and I would explain the order of Mass, the parts of the liturgy, and the meaning of the rituals, as I understood them. She would sometimes say that it all seemed patriarchal, with the old man in robes leading it all from the front. After more experiments and exploration of religion together in the earlier years of our relationship, we came to recognize how much more important faith and spirituality were for me than for her. Neither of us needed or expected the other to change in this respect, but it was also not an area of closeness or shared experience.

While "intellectual" was the newest part of my identity, the "Catholic" part was also morphing and developing. From early childhood, I knew I was Catholic. That was my religion, a group my family and I belonged to. In high school, I developed a spirituality, which is to say I learned to pray and cultivate my connection to the divine, a "personal relationship with God," as we Catholics would say in words that also resonated with American Evangelical Christian language. The spirituality that I came to practice in my teenage years looked to Ignatius—that Basque, 16th-century saintly spiritual master—for guidance on how to be with the Spirit. Attending to my desires, imagination, and the other interior movements of my heart and mind, I learned to apply the Ignatian motto of "finding God in all things" to my inner life.

The spirituality I developed at Creighton Prep was also very heavily influenced by Vatican II, particularly the heightened attention to social justice that coincided with the hippie generation and the American civil rights movement in the 1960s. The specifically Midwest American brand of post-Vatican II Ignatian spirituality that I grew into at Prep under the special influence of several former hippies (or so we imagined them) emphasized a "preferential option for the poor," a strong antiwar sentiment, and a commitment to equal rights for women and racial minorities. "Finding God in all things" thus also applied to the world outside my psyche, the world of politics and social movements, international relations and globalization, science and technology, art and culture.

At BC, I laid the intellectual building blocks and underpinnings of a theology that could likewise become part of me. Through my journey of learning to read the classics of Western thought, I began an integration between my religious and spiritual life and my newly emerging intellectual life. Though my studies focused primarily on languages and literature, not religion, philosophy, or theology, I was growing into this identity of a Catholic intellectual. For me, that identity meant above all that I experienced myself as connected to, created by, and even loved by the Divine, the ineffable and ultimately unknowable Spirit.

Though I learned new language to describe my faith at BC, that deep sense of being connected, known, and loved by God had lived in me and with me from as early as I could remember. Flashes of very early memories of sensing the presence of a truly great and benevolent Spirit coursed through my consciousness, just as memories of my earliest self-consciousness did: looking at my own hands, sitting on the red shag carpet of my childhood bedroom, and recognizing for the first time that I was *someone*, that I was separate from all my toys and my bed and from Mom and Carrie. *This body was me.* What I came to know as "faith" was first of all simply an admission of this recognition that *I'm someone*, and that I'm not alone in the universe. The powerful presence of Love, of Spirit, of the All-Powerful, the Creator, somehow touched me and held me. I might now call this a primordial faith, natural faith, or intrinsic faith. What has always felt most clear about this sense of the divine presence is that I did nothing to earn or deserve it. In my college years, I arrived at a very profound recognition of this ever-present divine presence as a gift. Someone, something, some power gave it to me from the very beginning and has (so far) never taken it away.

This understanding of faith gave me plenty of space to appreciate Carly's very different relationship to religion, ritual, and prayer. Putting this appreciation in terms I would later learn from reading Karl Rahner, SJ, the ineffable and unknowable depths within her had their own sacredness and dynamics, their own interplay with her personal history, family life, and psyche. *What could I possibly know of all that? How could I possibly judge her faith or lack thereof as in need of change or adjustment?* She was on her own path and schedule, and the Divine was undoubtedly with her in all of that, or so I believed.

The Plausible Deniability of Transgressive Titillations

Our sex life together was one particularly significant place where our values came into conversation. From nearly the beginning of my romantic relationship with Carly, I was ready and excited for all kinds of sexual play, except for baby-making intercourse. Throughout our years together, sexual intimacy stayed a steadily enjoyable, if somewhat careful, dimension of our relationship. By my sophomore or junior year, I started imagining us living together in an apartment in Boston or New York where having full-on sex would be a normal and fitting part of our life of love together. We were well on our way towards what I understood to be a standard, straight, modern American life as an adult couple.

But as we progressed on this well-lit and well-trod path, I increasingly noticed my rather neglected secret pledge to explore my erotic interest in other guys. (Neither the word "boys" nor "men" in those years felt fitting for the same-sex objects of my erotic attention. "Boys" felt too close to pederasty, and "men" felt too close to creeps or grandpas.) I became bolder in my fantasies and more honest with myself about how interested I was in seeing other guys' bodies—their dicks in particular. The main gym on campus, with its sauna and open showers in the men's locker room, became a place for this visual pleasure. Since I lifted weights and swam there regularly, being naked with other men at the Rec Plex became an additional corporeal pleasure before and after the pleasure of exercise.

Speaking of older guys giving off creepy vibes, I remember seeing one muscled, heavy-set, white-haired man quite often in the sauna, particularly on weekday afternoons. He would be there as I did my pre-workout stretching in the sauna and then again, forty-five minutes later, as I had my post-workout spa time. *Did he ever even workout?* I used to wonder. I imagined he was quite proud of his particularly large dick. A "show-er" (rather than a "grower"), we would have called it, that is, a dick that looks especially big when flaccid. Never did I observe any untoward move from him—we even exchanged modest pleasantries. Yet, I sensed he was there so often precisely to display, to be seen, and to impress the college boys.

I didn't know the gay term "cruising" back then, but the word captures how that man in the sauna gave off the energy of sordid sexual openness. He was an example of who I did *not* want to become: the figure in my head of *a dirty old man*, who preyed on younger men, or who wore a trench coat to flash unsuspecting passers-by, or the supposedly straight, married man who sought anonymous sexual release by frequenting parks in the dark or public restrooms.

The fourth-floor men's room in the main library at BC featured strategically placed holes, maybe two inches in diameter, piercing the metal dividers between two of the stalls. I liked studying on that floor because of the inspiring view of the John Hancock and Prudential towers off in Boston's distant Copley Square, and I discovered those holes in the stall walls which gave views between the legs of the person in the next stall. I also discovered that a certain man seemed often to sit there, waiting, quiet. I recognized him from the salt-and-pepper pubic hair and his tightly circumcised, rather short and thick penis, and figured he must be in his fifties or older.

I would keep my visits short, yet choose the stall with the hole and look to see whether there were feet under the next stall over. Plausible deniability. Those moments of voyeurism and exhibitionism felt at once quietly exhilarating, morally depraved, and slightly disgusting. Aside from looking and allowing whoever sat adjacent to me to look, I did nothing. Different men would be there besides the one with salt-and-pepper hair. Once, someone seemingly younger, with light brown hair, crouched down and extended his hand under the stall wall. I knew what he was offering. "No," I said firmly, as I stood, pulled up my jeans, and bolted. Another time whoever was next door suddenly put his eyeball to the peephole so we could look up at my face and know who I was. I bolted again, frightened and ashamed.

These transgressive viewings titillated me. I felt drawn to the erotic charge while managing my indulgence—not going *too* often, not lingering *too* long, and not doing anything *too* overt. I was managing the deniability to myself at least as much as to any imagined library security guard or campus police officer who might burst into the men's room to crack down on indecent behavior. That library men's room and the sauna at the gym—these were where my plausibly deniable gay side would peek out of the shadow for a few minutes during college before submerging again.

- *What settings or scenarios have coaxed you out of conventional performances of gender or sex into trying out ways of being and acting that liberated aspects of your true self?*
- *Where in your journey has the pattern of the **Double Life** shown up?*

Queen Harold

- *In what settings or scenarios does your **Queen** become most powerful?*

Having seen the heady, driven, and compartmentalized **Queen** that I was becoming in my college years, now could be a useful moment to return to *Boys in the Band* to consider the character Harold. He exemplifies a fully formed **Queen,** in all her bitchy power, perceptivity, and self-possession. For another bonus section with a full exploration of Harold, the character Zachary Quinto plays in the recent film version of the play, go to QueerFlourishing.com. Because of copyright protections of the extensive quotes from the play's text, this discussion can't be here in *Queer Flourishing* so is instead on the website for you.

For all its entertainment value, *The Boys in the Band* displays dark undersides of gay men's social personae and interpersonal patterns. Taking this group of friends in the collective as an example of **Pride Tribe,** Michael as an example of the **Best Little Kid,** and Harold as a **Queen,** we see how different characters have entirely different experiences of the same raucous evening together. Swept up in **Pride Tribe,** Bernard and Emory enjoy dancing their precision routine, then get emotionally decimated by playing along with Michael's "Affairs of the Heart" game. Donald, on the other hand, hovers on the edges of the gay friend group, feeling neither the benefits nor the pain of full membership in it. Each character makes his own meaning and constructs his own reality.

"We see the world not as it is, but as we are."
For even more fresh perspectives on the experience of someone in early **Self-Authoring** surrounded by friends operating from **Socialized** mind, let's leave gay New York for the fantasy land of *The Lord of the Rings*, with queer characters of an entirely different ilk. In the fictional world that J. R. R. Tolkien creates, we come to know "the fellowship of the ring." They are a set of characters on a quest to turn back the Shadow of evil that is coming over all of Middle-earth, by destroying the Master-ring through casting it into the Cracks of Doom in the Fiery Mountain of the land of Mordor. Every member of the fellowship of the ring regards their journey from one land to the next quite differently, just as we real-life humans look at the process of growth and development differently at different times, depending on our personality, culture, and developmental mindset or stage.

At the center of the story stands a hobbit named Frodo. Three other hobbits accompany him—namely, Pippin Took, Merry Brandybuck, and Samwise Gamgee—who epitomize the **Conformist** or early **Socialized** mind. These three companions carry the ways of the Shire with them even as they travel away from it. Not fully grasping what is at stake or the urgency or risks of the mission, they expect even on their quest to enjoy "second breakfast" and make a night fire to heat up a late-night snack, just as they would have back home in the Shire. The customs and expectations of their hobbit world shape their sense of the reality they see around them, even when the terrifying Nazgûl ring-wraiths hunt them. While they know full well that they are on a mission to destroy the ring, that goal does not preoccupy them as it does Frodo. In contrast, the journey has meaning for them because they are accompanying Frodo, who is for them an "important other."

For all of us, no matter which developmental stage we are operating from, "we see the world not as *it* is, but as *we* are."[62] That's what I mean by describing these mindsets as functioning like the lenses of *both* eyeglasses *and* projectors. This metaphor recalls for me the Saturday morning television commercials for Tootsie Rolls that I watched as a child. The lyrics "Whatever it is I think I see/becomes a Tootsie Roll to me" would be sung as the entire landscape of trees and sun and trains and houses morph into packages of Tootsie Roll candies. That old American TV commercial whimsically illustrates how that to which we are subject shapes our lived experience.

For his part, Frodo takes some time to discern what his role in destroying the Ring might be, at times wishing he had never seen it and dreaming of nothing else but returning to his simple life back in the Shire. In Peter Jackson's *The Fellowship of the Ring* (2001), a film adaptation of the beginning of Tolkien's novel, Frodo gradually comes to formulate an understanding of his singular role as Ring-bearer. At the end of that film, he leaves his companions and sets off, intending to journey alone to Mordor.

In terms of adult development theory, we can see Frodo in this film going through the transition from **Socialized** to **Self-Authoring** mind. Along the journey and indeed even before embarking on it, he learns a great deal, gathers expertise and tools, and starts separating and distinguishing himself from the comfortable surrounding culture of the Shire, as one does in the **Expert** stage. By the end, he has come up with a vision for his personal mission, with a clear goal to cast the Ring into the Fiery Mountain of Mordor. At the end of *The Fellowship of the Ring*, Frodo comes to see everything else in his life in relation to this mission and the values and commitments he has taken on that drive him to fulfill the quest. This developmental shift in Frodo sets him apart from his community of peers. Frodo gains an expanded sense of self and meaning for his life. Yet, he also suffers in new ways as he embarks on a more independent, even solitary leg of his journey.

- *What principles, assumptions, and beliefs do you notice yourself projecting onto circumstances and other people that you encounter?*

"Thus play I in one person many people"

- *What experiences of failure, like Richard II's being "unkinged," have annihilated some old version of yourself and thus allowed a new version with greater capacities to emerge?*

In my college years, I was well on my way to becoming the kind of person that my world wanted me to be—an independent-minded, go-getter, self-starter, hard worker, and, of course, married to a woman. I ruled over my interior castle, that version of myself I was busy as a bee constructing and erecting according to some mysterious blueprints, pages of which I kept drafting and discovering within my inner depths. Architect, bricklayer, and inhabitant, I was building a custom home, a keep, with secret gardens, "man caves," playrooms, and study. The castle I was erecting and inhabiting featured a very prominent ivory tower, where I kept my library, quill, and candle.

Ever so fittingly, in the last weeks of sophomore year, Professor O'Connor had us read Shakespeare's *Richard II*. We paid special attention to Richard's Pomfret Castle speech (Act V, scene v), a long soliloquy in which the deposed and imprisoned king reflects on what he has become. The once capricious monarch who spent lavishly—even disinheriting his cousin Bolingbroke to cover his debts—has now lost his throne, crown, and title. Bolingbroke has usurped Richard's throne to become King Henry IV. Yet, as depicted by Shakespeare, even in his fall, Richard gains a new perspective on himself. Indeed, from a developmental point of view, Richard remakes himself.

While ruler of his realm, Richard saw his powers through the lens of the divine right of kings. He did not see his own limits, and he never suspected he might lose his position. His sovereign will and regal vision reigned supreme. As he makes sense of his new position, "unkinged by Bolingbroke," a set of subject-object shifts take place, such that he grows larger than his kingly self. He gains a perspective wide enough to fathom a multiplicity of selves or parts, which he calls "A generation of still-breeding thoughts." Richard then goes on to describe some of those inner parts of himself, calling them "thoughts," yet personifying them:

> And these same thoughts people this little world,
> In humors like the people of this world,
> For no thought is contented. The better sort
> As thoughts of things divine, are intermixed
> With scruples....
>
> Thoughts tending to ambition, they do plot
> Unlikely wonders....

> Thoughts tending to content flatter themselves
> That they are not the first of fortune's slaves,
> Nor shall not be the last . . .

Observing these parts of himself, he plays out various real and hypothetical scenarios for his life looking backwards and forwards. Richard's reflection and introspection in response to his life circumstances have yielded a transformation wherein he grows larger than the **Self-Authoring** person he was when ruling his own realm:

> Thus play I in one person many people,
> And none contented. Sometimes am I king:
> Then treasons make me wish myself a beggar,
> And so I am. Then crushing penury
> Persuades me I was better when a king;
> Then am I kinged again; and by and by
> Think that I am unkinged by Bolingbroke,
> And straight am nothing.

Richard is annihilated, his old self-understanding shattered, and in this very loss of self, he has gained a new self, a new structure of mind, with wider capacities for embracing more realities previously unavailable to him.

> But whate'er I be,
> Nor I, nor any man that but man is,
> With nothing shall be pleased till he be eased
> With being nothing.

In this Pomfret Castle speech, which occurs in the play just a few lines before his assassination, Richard reveals signs of a structure of mind marked simultaneously by both greater fragmentation and greater self-possession. To put it developmentally, he undergoes a transformative expansion of his inner diversity and inclusion. What once was so clear and distinct for him is now undermined, redefined, and reframed. Transcending the conventions of his society, in which he had previously reached the apex, Richard expands himself and his purview to encompass his fall from power and his impending death. He may not be "pleased" with all he has lost, but he is no longer subject to the worldview that he had once taken in from outside and then remade in his own image.

Though as I graduated from college my powers reigned over no kingdom except the inner realm of my person, like Richard, I would soon find myself deposed and remade through an experience of both greater fragmentation and greater self-possession.

- *What Pomfret Castle experiences have given you occasion to reflect on the multiplicity of selves who people your own "little world," your inner realms?*

Flourishing into Personal Greatness

- *What understanding of personal greatness do you strive to achieve?*

When we are making sense of ourselves and others using an **Achiever** mindset, flourishing looks like reaching personal greatness. The definition of greatness naturally varies from one person to the next, as much as anything else that we "self-author." In this developmental stage, we elect our values, hatch our vision, and write our story. Self-possessiveness reigns supreme. For one person, becoming a great man might be expressed as *becoming my best self*. For another, greatness might mean achieving a position of nobility and dignity, or wealth and power, or some uniquely excellent accomplishment in any field of endeavor. Thanks to being "self-guided, self-motivated, and self-evaluative," those in an **Achiever** form of mind strive for greatness on their own terms.[63]

The development of greater inner diversity and inclusion features our own personal voice in a privileged position of authority for the first time. Despite the importance of other voices internalized during socialization, the work of personal growth at this stage principally focuses on recognizing the magnitude and stature of our own voice. Self-authorship requires enthroning the Self as the governing authority for one's life.

In a **Self-Authoring, Achiever** mindset, the love we most need could come in the form of someone seeing us in our greatness or supporting us in other ways to be our own person. Our highest dream in an **Achiever** mindset imagines making real the vision we have for ourselves and our lives: *Si, se puede. I can do it!* The greatest fear might be to fall back into the herd and remain undifferentiated from everyone else. For the earlier **Expert** mind this same fear of falling back into the herd looked like losing a sense of specialness based on superior knowledge or skills in certain areas. In contrast, the **Achiever** mind might understand this fear of falling back into the herd as the failure to realize a unique vision for greatness. Or perhaps even worse, we might find ourselves facing the possibility that our unique vision is nothing more than a fanciful mirage. *I'm a fraud!* We might also fear our relationships with other people devouring us. These fears express an aversion to developmental regression since our earlier, **Socialized** form of mind relied primarily on interpersonal relationships with *important others* to determine our worldview and our self-understanding.[64]

The ways I support my clients when they are operating from an **Achiever** mindset might help you take care of the **Achiever** part of yourself or in friends and colleagues. I make space for them to articulate their vision. I listen. I celebrate and amplify their vision by reflecting it back. I acknowledge what's wonderful and unique about their way of being and their way of seeing the world. I encourage them to live out their values and make real their hopes and dreams. Besides letting them know that I see them in their greatness, I also show them some of who I am in my own uniqueness. I allow them to know me, as I have come to know them. In addition, I get curious about the meaning such clients derive from their ongoing quest to achieve and accomplish. As we operate from an **Achiever** mindset over a number of years, at some point we might start to notice yearnings for fulfillment that further accomplishments cannot quench or even affect in any way.

When highly accomplished gay, bi, and queer men come to me with an interest in embarking on the Heroes Journey program, those primarily operating from **Achiever** mind typically have been experiencing some acute feeling of existential dryness combined with professional burnout. They no longer feel as excited or joyful when doing their work as they once had, yet they may still be working as many hours as ever. Many such men come to me as an executive coach saying that they want my help to recover the fire in their belly. Yet as we explore, they often find that the deeper shift that is wanting to happen redirects their attention away from accomplishment as such a vital source of meaning.

Flourishing—the distinctive aliveness that love makes possible for us—when in an **Achiever** mindset looks like the realization of our own version of greatness to such a degree that we set down the burdens of our struggle to achieve, we catch our breath, and we open our mind and heart to *what else* lies within . . .

PART III

Table 8: Queer Superpowers of Early Post-Conventional Stages

Developmental Stage			Queer Superpower	Adverse Circumstances that prompt superpower's emergence
Self-Sovereign	Self-Protective Opportunist	1	Chameleonic Passing	» Social exclusion » Mocking » Bullying » Shaming » Moral condemnation » Shunning by family / friends » Violent attack
		2	Shield of Hypervigilance	
		3	The Great Escape	
Socialized	Conformist	4	Gaydar	» Cultural values » Gender expectations » Romantic & sexual norms of the straight mainstream » Religious & moral condemnation » Legal persecution
		5	Pride Tribe	
	Expert	6	The Best Little Kid	
Self-Authoring	Achiever	7	The Queen	» Strictures of societal expectations limit creative powers » Socialized cycle of approval-seeking forecloses possibility of greatness
		8	Double Life	
	Redefining	9	Second Adolescence	» Self-imposed limits caused by personal adaptations made earlier in life to survive and thrive » Distressful self-awareness of unintegrated parts of self
Self-Transforming		10	No One Left Behind	

Queer Flourishing

Description	Heroic Possibilities & Powers	Pitfalls & Shadow
» Adapt to fit wide range of settings	» Shape-shifting » Cloak of invisibility » Avoid unwanted attention » Allow others to imagine you're one of them	» Not being seen or known for who we are » Loneliness » Fusing with our masks and forgetting who we really are
» Early alert system for possible danger	» Prepared to freeze, flee, or fight for safety » Avoid attacks, traps, & ambushes	» Fear & anxiety flood out other emotions » Skittish withdrawal inhibits relationships » Difficulty trusting even the trustworthy
» Depart toxic or abusive life situation to find supportive context	» Muster the courage, creativity, and determination needed for liberation	» Leave behind the good and the bad alike » Change of scenery without inner growth or change – "Running to stand still" » Flee into the clutches of new abusers
» Sense others' queerness	» Tap into intuitive knowing » See people's hidden faces » Empathy for others' shame	» Delusions of queer grandeur, imagining LGBTQ+ folks as superior to straight people » Project own queerness onto others
» Membership in a queer social group	» Strength in solidarity » Self-confidence to cultivate and use atypical gifts	» Gay groupthink papers over personal uniqueness » False sense of superiority
» Meeting and surpassing social standards and expectations	» Achieve excellence » Gain admiration in society » Earn one's way out of shame	» Fitting in to move up, lose sense of self and own unique "weird & wonderful" traits » Trapped by society's definitions of success, e.g., wealth, high position, prestige, luxury, etc.
» Accept and exercise "divine right" to rule one's own realm	» Claim own power » Impervious self-possession » Regal stature and poise » Sharp rationality » Relentlessly strategic in pursuing own vision and goals	» Self-sufficiency limits love – It's lonely at the top » Steamroll over others » Compartmentalization keeps valuable inner resources inaccessible » Haughty overconfidence leaves others impressed but distant
» Bifurcate life into separate domains	» Create space for expression and cultivation of queer self » Honor suite of personal values despite contradicitons	» Split life mirrors splits in the self that limit personal integration » Self-control verges on fraud and deceit
» A controlled coming apart and re-forming of adult self	» Shed conventional version of self in favor of greater authenticity and self-expression » Capacity for experimentation, follwed by rapid iteration, learning, and growth » Creativity and originality, despite societal flak	» Perpetually lost and not found, dissolution of conventional self never resolves into new coherence » Regress back to conventional self
» Return to scenes of wounding, to heal and more fully integrate all parts of self	» Wholeness » Integration of hidden resources and vulnerabilities » Revivification of spiritual scars	» Without sufficient support, re-traumatization can occur

CHAPTER 5:

Into the Desert

Humpty Dumpty Had a Great Fall

- *What have been the most disruptive and disorienting upheavals you have undergone in your life?*

Having recounted the collegiate chronicles of the rise of my **Queen**, I return now to my most regal moment as valedictorian in academic regalia addressing a crowd of ten or twelve thousand with my heady and heartfelt speech on "This Ignatian Village." Over the previous year, with much encouragement and support from Boston College professors, I had gone far in the application processes for Fulbright and Rhodes scholarships to study abroad. My great sending off, crowned with the highest honors that the University could bestow upon an undergraduate, sent me, however, not to Oxford for the Rhodes or Morocco for a Fulbright year, but rather to gritty Cleveland Circle, the nearest suburban hub to BC's campus. There, I felt overblown, puffed up by accolades. After all the pomp of Commencement, I moved into a dim, ground-floor unit, just behind Mary Anne's, the beloved BC dive bar so grubby I deigned only once to set foot inside, in the days of Senior Week just before graduation. Talk about anticlimax!

The rise of my inner **Queen** deflated into disillusion. I started to see all the accolades, awards, and regalia with which Boston College adorned me as empty pomp. Synchronicity, however, soon swept me in an unexpected direction, described in this account of the summer after college graduation written later in my 20s.

From Chestnut Hill to Fagallah

Invitations sometimes come in envelopes, marked clearly for what they are. The hoopla of 'commencement' in May 1997 left me well-read, credentialed, highly socialized, broadminded, bedecked with honors, and moved into yet another Cleveland Circle apartment. What seemed to have been such an illustrious college career ended abruptly, and with a hangover. The laurels, the lauds, the ruthlessly pursued personal growth, all these yielded no five-figure signing bonus, no prestigious fellowship, no impressive business cards or even any need to buy a new suit!

I did have a summer job, though. My girlfriend hired me. Her one-year lead coming out of BC at least put one person in the professional world who thought I was worth hiring. The three months I spent as a systems analyst at a leading biotech company put more in my bank accounts than all previous summer jobs combined. Plus, my well-honed skills in comparative literature were put to use on a daily basis. Right.

As I settled into my seedy Strathmore Road apartment a week after graduation, I began opening the mail my mother had brought from Omaha. What caught my eye was the Spring 1997 issue of *Company* magazine, which I received as an alum of a Jesuit high school. On the front cover was a cloth-covered man with a fancy Turkish-style drink dispenser on his back. The issue was entitled 'The Middle East.'

Fortuitous, I thought, as my trajectory had begun pointing towards that region during the second semester of junior year. A course on *francophonie* had introduced me to the Maghreb of North Africa, where Algerian, Tunisian and Moroccan novelists intrigued me with their fiction. My vocational energy senior year went almost entirely to applications for fellowships and programs that would have given me the chance to live abroad and develop the capability to understand Islam, the Arab world, and Israel.

More than anyone, Zehava Carpenter, my professor at BC senior year for modern Israeli Hebrew inspired me to pursue this new interest in the Middle East by teaching me from her own experience as a francophone Moroccan-born Israeli-American. Zehava's profound commitment to her students seemed the fruit of a close relationship with the Lord, an intimate knowledge of suffering, and a sense of mission to promote understanding between people of different cultures as a way for progress in human relations. She taught us vocabulary and grammar, but also opened discussions with us on what I today understand more clearly to be such highly sensitive topics as Jewish identity, Zionism, the State of Israel, the Shoah (Holocaust), and the rippling effects of all these for Palestinians.

No Fulbright to study Arabic and Maghreb literature in Morocco came through, the *kibbutz ulpan* programs for non-Jews to learn Hebrew were all too labor-intensive and study-poor, and the Peace Corps nomination to teach English as a second language in Central Asia for 27 months seemed too long and too scary. Nor was I accepted by the Walsh School of Foreign Service at Georgetown or awarded a Rhodes or Marshall scholarship to study international politics and economics.

In short, I finished senior year with all kinds of votes of confidence from former professors and all kinds of rejections from the world outside BC. I felt overestimated. I wondered whether BC's 'ever to excel' motto wasn't a sham. Having sucked the marrow out of the Boston College undergraduate experience, I felt both enriched and failed by alma mater.

Then this magazine comes with my family to me for graduation. The first article profiled this school in Cairo, *la College de la Sainte Famille* [CSF]. There were pictures of the Egyptian boys wearing plain school uniforms with neckties enlivened by Chicago Bulls caps and Nikes. There was a long interview with a Madame Nabila, who had taught English there for several decades. There were snapshots of other teachers and staff, including a young Frenchman, whose caption explained he was doing his national service there rather than in the French military. My head swam. I dreamed Egyptian. Quick queries on Yahoo!—Google hadn't yet appeared in the world—pulled up a website for the school. CSF alumni, now expatriates from their native Egypt who were spread all over the world, had created the site to keep in touch with each other. The email address of the school's director was listed on the site. I was nervous and excited, imagining the possibilities. While looking into Fulbright programs in the region, I had learned that Cairo was the most important city in the Middle East in terms of cultural life, academia, business, and politics. The only thing that had kept me from applying to study there rather than Rabat was that Egypt required two years of Arabic study even to apply for a Fulbright.

A great sweep of destiny and vocation seemed to bring me to Cairo. The pieces fell so easily into place that it felt meant to be. As soon as a vision started to form in my imagination and desire for what this experience could be for me, the universe began to present helpers and shift circumstances so that my vision would come to pass.

As I moved towards and past college graduation, a cyclical and multi-layered style of development emerged which then intensified as I acclimated to Egypt:

- On one layer, my **Conformist** form of mind had me performing certain scripts, as if I were an ant and some pheromone emitted by my colony directed my steps, my work, and my specialization. I had, for example, so internalized the Jesuit motto of being a "man for others," that

service to others pulsed powerfully and deeply within me, reverberating in my hands and limbs.
- On another layer, my **Expert** form of mind had me intently aiming to distinguish myself as so specially competent that I presumed to embody and transcend the Boston College motto, "Ever to Excel." My excelling in study and service would *surpass the high expectations* put on me by my family, peers, and professors—or so I said to myself.
- On still another layer, my **Achiever** form of mind had me as a college senior beginning to chart my own course, imagining myself taking my life journey to territory beyond the bounds of the map provided by my tribe.

Beyond these three so-called conventional stages of adult development—which were all simultaneously underway in my inner workings—I was also driving towards a profound upheaval, which would tip part of me into the first of the post-conventional stages, namely, the **Redefining** form of mind.

Introspective writing became a regular practice throughout these post-college years. I realized at the time just how remarkable so many of the experiences I was having in Egypt were, so I wrote to record them for the future me. I also wrote to seek meaning. *What is happening to me? What sense can I discern in the happenings of my life?* I put myself through an accelerating series of shifts. I cycled through stages and identities so fast I felt dizzy. I experimented like crazy. I tried on different versions of myself to see how they fit and how I felt wearing them. Writing reflective journal entries let me explore and notice in a way I hadn't before: *Who am I here? and here? and here? and now? and now? and now?*

Second Adolescence feels like an apt description of so much of what I experienced in these post-college years. The heteronormative, barely adult version of myself that I had constructed as I finished college came apart. Cairo shattered me. *Humpty Dumpty had a great fall!* I picked myself up and made and remade myself over and over, but *all the king's horses and all the king's men couldn't quite put Humpty Dumpty back together again.* I struggled to find inner coherence. Living in Egypt, I learned all over again how to behave, how to speak, how to be a man. I created a version of myself as a teacher in an all-boys school. Just after the two years there, I fashioned another version of myself as a graduate student. Then I tried on a life as a gay professional in Omaha and began learning how to date men. At some point, I also lived in community with Jesuits and formally began the process of applying to become one myself.

As if dying my hair wildly different colors, I tried on different lives. I put myself in new situations and watched to see what would happen. Telling the complete story of all these iterations, starts and stops, and spirals forward and back, would not serve our purpose here. Instead, let me draw selectively on my archive of reflective writings from these years. I will share fragments and snippets of some of the many lives I lived during this period to illustrate what **Second Adolescence** looked like in my life so that you can consider how it might show up in yours.

In the four years immediately after college, my personal development cycled through a pattern of painful disintegration followed by arduous recomposition of myself. Coming apart in successive waves, I would start the cycle in dazed depression, then move forward with hope. Multiple upheavals shook my world to cause those waves. The most disruptive of these upheavals emanated from the experience of having a boyfriend for the first time, though neither he nor I could bring ourselves to use the term "boyfriend." That relationship with Tom, a US Marine I met in Cairo, blew apart a great many aspects of who I understood myself to be and what I expected of my life. That relationship spanned the last semester of my two academic years teaching at the Jesuit high school in Cairo. Loving Tom, I no longer knew myself. One especially distraught moment, weeping in the shower, feels now like the emblem of that episode of distress. Gazing at myself in the steamy mirror, amazed and befuddled, I wondered desperately what was happening to me. Through the looking-glass, I saw myself in full-blown adolescent angst. As for so many other LGBTQ+ people, a **Second Adolescence** took place for me as my non-normative sexual orientation became undeniable.

- *What experiences of fate or destiny seemed to pull you forward into a major life move?*
- *What experience of* **Second Adolescence** *have you had?*

Becoming Adult All Over Again

- *Who do you know that has most apparently undergone a second adolescence?*
- *What influence does your interpretation of their experience have on how you receive the concept of* **Second Adolescence** *as a queer superpower?*

"**Second Adolescence**" might conjure up images of a man in his 50s wearing sneakers and T-shirts from some fashion brand trendy among teenagers, splurging on an extravagant sports car, or growing out his hair and piercing his ear for the first time. Living with abandon, unrestrained by convention or moderation, he makes seemingly rash decisions and heads in uncharacteristic directions. The trope for the straight family man in a mid-life crisis has him leave his wife, quit his job, and run away with his secretary to a tropical island. His kids, who might be in their 20s, are shocked at their father's wild behavior, which they see as immature and irresponsible. They see him as desperately and foolishly grasping for his lost youth instead of entering old age as they might believe he is supposed to—quietly resigning to personal diminishment and societal irrelevance.

Reframed as a queer superpower, **Second Adolescence** takes on some different aspects. In queer contexts, **Second Adolescence** connects to closeting and coming out. When an adult first comes out as gay, bi, or queer, the possibility or need for a **Second Adolescence** arises. He might now revisit earlier social experiences related to his sexual development during puberty. He might have graphic conversations with friends about sexual experiences or experiments, or point out to them hot bodies or protruding body parts that catch his attention. He might gleefully embrace what he and his gay friends call a "slut phase" of going on as many dates and having as much sex as possible, *making up for lost time*. Hypersexual expression in these ways could re-enact the teenage experience of having "raging hormones."

Beyond sexual expression, the queer superpower of **Second Adolescence** opens the gates to a deeper personal transformation. Just as a kid in their early teens might at a certain point throw off their childhood habits in favor of new clothes, hairstyles, friends, toys, ways of speaking, and cultural vocabulary, so does an adult who makes a courageous move on the closeting-coming out continuum. Perhaps that move towards more open and public identification as gay, bi, or queer dissolves a **Double Life**, in which he was closeted on workdays while keeping queer company on evenings and weekends. Bringing greater integrity to his social identity, he comes out to colleagues and clients, which allows him to drop the performative elements of a straight professional persona. New art might appear on his office walls, and new jewelry on his fingers, wrists, ears, or neck. He might start dressing in more colorful, tailored, and tasteful clothes.

Coming out and remaking one's social persona can, of course, occur at any age or stage of adult development. Someone in **Conformist** mind who comes out might need to switch social groups or find new important others. Someone in **Expert** mind might focus on learning gay lingo, acquiring queer cultural capital, and improving sexual skills to win recognition and approval from peers. Someone in **Achiever** mind might craft a new vision for life or set new goals to fit a newly acquired gay identity.

An Egyptian Sexual Orientation

Shazz. "Faggot," in Arabic, I figured.

"It's a bad word, an insult like the others I've mentioned," said Mohammed, my new colleague. "If you hear one of the boys call someone that, reprimand him. The boys use it a lot, and it's bad, but not the worst thing they can call each other. The word you really need to watch out for is *khawwal.* If one of your pupils uses that word, send him right to Mr. Waguih's office."

"So what does that one mean?"

"Well, it's like *shazz*, but much worse."

The lesson in Egyptian vulgarities from my fellow English teacher bonded us. There we were—two polite, respectable, professional men, having our first conversation ever, and we're clarifying the gradations of obscenity between *ibn mitnaka* ('son of a fucking bitch') and two words for 'faggot.' We each had our turns chuckling and blushing, wanting to seem to the other neither crass nor naïve.

Classes were to start the next day. Though the College de la Sainte Famille had a student body of boys evenly divided between Christian and Muslim boys, Mohammed was the first Muslim teacher I had thus far met. Most teachers at this French-immersion Catholic school in Cairo were Christian, except for the teachers of Arabic, who were required by law to be Muslim since they also taught religious education courses to the Muslim students. Mohammed and I had sat together at the meeting of all the administrators and teachers. He translated for me whenever anyone spoke Arabic, and I did the same for him whenever someone spoke French.

Afterwards, we went to a classroom to talk through the curriculum for the English courses we would both be teaching and get to know each other. Other Americans had come to CSF over the years to teach English there, and most had been volunteers like me who were connected to the New England Province of Jesuits. The Egyptian faculty had learned how important it was that these foreigners, who were routinely called *khawagat* (roughly, 'gringos'), be taught the cuss words our teenage students would yell out in their antics and rabble-rousing. Like the 'Penis!' game some of my friends liked to play at St. James in junior high, in which you kept saying the offending word intermittently with gradually increasing clarity and volume, but without the teacher catching what was being said, the boys at this French-immersion school in Cairo would let out Arabic vulgarities in the middle of class, so long as the teacher was a *khawaga* from France or the USA and thus unschooled in the local slang.

The point at which my private lesson in obscenities with Mohammed got truly awkward had to do with these two words meaning 'faggot,' *shazz* and *khawwal*. *Shazz* had the strength of mild insults like 'jerk' or 'dumbass,' while *khawwal* Mohammed put on par with *koss ommak*, the most vulgar phrase and greatest insult in Egyptian Arabic, meaning 'your mother's cunt.'

"But how can they be so different?" I asked. "What's the nuance between them?"

Mohammed blushed and delved delicately into the mechanics of anal intercourse. "The *shazz* penetrates. A *khawwal* is penetrated."

"Ah! Got it." I replied. "That's really interesting how one is so much more insulting than the other!" I spoke to Mohammed with the intellectual curiosity of one language arts teacher to another, but filed away for later inquiry my deeper wonder at this enormous emotional distinction between the Egyptian Arabic words for 'top' and 'bottom.'

Homosocial Cairo

This distinction between *shazz* and *khawwal* stayed with me as a puzzle to ponder throughout those first two years I lived in Egypt, in large part because Mohammed taught me these two words soon upon my arrival in Cairo as a fresh-faced volunteer teacher at this all-boys, Jesuit, French-immersion school. Gender and sexuality had not yet become topics of scholarly inquiry for me, but learning these two insult words got me thinking about sexuality as a system of meanings, like a language. Egyptians put values on sexual acts and roles that differed significantly from the sexual systems in my native culture.

Indeed, bodies in their entirety seemed to carry different meanings from those I knew. Unlike most American men, men in Egypt all seemed to shave their armpits, and many their pubic hair as well—a practice that goes back to pharaonic times, they would invariably tell me. Christians and Muslims alike very often wore mustaches, while certain styles of beard signaled conservative Muslim beliefs, following the practice of the Prophet and his Companions. Those same Muslim men would also wear swimsuits that reached past the knee to practice bodily modesty. Egyptians took offense if the bottom of someone else's foot faced them, so I learned to cross my legs with my feet facing the ground. My passing familiarity with the veil prepared me to recognize that women's hair bore different meanings for Muslims, but nothing prepared me to encounter families where the grandmother wore bright lipstick and no veil, while the mother and her 20-something daughter wore colorful garb that reached to their wrists and ankles with matching veils, or draping black dresses and veils that covered everything but their faces.

Across Egyptian society, I quickly discovered, men mostly socialize with men, and women with women. "Egypt is a homosocial society," I remember one expat professor explaining to me. Men express physical affection with each other, warmly kissing on opposite cheeks as a typical greeting. Sitting at outdoor cafés smoking large water pipes, they joke, tell stories, tease, complain, express joy or distress, and otherwise share the movements of their lives, usually over tea.

I was warmly welcomed into many male homosocial settings. Egyptians embrace hospitality and generosity as supreme cultural values, along with humor and affability. Their warmth matched my family's, and their emphasis on sociability fit my own. Still sorting out my sexual energies, I would regularly get confused by just how often, how affectionately, and how intimately Egyptian men would touch me. They would sit across from me so close that their bent knee would nestle between my thighs. They would drape their arms around my neck and lay their head on my shoulder. They would reach out and stroke my chin or caress my ear with a smile of genuine kindness and care. They would wrap their arm around mine as we walked, patting my hand. I came eventually to understand these as common gestures among friends, not come-ons, but I still found them confusing.

Cairo pushed men's bodies right up against mine in other ways as well. On thronged buses, I came to expect to feel other men's penises engorge as the jostling rubbed them against my hip or thigh. No apologies, no explanations, and usually no lewd gestures or overtures. Erotic energy just pulsed through these bodies.

The Europeans I met purported to understand all the ins and outs of gender dynamics in Egypt. They would authoritatively explain to me that sexual contact with women was sharply limited, and even social contact between the sexes was constrained. Indeed, predominant customs and morals did not allow an unrelated man and woman to spend time together, even in public, unless through social arrangement they had become engaged to be married. To reach eligibility for engagement, a man had to buy and furnish an apartment first—a financial feat that took men well into their 30s in many cases.

Egyptian Christians would also sometimes explain social norms like these to me disapprovingly, with subtle or not so subtle comments about Muslims imposing their ways on Christians. More affluent Egyptians would similarly disapprove of social norms like these. With attitudes ranging from compassion to disdain, many would characterize the tens of millions of people in the poor Egyptian masses as unthinking, uneducated, or ignorant. Egyptians with a stronger affinity for Europe or the USA would, in turn, explain these kinds of social norms as rooted in the influence of Saudis and other "Gulfies," whose customs and mores these Western-oriented Egyptians saw as moving Egypt backwards.

As I listened to these various observations, explanations, and interpretations, I shifted gradually from wide-eyed credulity to curious skepticism. *What is this interpreter's agenda? What in their experience and worldview is influencing how they are seeing and explaining Egyptian culture?* Everyone seemed to have a stake in knowing how gender, sex, and the body work in Egypt. I didn't judge these varying explanations as wrong, but I came increasingly to focus my attention on what each person's perspective revealed about who they were.

- *What disorienting experiences have you had of the body or a certain body part meaning something quite different to someone else, compared to the meaning you put onto it?*

Redefining Ourselves Beyond Convention

- *As you regard your own experience of growing up as a process of increasing individuation, what becomes clear about your developmental path?*

Second Adolescence as a queer superpower especially fits into the **Redefining** stage, because this stage marks the pivotal move beyond the so-called conventional stages of **Conformist**, **Expert**, and **Achiever** forms of mind into the post-conventional stages of **Redefining**, **Self-Transforming**, and beyond. The developmental shifts beginning in the **Redefining** stage radically challenge our sense of self in the world. Having previously received tremendous affirmation from heteronormative society for becoming self-authoring as **Achievers**—*the very form of leader lionized in mainstream culture*—someone in

Redefining mind begins to lose much of what had previously seemed like gains. They had succeeded in constructing a clear and distinct worldview, which organized reality into logical and bounded categories, a virtual beehive of compartments. The transition into **Redefining** mind begins a process of fracturing or melting that edifice of compartments. The **Queen's** realm is dissolved and then reconstituted—a disconcerting process to say the least!

The Heroes Journey program, where I bring together a few highly accomplished gay, bi, and queer men in an intimate developmental community, is designed especially to support the uncomfortable and often painful process of moving into and through **Redefining**. Entering and settling into a **Redefining** mindset presents formidable challenges. We can feel adrift or lost, like a misfit or even an existential failure. Old tropes and fears among queer people as "damaged goods" might return after years dormant. As the luster of life goals dims, the meaning of life itself can feel hazy. **Redefining** unsettles!

While contemporary Western straight culture seemingly most admires the **Achiever** mindset, contemporary queer culture idolizes certain central aspects of the **Redefining** mindset. Mainstream culture foments dreams of adults succeeding in the world through mastering rationality, ambitiously setting goals, and achieving them through grit and perseverance. Queer culture, on the other hand, prizes collective dreams of adults flourishing through searching for their *true selves* through skeptically reassessing what our culture programmed into us. The ascendant version of queer culture that treasures this vision of adult development adulates idealized gay or queer adults who have freed themselves from the prison of conventional cultural norms and strictures. Coming out allows something "natural" about us to come alive more fully.

Representations in mainstream straight culture often depict LGBTQ+ people with many **Redefining** characteristics and patterns, such as focusing on *being and feeling* rather than doing and thinking. Straight mainstream culture often regards queer people as fitting this description of people who are operating from a **Redefining** mindset: *spontaneous, expressing themselves freely and energetically, and keenly interested in finding their unique purpose.*[65] As so often with LGBTQ+ people, individuals of any sexual orientation or gender identity who operate from a **Redefining** mindset "may at times appear almost 'amoral' in their demand to be who they are and do what they want."[66] I see a close connection between the **Redefining** stage of development and queer culture in large part because the queer superpower of **Second Adolescence** so often serves as an on-ramp to the **Redefining** stage of meaning-making.

In this **Redefining** stage, we gain new perspective on all we know and start to see how our interpretation of the world always depends on our position in it. Other people's views, no matter how different from our own, become worthy of consideration to a much greater extent than ever before. Our *inner inclusion* expands as we become able to notice how the systems and cultures in which we live continually shape us. Our *inner diversity* increases as we shake ourselves loose from the self-created realm we had painstakingly constructed for ourselves and call into question all that we see and know. We see more than ever the dynamic give and take, ebb and flow, push and pull of autonomy and belonging, self and system.

The onset of the **Redefining** stage shakes our world, much like the surge of hormones in the pubescent body creates a cascade of physiological transformations that shake a child's world. In both cases, the very ground under our feet loses its solidity, stability, and strength. Once stolid and sure, we become more worried and anxious. As we begin operating from a **Redefining** mindset, mainstream society begins to look askance at us. We start to look ever weirder. Institutions and social groups question us, rather than affirm us. *What's wrong with you? Why don't you keep up the momentum of achievement you've had these past years? Have you lost your mojo? Are you giving up on all the ambitious goals for which we used to admire you?*

This troublingly pivotal stage typically looks and feels like a personal crisis that brings self-doubt, tension, and major life changes. Turbulence wreaks havoc in the calm kingdom of the **Achiever**. While the move into early **Self-Authoring** (i.e., the **Achiever** mindset) already involved a significant shift from living outside-in towards living inside-out, in **Redefining** we move even further away from external standards and expectations. We move further towards inner resonance and our own sense of what truly fulfills us, no matter the feedback from society.[67]

When coaching someone who is operating out of a **Redefining** mindset, I meet them in their unsettling process of reassessing what their culture has programmed into them, including influences from family of origin, national community, religious tradition, professional peers, and so on. I encourage them to keep noticing the manifold outside influences on their ways of seeing themselves, the world, and life in it. I affirm the value of this deprogramming, which can at times feel like a betrayal of those we most love. I also emphasize just how normal and natural their experience is. Untethering our meaning-making from "important others" liberates us to become ourselves ever more fully—even while we may still value and love those whose authority over our worldview we strip away.

Whereas learning about adult development theory can threaten the vaunted position we hold when in an **Achiever** mindset, the map of the developmental landscape can soothe the angst inherent to the **Redefining** mindset. *You mean nothing is wrong with me? I'm not damaged goods, a foundering failure?* Bringing together small groups of gay, bi, and queer men to share their experiences and support one another in their unique processes of becoming themselves particularly suits the needs of my clients who are primarily operating from a **Redefining** mindset. They experience a comforting sense of solidarity and affirmation that empowers them to continue their process of questioning foundational beliefs and truly authoring the axioms of their worldview.

This **Redefining** stage marks a shift in the developmental trajectory from increasing *individuation* to increasing *integration*.[68] If goaded by crisis or courage to call into question the very belief systems in which we are embedded—including those belief systems that we ourselves have constructed—we can begin to see the systems of interplay and interdependence that continually form and re-form us and all beings. Gradually distinguishing our sense of self apart from the knowledge we worked so long and hard to take in as well as from the personal vision of accomplishment we labored to construct, we come to find new levels of integration. This process advances our inner integration, bringing together into greater cohesion the manifold parts of ourselves, and also allows us to see how we fit into familial, organizational, societal, and cultural systems.

To form an **Achiever** mindset earlier in the developmental journey, we needed to embed our meaning-making into a version of our Self that we constructed as our own *realm* so that we could differentiate ourselves from everyone else. Then, if and when we get to the point of forming a **Redefining** mindset, we break our meaning-making out of that carefully compartmentalized Self we had constructed, so that now we can be more conscious of our interconnections with the many systems in which we abide. The **Achiever** form of mind embeds for the sake of greater differentiation, while the **Redefining** form of mind differentiates for the sake of greater integration.

- *Reflecting on younger and older people you have met, consider the varieties of unconventional characters, for example, members of an alternative subculture compared to eccentric misfits compared to unique figures who attract admiration. Where do you see individuals who appear truly post-conventional?*

Cairo, the Pressure Cooker

- *What experiences of not being fully honest with yourself about your sexual feelings, desires, and practices have you had?*
- *When in your life have you had the most conscious awareness of truly becoming your own person?*

Pressure pushed on Egyptians from all sides—sexual, economic, religious, and political. For this reason, one travel guide I had, *The Rough Guide to Egypt*, called Cairo "a pressure cooker" for its 20 million inhabitants. Cairo raised the heat and increased the pressure on me as well. The city accelerated the process of me becoming myself. This forward- and backward-moving process had me risking adventure and retreating to refuge, bringing forth visions and facing deep frustrations, connecting to new kinds of people and new parts of myself, while also at times finding myself profoundly disconnected and alone in the world. My daily life in Cairo took unpredictable turns, from which new challenges and opportunities emerged. Most important for this telling of the tale is the Egyptian environment where gender formed different boundary lines and groupings. They were different from what I had known in my home culture, and they pushed me to face more fully the secret pledge I had made to myself when first leaving Omaha for college in Boston.

Besides the physical interest in other young men, which I had noticed by the end of high school, I began to realize that I was creating a series of new friendships characterized by intense emotional, non-sexual intimacy. That first year in Egypt, Ramy and Chérif fit into this pattern. Both francophone Christian Egyptians, one a few years older and the other a few years younger, they felt like long-lost brothers to me. Chérif taught me the word "*akhouya*," meaning "my brother," which we would call each other with affection. With both Ramy and Chérif, I held a great many shared interests and perspectives and, at the same time, we also relished all that we learned from our differences.

In a journal entry in February 1998, I recorded some musings about these intense friendships:

> I have discovered that I have a deep need for intimacy with other young men. And I think this need stems from a lack of intimacy or contact with my Dad. While I had admitted/ acknowledged to myself some years ago that I had an unusual attraction to other guys, only now am I beginning honestly to separate & discern between desire for intimacy & desire for sexual contact.

While I considered myself with care and compassion in this and other journal entries, I did not exercise complete honesty. I did not write about how, in some of these intense friendships affection and companionship mixed with erotic exchange and sexual experiences.

The first of these intense friendships that turned erotic had erupted with a college friend back in Boston, at the end of my junior year. We had befriended each other through deep conversations over several months in the preparation process for a spring break service trip to Jamaica. Then, in his dorm room at BC, late on the night of St. Patrick's Day, after much drinking, we began kissing and groping each other. That became the first of many times over the next month or two that we got together for sex, despite my staying in a serious and purportedly exclusive relationship with Carly at the same time. The intensity of the sexual energy I felt throughout those weeks having sex with that close friend was like nothing I ever felt before or after. I felt like I was in heat. Even when sitting in class or the library, my entire body pulsed, remembering and anticipating sensations and convulsions, from the caresses and kisses exchanged with him.

Despite the power of these experiences, which ended as he graduated and moved away, this is the first I've written about them. I boxed up these experiences to contain the spread of these memories. I refrained from facing my duplicity, or what the intensity of these sexual experiences could mean for my identity or my future. Compartmentalizing, I constructed the beginnings of a **Double Life**.

Though my sexual interest in other guys peeked its head out in a few other furtive moments before I came to Cairo, I brought with me the story that I had not made good on my end-of-high-school pledge to explore my sexuality in college. I held that pledge more lightly and with greater curiosity as I moved to Egypt. While I did not set exploring my gay side as a goal for my time in Egypt, I did wonder what would become of this intention. At the same time, my move from Boston to Cairo gave me another go at a **Great Escape** from a relatively constraining context to one where new possibilities abounded.

Stepping out of the cultural contexts I had known in the US loosened up the rather rigidly rational morality by which I had lived in college. In Cairo, I crossed paths with an extraordinary array of people, some my age. I befriended Tamil-speaking Jesuit seminarians from India and French-speaking girls with diplomat parents from the Central African Republic, Burundi, and Congo. I encountered with some wariness Muslim Egyptian men of all ages who oriented to Saudi Arabia for models of piety and propriety. The hashish-smoking artists and intellectuals who cavorted late at night in downtown Cairo fascinated me and conjured up vague images of beatniks and Greenwich Village. Most foreign of all, villagers and country folk naïve to the ways of the city would occasionally walk down the side of busy streets wearing dusty *galabeya*s, the traditional ankle-length tunics worn by Egyptian men, accompanied by a small herd of sheep following as if in a pasture. Before seeing this sight, the word "peasant" had for me belonged to medieval times. From then on, peasants seemed to inhabit the contemporary world with me, at least in Egypt.

Returning to Omaha for a visit after my first year in Cairo felt like a watershed moment of self-recognition. I had become someone quite different. I had access to a world that seemed completely unknown to everyone I knew in Boston or Omaha. My life experience was starting to surpass that of my parents and grandparents and even those Jesuits and professors I had so admired in college. I began to see my value system and worldview as products of the culture in which I had previously lived my life. Relishing the power of life experience to shape each of us, I focused on honoring the multiple perspectives of which I was newly aware. I remember my students saying, "There you go again, *ya* Longo, with all this talk of 'experience'!"

Egyptians had their own ways of looking at reality, which I recognized as eminently valid while also extremely different from the worldviews of everyone I had known growing up in

America. Becoming increasingly bicultural, I came to reflect on how American society and Egyptian society (and French and Dutch and other societies) mold their members' minds and hearts. In Egypt, I had increasingly become my own. Defining myself, setting my own limits, and choosing what kind of person to be—I was individuating. *A Nebraska boy who went to Boston College, majored in French, minored in German Studies, and then moved to Cairo, Egypt as a volunteer teacher and began intensively learning Arabic.* I marveled at who I was becoming, so different from anyone I knew. I felt pride at living out such a unique life path, styling my life as art—reaching greater and greater differentiation and independence.

The cultural diversity of Cairo dizzied me and freed me to reinvent myself. In other words, I sought to find myself anew. Avoiding the company of Americans, I was finding new ways to be myself in Egyptian culture. I invented Dominique, an intercultural and polyglot version of myself who moved with increasing ease through Egypt. Sexual reinvention followed the cultural. In homosocial Cairo, I especially explored and experimented with different ways of being a man with other men.

- *How do you relate to the idea or practice of "reinventing yourself"?*
- *When have you tried it out, and to what effect?*

A Controlled Coming Apart

- *When have you found yourself psychologically swept up in a hurricane or sinking in quicksand?*
- *What new vistas on yourself and your life did you see from those topsy-turvy vantage points?*

Personal growth and development pertain to gaining access to increasingly more perspectives. You might remember from grammar the idea of first-person, second-person, and third-person point of view. When it comes to conjugating verbs in a new language or choosing pronouns, these three terms designate the direction of personal references. I talk about myself in the first-person, about you in the second-person, and about that other person who is not present for the conversation in the third-person. Playing on these ideas, the research literature on adult development uses these terms for the consciousness of self, the person in front of me, and the person who isn't present. In addition, theorists also use a fourth-person perspective, which refers to the perspective from which we see ourselves embedded in systems such as culture. While this notion verges on the abstruse, I beg your patience with this explanation. I believe the concept holds great value in expanding our understanding of this crucial element of development called multiplying perspectives.

In the **Expert** stage, we gained access to a third-person perspective, in which we can, in our mind's eye, get up on the balcony and see ourselves in life interacting with others down on the dance floor.[69] In this **Redefining** stage, our mind's eye can now ascend to a still higher perch, from which we can *watch ourselves watching ourselves*. From the new perch, we look down at the part of ourselves who watches from the balcony and see how that version of us is enmeshed and embedded in culture, family, gender, and other systems.

> The 4th person perspective allows individuals to stand outside the system they grew up in and observe themselves and their cultural surround from a new altitude. . . . One can look at the familiar (status

quo) through a new lens and query many of its tacit assumptions, values, and beliefs.[70]

This new perspective frees us to choose with greater agency which aspects of our cultural heritage to continue to hold as ours and which to release as not ours. To the extent we become members of both straight and queer cultures, we can, for example, gain perspective on what each of these cultures wants of us and offers to us.

Second Adolescence entails *a controlled coming apart* of the Self, to make possible *a coming together* of a new version of oneself, which is even more fully **Self-Authored** than was possible at the **Achiever** stage. In **Redefining** mind, we can reflect on how our various positions in systems back then used to affect us. We can project forward to anticipate how we could later be embedded in different systems, which will influence and change the reality we shall come to experience later in life. "The 4th person perspective allows individuals . . . to examine *how they came to believe what they believe* and feel and how one knows and proves things." (Emphasis mine.)[71] **Second Adolescence** puts to use this expanded horizon to fly more freely among personal possibilities. As we give adulthood another go with this new freedom, we move away from a focus on a personalized version of conventional definitions of success and instead move towards truly courageous authenticity.

In becoming wise, we become strange. We call into question everything which we used to hold as right and true, including especially those values, goals, and principles that we had selected and honed to rule our realm. We start to see how all of our and others' perspectives are mightily influenced by the cultural systems in which we dwell. We move beyond societal convention. Now relativism rules.[72]

Society resists this move. Through individual and collective action, society exerts a powerful developmental pull on those who operate from a **Redefining** form of mind. Institutions like universities, corporations, and professional guilds whose developmental orientation focuses on fostering conventional mindsets rally various kinds of pressures to counter post-conventional sense-making. *What's wrong with you?! You're taking your eye off the ball! Where is that old fire in your belly? You're getting soft.* The coalescence of external resistance with internal incertitude makes the **Redefining** stage acutely disconcerting and distressful. Indeed, depression for someone at the **Redefining** stage can often focus on "the realistic fear of being reabsorbed, that is sucked back into the 'rat race' of the **Achiever** mindset by the demands of society."[73]

Various external and internal factors can elicit this shift into post-conventional sense-making. Living in a foreign land, for example, can in some cases help us see the strangeness of our homeland.[74] Looking at my own life, I see that my move to Cairo catalyzed new access to this variety of meaning-making. The encounter with speakers of other languages who do not speak my own language starkly clarified what aliens we all are, depending only on the context in which we find ourselves. In the experience of cultural alienation, I found myself bereft of a great many cognitive and relational resources. I felt reduced and diminished to such an extent that I could not help but question who I was. With access to the language and customs of my home community sharply curtailed, I verged on losing my sense of adulthood. At times, I felt thrust back into a pre-conventional order of consciousness, before **Socialized** mind, when I was a little child not understanding the world which was so clearly ruled by big people. Once again in that foreign land of Egypt, I found myself with little understanding of how the world worked or what people were talking about. The **Queen** was knocked off her throne, blown off her steed. The one who reigned over a realm with mastery now became like a child once again. *Who am I? What is going on here?*

A similar experience of cultural alienation can take place without any travel to foreign lands. The powerful vehicle of introspection and reflection can transport us from **Achiever** mind into a psychological hurricane or quicksand, where everything we see and know becomes topsy-turvy. As we practice self-examination, the foundations we used to stand upon show themselves to be as temporary and contingent as sandcastles, as arbitrarily constructed as some secret sign language that young twins make up to communicate with each other. If we choose to allow ourselves not to unsee these new vistas within ourselves and our world, we become *a stranger in a strange land* without ever leaving home.

As the structures we formerly saw as solid and necessary reveal themselves to be located in the eye of their beholder, we begin redirecting our gaze in new directions and catch sight of what previously eluded us. With less single-minded focus on the vision and worldview we had constructed for ourselves with our **Achiever** mindset, we now become open to seeing and appreciating more of reality. For example, our view of time expands backwards and forwards, and our appreciation for its import increases. Experience of the present moment demands greater focus and holds greater interest than before. Looking back, we begin to see more clearly how past contexts and scenarios influenced us.

We gain the capacity to see beyond linear and mechanistic understandings of causality. We start to better appreciate the unforeseeable interconnectedness of events and phenomena. "No longer is the world a place of discrete objects, like billiard balls on a table, that cause subsequent events unilaterally and sequentially, based on an initially planned strategic act. Instead, causation is recognized as circular, relational, and system."[75]

Besides seeing more of reality out there, we also see more of the reality within ourselves. We gain access to new vantage points from which to peer into our own depths:

> Useful information can come from many sources that were previously considered outside the realm of scientific inquiry and viewed with skepticism, such as body sensations, intuition, dreams, reflection, and meditation. Therefore, the shift from conventional to postconventional stages also reflects a qualitative shift from a more linear, rational, intellectual to a more organismic and embodied awareness.[76]

Less analytic and more synthetic, the **Redefining** mindset gains capacity to make connections and recognize interdependencies that the **Achiever** and earlier mindsets miss. Now, "this new way of perceiving can foster the realization that the whole (the *Gestalt*) is more than its separate parts." With greater access to the depths within themselves, those in **Redefining** mind "appreciate that others have their own unique ways of doing things and being themselves. They recognize that different people have different needs and preferences."[77] In **Redefining** mind, we gain expanded capacity to see and respect the inner diversity in others, as well as in ourselves. We thus become "less apt to judge others."

The developmental trajectory of **Gaydar**, the queer gaze, offers another way to frame this expansion of the power to peer into inner reality and accept what we perceive. The gaze of the gay **Self-Protective Opportunist** mind looks through the reflection of the **Shield of Hypervigilance** to see threats, wherever they might be. The gaze of the gay **Conformist** mind using **Gaydar** looks to see social sameness, so as to find belonging in **Pride Tribe**. The gaze of the gay **Expert** mind looks to see social rank so as to find approval and distinction as the **Best Little Boy**. The gay **Queen** projects her own unique vision out into the world so as to claim the authority to author her own story. Becoming ever more **Self-Authoring**, the **Queen** recognizes that others may also legitimately construct and possess a unique vision of their own. From a **Redefining** place, **Gaydar** now looks within, to see inner layers of uniqueness in the personal preferences and needs of self and others which shift as contextual factors evolve and unfold.

Several fears characteristically plague **Redefining** mind. As we verge into a post-conventional way of making sense of ourselves and the world, the realistic fear of regression to conventional sense-making threatens at every turn. Another realistic fear is the feeling of hopelessness in the seemingly never-ending search for meaning outside of the conventions set by society. *I'm lost, adrift forever! I'll never find myself!* Amidst these intense anxieties, what powers the quest into the unknown is the ambition to deprogram from cultural brainwashing and unentangle from the webs of societal constraints and conventions.

Sex gets questioned along with everything else by **Redefining** minds. We give ourselves and others greater leeway for nonconventional sexual practices and experimentation, possibly with some direct rejection of the most conventional forms of sexual expression as inauthentic. From **Redefining** mind, we prefer to see how fluid everyone's sexual desires, roles, practices, and partners can be, so long as the strictures of convention are thrown off. We gain the capacity here to listen carefully and learn from sexual partners to discover more of what's possible for us and them in the realm of the erotic.

To take care of someone in **Redefining** mind, we can create conditions for vulnerability by modeling it ourselves and giving permission for whatever needs to emerge. Loving in a **Redefining** mindset looks like radical hospitality. It welcomes the stranger and the strange alike. Whoever walks or prances through the door receives acknowledgement, space, safety, and nourishment. In the **Redefining** stage of development, the aliveness made possible by love—flourishing—looks like *courageous experimentation*.

Many of the men who come to Flourishing Gays for support in their personal growth and leadership development have been so focused on achieving and accomplishing for so long that even those whose meaning-making verges into **Redefining** have not yet found their way to a **Second Adolescence**. So powerful are the pressures to stand up as a leader as conceived by conventional society and its institutions that many of my clients and so many others overhold certain habits and tenets of the **Achiever** mindset far beyond their usefulness. Raising my clients' awareness of **Second Adolescence** as a queer superpower often encourages them into the courageous experimentation that is so vital for **Redefining** mind.

- *In what domains have you endeavored to liberate yourself from cultural programming you received through your ethnic, national, religious, or family background?*

CHAPTER 6:

Spiraling

Keifo

- *What have you found most alluring or most difficult about the sometimes thin line between friendship and sexual relationship?*

A boy named Keifo played a pivotal role in all of this for me. With Keifo I stepped into a world that would otherwise be unknowable. The power of his loving friendship made possible courageous experimentation that unraveled me. A swindler, my age, he spent his days and nights mostly in the alleys and passageways of so-called "Islamic Cairo," the walled city from which the Fatimid dynasty ruled an empire a thousand years ago. Completely illiterate, Keifo had learned English from the tourists he relied on for his livelihood. When he approached me the first time asking in Arabic what time it was, he was sussing me out as a possible "client." He asked the question as a ruse, to find out whether I spoke Arabic and where I came from. Dark-haired, lean, musky, and a bit dusty, with an easy smile and a ready laugh, Keifo and I looked and smelled alike. Both my olive and his bronze skin shone, tan and smooth.

That day and many others when I would return to find Keifo, he walked me around the bustling district, into shops and up to colorful figures of all kinds, down passages and up stairways I would never otherwise have entered. Savvy and slick in many ways I was not, Keifo could not read. His formal schooling stopped after just a few years. He made his living from guiding and hustling tourists, taking a cut of their purchases from the shops into which he led them.

The third or fourth time we met, he dropped (most of) the ruse and told me how he worked. The magnetic pull we had towards each other made me something more than a "client." We enjoyed asking each other questions about our lives, our experiences, and the worlds we knew. We met up with his friends on a rooftop overlooking the historic Hussein Mosque to drink Stella beers and smoke *shisha*, that is, hookah. Keifo slept there, on a bed in the open air in a dilapidated ruin of a modern concrete building where he and his friends seemed to be squatting. The others worked the streets in different ways from Keifo, like making and hawking cheap flip-flops.

Some nights, when the hour got especially late, I would stay there and sleep next to Keifo on his mattress in the open air. With a thin sheet over us to keep off mosquitos and flies, we collapsed into sleep, leaning on each other in a gentle embrace for warmth and comfort. We cuddled and hugged with fraternal affection. At different times, we also exchanged gentle kisses on the cheek, the forehead, even once or twice on the lips. Never making out with sustained or passionate kisses, we shared a physical affection that went well beyond the brotherly kiss and shoulder squeeze with which Egyptian men would greet one another. The physicality with Keifo matched what

I had sometimes fantasized about having with other teenagers when I was in high school. With only spare and sideways verbal acknowledgement, we shared comfort with our bodies and our boyishness—the smells, the bulges, and the cycles of our bodies. We came together again and again for intimate and affectionate nights without ever becoming overtly sexual.

That thin line dissolved one night in the second year of our friendship. Late one weekend night Keifo came over to my apartment in Garden City. We talked and joked while enjoying the saltiness of peanuts and the boozy bubbles of beer. As we drank more and more Stellas, I observed that Keifo seemed to have been drinking before coming over.

"*N'amel tayyara walla tishrab cognac?*" he asked.

By that time, I had lived in Egypt and taken about a year of Arabic, so while I could make out the five words in his phrase, I could not grasp what he was asking me.

"Shall we make an airplane or will you drink cognac?" *What in God's good earth could he mean?* Keifo was joking around, I could tell. He had a glint in his eye and tipsily repeated the question again and again.

"*N'amel tayyara walla tishrab cognac?*"

Eventually, I understood that he was proposing sex, one way or another. I surmised what me drinking his "cognac" would look like, but I still couldn't figure out what us "making an airplane" might mean. We found our way to bed and exchanged more than our usual expressions of affection.

"*N'amel tayyara walla tishrab cognac?*" he kept repeating. Aware of the power dynamics at play in oral sex, I also didn't expect to enjoy sucking Keifo off or drinking his "cognac." I wanted mutuality, something we both would enjoy equally.

"*N'amel tayyara, y'ani eh?*" I asked more than once. *What would it mean for us to "make an airplane?"* Keifo never answered, but we took our clothes off, and he moved his body and mine so that we faced each other, with him on top of me. With his arms extended and hips gyrating while his penis moved up and down between my thighs, I finally got the image of an airplane propeller. *This isn't so bad,* I thought. *In fact, it feels good.* The thrill of crossing over the boundary of friendship into sex intensified the physical pleasure of our bodies rubbing together. I wanted to kiss as we had sex this way, but Keifo resisted that intimacy. Thoughts, feelings, and sensations crowded my mind and body. We fell asleep cuddling as usual, after both of us came. *What will be different because of this?* I wondered as I drifted into my dreams.

Curfew in the Barracks

- *What transformations has falling in love brought about in your life?*
- *To what extent has falling in love in some sense decided everything in your life?*

The experiences with Keifo made the musings about my gay side less vague and more concrete. I wanted more sexual experiences with men, no question about it now. The mix of brotherly affection with sensual pleasure excited and buoyed me up, even as it left my head swirling with questions.

During Sunday Mass in St. Joseph's Catholic Church, I would ponder these and other questions that came out of my dizzyingly rich life in Egypt. *What signs of God's invitations to goodness and love can I find in all that is happening in my life? What temptations are luring me away from goodness and love? How is the Spirit moving in my life?* Questions like these would course through my mind during Mass in those days, as they still do now.

"Peace of the Lord be with you all," announced the pastor.

"And also with you," I responded in sync with the whole congregation.

"Now let us share a sign of that peace," said the priest.

I turned to those next to me, extending my hand and saying, "Peace." As I turned to those in the pew behind, a cute, short, smiling guy with obvious muscles and a blond buzzcut extended his hand to me. "Peace of the Lord be with *you*!" I said, while thinking to myself: *So handsome!*

The Sunday Mass in English brought together Catholics from all over the world at this parish run by the Comboni Missionaries in the posh neighborhood of Zamalek, located on a large island in the Nile River, just west of Tahrir Square, the center of Cairo. Diplomats from all over the world came with their families, as did professionals posted in Cairo from NGOs and multinational corporations. After all the determined effort I put into avoiding other Americans, this hour of liturgy followed by community gatherings in the garden afterwards, afforded me a rare space where everyone spoke my native language, even if most came from somewhere in Africa, Asia, or Europe.

Where could this guy be from? Czechoslovakia? Germany? The contrast between his dark eyebrows and blond hair on a round face with such an easy and genuine smile conveyed a ready warmth that I didn't expect from an Eastern European. After Mass, I saw him outside church talking with my American friend Ken, an Air Force engineer who worked in the US Embassy as part of the massive US-Egypt Military Cooperation.

Ken introduced me, "Dominic, this is Tom."

"Nice to meet you, Dominic," said Tom, with a sideways look from his smiling eyes. *He's American*, I thought to myself, as I took in his way of speaking English.

"Tom is going to join us at Alice's tonight," Ken told me. Most every Sunday after Mass I went with Ken to Alice's, another American who worked in the Embassy. She opened her home with such generous hospitality that she assured me week after week to just come any Sunday evening I liked, whether or not I let her know ahead of time. The Morton salt, Skippy peanut butter, and Turning Leaf Chardonnay that I would see in her kitchen added to the reassuring sense of home during those dinners at Alice's my first two years living in Cairo. She had been an expat for many years, living in a Zamalek compound in owned by the US government and doing her grocery shopping in the commissary for American military personnel.

Ken first invited me to dinner at Alice's in my first few months in Egypt. I must have seemed like a lost sheep to him. Joining them once a week on their little island of American culture and colleagues in the midst of this megalopolis of twenty million Cairenes gave me much-needed succor and comfort. Now Ken was extending to Tom the same generosity and hospitality. This new lost sheep came from a big Catholic family in Michigan. Enlisting in the Marines after high school, Tom was stationed with the security detail of the US Embassy on the south side of Tahrir Square. Over dinner, I learned about his life in the Marines, who apparently provide security for every US embassy around the world. He lived in the barracks within the embassy compound, where the ambassador also had his residence. In terms of personnel, our embassy in Egypt at that time was the largest delegation of any country to any country anywhere.

Before Ken, Alice, and now Tom, I had never had any exposure to anyone in military life. All I heard about Tom's life and the Office of Military Cooperation where Alice was an executive assistant and Ken an officer broadened my horizons even as we all shared a common homeland. Tom intrigued me. Had I met a Marine in Boston, I imagine I wouldn't have felt we had much in common, even if like Tom he was my age, Catholic, and from the (upper) Midwest. Encountering each other in Cairo, we had much to talk about!

A week or two later, Tom and I met up for beers at El Horreya Café in bustling *wust al-balad*, downtown Cairo. A unique institution, El Horreya had open doors and windows, served coffee, tea, shisha, and cold Stella beer. Besides at El Horreya, alcohol seemed always to be relegated to bars and restaurants shielded from the streets behind closed doors or in posh enclaves. Tom and I drank and talked for a couple hours under El Horreya's bright lights until we decided to make a move to my apartment in Garden City. I had a quiet balcony perfect for continuing our night together. As we walked the twenty minutes to my place, I noticed the frat boy energy we had going on between us. Put next to each other in Cairo, we amplified the identities we shared as athletic, church-going, white American, Midwestern Catholics living in Cairo. He was twenty-three, and I was twenty-four.

While I could not overlook the draw between us, I had only the vaguest notion of anything happening back at my apartment beyond more drinking and talking. At some point in the darkness of my balcony, the comforting relief of making a new friend turned into the Egyptian-style physical affection of Tom laying his head on my shoulder and me resting my hand on his leg. His body's heat, smell, and touch enveloped me. My heart beat faster, my face flushed with beer and fear and excitement. I turned my head to his on my shoulder and kissed him. His rough stubble rubbed against mine, as we dropped our guard and expressed our desire for each other, lip to lip, tongue to tongue.

We moved inside from the balcony to my bedroom. Sitting next to each other on the bed, Tom started unbuckling his belt and impishly challenged me, "Show me what you got!" *I guess our dicks are coming out*, I thought to myself. His bold swagger felt playful and competitive. Unzipping, we showed ourselves to each other. Looking intently, we compared shape, color, texture, thickness, and length. His was shorter and pale, like the rest of his body in comparison to mine. We touched each other, feeling, examining, caressing, then grabbing and squeezing lustfully as our mouths met again to kiss voraciously. Shirts came off, then socks, khakis, and boxers. We touched each other everywhere, lying down on the bed, rolling one on top of the other, gazing deep into each other, then closing our eyes and embracing. Our play brought me to a sticky climax, followed by dozing in Tom's arms. He kept more awake than I, and whispered in my ear, "I have to go."

"Why?" I asked.

"Four o'clock curfew in the barracks. We have bed checks between 4 and 5 a.m."

"Oh wow, okay." I couldn't imagine living at our age in such a regime, which sounded to me like something from sleepaway summer camp or boarding school.

Tom pulled on his clothes. I stood up, and put on my boxer shorts. He took my hands in his. "This was fun. I'll see you soon, okay?" he said.

"Yes, sounds good, Tom." I smiled and kissed him good night before walking him to the door of my apartment. I went back to my room and fell into bed, smelling him on the pillow as I dropped into my dreams.

Nothing is more practical than finding God, that is, than falling in Love in a quite absolute, final way.

What you are in love with, what seizes your imagination, will affect everything.

It will decide what will get you out of bed in the morning, what you do with your evenings, how you spend your weekends, what you read, whom you know, what breaks your heart, and what amazes you with joy and gratitude.

Fall in Love, stay in love, and it will decide everything.

Often attributed to the Superior General of the Jesuits, Fr. Pedro Arrupe, SJ (1907–1991), this prayer of exhortation expresses the essence of my experience with Tom in Cairo. I loved him, and it changed everything. My world got turned upside down. *Who am I now?* The person I knew myself to be shattered into a thousand pieces. I no longer knew who I was. This new love could not be relegated to the shadows of a secret compartment that I opened only in the darkness of my fantasies.

Tom and I spent as many nights together as we could possibly manage. His rush from my place in Garden City the block or two back to the barracks in the embassy compound became routine. By the time I met Tom, my departure back to the USA was fast approaching. We had only a few months to luxuriate in our love and passion. As powerful as the magnetic attraction between us was, we didn't have language to describe our relationship. Love, yes. Friends, yes. Brotherly, yes. Friends with benefits, no, that felt too casual. Lovers, no, that felt too much like a soap opera. Neither of us could bear to use the word "boyfriend" either. At that point in life, I don't think I had ever heard anyone say, "We're boyfriends." Still, there was nothing platonic about our relationship or our love, which I would instead describe as lusty, sweaty, and physical, as well as tender, boyish, and vulnerable.

We had no gay community to help us make sense of what was happening in us and between us—or so we thought. In fact, many of the expat American men we knew had brought their lives to Egypt because there they could spend their time with men without raising eyebrows. With what in the US or Europe would amount to a middle-class income, these professors, professionals, and international aid workers could in Egypt enjoy a level of luxury and status that would otherwise be inaccessible to them. Inheriting colonial privilege, they could live their lives without the scrutiny or surveillance that typical Egyptians would apply to each other. As Tom and I suddenly started showing up at social engagements together, mostly with my friends though sometimes at parties put on by the Marines in the barracks, we gradually realized how many of the older American and European men who had befriended me were, in fact, gay. We never really came out as a couple to these or other friends. Many of them, however, intuitively knew that Tom and I were more than friends. They had much greater access to **Gaydar** than we did! Indeed, like the many older gay expats who had taken me in with avuncular care, many of our friends knew something more clearly about Tom and me than we knew about ourselves.

For all our sexual energy and play together, we did not really know how to have full-on sex with each other. We didn't even have language for it. The phrases that came to mind felt either too clinical, too euphemistic, or just plain dirty. *Sexual intercourse? Penetrative sex? Anal sex? Making love? Buttfucking?*

None of these words sufficed. Yet, as my departure approached, we wanted to share this intimacy. It seemed like the supreme expression of the kind of love we had for one another. Ahead of my eminent departure from Egypt, Ken loaned us his apartment, high in a glass skyscraper. He was going away for a week, and he figured we would like to have some time together.

There in Ken's apartment, we decided to try having actual sex. We had no concerns about STIs, so condoms did not feel necessary. For lube, we found olive oil in the kitchen, which worked all too well. Tom worried that I would not fit into him, so we decided he would go into me. Nervous, excited, and intent to express our mutual love by sharing this *first-time* experience, we kissed, took our clothes off, and put lots of olive oil all over both of us. I turned onto my stomach, with Tom lying on my back, his mouth at my ear.

"Ready?" he asked.

"Yeah," I replied.

Suddenly, all of Tom slipped deep into me. I yelped, and forcefully threw him off of me, my heart pounding in shock. I breathed in and out, quick and shallow breaths, my eyes wide. The pain of penetration permeated my body. As the unfamiliar sensations of soreness subsided, my heart rate calmed, and my breathing deepened.

"Are you okay?" Tom asked. "I'm so sorry!"

This experience of wanting, risking, not knowing how, my hurting, and his apologizing expressed the vulnerability, trust, and love that we intended. Only by eventually finding a **Pride Tribe** years later did I learn how to prepare and relax so my body could unite with another man's. My departure a few days later ended our relationship. We had no means of seeing each other, with me returning to Boston and him staying in the Marines for years to come.

I did not know what to make of myself in the wake of my relationship with Tom. The profound confusion and dizzying disorientation I experienced while trying to make sense of that relationship felt like an intensification of the extremely difficult experience I had gone through the first few months after arriving in Cairo. Both that earlier episode of distress at the start of those two years in Cairo and now this one at the end involved disillusion. Painfully releasing one set of hopes and dreams, I opened myself to others. In both cases, my distress came out of growing pains. Tracking back in the sequence of events to tell the story of that first episode of distress will, I believe, illuminate the contours and import of the second. These growing pains came over me episodically, like tremors before an earthquake.

- *What comes up for you as you consider the experience of falling in love to be an experience of "finding God"?*

Developmental Focus

- *To what degree do you focus on personal growth and development nowadays?*
- *I imagine you are pursuing certain questions in your own developmental process and that some of those questions are activated as you read this book. How urgent or pressing are those questions for you? How vital? How recent, or how long-standing?*

The new capacities to access one's inner life make possible new perspectives on the very process of human development, which captures greater interest in this **Redefining** and subsequent post-conventional stages. New capacities to see causality as more than linear, logical, and unidirectional further expand this capacity to understand human development, within ourselves and others. Recognizing the circular, relational, and systemic dimensions of causality, we can now make better sense of the human person and any other complex system, where randomness and unpredictability reign. In **Redefining** mind, we better recognize, respect, and appreciate alternative ways of making sense of reality. We gain awareness of the nonlinear path of developmental journeys. We no longer abide any illusion about some straightforward march along a linear path into ever greater maturity! With greater awareness of self-in-system and self-in-time, we notice that we bring various levels of maturity and resourcefulness to different domains of our lives. Such self-awareness humbles the proud **Queen**. Indeed, at this **Redefining** stage, noticing our inconsistency and incoherence can elicit profound confusion and "despair about ever finding one's true self."[78]

An acceleration of the developmental process and intensification of the quest for meaning occurs with these new insights. Attention to *the now* grows keen. Openness to noticing how the current context is influencing me, and how I'm influencing it makes every moment potentially intriguing. *What's here now?* is a question that can fascinate, always holding the potential to spark new connections and insights. Openness to incongruous data about self and system which reveal internal discrepancies, contradictions, and incoherence further enhances the interest in acting as a *participant-observer* in one's own life.[79] Indeed, this fascination with the incongruous can grab someone's attention so completely that they paradoxically settle into the unsettled state of an apparently eternal seeker, spending most of their adult life in **Redefining**—never landing, never settling, always searching for meaning, never fully inhabiting any place as *home*.

Whether or not we become an eternal seeker, the capacity of **Redefining** mind for self-awareness and self-witnessing allows us increasingly to notice the cyclical patterns in pathways of growth for ourselves and others. Everyone spirals up and down, backwards and forwards in their developmental process. Building on recognition of the nonlinearity of personal development, our observation and reflection may lead to a more or less thematic awareness of the fundamental developmental movements. Seeing our own inconsistency, we recognize consolidation as a developmental movement by which we engage with more domains of our life using the most mature mindset that we can easily access, rather than relying on an earlier, less complex form of mind. Noticing stages in our own or other people's maturation, we may understand something about how maturation consists of transition or transformation from one way of making sense of reality to another. We might also witness instances of significant illness or old age instigating overall regression in a person, whereby their capacities for seeing and handling the complexities of reality diminish for a prolonged period or even permanently. Noticing these and other patterns in the search for meaning, the **Redefining** mind can "become enthralled with watching themselves trying to make sense of themselves."[80]

- *Who do you know—maybe even yourself—who fits the description of an eternal seeker, always searching and never finding?*

The Stories We Tell

- *What stock stories do you tell about your life path?*
- *What motivations or desires—or other elements of your understory—do you habitually leave out of these stock stories?*

The story I've told for much of my life about what I was looking for when I catapulted myself to Cairo depicts multiple motivations. I sought adventure. I wished to see the world. The Mediterranean especially interested me, thanks to my Sicilian ancestry and my study of Greek and Roman classics. In ancient times, the lands on the Mediterranean operated as a region with strong cultural, political, and economic ties. *What happened to the Mediterranean?* In the modern era it seems split, even fragmented. Most of all, I intended to put myself in the service of people in a developing country. I felt privileged, and I wanted to give back before any other pursuits. Along the way, I wished to learn another civilizationally significant language.

Beyond all these reasons, this Jesuit all-boys school looked like a place where I could balance risk and safety, adventure and service, challenge and support. At Creighton Prep I had greatly appreciated my relationships with the young teachers who temporarily worked there as part of their Jesuit "formation," meaning their years-long program of study and training, punctuated by ordination. I imagined the College de la Sainte Famille as an Egyptian Creighton Prep, and I imagined myself like a Jesuit "scholastic" or "regent," temporarily teaching there before continuing my journey of study, training, and work.

My story about why I initially went to Cairo always referred back to my college spring break service trip in Kingston. Though I had arrived in Jamaica with the intention to serve, I discovered treasures beyond imagining. With a posture of openness, I stepped into cultural discomfort and found myself changed in ways I couldn't neatly identify. What I knew after this Jamaican experience was that much more growth and expansion awaited me in the so-called Third World.

My desire to confront the demonization of Arab Muslims added another layer to the story I told myself and others about why I went to Cairo. I was motivated by the radical command from the Gospels, "Love your enemies." Growing up in the 1980s, I feared a nuclear holocaust resulting from war with the Soviets. With the dissolution of the Soviet Union in the early 1990s, I had to look elsewhere for enemies. *Who are my enemies, that I might love them?* I asked my culture, and the world around me. Like some primordial poison, the demonization of Black people still pulsed powerfully through American society, even if the America I knew also disavowed racism, resisted it, and worked against it. The same seemed to be true about women, Jews, and even gay people. Dominant American culture recognized racism, sexism, antisemitism, and homophobia as forms of prejudice and hatred.

American culture in the mid-1990s seemed to hate and to be fine continuing to hate Arab Muslims. This was true in America even before 9/11, or so it seemed to me. I discerned virtually no countercurrent critiquing Orientalism or Islamophobia. America projected self-assured certainty about its fearful demonization of Arab Muslims. So, the most idealistic and most radically Christian reason I had for going to Cairo was to love my enemy, the Arab Muslim.

In telling this story for why I moved to Egypt, I always knew that this last piece usually garnered admiration. Looking back on myself as a fresh college graduate who embraced this kind of moral reasoning, I would even impress myself as I told the story! Even non-religious listeners seemed to find my story of moving across the world to a foreign land so that I might *love my enemies* to be not only impressive but genuinely inspiring.

Be that as it may, the story I told for years about what motivated me to go to Cairo as a volunteer teacher left out a couple of important elements that I kept to myself. One piece I seldom shared—admirable to some, ridiculous to others—was that I wanted to test out life as a Jesuit. Living in the Jesuit community in Cairo not only would offer safety and familiarity, but also the opportunity to try out what Catholics call "religious life," that is, living in community with others committed to a shared Christian mission in a certain tradition, such as that of the Jesuits, Franciscans, Dominicans, or other religious orders. I kept discreet about this part of my story, because I anticipated some listeners might judge me as old-fashioned or strange to have the kind of religious faith that might point to a vocation to become a priest.

Another motivation I kept to myself had to do with that rather neglected secret pledge I had made to explore my gay side in college. Somehow, the developing world seemed to offer better conditions than Boston College to allow me to experiment. I renewed my commitment to this secret pledge, curious as to how I might make good on it. I continued to keep quiet about this dimension of my quest not only because of heteronormative pressures but also out of embarrassment. *Wasn't I a coward for not exploring and experimenting more in college? What was wrong with me to be so late in sorting myself out?*

A last motivation that I hardly admitted to myself, much less to anyone else, built on the admirable "Love your enemy" part of my story. Hatred of the "Other" wove into more than the structure of American society and culture. The American caste system lived inside me as well. On some level, I did know that I had within me irrational fear and hatred for those different from me. I felt drawn to Egypt in part to face these shadows, whose existence within myself I only partially sensed, thanks to occasional attention to my dreams and fantasies. The most powerful dream revealing these demons in me had emerged on the first night of that Boston College spring break service trip in Kingston. I was sleeping at Kingston's Jesuit high school, St. George's College, before meeting the next day a kind woman named June, who with her two teenage sons, would host me in their home for the rest of the week.

My head swam with the sights, smells, and sounds of urban Jamaica. Later, the trip would be indelibly marked by the tragedy of a child dying by falling into a deep, open sewer in the shantytown in whose schoolhouse some of us volunteered. Days before facing that tragically disgusting smothering of a young boy, I slept fitfully and feverishly in the heat with no air conditioning. My imagination formed vivid fantasies drawing on the witches' fest, Walpurgis Night, depicted in Goethe's *Faust*, a play I had been intensively studying in my German literature courses at BC. A few years later, in my mid-twenties I already sensed how significant this dream had been for me, so I wrote this account of it at that time:

Walpurgis Night

> My first night's dream in the mythic Third World came in Kingston. Before the hepatitis, before that five-year-old boy's drowned-in-shit death, before June and her two-room house, of which I occupied half as an embarrassed guest while her two teenage sons and their 'uncle' crammed the other room with June and her constantly chirping TV (on which, by the way, we watched Richie Rich upon my first arrival at this host family's home for my week of 'service' in Spring Break 1996). The first night, though, Walpurgis Night, preceded June and her morning serving of

fried plantains and instant coffee packets. Walpurgis Night I was awakened alone in my room in a convent where we all stayed before moving in with our host families. Terror and sweat ran down my face and back. The dream: Cackling screaming hideous beasts pierced the black with their screeches. "Were those normal noises of the wildlife here in Jamaica?" my sleeping mind wondered. Devilish ululations from a throng of creatures as they sacrificed? or marched? Or danced? What horrible rites could such a hullabaloo signal? Were witches presiding, with pointy hats, sticking brooms, and gnarled grins?

This dream and the associations I discovered underlying it in my unconscious fed into my keen interest to go be with people whom my culture conditioned me to fear and loathe. A year and a half later, I was just noticing how that week in Jamaica changed me through shocks that tenderized my heart. For example, coloniality and cultural dominance became more apparent to my young eyes. I had read *The Heart of Darkness* in college; now I began to notice the darkness in my own heart. I awakened to curiosity about how these dynamics out in the world also lodged themselves inside my own inner workings.

In another excerpt from the spiritual autobiography I wrote as a step in the application process to the Jesuits at the age of twenty-six, I imitated Augustine's *Confessions* by directly addressing God and describing how I had seen grace unfolding in my life. The vision I had for my quixotic quest to serve others, live love, and bridge cultural and religious divides crashed against unanticipated realities.

Aphasia and Humility in *Misr al-Qahira*

This demonization of the other world, the 'third world,' so vivid in the fantasia of my dreams when I first encountered that other culture, tropical, dark, and incongruous to my rich white suburban experience, this demonizing, this otherizing reflex was what I went out to deconstruct by choosing a year and a half after that spring break service trip to live and work in Cairo, heart of the Arab world.

Your stirrings inside me, Lord, to grow, to understand, and to love have always been of a piece. As I envisioned how to follow up my lovely experience in the ivory towers of the Heights of Boston College, I determined by both chance and reflection that living in Cairo, home of the 'Other' whom we Westerners still allow ourselves to demonize, the Muslim Arab, was for me the way to most radically deepen my understanding, my growth, and my love. Personal growth at all cost was for so long my motto.

Cairo trampled me. Like a stampede of hungry, frustrated, marginalized Egyptians making their frantic sweaty daily commute, my innumerable experiences in Cairo crushed my ego. Bereft of language and thus stripped of my theretofore always handy intellect, I experienced myself in a totally new way. Deaf, dumb, and blind sums it up. Though languages had for several years by then been my friends, Arabic took much longer to warm up to, and for the first 6 months I lived in Egypt, I felt particularly disarmed, powerless, and isolated by my handicap of aphasia. [I had learned the word 'aphasia,' meaning loss of the capacity to speak or understand language, through studying linguistics at BC. The word captures so much of the frustration I felt at first in Cairo.]

Walking. Wet shoulders and middle back. Legs pumped. The slight breeze of my own motion cools me refreshingly.

The extremes of Cairo weather lie more in movement and stillness than in measurable heat or cold. It's what we do there that makes the experience what it is—whether sweaty slumber or refreshing walks.

In the hot nights I slept unclothed on top of the sheets wet with me. Fans simulated the motion I kept during waking hours. Still, summer sleep was restless. A groggy buzz became the inner static din of my overheated head. Only the sea relieved me of this white noise.

Desire for growth was not the only motivation in going to Cairo. I also yearned to contribute, to give back to a world that had privileged me, even in the midst of certain familial deprivations. Jesuit institutions were what had given me myself. Boston College and Creighton Prep were the venues for my maturation and self-discovery. In the communities of those Jesuit cultures I had flourished. At BC and Prep, Jesuits were most often the men I emulated for their integration of intellectual, emotional, and spiritual life at the service of others. My relationships with Jesuits were friendships. Sometimes, as in the case of Michael Buckley or Howard Gray, they have been more mentoring friends, and other times, as with Mike Lee or Grant Garinger, more peer friends. It seems a bit odd looking at it now that none has been much of a father figure. But I guess I never knew how to have a father, how to let someone be my father, so friends we were. Going to the College de la Sainte Famille (CSF) in Cairo was in part driven by a desire to live in a community of friends, men who I hoped to admire and be supported by, as I toiled to serve the students I would teach and to engage the country's culture.

But I felt bitterly disappointed in CSF as an institution and in the CSF Jesuit community as a group. They were not the kind of Jesuits I wanted them to be. They were rather cold, cranky, and difficult to talk with. The mood of the community was stiff and nostalgic, at least for the men who had been there long enough to remember when their mission of French education was relevant to the local culture. "Jesuit" as an institutional qualifier to these men and this school meant two things: French and prestigious. I wanted the school to be Jesuit in other ways, and held CSF to standards that were my own. Willful and self-righteous, I never got my way with the school. But I did eventually calm down somewhat and gave what

I could to the boys while taking what I could from the experience as a whole. The world outside of CSF became more important to me than I had planned—I had wanted to be like the regents who had taught me at Prep! Becoming fluent in Arabic and being present to Egypt on its terms rather than my own, I became quite rich in experience during my two years there....

The frustration and disappointment I felt during my first semester at CSF did not put me in a tailspin, but I later recognized that experience as a foreshadowing of later waves of depression that gave way to recovery efforts followed by personal growth and expansion.

My initial letdown in Egypt had multiple causes, including my disappointment in the Jesuits I met there, cultural alienation, and disengagement from "important others" whose expectations and approval had been so vital to me at Prep and BC. I showed up in Cairo with a vision inflated by both idealism and ideology, like many missionaries and colonizers—though I did not recognize myself as either. I fancied CSF to be another Creighton Prep. I imagined that the Jesuits of the Near East Province must be like those of the American Midwest Province. I projected my norms onto what I encountered and then criticized them for not living up to my values!

I recovered from this initial feeling of letdown gradually over the following year. Through observation, inquiry, and imitation, I learned many of the unspoken rules and norms of the society in which I found myself. Eventually, I did find my place. At first adrift in a culture so foreign to anything I had known previously, I gradually became part of it. I meshed with Egyptian society in various ways and nurtured myself so as not to collapse from the stress of it all. I came to dance the dance of Egyptians, awkwardly blundering, abashedly asking for help, assiduously practicing, and eventually finding some grace. Besides resocializing in this new culture, I also applied myself to building knowledge and skills to distinguish myself in that society, as a competent teacher, a foreigner who increasingly spoke Egyptian Arabic, and as a Cairene who knew how to navigate that great, bustling city.

Contributing to this process of inculturation, I put greater attention on my inner life. Chronicling my experiences felt crucial because I knew they were changing me irreversibly. I also knew I could not keep up with them all. Making sense of what I was going through would take me years, even after returning from those two first years teaching in Egypt. In fact, writing about those experiences now, twenty-five years later, I see new connections and gain new insights. But already then I was journaling, and so I possess precious documentary evidence of my developmental processes from that time. This journal entry gives some flavor of how that process unfolded. Experimenting in avoiding capital letters like bell hooks, I wrote this entry about three months into my two years teaching at CSF:

7 nov 1997

I feel no longer a newcomer in cairo. Yes, i am still foreign, but no longer a new foreigner. I grew a goatee and changed my room around—outer signs of an inner reality. I start to understand what people around me are saying. I listen—when i have the energy and the patience—intently to my friends talk to each other in arabic. Maybe i catch 20%, but something is communicated, so it's a start. I have so many new friends. So many people are so willing to reach out to me. Of course, the students more than anyone, but i explain or understand that as the attraction by teenagers to a new young adult in their midst–particularly from america, whose pop culture they are obsessed with. Last night at muqattam [an area of Cairo] we had a gathering of maybe about fifty teachers from csf. Felt like a family reunion. They never see each other–maybe twice a year. Two of the older folks, in particular, warmed up to me: raouf and mohamed. R is a science teacher, of lebanese origin, and speaks eng (& fr) very well.... Mohamed (abdou fata ...) is an Arabic prof. About 60+. He reminded me so much of grandpa longo. So engaging, funny, intelligent, and simple, in the best sense. Our friendship started when raouf had stood up to greet someone who had just arrived, and then i also stood up. Mohamed grabbed my arm so firmly! And the look In his eyes of such fear and surprise. I thought he was having a heart attack! The problem was the bench that we three were sharing. Mohamed was still sitting on one end of it and when r & i got up, he almost went flying. M said it reminded him of a benny hill episode.

Now i've left the jesuit house in muquttam and i'm sitting in a winchell's donut shop in heliopolis a half hour before my lesson with immanuel la foret. I guess i couldn't resist the possibility of good coffee and a clean, controlled environment even if i have to pay 6 pounds for breakfast! [under $2, but a great deal for breakfast here!]

Now that i feel past the initial stages of adjustment and establishment of a life here, i need to begin to think and act a bit more toward my mid- and long-term goals here in egypt and back in the us.

Teaching efl is not where it's at for me. Even if i were in a university or in a primary school, the challenges, joys, and possibilities of tefl would not be fulfilling over the long-term, i think. However, it could very well once again serve as a tool for living and learning in a foreign culture.

I relish, on the other hand, the opportunity to mentor young people. Talking about values, decisions, morals, life choices, friends, parents—all of this i find deeply fulfilling, worthwhile, and life-giving. And in some ways, doing it here seems more fulfilling than, say, at cp [Creighton Prep]. Csf boys don't have enough young men role models. There are the surveillants [proctors], but perhaps they are seen as a different (lower) class intellectually and socio-economically. I think of the scholastics and alumni teachers at cp who are at once intelligent, young, and role models for the students. Playing this role here is what i can best offer the students.

On the other hand, to the school my greatest potential gift is, i think, two-fold: 1) to establish some connection with American jesuit schools, and 2) to suggest some organizational change in the leadership or management for the next generation of administrators. [ie as the hoary colonial-generation missionaries dies out]

Rereading this entry now, I see how I had been using my **Conformist** mind to find my place in the professional community of teachers at CSF, my **Expert** mind to acquire Arabic (slowly), and my **Achiever** mind to begin hatching a new creative vision for the service I would do there. This cycle repeated, again and again throughout my 20s, always starting with a disruption causing disappointment. Some vision for my life and some version of myself would fall apart, and then I would move backwards and forwards through the developmental stages to put the pieces back together again—hence the thought of Humpty Dumpty falling off that wall. My vision would crash into reality. I would feel confused and at first evade facing the unexpected challenges, regressing and retreating into sorrowful rumination. At some point, I would then mobilize multiple mindsets to recover, grow, and expand.

Herein lie the similarities between the two episodes of distress that occurred, one at the beginning and the other at the end of my two years teaching in Cairo. Both episodes shook free certain visions I had held for my future. At the start of the two years, encountering CSF for the school it was, rather than what I had envisioned it to be and coming to know the Jesuits there for who they were, rather than who I wanted them to be shook out of my head the naïve visions I had had for what my time in Cairo would be. The realities I increasingly encountered forced me to recognize Egypt on its own terms, not mine.

In similarly disorienting ways, at the end of those two years living in Cairo, my erotic relationship with Tom disrupted my life by shaking from my imagination certain visions that I had held for my longer-term future. The queer realities I finally uncovered in myself forced me to let go of other naïve visions to which I had clung. I needed to grieve the loss of the dream my society had implanted in me of one day having a wife and a house with a white picket fence. Like some flesh-and-blood version of Ken and Barbie, we would produce 2.1 children, thus procreating precisely at the population replacement rate. *It would be perfect!* Now I had to let go of this artificial, simple, and straight version of the so-called American dream. Maybe I would still one day marry a woman, but I realized that my life would never fit this cookie-cutter mold.

By the end of my two years in Cairo, I recognized that I had moved outside of the sexual norms of society. My life had expanded beyond so many conventions that I had previously held as good and right and true. I had exceeded my bounds. So much becoming, growing, and developing had taken place in me that I could not keep up with myself. The love I shared with Tom burst apart certain fundaments of my self-image. I did not know how to make sense of myself now. *Who had I become?* Looking in the mirror of that steamed-up bathroom, weeping in the shower, cheeks runny with snot, eyes bloodshot and sore from the sorrow welling up through my face along with distress, confusion, and wonder. *What now?*

- *What realities have shaken out of your imagination dearly held visions for your life?*

Fallback

- *What triggers you and brings out a smaller, less resourceful version of yourself?*

Besides the longer-term developmental movements of consolidation, transition, and regression, which take place over years, greater immediacy in self-awareness makes possible the capacity for someone with a **Redefining** form of mind to notice changes of developmental state, that is, temporary, shorter-term shifts in meaning-making.[81] With practice, the time lag gets shorter and shorter between an experience and noticing one's own internal cognitive, emotional, and bodily dynamics during that experience.

In one such temporary developmental movement, we gain access to later-stage capacities that have eluded us. Such an experience can be called **uplift** or **springing forward**. The circumstances of a situation might call for such a capacity, and instead of reactively defending against the stress of such a moment, we rise to the challenge. Developmental scaffolding or support offered during a coaching or psychotherapy session might coax us into such access. This very book you are reading is designed to function as developmental scaffolding so that you can gain clearer perspective on the developmental movements within yourself and regard them with greater curiosity and compassion. When experiences of new compassionate self-understanding and self-regard occur, those moments might well be instances of springing forward to a way of making sense of yourself that typically is not available to you. Drawing on a distinction used by Sufis and other spiritual masters, we might call these temporary shifts changes of state, during which we visit for a short time a later stage. Though we might access these expanded perspectives in some moment or another, a practice of consciously returning to these new ways of looking at reality is needed for them to become our new normal way of making sense of reality.

Another temporary developmental movement or change of state might be called fallback. Here we find ourselves without recourse to our usual meaning-making resources. In a moment of stress or duress, a less developed—even childish—version

> **Uplift or springing forward:** A parallel to fallback in which a person temporarily visits a later developmental mindset. As with fallback, circumstances play an important part in developmental uplift. See Glossary for further explanation.

of ourselves takes the lead. Triggers that cause fallback can be physical or psychosocial, internal or external. Everyday experiences like "laziness, exhaustion, depression, group norms, stress, fear, tension, crisis, rage, shame, loss, overwork, failure, hunger, and jet lag" can trigger fallback, as can "uncertainty, ambiguity, complexity, and illness."[82] Social contexts such as our office environment or a classroom can exert a kind of developmental gravitational pull and bring down our meaning-making to an earlier form of mind. We could also be triggered into fallback by challenges to our identity in the form of "unemployment, bad marriages, the death of a loved one, illness or injury," as well as "new parenthood, taking a new job, moving to a new country."[83] *The story I used to tell myself and others about who I am doesn't make sense anymore, now that I have no job title other than full-time parent! All the things that used to matter to me seem less important now that I have a baby. Who am I now?* Social scientist Jack Mezirow describes these kinds of personal crises and life transitions as "disorienting dilemmas" that cause cognitive dissonance and unsettle our worldview to such an extent that they spur an expansion of our consciousness and a transformation of our basic worldview.

Threats to Status, Certainty, Autonomy, Relationships, or Fairness (SCARF) can trigger physiological responses in our brains that temporarily bypass the higher-level thinking capacities of the neocortex. We react as if physically threatened by a predator or an enemy. This SCARF model, developed by neuroscientist David Rock, sketches the biological underpinnings of a fallback experience. A more primitive operating system activates when we sense we are losing social rank (status), the ability to predict the future (certainty), control (autonomy), safety with others (relationship), or justice (fairness).

- *What individuals, situations, or circumstances most easily trigger you or tip you into "fallback"?*
- *When you or someone else is experiencing fallback, what helps you to bring compassion and understanding, rather than frustration and judgment?*

The Sinking Ship

- *What's the most significant experience of overwhelming personal distress that you've gone through so far in your life?*

I returned from Cairo to Boston College, with the stated goal of reading my way through the exceedingly rich experience I had had in Cairo. Enrolling in a Master's program in Theology, I wanted to read about Islam, Israel, Jews and Palestine, just war and *jihad*, colonialism and Orientalism. These topics now felt vital and of great personal relevance. I also knew my explorations of European literature and Western intellectual history only barely included any specifically Christian writings on the weighty questions of that "Great Conversation" among luminaries across the ages. From my two years living as a member of a religious minority in a country of mostly Muslims, I realized just how little I had explored Christian intellectual history or theology. Though in college I had taken on a sense of myself as a Catholic intellectual, I had not gone very far in exploring the Catholic tradition.

Besides all these valid intellectual motivations, I knew I needed comfort and community. Cairo had worn me down and poured me out. I needed to recover. Returning either to Omaha or to Boston College felt like the only two options where I would find the solace and support I needed.

Returning to BC gave me what felt like a bonus year of college, during which I could study with the professors I missed out on the first time around. I returned to a place where I received a warm welcome and abundant affirmation. There I happily regressed. Slipping into an academic mania, I registered for five courses a semester and audited five more on top of that. Besides courses with formidable titles like Catholic System Theology and the Hebrew Prophets, I took Mandarin Chinese, Intermediate Spanish, Intermediate Hebrew, and biblical Greek, plus courses in art history and musicology. I was on fire! Back and better than ever, gargantuan in my appetites for achievement and knowledge, I created an academic accelerator. Flexing the great strength of my brainy prowess, I returned to what I had excelled at while in college.

Frenetic intellectual pursuits enabled me to run away from the deeper questions that had arisen while in Egypt. On track to complete the ten courses I needed for a Master's degree in Theology by my second semester, I set myself up for another year of this maniacal academic intensity. In the summer I would go to Middlebury College for their renowned immersion language school for more Arabic, then to Jerusalem for the ordination of a remarkable Israeli Jesuit I had met in Cairo. In the Fall semester I would return to BC and start another Master's degree program at Boston College, this one in Philosophy. From my studies in the departments of Romance Languages and Literature, German Studies, and Theology, I came to understand that BC's Philosophy faculty included a remarkable array of scholars who specialized in Continental philosophy, plus unique resources in Catholic thought, such as the work of Jesuit philosopher Bernard Lonergan SJ.

Running this race, dashing from one intellectual delight to the next in full fallback, I pursued my evasive maneuvers as long as I could. Eventually, I collapsed. Feeling exhausted, I was actually depressed. Like a ship beginning to sink, my whole system went on red alert. The surface symptoms of fatigue and moodiness mixed with such profound confusion that I reached a state of effective paralysis, in which I could not manage the most basic quotidian decisions of what to do each hour. Tectonic plates deep in my psyche were shifting around. The tremors of episodic distress from previous years were now culminating in a seismic quake.

This narrative I wrote just a couple of years after my great depression describes the experience more vividly than I can today.

Depression and Lonergan

"To be unpractical is to keep blundering about."

– Lonergan, *Insight*

September 2000. Between Cleveland Circle and Chestnut Hill. I missed the first week of classes. But the ordination in Jerusalem was worth it. The first ordination Mass I'd ever been to, and David is such an extraordinary friend and person. Now, though, something was really wrong. Exhausted, my 'saturated self' found itself back in the familiar tour of classes and books.

Was it this cough that was the problem?

I visited the university health clinic my first day back on campus. An infection? Walking pneumonia? After a few quick questions, the nurse sent me off with packets of antibiotics that still after a week changed nothing.

I must be just tired. Sleep was the answer. A month-long return to Egypt and Israel after 9 weeks of intensive Arabic in Vermont would run anybody down.

The more I slept, though, the more I wallowed. No matter how long I'd wanted to read Foucault or Lonergan, no matter how objectively interesting the courses, there was just no energy or motivation inside me for scholarly activities. Instead, I was moping, escaping into sleep, waking up with no sense of purpose.

Where was the passion I used to have for studies?

What was I doing with my life?

The beginning of this semester was a period characterized by difficulty—little trivial tasks seemed insurmountable, next to impossible. Barriers, obstacles, complications seemed to abound. I had a sense of dryness in once delightful things. Inside was there only seriousness, gravity, and tragedy? This was indeed a period of spiritual desolation—feeling distant from God and dryness even in prayer. I experienced disorientation though in a familiar environment. What to do with my time? What are my priorities? What's important to me? And the moodiness—I was depressed when alone, in my own internal world, but easily drawn out of it, at least superficially, by friends who showed any degree of care or concern or love. But the happy face would go only on the outside, and only temporarily. I would want for the happiness to be realer, deeper, more enduring, but I would be fooling myself.

The elements of my life did not fit together. They formed a problematic more than a possibility. An overwhelming sense of dissonance, in need of harmonic resolution. Noticing this absence of intelligible correlation was an instance of what Lonergan called an 'inverse insight.'

The tension of my quest for a resolution to this dissonance was punctuated by heroic yet pathetic efforts to break the cycle of despondency: to go for a run instead of take yet another nap, to call up a friend instead of stewing, to arrange the apartment, clean the dishes, pay a few bills, go through the stack of papers on desk and floor. I tried to deal with a few of the tasks and obligations and responsibilities that were piling up, burying me deeper in an oppressive artifice of my own making.

I knew, of course, that something was wrong, but what exactly it was, I did not know. I did not even know what question to be asking myself. There were the health issues, but eventually the cough and lung problems were diagnosed as a mild asthma and yet the central problem continued unabated. What was the problem?!

Only in retrospect can I now identify, again to allude to *Insight*, what 'accurate presentation of definite problems' I was making to myself. In the midst of the problem, I did keep up a 'perpetual alertness to the little question, Why?' Why did I feel so bad? That was the 'definite problem' that I 'accurately presented' myself to solve. The tension of inquiry was particularly acute, because the problem was an inner, personal one.

> *"concrete situations give rise to insights*
> *which issue into policies and courses of action"*
>
> – Lonergan, *Insight*

The time was coming for a new pause from studies, and so I did some job searching. I attended the career fair held on campus, and one company that had been there contacted me the next day for an interview. The real possibility of working for this Washington, DC management consulting firm placed me far enough into a new concrete situation that a concrete solution to my formerly nebulous problem was soon to emerge.

Saturday walk: Go home! Old lady needing help from her old husband to get out of the car. Kids playing baseball in the schoolyard of a Brookline middle school, passing a kippah-toting Jew and greeting him with '*Shabbat shalom.*' Him turning and calling back to me, perhaps in Russian, wondering who I was and if he knew me. Saying hi to a mother and daughter resting in front of a U-Haul they had been loading or unloading. Being approached by a middle-aged woman for directions in front of Sports Depot. Friendly banter of figuring out together the unclear directions she had. Heading home, and stopping by a house church 'in the Eastern Orthodox tradition' along Harvard Ave., whose light posts were decorated with colorful banners inscribed with 'Welcome' in about ten languages. Noticing on a Chinese restaurant a few character radicals that I recognized. *Chong guo fan.* Dreaming about inter-religious dialogue in Omaha, and the Islamic center nestled in a concrete building amid a lower-middle class neighborhood near Prep. Wondering about Qur'an study in Omaha, and where the Muslims in Omaha come from. What would happen if we had a public dialogue with local Jews and Muslims about the newly rekindled warring in Palestine and Israel? My grandparents' twilight years, my niece's first year, my sister the mom, my mom in her post-cancer recovery sabbatical, my dad…

Opening, fertility of mind, clarity, obstacles receding. And so it was indeed like a certain 'Eureka' called out from a Syracuse bath that I had the insight that moving to Omaha was somehow the beginning to the resolution of my inner problematic.

And so, I wound down my studies and left the Heights to return to my hometown, Omaha.

- *What experiences of failure and setback have most powerfully shaped your life? What unexpected gifts did those experiences bring?*

There and Back Again

- *What experiences of suffering have most formed you as a person?*
- *What primal wounds mark and make your identity?*
- *Who in your life recognizes the scars you bear from these crucial wounds and formative experiences of suffering?*

Superpowers in myth, lore, and legend of contemporary and classical culture often trace back to trauma. Physical and emotional wounds scar a young character. As a consequence, they embark on valorous quests, grow great powers, face future foes, and find wise guides and resourceful allies. Batman witnessed the murder of his parents. Superman's planet was decimated, his parents killed. Harry Potter's parents likewise were murdered, and the lightning strike scar seared on his forehead mysteriously connects to their murder. These characters become heroes in response to their traumas.

The intellectual in me wants to highlight an ancient example of a more profound story influencing these recent tales: In Book XIX of Homer's epic about Odysseus, the hero returns home but keeps himself disguised so he can slay the suitors vying to marry his wife, Penelope. Washing Odysseus's feet upon his arrival is Eurycleia, the now old woman who had been his nursemaid in his youth. She recognizes the hero when she sees the scar on his inner thigh. The poet then recounts how Odysseus got this scar as a young man when visiting his maternal grandfather Autolycus, the ancestor who years prior proposed to Odysseus's parents a name for their newborn son that meant "man of pain" or "man of suffering." The scar marks Odysseus. It identifies him to Eurycleia, just as he received the wound in the company of his grandfather Autolycus, who named the hero as someone with a special relationship to pain and suffering.

Suffering and scars mark the bodies and lives of LGBTQ+ people—myself included. Queerness implies a certain relationship to personal pain and wounds, emotional and otherwise. Bearing these marks, variously hiding or revealing them to those we encounter, LGBTQ+ people embody the heroic archetypes of myth and legend throughout the odyssey of our own queer lives.

Stress, Tension, Trauma

Heroes of lore rise to the occasions presented to them. Their burgeoning powers derive from a mix of unusual innate qualities and the great needs pressed onto them by crisis. Similarly, researchers have noted the crucial role of "adaptive tension" in human development. As with Odysseus, Harry Potter, Frodo, and so many other heroes of myth and lore, the growing and developing of people in real life also requires stress caused by change and challenge. We grow and mature when we find our current way of operating to be inadequate for the demands that our lives present, whether those demands look like a cyclops, Voldemort, ring-wraiths, or our firstborn child.

As I consider the developmental journeys of the gay, bi, and queer men whom I know as friends, boyfriends, and clients, "adaptive tension" in all its various forms feels especially relevant. But above all, *trauma* crucially defines, delimits, and intensifies queer lived experience. Thinking about adaptive tension, I remember learning in a high school gym class about the difference between *distress* and *eustress*. Weightlifting, for example, puts stress on our muscles and breaks them down, so they rebuild themselves stronger. The pain of normal post-workout muscle soreness and tenderness signals that this self-inflicted process of breaking down to build back up is underway. In other high school classes, teachers would start class with pop quizzes to inflict a measure of unannounced stress and discomfort so we students would gradually develop good study habits. In professional life as adults, our employers give us more responsibilities in part to stimulate us to find new ways to be efficient and effective as we prepare for our next promotion.

In contrast to eustress, which brings developmental benefits or stimulates high performance, day-to-day stress that does not spur growth or bring benefit is called distress. It can be painful and difficult but is not generally overwhelming. Distress might arise from being fired from a job, or losing one's wallet, or having a heated argument with a close friend. We might experience distress witnessing the suffering of people living on the streets, or reading about famine in a far-off land. Death can be the cause of distress that is extremely painful and difficult yet not truly overwhelming. The grief from an elderly loved one's natural death might, for example, occasion distress, but not the overwhelm of trauma.

For you personally what enables you to experience situations of difficulty as "eustress" rather than "distress"?

Beyond distress, *trauma* applies tension and stress that cracks, breaks, and splits us in overwhelming ways. We experience helplessness, terror, or an existential threat that is more than we can take in or integrate. Trauma is too much for us. It is a division, a separation, a fragmentation that we cannot make whole. We lack the capacity to include it into ourselves. The examples named above—experiencing an argument with a friend, the loss of a job or a wallet, or the death of a loved one of any age—could all result in trauma for someone, depending on what happens within them as they face those circumstances.

The word "trauma" means "wound" in Greek. When struck by force, an organism bruises. Cells and vessels are crushed, and bodily fluids escape their normal containers. When cut or pierced, somatic ligatures and tissues are sliced apart, cohesive wholes are sundered. When hit suddenly or sharply, strong structures like bones crack, break, and shatter.

Psychological traumas also wound through crushing, piercing, breaking, and shattering. Molestation, for example, forcibly extracts erotic energy from children without their yet having the capacity to consent. Rape divides free will from sex. The victim has someone enter their body, transgress the physical boundaries of their very person, and violate their somatic integrity through channels normally reserved for intimacy. Helplessness, overwhelm, and existential threat characterize trauma, whether psychological or physical. Indeed, a more formal definition of trauma entails serious injury, sexual violence, or exposure to actual or threatened death, accompanied by an experience of helplessness in the face of that feared or actual harm.

The developmental journeys of LGBTQ+ people bear the marks of trauma and distress. Other particularities also shape our journeys, but the prevalence and influence of trauma have powerful and specific effects. Adverse experiences compel LGBTQ+ people to adapt, even when we do not wish to do so. As previously noted, the adversity of "minority stress" provides stimulus in response to which LGBTQ+ people must evolve new abilities, as ingeniously as we can muster. Minority stress theory explores how, for LGBTQ+ people and members of other minorities, stigma generates excess burdens by compounding with the stresses typical of anyone's life.[84] Whether or not these excess burdens meet the clinical standard for trauma in any particular case, they create hardships for LGBTQ+ people.

The experience of trauma, including avoiding and recovering from it, accounts for two characteristics of queer development, namely its *jagged* nature and *recursive* cycles. As we explored early on with **Expert** mind, by "jagged" I mean a developmental profile with extreme highs and lows, a collection of expansive capacities and tight narrow spots. In one realm of life, we might routinely operate with grace, compassion, and dexterity, while in another we are easily and frequently tripped up and triggered into an irritable, frightened, and reduced version of ourselves. Every adult holds some such contrasts, of course. In jagged development, these towering heights and dreadful pitfalls are more numerous, with higher highs and lower lows. Beyond the **Best Little Kid**, *all* the queer superpowers we have been exploring throughout this book highlight common features of the jagged topography of queer developmental journeys. The formidable heights reached by queer superpowers come paired with fearsome sinkholes, wherein our unresolved traumas fester.

By "recursive cycles," I mean the developmental pattern of visiting earlier mindsets and developmentally significant moments, as we are doing in this book. In our lives, we cycle backwards and forwards and back again, to attempt repair, to shore up defenses or to dismantle them, to replay scenes that marked us and thus fascinate us still. Recursive cycles create a spiral dynamic in our development, which intensifies and accelerates as we move beyond the **Achiever** mindset. Some recursions happen without our willing them; others we purposefully intend. In these pages, I aim to incite, with care, recursive and reflexive awareness in you, so that you might gain new perspectives on yourself and thus expand as a person.

The superpowers that arise in the **Redefining** and **Self-Transforming** stages relate to the jagged and recursive aspects specific to queer development. **Second Adolescence** allows for *a controlled coming apart* of the conventional version of the adult self. Getting a second go at adolescence resembles the purposeful re-breaking of a misaligned bone so as to re-set it for greater cohesion. **No One Left Behind** similarly returns to earlier life experiences, but this queer superpower does so recurrently, to multiple moments of dis-ease, rupture, and overwhelm. Its purpose is to scoop up in our safe arms the terrified part of ourselves left behind enemy lines, at some scene of violence or other harm. With the queer superpower of **No One Left Behind**, we perform rescue missions within ourselves.

Insidious Trauma

Encountering someone or something that resembles some aspect of an unresolved trauma makes for another trigger of fallback. Unresolved trauma and the fallback brought up by triggers related to trauma hold special significance in LGBTQ+ life journeys. Research shows that sexual minority individuals experience a higher incidence of psychological and physical abuse by parents, intimate partner violence, sexual assault, and other victimization events. Of particular relevance here is the term "insidious trauma," which refers to prejudice-related events based on the social status of the person being devalued because of characteristics intrinsic to their identity, such as gender, race, ethnicity, sexual orientation, or physical ability. The experience of insidious trauma by people of color can inform our consideration of the developmental journeys of LGBTQ+ people.

> [E]vents motivated by racial prejudice—regardless of whether these events involve actual or threatened death—can be considered cognitive and affective assaults on one's identity, and therefore they 'strike the core of one's selfhood.' Thus, scholars have proposed that exposure to non-life-threatening racism-related events can also contribute to posttrauma symptoms, such as avoidance and numbing, self-blame, feelings of shame, and hypervigilance.[85]

Like Black people and other racial minorities that face systemic racism, LGBTQ+ people may experience post-trauma symptoms resulting from traumatic events or experiences that are stressful and deleterious, but not technically trauma.

Trauma overwhelms and shatters. It is more than we can handle or make sense of at the time when we experience it. We may ingeniously and creatively innovate some adaptation to survive the experience and move forward in our lives. However, some part of ourselves also drops anchor in trauma and gets stuck there. Parts of us break into a thousand pieces. We compartmentalize, freeze-frame, and numb those overwhelming moments or experiences. We encapsulate the broken parts of ourselves and build an exoskeleton around them, like a cast for fractured bones. These adaptations permit us survival but do not in themselves instigate repair. Instead, these encapsulated traumas stay inside us, like frozen pellets or boarded-up compartments of suffering until we find the wherewithal to heal these wounds by processing, metabolizing, and integrating these hurts into ourselves. We psychologically remove ourselves from the overwhelming experience in an out-of-body experience called *dissociation*. Kegan notes that while dissociation enables survival, "it has a big cost, which is usually that some piece of your experience gets bracketed off, or encapsulated."[86] This bracketing off of parts of the Self underlies the jagged development so common among LGBTQ+ people: "while the rest of the self develops and becomes more complex, the bracketed self is left at that historical and developmental time, and that way of meaning is preserved until one is psychologically strong enough to reintegrate parts that were left behind."

The queer superpower of **No One Left Behind** arises in the process of going back for these younger parts of ourselves that previously did get left behind and still need rescuing. In military contexts, the slogan "No one left behind!" rallies the rescue of soldiers captured or lost behind enemy lines. With the queer superpower of **No One Left Behind,** we go back for parts of the Self that are still caught in a past experience of overwhelming danger or terror.

Experiences of fallback occasioned by reactivations of unresolved traumas provide geographic data on our inner landscape. Fallback helps us learn where we retain sinkholes in whose depths lurk encapsulated trauma and bracketed-off parts of ourselves. As our capacity to see more of ourselves grows, including memories that we used to avoid, we gain the courage and strength to face our greatest fears, most searing pain, and most terrifying monsters.

- *What moments or scenes from your past haunt you?*
- *What younger versions of yourself are frozen and stuck at some site of suffering, left behind on some "battlefield"?*

Therapeutic Thawing

- *What underlies your attitude towards psychotherapy?*

For the first few months back in Omaha, I boomeranged back to the home of my mother and stepfather. I started a job search, but my real work took place through psychotherapy. Until the sense of crisis calmed down, I visited the office of Stephen Skulsky twice a week. We explored my distress and confusion. He made space for me to unearth the powerful feelings that welled up.

The therapeutic work I did with Dr. Skulsky felt like thawing frostbitten limbs and digits. I had the sense that earlier in life I had flash-frozen memories of moments. What my younger self couldn't handle, he placed in the deep freeze. Now I was bringing these memories and moments back to life. Like running room-temperature water on frostbitten hands, the thawing burned. I returned to earlier scenes in my family life, in grade school, as a teenager, in college, and in Egypt, revivifying what I had previously numbed or passed over.

In some cases, we imaginatively rewrote the script of scenes. *What would I have liked to have happened there? What do I wish my mom would have said instead of staying silent or saying what she did? What did ten- or twelve-year-old Nick need at that moment that he didn't get from Dad?* In other cases, we considered the power dynamics at play among the characters in a scene. *Because of them doing or saying that, what possibilities opened up or closed off? What indirect impact did that have on you?* Dr. Skulsky also had me turn my curiosity to the inner workings of my parents, grandparents, and sister. *What unspoken needs might they have been trying to get met in that moment? What scene from their own earlier life might they have been re-enacting? What role did they cast you to play for that scene, Dominic?*

Opening up those cryogenically stored memories brought a developmental perspective to various versions of myself and other characters in my life. I extended empathy to these younger and current versions of them and myself, and I came to see how various parts and versions of myself interacted with multiple parts and versions of my parents and others. This new way of seeing the important others in my life dethroned and humanized them. Instead of regarding my mom or dad or grandparents or older sister as family royalty who were powerfully unquestionable by dint of their position, I saw them more fully, with their layers and foibles, inner struggles, highest hopes, and dashed dreams. Crucially, I untethered my fate from theirs. Dad's downfall was his own, not mine. Mom's despair or triumph was her own, not mine. I learned to love them, without fancying their paths as mine, or mine as theirs. Dynamics and patterns I had always taken for granted I now came to understand as unnecessary, in the sense that something else could have been the case. I came to recognize how characters in the drama of my family life were expressing or meeting needs of their own as they created these dynamics and patterns in my life.

Among the most surprising discoveries, I began to recognize more similarities between my mother and father than I ever had been able to see before. She functioned so successfully in the world, even in taking care of my sister and me, that she appeared to be utterly different from my dad, who was so limited by his mental illness that he could barely take part in society. Like him, however, she had demons who tortured her and against which she defended herself in a variety of ingenious ways. She also had her unpredictable moments of rage, which disturbed the peace of our family life. Full-throated yelling matches laced with emotional, not physical, violence had punctuated our family life. Of course, I could never really know what demons tortured my mom or my dad. I could never fully see the vulnerable or helpless child versions of either of them, the inner exiles whom they raged to protect.[87] I did, however, come to see and recognize shadows and traces of exiled, abandoned, terrified, ashamed, and overwhelmed child versions of each of them.

Like a search and rescue team returning to battle scenes to find and care for the wounded left there, I sallied forth repeatedly. "**No One Left Behind**" could have served as the motto of this life-saving work of returning and retrieving. I went back for Nicker Kicker, whose mother spent months recovering from his childbirth after a loose suture led to a great loss of blood. His needs to be held and to breastfeed were not fully met, through no fault of his own. I went back for three-year-old Nicky, the toddler who witnessed rage and violence in his home, and I felt pain that little Nicky didn't have the capacity to hold. His needs for safety and steady attachment were not fully met, through no fault of his own. I went back for Nick the schoolboy, who was made a misfit by his "broken home," prodigious intelligence, and the occasional apparitions of his strange father. His needs for belonging, to fit in as just another boy, were not fully met, through no fault of his own. I went back for F. Dominic "Nick", the teenager turned golden boy, who played the role of "Joe Prep" to demonstrate his worth through competence and achievement. His need to drop the masks to be known and loved as he was, with or without his talents or skills or achievements, was not fully met. Through a practice of revivifying empathy and compassion, I took strides to integrate these and other parts of my Self.

Though deep confusion and great suffering had been needed to bring me to the point of accessing this queer superpower of **No One Left Behind**, these salvific sallies tremendously enhanced my inner life. This work exponentially increased my inner diversity and inclusion. Going back for those young, misfit versions of myself and retrieving so much that I had socked away in cold storage to survive now made possible a new kind of self-possession. This work of retrieving and revivifying also allowed me to compose new music from the cacophony of my many parts, especially the gay and straight parts, the American and Egyptian, the Omahan and Bostonian and Cairene. I allowed more of my inner melodic lines to play aloud, and I harmonized them. I arrived at a new understanding of myself and my world, which had started to take shape in Cairo. Digesting the overly rich buffet of stimulation and experience I had consumed in Egypt took years of slow painstaking work (and rest!), with the professional guidance of my therapist.

Besides cycling backwards in time to retrieve and rescue these much younger versions of myself, I also cycled forward once again through the stages of adult development I had begun while living out a straight version of myself. This time, I went through them again with my emerging gay, bi, and queer self. Acquiring the trappings of contemporary adult American life, such as a cubicle, an apartment, and a paycheck, I re-formed an age-appropriate **Socialized** Self, but now one who fit into both gay and straight societies.

To make this possible, I found a **Pride Tribe** with two gay professional friends my age, Jason and Scott. In their company, I played my part in some real-life queer version of "Sex and the City," set not in NYC, but in Omaha, our Midwestern metropolis. I learned anew to dress, flirt, date, and have sex in distinctively gay ways. I learned to handle queries and assumptions put on us at the office about the women we must be dating, the bodies that we must find attractive, and the sports pages we must read. I learned anew to draw on the powers of **Chameleonic Passing** in professional settings and to wield at the office the **Shield of Hypervigilance**. Jason and Scott helped me hone my **Gaydar** so I could suss out all kinds of queer creatures whose coping strategies differed from my own, and learn the language of "looking" that signaled erotic interest between men. In this **Second Adolescence**, I learned anew to operate as an adult in society, this time as a man who fell in love with other men.

- *What conditions are necessary (and conducive) for you to be able to revisit difficult chapters of your life?*
- *What would enable you to make peace with these difficult experiences so as to gain a greater integration of all parts of yourself?*

Trauma Recovery

- *What benefit has this book brought you so far in its attempt to offer a "trail guide" for personal growth and development?*

- *What personal experiences of physical or emotional recovery can you draw upon in considering what it takes to heal and move on from trauma?*

In seeking to flourish, everyone must face their individual and collective trauma. Knowing ourselves means knowing our wounds and all of the rest of what makes us who we are. The journey of personal growth and leadership development each of my clients undertakes involves facing the effects of trauma.

In some cases, I'll work with a client who has done significant healing of their inner wounds but still moves through the world in a defensive posture of one kind or another, such as guardedness or cynicism or conflict avoidance. While these defensive postures might have helped the person to survive some earlier phase of life, he finds himself still making these maneuvers though no longer facing the same threats he once did.

In other cases, a highly accomplished gay man will come to me wanting to grow into a more effective leader, say, following a promotion to an executive position with greater scope than ever before in his life. As we explore his behavioral patterns and his inner world, we discover untouched compartments inside him where long ago he packed away some traumatic experience. In such a case, our leadership development work together prepares him to start working with a psychotherapist who is trained to help heal psychological wounds.

These two examples illustrate some of the range of possibilities for how coaching and leadership development can intersect with trauma recovery. Working with LGBTQ+ clients in particular necessitates a trauma-informed approach to leadership development and personal growth. Besides our individual traumatic experiences, trauma affects queer culture and LGBTQ+ people collectively. Consequently, queer people stand to gain much in their friendships and sexual relationships from learning about trauma and trauma recovery.

Psychologist Gretchen Schmelzer, Ph.D., in her book, *Journey Through Trauma*, provides a "trail guide" for wayfarers retracing their steps, circling back to rescue themselves and repair their shattered bits and pieces.[88] In the context of queer superpowers, we can use Schmelzer's book as an invaluable reference for embracing the queer superpower of **No One Left Behind**.

Schmelzer focuses on repeated relational trauma, that is, psychological trauma that takes place within human relationships, which describes my own early trauma related to my dad. Relational traumas can only be healed through the same medium in which they occurred, namely, through human relationships, most directly in therapeutic relationships, like mine with Dr. Skulsky, but also in other loving relationships of trust, vulnerability, and intimacy.

Schmelzer compares the cyclical journey of the rescue missions we undertake to retrieve and revivify traumatized parts of ourselves to intense mountaineering, like climbing Everest. She describes five phases to this cycle: Preparation, Unintegration, Identification, Integration, and Consolidation.

Preparing for this epic journey requires considerable time, skill-building, hard practice, easy rest, acclimatization, and a trusted support team. Just making it to Base Camp, the staging ground for the climb, takes great dedication and effort. What Schmelzer describes as the Preparation phase entails getting to Base Camp, assembling the resources and support team, and building strength, skill, and knowledge for the arduous high-altitude climb that lies ahead. Looking back, I see that I returned to Boston College for those three semesters of graduate school after the extremely challenging two years I had had in Egypt in order to recuperate and gain strength for the inner work that needed to happen for me to put all the old and new pieces of myself together into a coherent whole.

Unintegration requires dismantling with great care the protections and defenses put in place to survive the trauma. Just as a cast only serves to heal a fractured bone for a limited time, the defense mechanisms we create to shield ourselves from relational trauma eventually constrain us in unhelpful ways. A plaster cast worn too long keeps the once-broken limb underdeveloped, inflexible, and atrophied. Schmelzer draws on pioneering psychoanalyst D. W. Winnicott to describe unintegration as "a relaxed state of coming apart to reconnect."[89] Unintegration requires safety and support, someone on which to lean so that what trauma shattered can begin to heal. As a cane bears some of the load for someone healing a broken foot, the safe support of a therapist or others helps us exercise our tender inner parts, which once were broken and have long kept shielded.

For me personally, the cultural, social, linguistic, political, and sexual experiences I went through in Egypt put pressure on the version of myself I had previously assembled. As I ran away from the disintegration that was happening, especially during and after my relationship with Tom, the U.S. Marine from church, I attempted and temporarily succeeded at patching back together my old self. Returning to Boston College and the straight, young adult version of myself helped in this regard. But then, when all that was stewing and brewing inside me erupted into a major depressive episode, I could no longer stay in the Preparation phase. With able support, first from therapists at Boston College who offered emergency aid and then from Dr. Skulsky in an ongoing manner, I started to remove the patchwork and released the effort of holding myself together in this old way. Instead, for the first of many times to follow, I began disassembling and deconstructing old versions of myself that could no longer contain the sheer degree of complexity that I had taken in and created within myself.

Next, Schmelzer compares the Identification phase to when all the pieces of a jigsaw puzzle get dumped out on the table for examination and sorting. This phase of recovery entails reconsidering the fragments of memory or the provisional story made up in the aftermath of trauma to make sense of the protective measures taken to survive it. For me, the project of revisiting so many earlier experiences and reconsidering the sense I made of them began to happen through psychotherapy. Then about a year into seeing a therapist, I wrote the thirty-page spiritual autobiography which I have quoted several times within these pages. In it, I clarified and expressed my new understanding of some of the stories I had constructed about major features of my life up until that point. Sensing how pivotal that autobiographical writing would be for me, I titled it "Beginnings."

In what Gretchen Schmelzer describes as the Integration phase of healing, the jigsaw puzzle pieces come together in a new configuration. The reconsidered fragments come together into a new whole. Back in my mid-20s when I was recovering from depression through my first foray into psychotherapy, this integration phase of trauma recovery would arrive with feelings of expansion, even elation. The newly expanded and more coherently whole versions of me who came more fully to life through this process enjoyed greater inner resources and more options at any given moment for how to respond to whatever situation arose in the world or inside of me. This gain of function, freedom, and options, with increased integrity and fullness of life, epitomizes "personal growth," as I understand it.

Schmelzer uses the word Consolidation for the fifth and final stage of this recurrent cycle of trauma recovery. In Consolidation, we take a respite from the arduous work of retrieving, revivifying, and reorganizing parts of ourselves. We might consciously be putting our energy and attention on other matters, not trauma recovery. Yet as we rest and recover from the Alpine trek through our interior wilderness, our new inner structures grow roots. The stalks of new growth thicken, the leaves widen and multiply, buds bloom. We flourish in this new lushness of greater aliveness. My first profound experience of Consolidation came about three years after I started intensive psychotherapy to recover from debilitating depression by putting together a new and bigger version of myself. At the age of twenty-eight, I quit my job, broke my lease, packed up my car, and moved to Seattle for what I called a "personal sabbatical." As the ripe old age of thirty approached, I wanted to play more. I dreamt of hiking in the forested mountains of the Pacific Northwest—with the explicit goal of doing nothing that year that added anything to my resumé. I just wanted to enjoy life and all the fruits of the arduous inner (and outer) work I had done the previous years.

Trauma recovery seems to entail a specific kind of transformative shift in meaning-making. In trauma recovery, we go back to retrieve and rescue a part of our inner self that was shattered and that we freeze-dried or cauterized in order to survive and keep on living. Revitalizing those freeze-dried fragments, we metabolize in recovery what we could not when the trauma first happened. We un-encapsulate these fragments and make them part of us once more. Trauma recovery releases energy while expanding us. Nothing else can increase our inner diversity and inclusion in the ways recovery from trauma can, through revitalizing and integrating these freeze-dried fragments of ourselves.

As Schmelzer describes, the cycle of trauma recovery involves letting go, coming apart, re-knowing. We disentangle our old worldview and metanarrative into its component parts. As with any process of transformational growth, we feel disoriented, even terrified, by releasing our old ways of being, thinking, knowing, and understanding. At some point in the process, we are like a monkey holding two branches, going nowhere, ready either to move into the unknown or stay stuck. When we grab that new, unknown vine, we swing into a new configuration of self, a new story of our life, the world, and our place in it. My sabbatical in Seattle gave me time to revel in the new branch I had grabbed and to somersault into the new territory where that swinging limb brought me.

While trauma recovery holds extraordinary power for anyone who goes through it, when we recover from queer trauma, which especially relates to queer identity or queer experience, then I regard trauma recovery as the queer superpower I'm calling **No One Left Behind**. Like all the queer superpowers highlighted throughout this book, **No One Left Behind** specifies a queer version of a pattern or posture that in other variations could feature in any person's developmental journey, including straight folks.

- *What difficult or overwhelming experiences have you freeze-dried or cauterized so as not to have to face them or deal with them?*
- *What would it take for you to consider bringing back to life these parts of yourself?*

A Queer Cycle of Violence

- *What experiences of "narrative violence" have you had in your life—someone trying to control the narrative of your life by imposing onto you their version of you and their interpretation of your story?*

Gretchen Schmelzer wrote her book as a trail guide for the recursive and cyclical journey of healing from trauma. She explicitly disavows the genre of self-help for her book. "This is a how-to-understand-and-use-help book. It is a what-to-expect-from-trauma-treatment book. This book demands that you get help, but it also provides the information you need to feel empowered and secure in your helping relationship."[90]

In his books, French novelist Édouard Louis (b. 1992) vividly portrays several experiences of trauma and its aftereffects. I draw upon Louis's writings to present different examples of how queer trauma and queer superpowers can show up in someone's life. In what he calls an "autobiographical novel," titled *Histoire de la violence* (2016), that is, *History of Violence*, Louis focuses on an episode from his early adulthood which terrified and marked him.[91] In terms of queer superpowers, Louis as narrator embodies **No One Left Behind**. He goes back and retrieves a version of himself which was split off and left behind at the time so that he could survive and move forward in life. I mean for *Queer Flourishing* to resemble both Schmelzer's book and Louis's. As Louis draws on his lived experience and life story to create in his novel a world that readers can step into, so have I been telling some of my own story so that you can enter my world.

A gay white man who grew up in poverty in a working-class town of northern France, Louis recounts a "history of the violence" endured one Christmas Eve in Paris after celebrating with friends. He also tells the story of his "story," which is another meaning of the word *histoire* in the novel's title. Louis structures the narrative as a layering of story upon story, version upon version, interpretation upon interpretation. He tells how the very story of his experience of assault and rape gets taken from him by the police interrogators and by his sister. Like the man who raped him, the police "rob" and do a kind of violence to Édouard (the main character). Louis thus portrays his own and other characters' processes of making sense of what happened to him, as I have been doing in my own autobiographical writing.

In *Histoire de la violence*, the author works to make sense of his trauma. Through telling his story, Louis knits together fragments of desire and fantasy, memory and sensation, emotion and thought, stemming from that fateful night when hearing footsteps behind him leads to a beautiful man coming up next to him and striking up a conversation. The violent events that germinate the book took root that Christmas Eve when the beautiful stranger, whose name was Reda, goes home with Édouard at his invitation but then attempts to rob and strangle our narrator before raping him at gunpoint.

However, it is not this physical violence but the narrative violence done by Édouard's sister and the police that structures the novel. Some days or weeks after his encounter with Reda, Édouard is at his sister's house in their hometown. Édouard stands behind a door listening furtively as his sister recounts Édouard's story to her husband. Édouard's silent thoughts provide commentary on her version of the story (*italicized*), including where she lies or demonstrates misunderstanding elements of the "story of violence" that Édouard told her previously, outside of what the author includes in the novel. Like the police investigators, Édouard's sister imposes herself onto his experience. She makes a new story out of his account, shaping it to match her reality rather than faithfully conveying his. Indeed, she tells her husband that Édouard exaggerated and even lied in his own account of what happened with Reda, as—she claims—Édouard also lied in portraying his family as intolerant of his gayness.

> . . . when he told us that he was different, the day that he told it to us, I remember like it was yesterday, I guarantee you, we told him that it changed nothing and that we would love him nonetheless (*she's lying*), always, and that for us he would be the same person. We told him that the important thing was his happiness, that he be happy (*she's lying*), family before all else.[92]

The italicized parentheses share Édouard's silent thoughts as from behind the door he listens to his sister tell his story. While watching his sister tell her version of his story, Édouard relives the events of robbery, rape, and attempted murder. Now not quite helpless as he writes the novel, Louis (the author) has Édouard (the main character) correct his sister's account silently, in italics, from the place of parenthesis.

Histoire de la violence captures and expresses something important about queer trauma, particularly the trauma of gay men. These particularities come out through many small moments and details. For example, Édouard gets cruised. He invites a man he just met on the street into his apartment for a hookup. At the police station, an apparently straight officer taking Édouard's crime report questions how this could happen:

> He [the police officer] posed this question: "And you let someone you didn't know come up to your apartment like that, in the middle of the night?" I responded, "You know, everyone does that . . ." and in an ironic, mocking, sarcastic tone of voice, he doubled down, "Everyone?" It wasn't a question. He was obviously not asking me whether or not everyone behaved that way, but rather he was trying to have me know that no one did.[93]

Édouard then clarifies, not everyone has strangers up to their apartment in the middle of the night, just "people like me." Louis tells this history of violence, the story of his rape, the word for which in French is *viol*—a fundamental sort of human violence, which is a bodily violation. In so doing, he works through his experience of being betrayed, violated, and ravaged by a man to whom he had trusted both his body and his affection.

Though I have neither endured nor perpetrated rape, I know from personal experience this cycle of encounter, invitation, intimacy, affection, tenderness, betrayal, and harm. Indeed, I believe that this cycle makes part of the collective experience of queer people generally, and gay men specifically. Perhaps in harming those who allow us in—to their homes, lives, hearts, and bodies—we reenact the hurts we ourselves have endured at the hands of those we have trusted, those who have held us tenderly, even as young and vulnerable innocents. In living out this cycle in my own life, I have been Édouard, I have been Reda—both someone who has been harmed and caused harm.

Louis's novel touches on most of the examples of relational violence given by Schmelzer: domestic violence, child abuse, sexual abuse, clergy abuse, police violence, genocide, and war.[94]

While no clergy abuse appears in *Histoire de la violence*, the French war in Algeria marks Reda, who thus merits regard as both perpetrator and victim of relational trauma. Indeed, (the character) Édouard's regard for Reda and his story makes for a resistantly tender thread through the novel. Even as Édouard endeavors to recover and repair the shattering caused by Reda, he cares for him.

Histoire de la violence belongs to a genre called auto-fiction. With the label "novel" printed on its title page but a main character by the same name and biographical details as the author, *Histoire de la violence* asks readers to take its contents seriously as actual human experience but not evaluate it as actual "history." In that spirit, I recognize from Schmelzer's framework for recovery from trauma that sense-making and storytelling are vital components to healing from repeated relational trauma. I imagine that in the process of composing *Histoire de la violence* Louis may have gone through the five stages of Schmelzer's cycle of healing—namely, Preparation, Unintegration, Identification, Integration, Consolidation.

In Louis's novel itself, we as readers handle the fragments of trauma that arise and slowly get sorted through the course of the narrative. During the moments when Reda was raping him, the character of Édouard concentrated on the "more or less realistic peach smell of laundry detergent" emanating from the beige bedsheets onto which his face was smashed.[95] By numbing his emotions through dissociation, Édouard survives the rape. As he narrates the experience, he presents all manner of sensations, thoughts, minute observations, feelings, and fantasies. Schmelzer emphasizes that trauma comprises not only the traumatic events themselves but also what measures we take to survive. Édouard's focus on the peach-scented laundry smell of his sheets while Reda was doing sexual violence to him illustrates the fragmented memory of such a protective measure. Numbing and dissociating enabled Édouard to survive. However, in his eventual recovery he has to drop these shields to resume a vibrant life.

Ultimately, in the context of trauma recovery, we can regard Louis's novel as a product of what Schmelzer terms the Integration phase of healing. Édouard, the narrator, makes sense of what happened to him in constructing and telling his narrative. In this telling, Édouard's experience of trauma becomes something that he sees he survived. For Édouard the narrator, and perhaps even more for the living breathing Louis the author, the past finally becomes for him the past, rather than an ongoing nightmare. In assembling the fragments and weaving them into a story, he makes meaning of them. He shifts the trauma from subject to object, something he can now see as other than himself.

Novelists excel in perspective-taking. Switching points of view from character to character as well as that of a sometimes unreliable, sometimes omniscient narrator, novelists layer perspectives and interweave them. Attentive readers come to see and hold the complexity of alternative versions of reality. Reading fiction like *Histoire de la violence* thus provides an imaginative path to experiencing and recovering from queer trauma.

We as readers get to be with the narrator and characters. As we take in the words on the page, we imagine living through their experiences. We take on their perspectives—sometimes one after the other and sometimes simultaneously. Staging the scenes in our minds, we position ourselves in numerous places as we read the narrative. We play all the roles. Our own memories, knowledge, desires, and dreams interact with the characters whom we come to know. We become witness to their dialogue, bodies, thoughts, and feelings. Safe in our own space, wherever we are as we hold their story in our hands, we feel their fears, enter their terrors, and experience their violence.

Similarly, I hope you keep bringing your memories, knowledge, desires, and dreams as you explore my world. Let yourself reminisce and relive episodes from your life. Revisit earlier chapters of this book as part of your own recursive cycles to earlier versions of yourself and past experiences that stay encapsulated within you. Take a fresh look at your path, the challenges you faced, and the moves you took to overcome them. Relax into allowing fragments of memory to arise for you. Even as you revisit, hold lightly your old story, and ask anew whether anything else may (also) be the case.

- *What elements might be missing from the stories you've long told (to yourself and others) about yourself?*
- *What alternative and equally valid sense-making might also apply to who and how you are?*

PART IV

Table 9: Queer Superpowers of Self-Protective Opportunist

Developmental Stage			Queer Superpower	Adverse Circumstances that prompt superpower's emergence
Self-Sovereign	Self-Protective Opportunist	1	Chameleonic Passing	» Social exclusion » Mocking » Bullying » Shaming » Moral condemnation » Shunning by family / friends » Violent attack
		2	Shield of Hypervigilance	
		3	The Great Escape	
Socialized	Conformist	4	Gaydar	» Cultural values » Gender expectations » Romantic & sexual norms of the straight mainstream » Religious & moral condemnation » Legal persecution
		5	Pride Tribe	
	Expert	6	The Best Little Kid	
Self-Authoring	Achiever	7	The Queen	» Strictures of societal expectations limit creative powers » Socialized cycle of approval-seeking forecloses possibility of greatness
		8	Double Life	
	Redefining	9	Second Adolescence	» Self-imposed limits caused by personal adaptations made earlier in life to survive and thrive » Distressful self-awareness of unintegrated parts of self
Self-Transforming		10	No One Left Behind	

Queer Flourishing

Description	Heroic Possibilities & Powers	Pitfalls & Shadow
» Adapt to fit wide range of settings	» Shape-shifting » Cloak of invisibility » Avoid unwanted attention » Allow others to imagine you're one of them	» Not being seen or known for who we are » Loneliness » Fusing with our masks and forgetting who we really are
» Early alert system for possible danger	» Prepared to freeze, flee, or fight for safety » Avoid attacks, traps, & ambushes	» Fear & anxiety flood out other emotions » Skittish withdrawal inhibits relationships » Difficulty trusting even the trustworthy
» Depart toxic or abusive life situation to find supportive context	» Muster the courage, creativity, and determination needed for liberation	» Leave behind the good and the bad alike » Change of scenery without inner growth or change – "Running to stand still" » Flee into the clutches of new abusers
» Sense others' queerness	» Tap into intuitive knowing » See people's hidden faces » Empathy for others' shame	» Delusions of queer grandeur, imagining LGBTQ+ folks as superior to straight people » Project own queerness onto others
» Membership in a queer social group	» Strength in solidarity » Self-confidence to cultivate and use atypical gifts	» Gay groupthink papers over personal uniqueness » False sense of superiority
» Meeting and surpassing social standards and expectations	» Achieve excellence » Gain admiration in society » Earn one's way out of shame	» Fitting in to move up, lose sense of self and own unique "weird & wonderful" traits » Trapped by society's definitions of success, e.g., wealth, high position, prestige, luxury, etc.
» Accept and exercise "divine right" to rule one's own realm	» Claim own power » Impervious self-possession » Regal stature and poise » Sharp rationality » Relentlessly strategic in pursuing own vision and goals	» Self-sufficiency limits love – It's lonely at the top » Steamroll over others » Compartmentalization keeps valuable inner resources inaccessible » Haughty overconfidence leaves others impressed but distant
» Bifurcate life into separate domains	» Create space for expression and cultivation of queer self » Honor suite of personal values despite contradictions	» Split life mirrors splits in the self that limit personal integration » Self-control verges on fraud and deceit
» A controlled coming apart and re-forming of adult self	» Shed conventional version of self in favor of greater authenticity and self-expression » Capacity for experimentation, follwed by rapid iteration, learning, and growth » Creativity and originality, despite societal flak	» Perpetually lost and not found, dissolution of conventional self never resolves into new coherence » Regress back to conventional self
» Return to scenes of wounding, to heal and more fully integrate all parts of self	» Wholeness » Integration of hidden resources and vulnerabilities » Revivification of spiritual scars	» Without sufficient support, re-traumatization can occur

CHAPTER 7:

Returning and Retrieving

The work of **No One Left Behind** gradually deepens, one cyclical foray to the next. We go back recursively to those sites of suffering to recover parts of ourselves left in the lurch. We thaw out frozen feelings and revivify deadened extremities. With this magnificent queer superpower, we do inner work to integrate more of ourselves and move toward wholeness. As has become familiar in popular culture, we locate and care for our "inner child." In order to move forward, we look backwards. To grow larger, we return to our smaller selves.

Like other aspects of personal development, this inner work has specific contours and characteristics for LGBTQ+ adults. **No One Left Behind** takes us back to pre-socialized versions of ourselves, who hadn't yet become real members of society or come to understand the ways of the world. At this point in the journey of *Queer Flourishing*, we therefore delve into the not-yet-adult, pre-conventional sense-making that immediately precedes the **Conformist** form of mind. The queer superpowers of this early developmental stage belong properly to child development. Nonetheless, at some point in our adult development, starting in the **Redefining** stage, when we acknowledge more of our shadow material, working with these pre-conventional queer superpowers becomes a significant developmental edge that demands our attention.

Developmental Defenses

- *What standard moves do you make to seek safety when you feel under attack?*

Everyone needs to feel safe, and how we find personal safety to a large extent defines how we are in the world. In a sense, each stage of development amounts to a strategy for finding and creating that safety that we all need. For example, in **Socialized** mind we find safety through our communities of belonging; in **Expert** mind, through our knowledge and skill; in **Self-Authoring** mind, through our ideology or worldview. Defenses are "what makes a system a system," by giving integrity and coherence to a person's structure of mind.[96] We are defined by our limits and boundaries, the structures of self that keep threats out and our sense of self in. For this reason, we mobilize ourselves to fend off threats to our ways of making sense of the world.

Defenses shore up boundaries. Those moves and maneuvers, called ego defenses or alternatively, creative adaptations, define the boundaries of the Self. Using various maneuvers and habits, ego defenses determine what is in me, and what I exclude from my Self. Queer superpowers comprise a set of creatively adaptive defensive styles and strategies that LGBTQ+ people use. This concept of ego defenses thus further illuminates the connection between queer superpowers, inner diversity and inclusion, and human development.

While all people experience a need for safety and security, as we develop, our need to fend off threats to our ways of making meaning diminishes. We lower our defenses as we grow in our capacities to be with the complexity of reality. In other words, the later the developmental stage, the less we need experiences to be different from what they are, and so the less we need defensive maneuvers.[97] We can increasingly let more of reality in. We can *include* within ourselves more of the textured, layered, and interwoven complexity and diversity of reality.

The defensive styles we turn attention to now belong to the forms of mind called pre-conventional. They have this name because they *precede* that point in development when a person can internalize the conventions of society. After adolescence, few people primarily use pre-conventional mindsets to make sense of their world. These forms of mind allow relatively narrow windows through which to see and understand reality. They are less sophisticated and less capacious than later stages. From these forms of mind, we possess only blunt instruments with which to protect ourselves or exert power. Like a young child wandering alone in the streets of a bustling city in a foreign land where they don't speak the language or fully understand the customs, when in a pre-conventional stage of development, we easily experience overwhelm and fear. Threats abound. We watch, hide, escape, disguise.

Our pre-conventional forms of mind do not die or dissolve after we move on to a developmental place where we primarily rely on other forms of mind with wider scope, access to greater nuance and subtlety, and more powerful, flexible means for handling the challenges that life presents. Even when fully settled into a later stage as our primary operating system for making sense of reality, we always retain within us those younger versions of ourselves who can only resort to blunt instruments and gross measures to stay safe.

The particular pre-conventional form of mind that we now focus on is called **Opportunist** or **Self-Protective**, depending on the defensive style of a person.[98] One distinctively gay or queer style of *staying safe* that has become well known in mainstream society. It is a way of hiding and disguising in the structures and strictures of straight life. From a developmental point of view, this practice, called "closeting," belongs to the **Self-Protective** version of this stage. Among the queer community and our allies, who both understand and love LGBTQ+ people, we celebrate coming out of the closet as an important developmental step. No matter the biological age of the person who comes out, the psychologically young, adolescent version of that person makes a transition in the process. The closeted, self-protecting kid comes out of hiding and joins society more fully.

If it is the **Self-Protective** part of us who closets and eventually transitions into the paradoxically greater vulnerability of openness and integrity, then it is also that same part of us who undergoes the kind of trauma related to identity degradation. When we are overwhelmed by hurt caused by others devaluing us and relegating us to some despised low-level social status on account of our queerness, we are cast back into our **Self-Protective** form of mind. The particular experience of insecurity and danger that comes from not belonging and not finding community calls up our pre-conventional selves, that part of us who is not yet **Socialized**, has not yet found any communities of belonging, and thus is not yet a true member of society.

To create maximal safety at Flourishing Gays events so that pre-conventional versions of participants can feel at ease, I ask everyone to assent to a set of agreements regarding presence, purpose, and trust:

Presence

Be fully present. Leave your devices in another room. Turn off all notifications, take off your Apple Watch, put your phone on airplane mode, and let me hold time for you.

- Be sober and not under the influence of alcohol or recreational drugs during our session
- Be stationary (not walking or driving) in a quiet place
- Turn your video on, except in case of technical difficulties
- Give full attention to the group process
- Do not read text messages, emails, or otherwise multi-task
- Arrive before the start time and stay till the end

Purpose

Bring your real stuff, and use this event and this community in the most valuable way you can.

- Bring to the work of our session (at least one of) the most high-stakes challenges or opportunities that you are facing in this period of your life
- Experiment with greater vulnerability, revealing parts of yourself that you usually guard
- Tell others what it feels like to be in this group and share with others what you learn about yourself—Talking about your experience can help you integrate what you learn

Trust

Create a safe container.

- Hold in confidence what others share—Tell your own story, but no one else's
- Express your feelings and thoughts genuinely, candidly, and courageously, even (especially!) those feelings and thoughts that you are not used to expressing
- Ensure privacy for yourself and the other participants— If you live with others, go to a room with a closed door, and consider using earphones
- Take responsibility for your impact on the group (not just your intentions)

These requests benefit each of you individually and all of us as a group so we can make the most of our limited time together, to focus on mutual support and connection.

While these agreements sometimes strike new participants as more elaborate than anything they are accustomed to, many also report feeling a sense of security knowing they will be carefully held in the event they are about to attend.

- *What parts of yourself do you do your best to hide from other people's notice?*

The Closeting–Coming Out Continuum

- *What social identities do you downplay or even obfuscate? Consider your background and identity as widely as possible, e.g., socioeconomic class, ethnicity, religious community, medical history, (hidden) disabilities, addiction/recovery status, survival of rape, veteran of war, geographic origins, native language, neurodiversity, etc.*

- *What cherished aspects of yourself might you soon be ready to reveal to those who know you?*

Coming out cannot be extricated from queer development or LGBTQ+ identity. For those of us who find our sexual orientation or gender identity to belong to the basket of identities dubbed "LGBTQ+," coming out marks our lives. Whether we put it off indefinitely or direct life around it, whether we hit it before we wanted to or struggle for years and years to grasp at it, coming out features prominently in our developmental journeys. Moreover, our stories of orienting ourselves sexually intertwine inevitably with the development of our gender identity and expression. Only in tandem do these aspects of the Self make sense.

Looking back now, from the age of forty-seven, to the years when I was first looking for my place, my people, and my path, I get curious about my experience back then of coming out and closeting. I have also come to understand that closeting and coming out continue throughout life. Not binary opposites, but rather poles of a continuum, closeting and coming out remain ever-present options as I move through the world. Over and over, I reveal or conceal parts of myself, to be seen or to take cover. Living along this continuum, I come out, or I do not, to various degrees, again and again, in an ongoing and never-ending process.

To straight folks, coming out might sound like it is analogous to letting others know your nationality or your professional background. It may seem like some relatively important and non-apparent aspect of your personality and personal history. To a limited degree, coming out is indeed like that. However, for many queer folks—me included—coming out is more personal and more profound. Coming out is about being seen and known, being loved and lovable, being accepted and acceptable. Coming out is about being worthy and worthwhile.

I learned a good deal about coming out from the recent book of my friend and colleague Kathleen Talvacchia. As a queer theologian, she explores "coming out as an erotic ethical practice." Drawing on many sources of insight, including her own experience being in an interracial queer couple, Talvacchia arrives at a view of coming out as "a transgressive action of embodied truth-telling that is formed from moral convictions for the purpose of resisting normative discourses that perpetuate injustice."[99] Her take on coming out helps me understand the power dynamics in bucking the trend and resisting the normative sexual and gender expectations that bear on LGBTQ+ people, including myself. At times, we shrink back to the closet for protection, and at times we transgressively stand taller to resist.

What Does Your Daddy Do?

The story of my closeting and coming out begins not with my gayness, but with my queerness, my difference, my weirdness. As I have recounted previously, my father's emotional and psychological difficulties led to my parents divorcing after about a decade of marriage. I was three years old, and my sister was six. That summer Mom made for the three of us a kind of "great escape." We flew from Omaha to San Jose, where we stayed for some months with my dad's sister, who had become one of my mom's dearest friends. Before this furtive escape from my dad and the emotional and physical violence between him and my mother, my sister and I were witness to scenes of painful combat between them.

Seeing my father strike my mother seared me. Images and sounds and feelings from those scenes mark me indelibly. On some level, even as a toddler, I sensed something of the intricate and powerful emotional energy as these two people, my parents—who fell in love as teenagers and married as college students—faced each other with fury and rage. From close proximity, I witnessed great harm, and the threat of still greater harm. At its most intense and destructive, the energy between my parents was murderous.

Witnessing this violence and experiencing the break-up of my parents, which saved us from more of this violence, confused and terrified me as a child in ways I could not handle. I learned much later in life to call overwhelming experiences such as these "trauma." As a child, I knew nothing about the psychologists who treated veterans of the First and Second World Wars who struggled severely after the overwhelming experience of seeing bombs blow their fellow soldiers apart. After enemies had powerfully and repeatedly threatened their safety, those men returned home shaken, marked, and changed. Researchers came to call "trauma" the wounds that injured those soldiers' spirits and minds, as I had been injured emotionally by the violence I witnessed as a very young child.

In my earliest years, bombs of familial war blew apart my home. After some months of refuge at my Aunt Marilyn's home in San José, California, my mother, sister, and I returned to the house on Queens Drive where we had previously lived with my dad. Some of the bathroom doors remained marked with bruises where he had kicked when my mother had locked herself in for protection. Those bruises marked us too. They were the scars of wounds not fully healed. The searing wounds of trauma scarred each of us differently—my mom, my sister, myself, and my dad, too.

This story of my sexual orientation and gender expression begins inevitably with my family of origin. The wounds I have described and the violence that caused them had complex causes and effects. These wounds and scars also marked me with certain information about gender and sexuality, coupling and intimacy. Still today I can recognize and organize only certain parts and pieces of this information that lies entrenched in my unconscious depths. What I do know is that these violent scenes of the two lovers whose lovemaking generated my very life conveyed much to me, for example, what it is to be a man, to be a woman, and what it is to couple. This knowledge in my depths resonated powerfully when, at Boston's Hatch Shell, in 1994, the summer after my first year of college, I thrilled to the '70s groove of Lou Rawls performing his classic song "Love Is a Hurtin' Thing." His mellifluously masculine bass voice sang out a truth that reverberated deep within me. Though his lyrics depict romantic travails, Rawls' poetic lines named the hurt that, from my earliest memory, I knew love could do.

Reflecting on these memories, I recognize many of the "adverse childhood experiences" that public health and trauma experts today regard as impediments to human flourishing and thriving.[100] Among these adverse experiences in my childhood were witnessing the terror of domestic violence, the ruptures of divorce, and experiencing my dad's cognitive distortions and emotional aberrations.

Mom taught my sister and me the term "mentally ill" for us to use when other kids' parents would ask, "What does your daddy do?" Reciting the sentence as if showing some badge of identification, we would reply, "He's mentally ill." My sister and I hated having to say this, and yet we would pretend normalcy in declaring our dad's abnormality. The phrase was like a hall pass at school for us to show to adults so that they would stop scrutinizing and let us carry on with our childlike ways. *Here's your answer! Can I go now? Stop looking at me like that. I just want to pass like any other kid.* I needed **Chameleonic Passing** not to look straight, but to seem normal in other ways.

Dad's mental illness pervaded my sense of self as I was growing up. It marked me as utterly different, even from the other kids with divorced parents. As I write about this now, all of the politics of the closet feel relevant. We wanted so desperately to be other than we were, children with a mentally ill daddy. And we did pass as normal, until asked that fateful question, "What does your daddy do?" which usually seemed intended as a way to gauge our place in the socioeconomic hierarchy. "I have a mom and a dad, just like everybody else, and everything at home is just fine." Something like this was what I wanted everyone to see when they saw me.

In his book *Covering*, the gay Japanese-American legal scholar Kenji Yoshino identifies patterns in gay Americans' relationship to closeting and coming out in order to demarcate three stages in queer history in America.[101] In the first stage, gays wanted to "convert" into straights, and conversion therapists showed up, peddling false hope to gays who wished to embrace a false consciousness as straight. Yoshino sees a second stage in an era of "passing," emblematized by the US military policy of "Don't Ask, Don't Tell." *Fine to be gay, just don't let us see it. Pass as straight, and we won't throw you out.* In the third stage, in which Yoshino saw America in 2006 when he published his book, he saw "covering" to be the issue of the day for LGBTQ people. Muting or downplaying our queerness, not flaunting it—that's what society seemed to be asking of us.

Considering my "queerness" as a youth in light of these three stages that Yoshino identifies, I see no "conversion" stage in my past. I held no hope that he would return to some state of mental and emotional health that he may have enjoyed earlier in his life. I harbored no illusions that he would turn back to some state in which I had never known him to embody. I never imagined he would become a normal father and thereby make me a normal boy with normal answers to questions like "What does your daddy do?" Looking back, perhaps such a fantasy would have been helpful. It may have provided me succor or given me greater access to the needs and wants for a father who could be more fully present to me. Thanks to many conversations with uncles, aunts, grandparents, family friends, and, yes, even with my mom, I came to know something of my dad, Fred Longo, before he became so disturbed. But from my earliest memory, he abided on the margins of society, strange, estranged, unable to cope with jobs or stores or bills. He could not even maintain relationships with his cousins or others who knew and loved him as a young man.

Instead of wishing for conversion to normalcy, I dwelt in the land of "passing," the second approach to queerness that Yoshino highlights. *If I don't bring up the subject of my father, no one else will, right?* Even in the Longo family, amidst the many clans and generations of Italian-American kin we kept connected to, I usually wanted to slip away from the topic of my dad.

Some of the more distant kin, say, cousins of my grandparents, wouldn't bring him up in front of me, but whisper condolences and *tsk tsk*s about Fred to Grandma. Others who had known Dad in his youth and his married life with my mother would sometimes ask me if I had seen my dad lately, as if my not seeing him stemmed from a lack of filial piety.

Closer family—my uncles, my dad's cousins, other contemporaries of his—sometimes, after a family feast and a few drinks, would regale me with stories of Fred. Imploring me to know who my dad was, they would forcefully and affectionately tell their tales.

I felt shame, just wanting to slip away.

Can't we return to the fun family gathering where I'm just another kid like the other cousins here? Is there a closet I can hide in?

- *Which of your social identities do you yearn to escape or convert into something else?*
- *Which parts of your identity do you mask to pass as something else?*

Self-Protective Opportunist Queer Superpowers

- *What kinds of personalities or social threats do you especially watch out for, on account of previous negative experiences?*
- *In what social situations do you shape-shift to fit in?*

The recursive sallies of **No One Left Behind** bring us back to many versions of ourselves who need our attention. Some of those younger versions of ourselves stuck at scenes of trauma require a healing process best guided by a psychotherapist. Other young parts of ourselves needing attention might be gripped by less wounding experiences in our past that still influence how we show up in the present. Indeed, as we continue to expand our capacity to see and honor the tremendous inner diversity of our psychic landscape, we unearth ever more parts of ourselves long locked in some or other defensive posture. We rediscover versions of ourselves from before we really joined society, that is, our pre-socialized self. In our early years, before we grasped the mostly implicit rules and expectations that govern speech and behavior in our culture and society, the world felt overwhelmingly difficult to fathom. In the safety of the coaching relationships I create with my clients, they often allow quite young versions of themselves to emerge. As we explore especially difficult moments that trigger "fallback," my queer clients often get in touch with parts of themselves that might still believe major defensive maneuvers are needed to keep them safe.

In the **Self-Protective Opportunist** stage of human development,[102] which immediately precedes the conventional stages starting with the **Conformist**, the person emerges "out of total dependence on the care of others."[103] The two stage names of "**Self-Protective**" and "**Opportunist**" reflect various expressions of this form of mind "depending on the individual's physical power and temperament." When generally feeling weaker, the person shows up in **Self-Protective** mode, and when they sense a gain to be had, in **Opportunist** mode. For the middle-schooler, teenager, or adult who knows or senses his sexual difference and operates from this stage of development, the dangers of the straight world loom large. Through the slights, insults, or bullying directed against him, he hones his skills at risk calculation, evasive maneuvers, and perhaps also some dirty tricks. Sensing some of the complexity of life, he feels overwhelmed and "in over his head" with almost any situation in the adult world. Researcher Cook-Greuter notes that people in this stage often "get into trouble."[104]

Leading adult development expert Robert Kegan based his book *In Over Our Heads: The Mental Demands of Modern Life* (1994) on the premise that life in contemporary society demands of adults the sense-making of at least a **Self-Authoring** form of mind. Encountering these demands from a **Self-Protective** or **Opportunist** mindset creates overwhelm and confusion for anyone, including the (young) queer person whose developmental experience we are now focusing on. Increased awareness of our distinctiveness as a person, including our gayness and queerness, emerges concurrently with greater experience of the threats and difficulties posed by other people and institutions, whose workings remain generally mysterious and incomprehensible to us when operating from this form of mind.

Some gay kids—far too many—find themselves unable to withstand the attacks that come at them. Lacking sufficient support or empathetic understanding, they see no way out of the conundrum their life becomes. They kill themselves. Regarding the epidemic of LGBTQ+ teen suicide from a developmental perspective, we can appreciate the precarity of queer youth in **Self-Protective Opportunist** mind. Like all children, they have vital needs for safety, acceptance, and love, yet bullying communicates to queer kids that they do not belong, are not safe, and are not welcome. It tells them they differ so profoundly from the norm that they deserve pain and hurt. Bullying tells them that they deserve to die.

The It Gets Better Project founded in 2010 by Dan Savage and his husband Terry Miller aims to support LGBTQ+ kids so that they don't resort to suicide, but rather wait out the most trying travails of their youth and stay in the land of the living. Another benevolent organization, The Trevor Project, offers a suicide hotline for LGBTQ+ youth, with trained volunteers at the ready to talk kids down from the ledge of despairing self-destruction.

The It Gets Better Project aims to speak to children and teens in such a situation. As part of this project, more than 70,000 people have now told their story of how "it gets better." Ft. Worth, Texas City Councilman Joel Burns told his story of being bullied as a "skinny, lanky, awkward" thirteen-year-old. Older kids cornered him and told him he was a faggot and that he should die and go to hell where he belonged. "Ashamed, humiliated, and confused," teenage Burns felt like his secret had gotten out. Burns became so choked up during the city council meeting during which he told his story that he couldn't bear to read aloud the lines he wrote about his temptation to kill himself at that age. But showing the photos and saying the names of several middle schoolers and teenagers who had recently hanged or shot themselves, Burns mustered the strength to tell his story and how, over the years, it got better for him as a gay man. Through YouTube more than three million people viewed the video of Burns telling his story, including later highlights of his life, such as the moment on a West Texas hilltop when he proposed marriage to his now husband.

Filmmakers James Lecesne, Peggy Rajski, and Randy Stone founded The Trevor Project before their Academy Award-winning short film *Trevor* aired on HBO in 1998. In the movie, the fictive title character finds himself at thirteen years old in 1981 obsessed with two things: Diana Ross and his best friend Pinky Faraday. Spurned by Pinky and his other friends at school, Trevor looks to his parents for attention and understanding but gets neither. Vying for his mom and dad's attention, he melodramatically feigns his own death over and over, playing dead before their eyes

> in the yard, the bathtub, and the living room. He is foiled both in his attempt to take a bus to San Francisco and to take his life by popping aspirin while lip syncing Diana Ross's part in her duet "Endless Love" with Lionel Richie. A dramedy, *Trevor* approaches the gravely serious topic of teen suicide with tenderness and a highly effective sense of humor. We come to feel delight in Trevor's campy verve and compassion for his problems which seem to him unresolvable. Knowing that some viewers might find themselves in similar circumstances, the filmmakers created what became the first twenty-four-hour suicide prevention helpline for LGBTQ+ youth in the United States. Today with dozens of staff, hundreds of volunteers, and millions of dollars in funding, The Trevor Project offers a range of crisis and suicide intervention and prevention services for LGBTQ+ young people under the age of twenty-five.

With the queer superpower of **Chameleonic Passing**, we blend into the surround until "It Gets Better." The downside of protecting ourselves in this way is not being seen or known for who we are. Indeed, long after our middle or high school years, many of us keep masking with elaborate personas in an attempt to create psychological safety. From my personal and professional experiences, I've come to believe that a profound experience of *not being seen* characterizes the lives of LGBTQ+ people. This experience of not being seen occurs not only in society at large but also when with other gay and queer people. The personas we present provide protection from threats, but also become barriers to intimacy. This dynamic accounts in part for "the epidemic of gay loneliness" described by Michael

Hobbes in his March 2, 2017, *Huffington Post* article, "Together Alone."[105]

Those of us who don't kill ourselves learn to mask and defend. We devise shields and cloaks to disguise who we are, seeking safety in inauthenticity. When honed and developed, these survival skills allow us as LGBTQ+ kids to pass as straight. We become chameleons, shapeshifters who adapt our appearance and behavior so as to play by the rules of the games in which we find ourselves trapped. We strive to move in the world invisibly, unnoticed as distinct or different. We fit in. We playact. Virtuoso actors trained only by our instincts and our powers of observation and imitation, we mesh into the scene. Our true selves fade into invisibility. We disappear.

Masking the true self they are still discovering, gay and queer kids who develop the **Chameleonic Passing** superpower dissimulate so effectively that many people in our lives cannot see us for who we are. Thus, while surviving and getting some of our most basic needs met through **Chameleonic Passing**, those LGBTQ+ kids who grow this superpower sidestep their own deeper needs to be seen and known. Their inventive and creative means to survive through invisibility chokes off their sense of self from the oxygen and nourishment they need to develop further.

As awareness and complexity develop, people operating from **Self-Protective** or **Opportunist** mind gradually gain in understanding that other people have wants of their own. We start to see others as competitors in this "zero-sum" game of life. *It's me against the world.* If LGBTQ+ kids remain primarily in a **Self-Protective** or **Opportunist** form of mind later into adolescence or even adulthood, they experience the world as so dangerous and threatening that they can develop another queer superpower, the **Shield of Hypervigilance**. They create for themselves an early alert system that can sense any whiff of a predator or opponent who might overpower them. This hypervigilant early alert system erects antennae to take in any possible signal of threat so that evasive maneuvers or pre-emptive attacks can be undertaken. We can recognize this hypervigilance as a step towards developing **Gaydar**.

In Greek mythology, Perseus approaches snake-haired Medusa by regarding her through her reflection in his shield. Seeing her directly turned anyone into stone. Reflecting on this mythological moment of Perseus stalking Medusa, we can grasp both the shadow side of the **Shield of Hypervigilance** and the potency of its power for keeping its possessor safe. With this queer superpower we look at the world through its somewhat warped reflection on the shield we have fashioned. We cannot and do not see reality directly or as it is. Rather, we see a version of reality that is limited and determined by our fears and the protective barrier we hold up around us, the **Shield of Hypervigilance**. Imagining danger where it might actually be safe, we thus move through the world fearing some version of the monsters under the bed and in the closet. All these threats keep us from resting soundly and recharging.

Fragility characterizes those adults who go no further than **Self-Protective Opportunist** mind. Not (yet) reaching **Socialized** mind, these individuals prowl around the edges of society, sniffing out opportunities to advance their self-interest. They often make trouble and get in trouble. They snatch "goodies" whenever they can. They sneak. They troll. They flex and boast. Unable to manage adult life in society, they find some other way to get the structure and protection that they need to survive. They may leave mainstream society by being institutionalized in an asylum or a prison. Or they may somehow operate on the margins of society. In urban settings, they may join a street gang or work in a brothel. In rural settings, they may be taken in by a farm or ranch family to live and work on the grounds in a circumscribed world. **Self-Protective Opportunist** teens and adults are prone to abuse. If unlucky enough to be taken in by the wrong people, they can fall victim to trafficking or other forms of exploitation.

Those relatively few adults who primarily operate from a **Self-Protective Opportunist** form of mind would, I imagine, never find their way to reading a book such as this one. I address this early developmental stage in a book focused on adult development because, as I have already emphasized, these younger parts of ourselves are still in there and can still take charge of us at times. Not only can we unearth them through inner expeditions of introspection and exploration, but sometimes we regress suddenly. For many LGBTQ+ people, experiences of queer trauma bring forth this earlier, smaller version of ourselves who needs either to focus entirely on protecting ourselves from the world or to grab whatever small advantage we can gain, by hook or by crook. In the work I do with my clients individually and in small groups, such as in the Heroes Journey program, we develop their use of the queer superpower of **No One Left Behind** so that they can rescue versions of themselves who still cower in closets or still flex for the fight in some long-ago battle scene. We show up with compassion for those parts of them standing ever still with their **Shields of Hypervigilance** raised. We recover and release into the freedom of authenticity those parts of them who still shapeshift to hide ingeniously using **Chameleonic Passing**. Our embrace of the queer superpower of **No One Left Behind** requires repeated returning to the pre-conventional self for exploration, compassion, and nurturing.

- *How does the queer superpower of **Chameleonic Passing** apply to your life?*
- *Where do you notice yourself holding up a **Shield of Hypervigilance**?*

"Itsasecretia"

- *When reading this section, look inside yourself to locate that **Self-Protective Opportunist** part of you and let that part of yourself resonate with whatever in my story or explication touches you.*
- *Notice the self-judging recriminations, the vaunting boasts, or whatever else comes up in yourself.*
- *See if you can locate your multiple selves, notice your affective attitudes about these younger inner layers of yourself, and see whether you can come to know these layers with compassion and appreciation, as well as recognition of their limitations.*

One June evening on Grindr I first encountered the person who I came to know as "Ig" (who uses the pronouns they-them-theirs). I was cooking dinner and listening to NPR, my iPhone sitting on the kitchen counter next to me with the gay dating app open. A portal into connecting with other gay men, for me Grindr functions like a virtual gay bar where I can spend downtime socializing and flirting. Ig's first missive was a nude photo of themself from behind, kneeling with ass up and head down—a version of what in yoga is called "child's pose." Completely shorn and shaved, their girthy uncut dick and big balls hanging down between two muscular legs. Along with the photo, Ig sent three messages in quick succession:

"Hi gen? / Well that's not necessary / U can fuck me now."

My response back was the emoji of a face with a scrunched-up face and a monocle, conveying something along the lines of "Huh?!" They re-offered the deal:

"I just need money a lil / U host now?"

Something about this person, their profile, and their confusion caught my attention. Using "gen" (short for "generous"), they were using Grindr lingo to ask about my willingness to give money in exchange for sex. Ig's opening messages thus placed our exchange in the territory of prostitution. Sex workers come across a Grindr feed somewhat regularly, though escort services are explicitly prohibited by the app's guidelines. I typically block them immediately, but this time, I wrote back:

"I found you interesting / Not looking for a transaction–sexual or financial."

From there we engaged in an intermittent back-and-forth exchange of messages for maybe a half hour, as I continued to prepare dinner. I asked questions like whereabouts in NYC Ig lived and what they had studied. From the Slavic look I saw in the face pics of their profile and their chosen name, which I figured might be short for Igor, I supposed Ig to be from Russia or maybe Poland. To the question about studies, Ig replied that they were an artist and fashion designer, but had also studied translation between their native language and English. At this self-revelation, Ig peremptorily foreclosed any inquiry into their native land.

"Don't ask me where I'm from / That's the worst thing to ask someone"

The way they put it was so defensive that I could tell that for Ig this topic held special significance and sensitivity. Vigilantly fending off questions that might reactivate the pain of their home, Ig preemptively raised shields of privacy.

Here I found another hint that the person on the other side of this chat was different from the men I typically encountered on Grindr. Ig intrigued me. I imagined great travails and longings underneath these many maneuvers. Ig wanted sex from me, seemed puzzled when I rebuffed the offer, and then showed a willingness to stay engaged when I expressed my interest in them.

"I'm asking these questions because I want to know you for who you are," I wrote.

Perhaps Ig found me as oddly intriguing as I found them.

As I tasted the tomato sauce I was making, I found myself piecing together my own imagined version of Ig's backstory and understory. Their forceful insistence that I not ask where they were from brought my attention precisely to that question. They are Russian, I speculated. Unusually beautiful and with a high IQ, maybe Ig grew up in some small or medium-sized Russian city, where virulent homophobia combined with physical and sexual abuse from older boys or men to cause Ig profound suffering. Artistic expression and linguistic inquiry might have given Ig creative channels through which to escape the world into which they were born. Art and language studies also perhaps allowed Ig to cultivate competence and independent mindedness, plus vent and express their powerful feelings.

I projected my own childhood experiences onto him as a screen.

Half consciously referencing my mother's "great escape" from my dad, with my sister and me in tow, I imagined Ig's hurts and resentments festering and intensifying. I wondered how long they were scrimping, saving, plotting, and planning to get away, get safe, start anew. Perhaps they used college to plot a **Great Escape**—out of Russia, away from abuse, far from betrayers, into a place where Igor could become Ig. The gifted and beautiful queer Russian boy could change his pronouns to they-them-theirs, wear dresses when and if they fancied, and sever ties to the land of their birth. Ig escaped to survive. In New York City, thanks to their striking Slavic face, large penis, and smooth muscular body, Ig must have found enticing opportunities, I imagined. Ravenous men must have offered Ig money for sex, and with such sharp street smarts, Ig swiftly grasped what such offers made possible—rent, tuition, food, survival, independence.

Ig's social media feed consisted entirely of images of their own art, which was psychedelic and complex—much of it political, with intertwining themes of antifascism, for Black Lives Matter, and against anyone asking anyone "Where are You From?" This last theme fascinated me, given how Ig had brought up this question so forcefully and preemptively in our chat. We continued to chat on Grindr from time to time. One image they posted some months after our first chat had a red plaid cloth background, with green words in all caps, asking and answering a riddle:

WHERE

FROM?

ITSASECRETIA

A hand holds a revolver in the foreground. From the center of "O" in "FROM," a stream of blood spurts, coming out of a fiery hole, presumably the perforation of a fired bullet. Ig's commentary reads "I always answer this question with the question 'It's a secret' and perpetrator always asks again 'Where is that?'—as they expect me to say the name of the country. So my country is Itsasecretia."

A week before the plaid "ITSASECRETIA" post, Ig made another couple of posts on this theme.

Against question "Where are you from?" If you hear immigrants' accents first thing you do is harass them with this irrelevant and very personal question. Like a new souvenir it's interesting to pull information from that person like it's an object of your research. It might be triggering and reminding of trauma. #triggered #harassment #whereareyoufrom here

As I write this story of Ig, I wonder whether my reflections on our interactions or my interpretations of their art would strike Ig as a triggering attack. Would they experience my wonderings about them as narrative violence? Wanting to treat this person and my memories of our interactions with great care and consideration for their dignity and their hurts, I'm giving them a fictionalized name and changing some details to produce a protective cloud. I take to heart Ig's request not to be treated like "an object of research." I hope not to trigger or re-traumatize anyone. I behold Ig with empathy and appreciation. Moreover, I recognize that my interest in them largely originates in my own experiences of childhood trauma.

The Great Escape

Whether the **Great Escape** entails boarding a bus for San Francisco, or, like Ig, emigrating across the globe, escaping for the sake of survival takes tremendous courage. Leaping over a chasm filled with doubts and fears, these courageous kids catch hold of safety—even if just by their fingernails—and claw their way up to clear ground. The **Great Escape** requires hope, the very opposite and antidote to despair. These kids hope for a time and a place where "it gets better."

In the shadow of this queer superpower, we can recognize the **Great Escape** in some cases as running to stand still. While physically separated from parents and other abusers, runaways far too often find themselves delivered into the hands of pimps and johns and madams who exploit these queer kids and abuse them all over again. Chums share their meth or their heroin as an offer of pleasurable relief. Gangs of vainglorious hoodlums, themselves runaways and rejects, take in the new kid and initiate him into their flexing, boasting, and ruthlessness. They tag neighborhood walls with spray paint and their bodies with tattoos. Too easily the **Great Escape** can catapult a fragile young person from one land of dangers and threats into another.

All of us escape at times, no matter our age. LGBTQ+ adults sometimes escape circumstances that pose discomfort or greater threats due to our sexual orientation and/or gender identity. The paradigmatic example of queer teens and young adults who run away from home fits other versions of the **Great Escape**. We move away from our hometown or home country, to depart from the social pressure or religious condemnation that batters us in our family of origin or native community. We might divorce our opposite-sex spouse and escape from a straight life into which social momentum had previously swept us.

- *What **Great Escapes**, if any, have you made in your life?*

The End of Eddy

- *To what degree did you witness, experience, or perpetrate bullying as a kid?*
- *What difficult childhood experiences do you find yourself repeatedly reliving as an adult?*

Before *Histoire de la violence*, Édouard Louis wrote another autobiographical novel, *En finir avec Eddy Belleguele* (2014), titled in English *The End of Eddy*.[106] It chronicles his early life in

Hallencourt, a poor working-class village of Picardy, a region in northern France. The book depicts the backstory and understory of the author's own **Great Escape**.

The pairing of this autofictional novel with his later work, *History of Violence* (2016) illustrates how the **Self-Protective Opportunist** form of mind can stay important into adulthood for gay and queer people. The young, relatively powerless, bullied gay kid remains powerfully and painfully present in his adult life, particularly in Édouard's experience of rape. The violence of Édouard's childhood in Hallencourt, where his birthname was Eddy Bellegueule, echoes in the violent rape, robbery, and near murder that he suffered as a young twentysomething in Paris.

Louis's writing of these novels seems to make part of a recovery from a suite of relational traumas, all suffered by the author at the hands of other men, all due to his being gay. His recovery from one trauma is intertwined with his recovery from the other. He was raped on Christmas Eve 2012, published *En finir avec Eddy Bellegueule* in 2014, and then *Histoire de la violence* in 2016.

In the two books, Édouard Louis retraces the cycle of violence, trauma, defense, and recovery. Indeed, *The End of Eddy* begins with a "history of violence" done to young Eddy, who cannot help but be an effeminate, pretty boy. As Louis makes sense in the two novels of repeated relational gay traumas, he focuses recurrently on his *gueule*—his face, his throat, and his original family name, Bellegueule, which literally means "pretty face." This identity imprisons and exposes the boy.

Author Édouard Louis thus returns again and again, through the language of his personal "history of violence," to the special site of his trauma, his *gueule*. The word in modern French means face and derives from the Latin *gula*, meaning throat. As we shall see, the *gueule* is a primary site of trauma on Eddy's/Édouard's body in the two novels. Tracking this word *gueule* illuminates a theme that runs through both novels, pointing to the persistent vulnerability, shame, and trauma which the **Self-Protective** boy continues to carry within Édouard as an adult. The thematic recurrence of this word *gueule* demonstrates just how tough it is to find "the end of Eddy" Belleg*ueule*. Our younger selves remain inside us, even as we grow more complex and capacious forms of mind.

Ready to read how this effeminate French pretty boy mustered queer superpowers to find his way to greater flourishing? Go to QueerFlourishing.com to download this and other *Queer Flourishing* bonus material.

Finding Flourishing for Our Self-Protective Opportunist Self

- *When and how does the **Self-Protective Opportunist** version of you show up in your life nowadays?*
- *How well do you respond to this younger part of yourself with compassion and care?*

In the **Self-Protective Opportunist** form of mind, flourishing looks like safety and security. The queer superpowers of **Chameleonic Passing**, the **Shield of Hypervigilance**, and the **Great Escape** help us find the safety we need so vitally. Besides the absence of harm, safety in this form of mind is understood as *getting what I want*. The greatest fear of someone in this mindset might see the prospect of not getting their basic physical needs met for food, shelter, clothing, and physical wellbeing as if it were murder. *They'll kill me!* The highest dream of someone in this mindset might imagine a world where they would not need to worry about safety or getting other basic needs met, thanks to them abiding in an impenetrable fortress or wielding an all-powerful weapon. In this developmental stage, a person's inner world is populated with dangers and evasive measures. Inner diversity and inclusion entail threats to personal safety and tools to mitigate harm. Living seems mostly about risks and rewards—pains and punishments or treats and pleasures. Learning to move successfully among these diverse features requires the mastery of tricks and hideouts, maneuvers and ruses, blocks and attacks. Above all, the **Self-Protective Opportunist** form of mind notices power and how it impacts getting needs met. *Will this power help or hinder me in getting me what I want?*

Like all earlier forms of mind, the **Self-Protective Opportunist** mindset persists into and throughout adulthood. It is not the exclusive territory of preteens, or any one group who faces dangers, such as runaways, gang members, or sex workers. All our lives, no matter how long ago we began operating from more expansive forms of mind, the **Self-Protective Opportunist** mind perdures within us. When in this mindset, we regard other people merely as a means of meeting our own needs. When they do, they are esteemed as "good." If not, they are demeaned as "bad." Within gay male sex culture some segments reflect a **Self-Protective Opportunist** mindset, such as when an anonymous Grindr "sex date" might end abruptly with a man saying after his climax, "Now that you've helped me get off, go finish on your own . . . or not, I don't really care."

As we encounter the **Self-Protective** or **Opportunist** within ourselves and others, we do well to be especially caring and cautious because they might be seeking advantage over us. Unbound by rules not enforced by power or force, people in this mindset can seem unpredictable to someone who respects and adheres to rules and expectations. At this stage, a person does not yet understand or bind themselves to the social contracts implicit in any society.

Loving someone in this stage requires caretaking. When encountering the **Self-Protective** or **Opportunist** self, if we can be careful—in the sense of "full of care"—then we might be able to create or convey the sense of safety needed to coax the **Self-Protective** or **Opportunist** mind to calm down and relax its habitual hypervigilance. The care we might helpfully offer could entail physical protection and comfort through meeting basic needs for food, water, clothes, warmth, space, movement, gentle touch, or shelter from harm. Other ways of helpfully taking care of such a person could entail more intangible elements. We can, for example, provide them with structure, routine, consistency, play, personal dignity, respect, due attention, companionship, and the permission just to be as they are.

For someone in **Self-Protective** or **Opportunist** mind, love might be understood as doing favors, giving goodies, making good on promises, or not making good on threats. At a deeper level, love in this developmental stage feels like the secure trust that *you won't harm me* and means putting down their guard and trusting they are safe with that person. When they calm down and feel safe, they can access inner resources such as curiosity, confidence, connectedness, clarity, creativity, and courage. They can take risks to explore and learn while staying within the bounds of security. They can begin to tune into others and start noticing how other people act, which may elicit curiosity about the social rules and expectations that often guide others' behavior.

In short, for someone in the **Self-Protective Opportunist** mindset, flourishing looks like lowering the defenses enough to be open to other people. That's the aliveness made possible by love at this developmental stage. Eventually, as they experience sufficient safety and reliably get their needs met, they can begin to feel a sense of common cause with others in certain social groups. They don't have to stay in the attitude of "Me against the world," but instead can find greater strength in numbers and move into the **Socialized** mindset of "Us versus them."

When we who generally operate from a more complex form of mind find our **Self-Protective Opportunist** self to be activated, we can profitably attend to that younger part of us with similar care. To regain access to more grown-up versions of ourselves, we first must take care of our basic needs for physical and psychological safety. We might feel under attack at those moments, either literally or figuratively. Fear might be driving us to desperation. Cognitive distortions like catastrophizing or self-punishing self-judgment might be making our lives needlessly difficult or dire. As we find our way back to self-regulation and a sense of safety, the **Self-Protective** or **Opportunist** parts of ourselves can calm down and stand back so that our more grown-up self can appropriately take care of those younger parts.

- *Reflecting on the material in the last couple of sections, what are you learning about your own **Self-Protective Opportunist Self**?*

No Longer Afraid of Our Shadow

- *What aspects or parts of yourself are you most hesitant to look at or even acknowledge?*

Very often I support highly accomplished gay, bi, and queer men as they leave an overheld **Achiever** stage and make their way through the wilderness of **Redefining**. As we find our feet with **No One Left Behind**, circling back and then returning to the present with greater access to more parts of ourselves retrieved and revivified, we intensify the magnitude of transformations of self that we have been going through all along. The repeated return to pieces and parcels of self that had been encased for the sake of surviving overwhelming difficulty feeds into an acceleration of the developmental process.

At some point, the shifting nature of reality and of our very self becomes something to treasure, even a reason for celebration. No longer do relativism or personal transformation result primarily in worry or anxiety, as is so often the case in **Redefining**; now we revel in the endless opportunities to learn. While in **Redefining** mind, we gained capacity to recognize the range of developmental stages and meaning-making mindsets, now our appreciation for each stage and mindset deepens. The permission we gave ourselves in **Redefining** mind to notice our inconsistencies and discrepancies now opens into a capacity for accepting, owning, and integrating the varying facets and disparate parts of ourselves.[107]

The persistent *coming apart* of the **Redefining** form of mind *comes back together* in a new more integrated self. This form of mind, called the **Self-Transforming** stage of development, feels like coming *home* to oneself.

> **Self-Transforming or Transforming:** Terms used to refer to a post-conventional developmental stage or mindset that grounds itself in the ever-shifting dynamics growth, change, and development—within the Self and in systems. Moving further beyond convention, Self-Transforming mind sees more of its own multiplicity and internal contradictions, including more of its shadow sides, which previously were to be avoided. The developmental process within oneself accelerates and becomes an increasingly fascinating object of attention. See Glossary for further explanation.

As gratifying as this homecoming can feel, new developmental challenges arise as we move into a **Self-Transforming** form of mind. We find fewer peers. *Who can I now relate to? Who can relate to me?* In this stage, we can genuinely exercise deep compassion for others, whether they be in fallback to much earlier versions of themselves or stretching into any variety of **Self-Authoring**. But few others can put themselves in our shoes and see the complexity of the world that we can now see.

In my work with clients who operate primarily from a **Self-Transforming** form of mind, I offer this companionship. I enter their world, as best I can. In finding solidarity with me or other gay, bi, and queer men in a cohort of Heroes Journey, such clients gain fortitude and resilience for continuing their beautiful work of reclaiming ever more of themselves, using the **No One Left Behind** superpower and other kinds of shadow work. To grow them as leaders, I help my clients who operate from this form of mind to flex their developmental range with greater agility. **Self-Transforming** leaders can easily get bored when their colleagues might approach a matter from **Expert** mind. Similarly, **Self-Transforming** leaders might not speak the language of goals and striving that their clients, supervisors, or direct reports in an **Achiever** mindset might need to hear.

From the **Self-Transforming** form of mind, we see reality through the lenses of personal transformation, the multiplicity of selves, and the interpenetration of selves and systems.[108] The process of development increasingly fascinates us and itself becomes an object of focus more than ever before. As a result, we can all too easily stay in this realm while missing the concerns of those around us who do not see what we see. As developmental thinking becomes integrated with our cognition, the mysterious and wonderful process of *self-actualization* takes center stage.[109] No longer do we relentlessly pursue the goal of becoming *the very best* we can be, as we did when in **Achiever** mind, nor do we focus anymore on the profound questioning and cultural deprogramming of **Redefining** mind.

The ever-shifting dynamics of our own inner life become increasingly familiar and worthy of attention. In **Self-Transforming** mind, we allow ourselves to be surprised by ourselves, yet we are not threatened by the unpredictable elements that emerge from within us. We grow more comfortable with ambiguity and polarities.[110] Paradox and the very process of making sense of the most intractable dilemmas feel like especially valuable places to direct our energy.

Consciously working with our queer superpowers becomes increasingly possible from a **Self-Transforming** form of mind. From here, we can gain perspective on how each queer superpower has both tremendous heroic potential and significant shadow sides. Indeed, we come to appreciate queer superpowers as *gifts of the shadow*. In other words, we see how these treasures sprout up through the discarded parts of ourselves. As we work through what we had dismissed as rubbish, we turn it into rich fertile soil in which these superpowers take shape. Jung elaborated the idea of the shadow as always there, just behind and next to us, so easily ignored, an imp to chase, impossible to catch hold of, but necessary to grapple with if we are to journey to wholeness. With **No One Left Behind**, we develop "night vision" so as to see the imps in our own inner darkness without being blotted out by the bright personae which we more consciously bring to light.

Moreover, we can also see on a macro-level, how we and other LGBTQ+ people function in certain ways as a shadow for the rest of society. With our increased capacity to recognize self-in-system, we see how we can sometimes become for straight folks the scapegoats freighted with their unwanted baggage, which rightly belongs not to us but to them.

From **Self-Transforming** mind we can hold our considerable and ever proliferating insights and connections with an air of superiority. We can become so intent on growing, learning, changing, exploring, and expanding that we present ourselves as "exemplars of humanity."[111] Allowing even mistakes and failures to fuel the fire of self-fulfillment and personal transformation can lead to a "whitewashing tendency." The search for enlightenment or self-actualization can become the all-encompassing dream. People in **Self-Transforming** mind might hold as their greatest fear the possibility of not realizing their human potential, not self-actualizing, not reaching enlightenment. *What is life for, if I do not become all I can be?*

Sex may itself become a consciously developmental practice in this stage of development. We can increasingly hold both animalistic and spiritual aspects of erotic expression and sexual union with ourselves and others. We gain greater access to real-time attunement to what each ephemeral moment offers for the generation and exchange of erotic energy. The range of sexual possibilities proliferates even further than before, including the most conventional and nonconventional forms. Having sex and not having sex could even become equally interesting.

To take care of someone in **Self-Transforming** mind, we can give them space for the ebbs and flows of their unfolding inner processes, the contractions and expansions, the dark and the light. We can support and encourage them as they cycle through ongoing evolutions of their being. We can hold space for them, like a womb, in which they can undo themselves and knit themselves back together again. Such a womb may well be how someone in **Self-Transforming** mind might conceive of love. Flourishing for **Self-Transforming** mind looks like healing, learning, and expanding toward wholeness. The highest dream might thus be something along the lines of *yearning for you to flourish so that I may flourish, and yearning for myself to flourish so that you may flourish. Queer flourishing for all!*

- *To what degree do you see your own superpowers (queer or otherwise) as gifts of the shadow?*
- *What might it look like for you to make sex a developmental practice in your own life?*

The Cycle Continues

- *What world events have most impacted your worldview or life choices?*
- *What instances of role reversal have you had with your parents? What about these situations most changed your sense of yourself?*

As I continued the therapeutic thawing, a gay version of myself increasingly came to stand together with the straight, heteronormative version. This second pass at growing up freed me profoundly. With this newfound freedom, I finally faced head-on my attraction to the Jesuits, the Society of Jesus. Since first meeting Jesuits while a student at Creighton Prep, I noticed a strong draw towards becoming one of them. Yet I knew I had important things to take care of before I could or should start that process. In high school, I knew I first needed to grow up, see the world, and gain a much greater sense of self-possession. *How could I give myself away to a life of service, if I did not yet enjoy genuine self-possession?* Life as a Jesuit would entail vows of poverty, chastity, and obedience. To prepare for even considering such perpetual promises, I knew that I needed first to explore sexual life. Otherwise, how could I in good conscience sign up for celibacy? The profoundly loving relationship with Carly over so many years and the new liberating experiments and explorations of gay life felt like sufficient exploration of romantic possibilities to free me to face the prospect of starting a life of celibacy.

In the winter of 2001, I began the process of formally applying for the Jesuit novitiate—a period when I would be a novice in the religious order. I've been quoting passages from a spiritual autobiography that I wrote as part of my application process. Entitled "Beginnings," the essay adopts features of Augustine's voice and style in the *Confessions*, which I knew as the first autobiography, the book which formed a genre of Western literature. Imitating Augustine, I address God directly, in second-person discourse, as he lays bare intimate thoughts, feelings, temptations, and triumphs throughout his life.

I

What, Lord, can I write about your workings in my life? What in my life is not your work? But a complete record of the mysteries of your urgings, proddings, and curbings is more than I can remember. Writing from now is all I can muster.

How did I get here to this cube on a floor of corporate America? What is the shape of my life? How was it that you brought me home to the same zip code in which I grew up? Is allusion to Jim Croce's "All My Life's a Circle" fitting? Or to Sisyphus? Or, my Lord, are your ways more mysterious and meaningful? In faith I see your workings; of myself alone I come up with only doubts, anxieties, fears, and disappointments. How fragile I am and how fitful! Fraught with weakness, apt to despair, wounded by disappointments, and sometimes paralyzed by fear, I am nothing like I once thought—powerful with potential, accelerated in growth, exceptional in outlook. I am but a man: my gifts are my wounds; my talents avail me nothing. For what good are my strengths if they lure me away from you?...

With the following description of the previous year of my life in Omaha, I depicted the immediate context of my writing that spiritual autobiography:

Now

I come before you now, O Lord, broken and yet calm. Having been back home in Omaha for a full year, I have tended my wounds and laid bare my scars. No longer are there such dark corners of my inner landscape where I tremble to gaze. This has been a year of inner work, with the help of an able therapist, and relational work with so many of the key figures in my life. Here I have found new beginnings to the ordering of my soul.

The most striking relational development is the re-entry of my father into my life. His absence, his pained way of life and disturbed personality have caused such hurt to me, my sister, and all of the family we share with him. But in this year, 2001, you used the twin crises of his uncle's and his father's deaths in addition to his own heart attack to bring him back not only to Carrie and me, but to all of his extended family. The day before Uncle Charlie's wake was a special time for Carrie and me to share about how, from childhood to young adulthood, we had dealt with having a father who was severely mentally ill and absent yet close by. We prepared each other to encounter our father at his uncle's funeral—an encounter, which Dad referred to last weekend as an 'ambush' at the wake. On that one Sunday afternoon of sharing and crying and laughing, she and I came a long way toward remembering that our journey was shared and that our burdens were not just our own to bear in isolation. Just so, several months later, when Dad himself was near death, in the ICU, his three siblings, two parents, Carrie and I sat around a patio table and began more intently to share the pain Fred's sickness had caused each of us and to bear together the burdens of his failings. The despair and tortured sense of loss we each had experienced over the last 25 years suddenly became much more of a shared burden, borne on the strength of the love bonds between us. For me, Lord, those 6 weeks when Dad was in intensive care were a special time of healing. I found myself the adult family member most able to deal with many of the issues that came up, from the legal and financial decisions to the communication and coordination demands. How perverse to become a caretaker at age 26 of a father who had never parented me! And yet how necessary were the nitty-gritty tasks for me to find ways to incarnate my frustrated filial love for him....

This year in Omaha has been a time of convalescence for myself as well. The only novel I read this year was *The Magic Mountain*, and, like Hans Castorp, I have taken great care of myself this last year, in hope of a cure. The passage of this period of a year has been extraordinarily slow, though not because the time was unfilled. Unlike Castorp's long slow passive convalescence at the mountain sanatorium high above and removed from the world, this time for me has been quite active and thoroughly in the world. In fact, what I have been removed from this year have been the academy and the monastery. While focusing first on my project of inner excavation and second on enlivening my relational life, I have been living the typical adult life of the society in which I grew up. Eight to five, office, car, commute, dry cleaning, paydays, boss, desk, routine. Somehow living this lifestyle if only for a year has been as necessary as the more daring or unusual inner and outer moves of my life.

Following that year of living the adult American life that my world had presented as the norm, I left it. I quit the job and moved out of my downtown Omaha apartment. I made vocational discernment about whether to become a Jesuit my top priority and full-time occupation. It felt like a risk, at once exciting and scary. Like when I left Boston for Cairo, I was once again giving up solid ground and leaping into the unknown. I remember feeling as if I were jumping off a springboard without seeing what abyss I was diving into. That image of flying and falling filled my dreams and waking fantasies. The Jesuit novitiate would take in a new group of novices each September, so I had almost a full year to float and flutter.

In strange ways I cannot fully understand, the catastrophe of 9/11 contributed to the courage I needed to make that leap of faith. Because of my deep personal ties to the Arab world, 9/11 seemed to raise the stakes of my own life. I knew I was already something of a bridge between the worlds I had inhabited. *If not me, then who?* Like any visceral experience of death, 9/11 highlighted how ephemeral life is. *If not now, then when?* In the immediate aftermath of 9/11, I felt a stronger impetus to meet my fate, to follow my course, to risk my life in order to gain my life. Finally facing my attraction to Jesuit life now felt urgent and timely.

But besides 9/11, more personal encounters with death also shook my world and gave me back a larger sense of agency in my own life. Grandpa Longo died the November after 9/11, and I lived with Grandma for the year after she was widowed. We comforted each other as we each wondered what life would bring us next. His death, at 88, turned her world upside down. From me, his death removed from my life the one man who had steadily been in my life from its beginning. Imperfect as he was, Grandpa's presence and his love stayed always available to me, in ways that no other man's was from the time I was born. Without his fierce and formidable love, I now had to look elsewhere for the unflinching support he always gave me.

Besides losing Grandpa, we had also nearly lost my dad, who spent the August before 9/11 in intensive care. He had had a massive heart attack and quadruple bypass surgery, followed by his lungs going into acute respiratory distress after decades of smoking. Dad was intubated and kept in a medically induced coma for a month with a respirator to aid his breathing. For fifty years, Grandpa had cared for patients in that same hospital where Dad now struggled to live. But now that the patient was his son Fred—my dad—who teetered on the verge of death just over the age of fifty, Grandpa could not bear it.

The emotional distress of that crisis brought to a climax a sequence of so many other crises in my dad's life which Grandpa and Grandma had weathered, along with the rest of us. I took the lead in managing Dad's healthcare. Convening calls with his sister, my Aunt Marilyn, and his two brothers, my Uncle Joe and my Uncle Chuck, who were both physicians themselves, but living in Arizona and California, I would gather perspectives and questions to bring to Dad's care team. Dad survived, though his heart endured massive damage.

He had no health insurance and virtually no assets to pay for the six weeks in the hospital. While he was comatose, I worked with the hospital's finance office to understand how to take care of his bills. They recommended enrolling him in Medicaid and having him declare bankruptcy, which we did. Though I bore gargantuan burdens that month, never had it been easier to love my dad. The strains on my capacities for stress, communication, decision-making, and emotional duress did not compare to the hardships of growing up as Fred's son. In the midst of that crisis, I saw clearly that I had never in my life done anything as important.

That month had a redemptive quality to it. Perhaps on some spiritual plane, Fred spent that comatose month in purgatory. Whatever transpired in his brain chemistry or in his soul, when Fred returned to the land of the living, he returned to himself in other, more profound ways. He found much atonement. In the weeks that followed his recovery, he showed up with the humor, charm, affection, and infectiously roaring laugh that his parents, siblings, cousins, nephews, and nieces all remembered. At the family gatherings for Grandpa's funeral, they all marveled and cried tears of joy, "The old Fred is back!" I had only ever partially glimpsed that "old Fred," the charismatic, affable, and impish young man he had once been. Still, I joined my older relatives in celebrating Fred's return.

The sum of these events, including both personal and political crises, somehow freed me to move forward in my life. I felt serenely determined to discern my path. The draw of Jesuit life had dogged me for years. Time to sort it out!

To help inform my discernment, I returned to my former high school as a volunteer, called in Jesuit parlance a *donné*. The Jesuit community who lived in a part of the school building gave me my own room in their residence and free rein to live there and share in their community meals and Masses, to whatever degree I wished. I directed a retreat and contributed to some French and Theology classes for the high school. Though I used my room in the Jesuit residence for afternoon naps, I never spent the night there. Even after joining for Mass and dinner with the twenty or so Jesuits who lived there, I would make my way from the school to my grandparents' home, as I had done so often when a teenager.

Larry Gillick, SJ, my spiritual director during this period, would listen, ask questions, reflect what he heard, and sometimes share something from his own life. I had known Fr. Gillick since being a student at Creighton Prep. Blind from a young age, he used his formidable powers of insight and empathy to help me see. Many Jesuits specialize in discernment and spiritual direction. Their founder, St. Ignatius of Loyola had written a handbook called *The Spiritual Exercises* for Jesuits to use in helping other people (and each other) to discern the workings of God in their lives. Ignatius gives the spiritual director guidance on how to help people sift through their feelings, thoughts, impulses, fantasies, and attractions, to discern which come from God and which come from the Adversary, Satan.

Almost as soon as I stepped into life as a *donné*, I became smitten with someone I met through friends at a bar downtown. In another soft start to living a **Double Life**, I started dating him. In my regular meetings with Fr. Gillick for spiritual direction, I opened up about this relationship and everything else going on in my life. This included how it felt being welcomed into the Jesuit community at Prep, contributing to the work of the school, leaving my office job—everything. I also continued my weekly sessions with Dr. Skulsky through it all. After several months, I recognized how much I was enjoying time with my boyfriend, while my doubts about fitting into Jesuit life persisted and strengthened. As I came to terms with where my discernment was leading me, Fr. Gillick said to me, with great compassion and wisdom, "You need to be loved more, Nick."

By the end of the spring semester, I ended my application process. The Spirit of God seemed to be calling me not to life in the Jesuits, but to a different kind of life loving men. Within a couple of weeks after withdrawing my application to the Jesuits, my boyfriend and I broke up. I realized that my attraction to him, though genuine, had above all served to clarify my deepest needs and desires—my vocation. Love worked through our relationship to divert me from the path of religious life.

The discernment, however, continued in different forms. I returned to corporate life, finding a fantastic job that brought me much learning and made good use of much of who I had become. As the Middle East business development manager for Valmont, the largest agricultural irrigation company in the world, I spent half my time in the Middle East—Saudi Arabia, Dubai, and Egypt—working with colleagues, key clients, and local partners. The professionalization I had gained from my previous job served me in this new one, where I had much greater responsibility and leeway for innovative initiatives. I also relished the mentorship of two men, my immediate boss and another executive, who brought brilliance, grace, and deep integrity to our shared work, which focused on growing more food with less water.

I threw myself into this work wholeheartedly and found great meaning in our mission to alleviate hunger and water scarcity through efficient irrigation technology. Indeed, I forged my own vision to contribute to this mission through creating more conversation and collaboration between Valmont and both governmental and non-governmental actors. Though much distrust impeded relationships between the private, public, and non-profit sectors, I saw potential to move forward together, if each party could listen and learn more from the others. This personal vision culminated in my writing a white paper to use in those conversations and to present in Japan at the World Water Forum.

Despite all the personal expansion through exposure, learning, mentorship, and opportunities for leadership at Valmont, I eventually reached a point where I could see that my future lay elsewhere. My contributions to the post-9/11 world would not focus on water or agriculture. Once again, I prepared to leap into the unknown. This journal entry, written on a Lufthansa flight to Cairo, portrays how that moment in my development looked and felt as I was living it:

15 July 2003
LH 594 One hour from Cairo

Reading Po Bronson's *What Should I Do With my Life,* along with a last-minute phone conversation with Bill L. on my way out of Chicago, has calmed down the turmoil in me quite a bit. I'm still scared about quitting my job and building some space into my life to read, play, pray, think, exercise, and love. What's scary is leaving off the respectable for a time– not having an ambitious answer to the 'And What Do You Do?' question that will impress all hearers. In fact, it's clear that only a few people in my life will approve of or understand the value of taking some time in my 20s to *be* more and *do* less. My heart has cracked up/ cracked open in so many ways these last 2½ years in Omaha. I have fallen deeply in love; I have felt deeply betrayed, I have recognized/ let up the pain from my experience of family as broken & wounded. I have been utterly present to my grandfather in his death & to my grandmother in her grief. I have gotten closer to each of my parents and then seen the limits of my relationships with them. I have learned to know my wincing, desperate need for the unconditional love that neither of them has been able to give me. I have learned how different, how special, how odd, how intense, how wanting I am. I have found strength and ability in me that I never knew I had during the same period when I have come to know lovingly my great weakness. I am on my way to becoming compassionate and understanding with myself, so that I can be compassionate and understanding with others....

These 15 months at Valmont have been good–very good. Rich & Bob have been such good mentors to me, and I have seen myself succeed in a business environment. I have seen myself make a major contribution in a core business function–marketing, and I have seen my passion for [economic] development & for participating in the larger international community pull and push along my company into seeing with wider eyes its place in the world. For most of the year, I had a spring in my step as I got out of bed every morning & even got a speeding ticket once at 7AM because I was so excited to get to work!

But I have also seen that the greatest part of the joy of this job has been learning the process of leadership in business and the collaboration with outstanding people like Terry Rahe & Rich Berkland. Writing the research paper on "Water Scarcity & Modern Irrigation" was also a joy–the intellectual process of learning a new field, writing about a vital issue for the world, and elucidating how the technology of my company could make an important contribution to solve this problem.

My reason for coming home to Omaha, though, was not for Valmont, but for me. As Providence had it, I re-entered the life of my family at a crucial time. My availability to manage the crisis of my dad's heart attack and to support Grandma in the first year of her widowhood made this whole turn in life worthwhile.

These two things are now among my proudest accomplishments. I have healed the wounds of my childhood to the extent they can be healed for now. The pain from my own wounds and the collective wounds of our little family is now a conscious part of every cell of my being. That pain is now no mystery to me. Like the Classical Greek statue of the woman gazing at the thorn in her foot, I have lovingly & compassionately gazed at my wounds, cleaned them out, & come to understand them. My wounds, though much healed, are still there and always will be. They still fascinate me, though I am much less self-absorbed than I used to be. Most important, I am beginning to find the strength to grow new flesh in those wounded areas. I am finding the courage to fall in love & to be loved. I am beginning to find a glimmer of faith in myself to follow my dreams, to live my life well, dance to the beat of my own drum, to sing my song.

The image of attending to my wounds gives another way to regard the work of the **No One Left Behind** superpower. I gazed at those wounds with compassion, cleaned out whatever debris or infection festered inside, and began growing new tissue over those areas of puncture and hurt.

Enlivened by all the risk-taking, experimenting, healing, and growing I had done in Omaha for the three years I lived there, I once again left corporate America and dropped out of mainstream life. This time I was not heading off for service and adventure in Egypt or any other a far-off land, nor putting myself on track for ordination and life in a religious community.

Instead, I honored my developmental process by simply creating space and giving myself time. What Gretchen Schmelzer calls Consolidation, I called a personal sabbatical. Having worked so damned hard for so many years, I gave myself time to pause, rest, and play. The overdrive of the overachieving version of myself had served its purposes. Endeavoring both to compensate and escape, my intense, hard-charging Self had consumed my teenage years and almost all of my 20s. Even as a younger kid, I had had to handle too much. I deserved dilation, the easy expansion of *otium*, the Latin word for leisure and play that I had learned from reading Augustine.

I packed up and moved to Seattle to reflect, regroup, discern, and decide what was next, and who to be in the post-9/11 world. *What does this moment require of me? Where lies fulfillment? What iterations of myself might come next? How might my becoming myself be in service of others?* I established one organizing principle for the year before me: I shall do nothing in this year that changes my resumé! No new accomplishments, no new credentials. I had not played enough, and now my 20s were drawing to a close. It was time to put myself in a space of calm openness and utterly unambitious learning to allow myself to find joy and beauty in the mere experience of becoming.

- *For what life decisions have you undertaken the most serious and intentional process of discernment to find your path forward?*
- *What discoveries from those periods of discernment have had enduring value for you?*

CONCLUSION:

Languishing, the Diminishment of Love That Deadens

Since Covid, languishing often feels closer at hand than flourishing. I don't mean depression, that paralyzing despondence of bewildering emptiness, but languishing, the grim gritty gray, dull and distracted, mediocre way of living. We feel down nowadays, perhaps because our worst collective memories from the 1960s, 70s, 80s, and 90s seem to be recurring: Inflation, invasions, and demagogues on the rise; viruses mutating and spreading, killing millions and terrifying millions more; the earth's ecosystems deteriorating under the strain of humanity. The world even faces the prospect of nuclear arms attacks.

A year into the pandemic, organizational psychologist Adam Grant published a piece in the *New York Times* which locates languishing as a blah mid-point between depression and flourishing.[112] "In psychology, we think about mental health on a spectrum from depression to flourishing. Flourishing is the peak of well-being: You have a strong sense of meaning, mastery and mattering to others. Depression is the valley of ill-being: You feel despondent, drained and worthless."¹¹³ From a mental health perspective, flourishing is the presence of mental health, languishing as its absence.¹¹⁴ In coining the term "languishing" some twenty years ago as a word to refer to the blank space between depression and flourishing, researcher Corey Keyes aimed to draw attention to the experience of "emptiness and stagnation" and those people who lead "a life of quiet despair."¹¹⁵ Since mental health professionals typically focus on curing illness more than building health, Grant calls languishing, "the neglected middle child of mental health."¹¹⁶ This "joyless and aimless" feeling, Grant declared "the dominant emotion of 2021."

Still now, languishing persists, a pandemic of souls. From my perspective, the persistent problem of languishing has to do with love. When bereft of love, we languish. If we regard flourishing as the aliveness made possible by love, languishing refers to a human diminishment, a deadness of the soul that occurs when we are starved for love.

Queer Ghosting

Bringing LGBTQ+ perspectives to this broader phenomenon of languishing, I see the outlines of specifically queer varieties of languishing, which seem akin to what has become known in popular culture as "ghosting." Commonly used to name the unexpected communications blackout following a first date, ghosting evokes confusion, self-doubt, sadness, and loss. *What happened? Where did he go? What spooked him? Did I do something wrong? I thought things were going so well. I liked him. We had such meaningful conversations, so many laughs, such tender caresses. How could he just disappear on me?* Yet the unreturned messages eventually cannot be mistaken for oversights.

Queer artist Colin J. Radcliffe (Instagram handle @colin-memaybe) has represented ghosting in ceramic glaze sculptures that liken it to death. In his 2020 piece, "You Ghosted Me," Radcliffe depicts a humanoid ghost figure holding his erect penis, in cotton candy pink, with a scrotum chromatically evoking the phrase "blue balls." The figure is lying on grass in front of a gray tombstone topped by the *Memento mori* trope of a winged skull, with the following inscription:

YOU

GHOSTED ME

TODAY–???

Another piece, made in 2021, titled "Respect the Dead, MOVE ON" depicts a similar figure with human arms, legs, penis, and scrotum but a ghost torso and face, with sad eyes and a blue New York Yankees baseball cap. The ghosted figure holds a chocolate chip cookie, and leans on a gray tombstone, inscribed with these words:

SORRY

I didn't answer

…

I just need

more time

These sculptures brilliantly capture the effects of ghosting on both parties. Ghosting deadens us, whether we are the ones doing the ghosting or the ones being ghosted. The one who does the ghosting is nowhere to be found. Only a tombstone remains to mark the spot where his body once sat. The left lover has partially died in the wake of the departed. The upper half of his body has become a ghost, a phantom of his former self. Blue balls symbolize erotic anticipation without consummation, the unrealized sexual connection with the one who ghosted the other. The headstone leaves the one who pines for his absent love with an iconographic reminder: *Memento mori*, "Remember to die."

To Be or Not to Be

Flourish or languish, to be or not to be, that is the question. Deciding for flourishing means expanding our lives by choosing greater aliveness, which overflows to enliven those around us. Queer flourishing benefits all. By contrast, in ghosting all involved become less. We move towards annihilation. In annihil-ation, we head *ad nihil*, towards nil. Step by step we get closer to nothingness. Ghosting diminishes our presence, our existence, our very being. Just as queer superpowers such as the **Queen** or the **Best Little Kid** represent styles of flourishing, queer ghosting represents a style of languishing.

Ghosting avoids love. In ghosting, we lack the courage to have difficult conversations, face feelings, and take responsibility for our impact on others. In ghosting, we skip solving our personal problems and instead ignore them. We run away, disappear, put our heads under the covers and close our eyes to reality while holding the fantasy that the world thus goes away.

Ghosting takes a detour around the "swamplands of the soul," those difficult but eminently real parts of life like loneliness and grief, fear and anger.[117] Instead of increasing our life force by moving through these dismal swamps of life, we carefully avoid them. In ghosting, we apply a blindfold to our hearts, and pretend that the messiness of our lives and our relationships does not exist.

Ghosting is not restricted to the realm of romance. It happens in friendships too. Indeed, in the pandemic of languishing, I lost several of my closest friends to Covid. They didn't die, but they left my life. Some friends moved away, deciding that wherever they had retreated to for the pandemic felt like the place to stay. Others found comfort in socially isolating, and discarded as dross relationships they had nurtured for many years. Still others reprioritized and redirected their time and energy. Not all losses of friendship or love qualify as ghosting, of course. The greater the number of unreturned calls and texts and the less the explanation for the silence and absence, the more an exit counts as ghosting. Experiences of ghosting and other examples of queer languishing stand as cautionary tales to inform our quest for queer flourishing.

Greyson Ghosting

For over seven years, Greyson had been one of my closest friends. Living just a few blocks from each other in New York City and sharing an abundance of common interests, we companioned each other through a great deal of life, usually meeting up twice a week. We talked through challenges and joys in our work, our families, our love lives—and together created innumerable experiences of culture, nature, friends, and fun. When he asked me the summer before Covid to become one of the executors of his will, I felt honored and saw the request as formally recognizing the lifelong quality of our friendship. Chosen family.

Then, starting in March 2020, Covid required social distance. Our usual banter, exchanging book recommendations and quips, intermixed with plans for walks and drinks continued normally for the first couple of months. But then his responses abated. He would sometimes respond, but only after letting a few messages go unacknowledged. I kept reaching out, saying hello every few weeks, saying hello, asking how he was, maybe adding some news of a mutual friend or a book I was reading.

Greyson's ghosting was gradual. By mid-May, when several weeks had passed without our seeing each other, he texted some explanation, "Paradoxically I have been feeling less sociable, not more, in this time of social distancing," adding the emoji of a figure with upturned hands. *Who knew?* How unexpected that staying away from friends would build inertia for even less social connection!

We saw each other a couple of times that summer. The last time he ever showed up as my friend, we met at a pizza restaurant in October of that year. Soon thereafter he left the country for a few winter months. When he returned in the spring of 2021, his intermittent responses diminished further and became even more distant. Eventually, as months passed, the pattern of his withdrawal became more apparent. The question I had been asking implicitly became explicit: *Are we still connected?* I texted him this message:

> "Umm, so, what's the story with our friendship, mister? Have you opted out of it? Do we resume as normal at some point?
>
> You are very special to me, and I have been confused by your absence from my life–and don't know what's happened…"

His response, which came that night, felt trite and wooden: "Nothing has happened beyond the ebb and flow of relationships, including friendship. I'm more solitary these days. Can we leave it be, and see what the future holds?" In response to this question, I emailed him a letter the likes of which I had never before written. In the subject line, I put "Holding." My Covid loneliness was turning into the fear of losing this dear friend, who I still was holding in my heart. I thought a wake-up call reminding him of how our friendship had enriched both of our lives might bring him back to me.

> Dear Greyson,
>
> I mean for this to be a love letter from me to you. You are one of my favorite people and most cherished friends. I love you, and I opted into a lifelong friendship with you.
>
> My experience of our relationship since Covid hit NYC has not at all been some natural cycle of ebb and flow, as you wrote me last week. Rather, I have stayed as committed to our friendship as ever and as mindful of you as ever, while you have withdrawn from me.
>
> Your withdrawal from me has occasioned a great deal of suffering and pain for me. I have told you that before, in a number of ways. The general loneliness of Covid was exacerbated and amplified for me by you pulling away from me.
>
> Back in November you apologized for being scarce, and from early on in the pandemic you noticed how you paradoxically were feeling less sociable in this time of social distancing.

Since you have not made yourself available for conversation about this, I'm writing this letter to you. Our friendship is worth this effort—and much more than this. You are worth it. I am worth it.

Loving you, I want you to thrive and flourish in life. Knowing you as intimately as I do, I do not know what is going on in you that you would suffocate or starve one of your most intimate friendships. Sometimes I have thought that perhaps you are trying to prove to yourself that ultimately you are alone in the world, that personal connection must be ephemeral, that attachment is pointless.

How many friendships have you had that were as intimate as ours? We opened up to each other about our families, our romances, our professional dreams and struggles, our intellectual interests. We met each other's families and loved ones. We celebrated important moments together and comforted each other in times of difficulty. We talked politics and religion and sex. We learned from each other and made sense of the world together.

We met at Romba in New Orleans in October 2013 and in March 2014, you wrote me after what must have been one of our first outings together:

> I really enjoyed spending time with you last night—the dance performance was great, and I was also both excited and challenged in good proportion by our wide-ranging conversation, from furnishings to faith. I look forward to more.

For our next cultural event, how about Tuesday 11th March or Wednesday 12th March for *The Book of Mormon?*"

For me, the eagerness and delight that I have for you still now feels like what you conveyed to me back then! And now there are deep levels of love and trust, after so much shared experience, so many profound exchanges. You know me, and I know you. You see me, and you have allowed me to see you. I have wondered at times if it is precisely because of our intimacy that you have backed away from me.

My life has been greatly enriched by your being in it these past seven and a half years. From what I have seen of you, your life too has been enriched by me.

Since around the time of your departure [from the US] last November, you seem to have let go of our friendship, and let me drop from your hands to the ground.

Confused and heartbroken as I experience this, there are times I have wondered if I did something wrong, times I have felt unloved or even unlovable. There are times I have wondered if you were in crisis, or depressed, or losing your will to live.

I am truly at a loss.

Last week when I wrote you asking what happened with our friendship, you responded by asking if we could leave it be and see what the future holds. In this, you sound listless, despondent, fatalistic.

I am too alive to be languid in return. I care too much for you and too much for myself to let you drop, even as you have dropped me.

Of course, our friendship can and must change and grow and develop through various phases and cycles. I am by no means insisting on a return to our pre-Covid patterns of seeing each other twice a week, sometimes spontaneously and sometimes planned.

Indeed, I demand nothing. I recognize your agency and will—which could continue to opt for dropping me and letting go of our friendship. However, at least in writing you so expressively, I am exercising my agency and will in this.

Rather than passively leaving it be and seeing what the future holds, I am actively extending my heart to you. I love you. I miss you. I hold you.

Fondly and devotedly yours,
Dominic

This *cri de cœur* received no response from Greyson. It became one more in a string of unreturned messages letting me know that Greyson was ghosting. Over the following year, Greyson faded to black. In the face of Covid, I needed reassurance I was not in fact alone, while Greyson seemed to need to prove to himself that he was indeed alone.

Ultimately, I do not and cannot know whether cutting me out of his life increased or diminished Greyson's well-being, but the wooden tone of his spare explanations fascinated me. *I write to him from my heart, and he responds with trite truisms from his head.* Besides the comfort he was finding in a life of social distance, Greyson pointed to the natural waxing and waning, ebbing and flowing of friendships. How banal Greyson's reasoning for banning me from his life! Knowing how intellectually and socially adept he could be, his reliance on cliché confounded me. He seemed to be numbing, deadening his thoughts and feelings in order to go through with this severance. And as he deadened parts of himself, I experienced a death, losing him as if he had died. I went through the stages of grief, including denial, anger, intense sadness, and eventually acceptance.

Many to whom I have told this story of ghosting asked if some romantically crossed wires were at the heart of the story. Had that been the case, I wouldn't have felt so baffled by Greyson's withdrawal. Ours had been a platonically intimate friendship of two gay men without sexual tension between us. The confusion and hurt I felt at losing this beloved friend had me instead reflect on how the social fabric seemed to fray during the age of Covid. From what I could see, he was diminishing himself and his aliveness by ending our relationship the way he did. It looked and smelled like languishing, that diminishment of love that deadens.

Queer Forms of Ghosting

Besides surreptitiously ending intimate relationships, other varieties of ghosting make part of queer culture. Men who fashion themselves as shiny gays may provide the most pervasive example. Shiny gays glow. They sparkle. Eyebrows sculpted, muscles toned, body hair manscaped, everything looks just so. The fabrics and textures, colors and name brands, accessories and coiffe, all are chosen and placed for maximal perfection. With an extreme emphasis on the exterior at the expense of the inner life, the interior substance of the self, some gay men ghost as their fundamental stance in the world. *I'm not real but rather ethereal. My being is ether—pure, colorless air, highly volatile, aromatic to smell and sweet to taste.*

In another variety of ghosting, the deadening goes further than skin-deep. This style of a deadening of the soul that tries to kill the body can take many forms, some sudden, some gradual, some violent, some quiet. The higher suicidality of LGBTQ+ individuals compared to straight ones applies especially but not exclusively to youth.[118] I can hardly bear to remember or write about the actual or attempted suicides of those I love. Hearing from one of my dearest friends just a year ago that he had unsuccessfully (thank God!) tried to hang himself in London instilled in me a singularly heart-wrenching relief.

Another close family friend drank himself to death in the social isolation of the pandemic. Having decamped from San Francisco for more permanent residence at his vacation home in Palm Springs, Mitch's day drinking became incessant. We spoke just a few weeks before he died. He had heard I was writing something autobiographical and wanted to encourage me and offer help. Though I had noticed his problem drinking, I had no idea how severe it had become, nor do I know what demons or despairs plagued dear Mitch.

One part of Adam Grant's description of languishing feels applicable to what I imagine might have happened with Mitch: "You don't catch yourself slipping slowly into solitude; you're indifferent to your indifference. When you can't see your own suffering, you don't seek help or even do much to help yourself."[119] In Mitch's case, I imagine he didn't exactly mean to ghost, even if he kept choosing to drink so excessively and so continuously. These and so many other gay men turn from despair towards death as a final solution. Whether in an instant or over a long stretch, self-annihilation feels easier to them than facing life, and they ghost.

The Inheritance

Matthew Lopez's play, *The Inheritance*, offers us the occasion to reflect on gay ghosting in queer culture from a few other angles, from which we can see more sharply both languishing and flourishing. *The Inheritance* plots gay men on multiple storylines, the trajectories of characters following their fates, up mountains and down into pits, around and through excruciating feelings of pain and loss and fear and hope. The play presents possibilities for what to make of ourselves. *What to do with our life before we give up the ghost? Languish or flourish? What aliveness and what deadening do we choose?*

The plot revolves around Toby Darling and Eric Glass, a couple when the play begins. Neither knew himself nor saw his own greatness. Eric saw himself as "painfully ordinary,"[120] but in fact, he "possessed the ability to change the world to an extent far greater than he could possibly imagine."[121] Toby, on the other hand, entertains delusions of grandeur. He writes *Loved Boy*, a novel of autofiction, purportedly based on his life, with a central character named Elan whose blessed and privileged childhood does not match Toby's. Toby fancied himself as a writer already on par with J. D. Salinger. Eric, however, saw through Toby and "recognized within the first few minutes of their first date Toby's potential for greatness" as well as "his capacity for destruction."[122] Toby "shone with life," such that Eric thought the first day they met, "This guy is a lot, but this guy is alive."[123]

As the play progresses, the two break up and follow disparate paths. We come to see that Toby Darling, true to his name, strives for nothing more than *to be darling* during his days on earth. With a fictional alter ego named Elan, Toby presents nothing but showy flair. He glimmers his way into an empty, shiny gay version of the **Best Little Kid**. Frenetically and pathetically languishing, Toby does not grasp his greatness but rather fades to black. He evades his swamplands and leaves behind his difficult inheritance of boxed-up memories from his impoverished past with parents long dead. Long after they break up, Eric keeps for Toby an actual box full of Toby's mementos and childhood memories, in the hopes that Toby will come back for it, face his truth, and finally feel his feelings of loss and sadness.

While Eric does not tumble and slide down to self-annihilation as Toby does, he is no paragon of perfection. He does, however, face the messiness and imperfection of his life—and therein finds his way to flourishing. The action of the play opens in the Summer of 2015 with Toby in the Hamptons at a posh party hosted by billionaire businessman Henry Wilcox and his partner Walter Poole. As Toby gets progressively drunker, he leaves Eric a stream of excited voicemails, until finally disgracing himself by puking in the lap of one of the other party guests, namely, Meryl Streep. Eric faces this mess by phoning Walter the next day to apologize for his boyfriend. Toby, by contrast, implores Eric thereafter to avoid Henry and Walter so that they might forget Toby and Eric entirely.

Eric apparently complies, because a year later, when Eric encounters Walter by chance, he tells him, "Listen, Walter: I feel really bad about ghosting on you like I did last year."[124] Following this apology, the two men, more than a generation apart, strike up a fast friendship though it only lasts a couple of months, cut short by Walter's death. From the beginning of the play, Walter Poole is already likened to a spirit. Toby says that Walter has "this ghost-like spirit about him. Like a sheer curtain in front of an open window."[125] When Eric runs into Walter a year after Toby's disgrace, the older man has a new frailty and looks "positively spectral."[126]

This spiritual aspect of Walter is accentuated by his character being played by the same actor who plays the ghost of English author Edward Morgan (E. M.) Forster (1879–1970), who appears from the beginning of the play as a narrator or, perhaps, a prophet of queer flourishing. The stage directions say at Forster's entrance, "*We, like all his intimates, shall call him Morgan.*"[127] In narrating and commenting on the events of the play, Morgan interacts with a kind of Greek chorus of nameless modern-day gays, a **Pride Tribe** in which each is given a number and called "Young Man." Speaking for a generation of lost gay men, who in their cultural context could not find full freedom of sexual expression, Forster (and thus also Walter after his death) hovers over the stage like a holy ghost, a saintly intercessor.

Throughout *The Inheritance*, playwright Matthew Lopez invokes E. M. Forster's spirit for inspiration, even taking as models certain characters and contours from Forster's novel, his masterpiece, *Howard's End*. Despite Forster's literary greatness, the demands of the closet kept Forster from becoming himself more fully. He nonetheless bequeathed to queer culture a singular story of gay love, in his posthumously published novel, *Maurice* (1971), which shows up in *The Inheritance* as Eric Glass's favorite book.[128] Speaking to Leo, one of the lost gay men in the play who eventually finds himself, Forster's character says of *Maurice* that his aim was to write a simple love story about two men that had a happy ending. "Writing *Maurice* was the most terrifying, and the most exhilarating thing I had ever done. Hiding it from the world was the most shameful."[129] The character of E. M. Forster goes on to tell this lost gay man Leo, "you have shown me that my book was then, as you are now, a link in this chain of gay men teaching one another, loving one another, hurting one another, understanding one another. This inheritance of history, of community, and of self." In both Toby Darling's *Loved Boy* and Forster's *Maurice*, the authors fictionalize lives that they never lived. They take to writing to reach for the queer superpower of a **Double Life**. Yet Darling's yarn evades truth and spins lies, while Forster's story passes on to other gay men the hope of true love.

On multiple levels, *The Inheritance* returns repeatedly to the theme of gay men passing on stories, one generation to the next. The play powerfully conveys how crucially queer flourishing depends on our telling our stories truthfully to ourselves and to one another. In the play's Prologue, the chorus of young gay men asks Morgan, the great novelist, for his help telling their story—who we gay men are, how we got here, and what we mean to one another.[130] Morgan responds affirmatively. Herein lies the theme of *The Inheritance* and a central goal of *Queer Flourishing*: We help each other tell our true story so that we all might live our truth. In this reciprocity, we find the antidote to ghosting.

Walter Poole passes on his story to Eric Glass, who worthily receives it. Walter also intends to leave Eric another inheritance. On his deathbed, Walter writes a letter to his partner Henry that he should like to leave Eric his country house, a home which holds immense spiritual significance. This country house at first shielded Henry and Walter from the HIV/AIDS epidemic. They took refuge there for a year in the late 1980s, after attending too many friends' funerals. One day, however, Walter brought to the house a friend dying of the deadly plague that gay men were passing on from one to the next. Later in that same house, Walter loved many more men unto their early deaths from HIV/AIDS. He cultivated aliveness through love, even as the Human Immunodeficiency Virus turned so many young men there into ghosts.

Feeling betrayed and terrified, Henry responded by locking away his feelings of love for Walter in an attempt to avoid the future pain of loss. The next thirty-six years of his life with Walter, Henry spends as an **Ice Queen**, enclosing himself in a castle of frozen chambers. Nonetheless, Walter's death eventually brings the pain Henry had endeavored to evade. When Henry's adult sons read Walter's inheritance letter about the house, they talk their father out of heeding Walter's wish to give the property to Eric, someone they do not know. Eric is thus robbed of the inheritance that Walter left him, just as HIV/AIDS robbed the world of a generation of gay men.

In an unexpected turn following Walter's death, Eric and Henry strike up a friendship that turns into love and marriage. In the final scene of Part I of *The Inheritance*, Eric walks into the inheritance intended for him. Eric asks Henry to take him to Walter's house for the first time. He reveres all that was lost there, so many gay men whose lives were cut short. "Eric wondered what his life would be like if he had not been robbed of a generation of mentors, of poets, of friends and, perhaps even lovers."[131] HIV/AIDS ghosted a generation of gay men. It curtailed their stories and their capacities for self-authorship by making them languish physically and then annihilating them. The ghosts of the gays who died from AIDS as Walter loved them to their end greet Eric and welcome him home.

Eric embodies *queer flourishing*, the aliveness made possible by love. He possesses that *queer inheritance*. He risks loving Toby, and then Henry, whom he marries after Walter's death. Eric sees both men's greatness and their imperfection, and he loves them, nonetheless. Eric dares to love and to face his feelings of pain and loss. He acknowledges and apologizes for his mistakes and missteps and learns from them. He lives honestly and openly, as a gentle, kind, and eventually wise man. Eric Glass finds flourishing by staying alive to both his loves and his losses, by moving through, not around, the swamplands of his soul.

As for Toby Darling, instead of telling his actual story, he fabricates a false story of élan and loses himself in it, even as *Loved Boy* is produced on Broadway. Toby squanders his life. The thrills of fame and meth and celebrities and orgies entirely capture his attention. This lustrously shiny gay dims to a shadow.

As Eric's life starts to become intertwined with Henry's, he and Toby pack up the home they had shared for seven years. In this conversation with his ex, Eric realizes in an "epiphany" that Toby never learned how to love. He asks Toby, "What happened to us?" Toby replies that they just grew apart. "But Toby, you haven't grown," observes Eric.[132] The two bicker about their new love interests, exchanging sarcasm, then insults:

> **Toby** Fuck you, Eric.
>
> *He turns to leave.*
>
> **Eric** Wait—please.
>
> I love you, Toby. And the fact that you don't seem to understand how badly I'm hurting right now hurts me even more. Did you ever love me?
>
> **Toby** I mean, obviously.
>
> *Eric seems to have an epiphany.*
>
> What?

Eric No one ever taught you what that means, did they?

Toby What the fuck are you talking about?[133]

Toby languishes because he does not know how to give or receive love. Deadening and diminishing himself by staving off love, Toby eventually ghosts himself into oblivion.

Spiraling from one disgrace to another, Toby makes a **Great Escape** that takes him from languishing to perdition. He flees from the opening night performance of *Loved Boy*. He flees from New York, after showing up to Eric and Henry's wedding drunk and high with an invitation to Eric to "escape together."[134] Toby disappears to Alabama, where his mother had taken him at the age of seven after his father's bloody suicide. There, Toby holes up in a luxury hotel as he faces a choice, either to forgive and heal and grow into "a life that is real" or to burn into annihilation "his memories, his past, his anger, his pain, and ultimately himself."[135] Facing this fateful decision, Toby does something utterly uncharacteristic. He prays, asking God to "teach me how to be loved, show me how to forgive. . . . God, please forgive me for being me." With this prayer, Toby mounts a desperate and courageous attempt to face his truth and climb out of the pits into which he has fallen. In the months that follow in that hotel room, he writes the true story of his childhood poverty, abuse, and suffering. Calling the new play *Lost Boy*, Toby cannot find himself in his aloneness.

Table 10: The Queer Superpowers Revisited

Developmental Stage			Queer Superpower	Adverse Circumstances that prompt superpower's emergence
Self-Sovereign	Self-Protective Opportunist	1	Chameleonic Passing	» Social exclusion » Mocking » Bullying » Shaming » Moral condemnation » Shunning by family / friends » Violent attack
		2	Shield of Hypervigilance	
		3	The Great Escape	
Socialized	Conformist	4	Gaydar	» Cultural values » Gender expectations » Romantic & sexual norms of the straight mainstream » Religious & moral condemnation » Legal persecution
		5	Pride Tribe	
	Expert	6	The Best Little Kid	
Self-Authoring	Achiever	7	The Queen	» Strictures of societal expectations limit creative powers » Socialized cycle of approval-seeking forecloses possibility of greatness
		8	Double Life	
	Redefining	9	Second Adolescence	» Self-imposed limits caused by personal adaptations made earlier in life to survive and thrive » Distressful self-awareness of unintegrated parts of self
Self-Transforming		10	No One Left Behind	

Languishing, the Diminishment of Love That Deadens

Description	Heroic Possibilities & Powers	Pitfalls & Shadow
» Adapt to fit wide range of settings	» Shape-shifting » Cloak of invisibility » Avoid unwanted attention » Allow others to imagine you're one of them	» Not being seen or known for who we are » Loneliness » Fusing with our masks and forgetting who we really are
» Early alert system for possible danger	» Prepared to freeze, flee, or fight for safety » Avoid attacks, traps, & ambushes	» Fear & anxiety flood out other emotions » Skittish withdrawal inhibits relationships » Difficulty trusting even the trustworthy
» Depart toxic or abusive life situation to find supportive context	» Muster the courage, creativity, and determination needed for liberation	» Leave behind the good and the bad alike » Change of scenery without inner growth or change – "Running to stand still" » Flee into the clutches of new abusers
» Sense others' queerness	» Tap into intuitive knowing » See people's hidden faces » Empathy for others' shame	» Delusions of queer grandeur, imagining LGBTQ+ folks as superior to straight people » Project own queerness onto others
» Membership in a queer social group	» Strength in solidarity » Self-confidence to cultivate and use atypical gifts	» Gay groupthink papers over personal uniqueness » False sense of superiority
» Meeting and surpassing social standards and expectations	» Achieve excellence » Gain admiration in society » Earn one's way out of shame	» Fitting in to move up, lose sense of self and own unique "weird & wonderful" traits » Trapped by society's definitions of success, e.g., wealth, high position, prestige, luxury, etc.
» Accept and exercise "divine right" to rule one's own realm	» Claim own power » Impervious self-possession » Regal stature and poise » Sharp rationality » Relentlessly strategic in pursuing own vision and goals	» Self-sufficiency limits love – It's lonely at the top » Steamroll over others » Compartmentalization keeps valuable inner resources inaccessible » Haughty overconfidence leaves others impressed but distant
» Bifurcate life into separate domains	» Create space for expression and cultivation of queer self » Honor suite of personal values despite contradicitons	» Split life mirrors splits in the self that limit personal integration » Self-control verges on fraud and deceit
» A controlled coming apart and re-forming of adult self	» Shed conventional version of self in favor of greater authenticity and self-expression » Capacity for experimentation, follwed by rapid iteration, learning, and growth » Creativity and originality, despite societal flak	» Perpetually lost and not found, dissolution of conventional self never resolves into new coherence » Regress back to conventional self
» Return to scenes of wounding, to heal and more fully integrate all parts of self	» Wholeness » Integration of hidden resources and vulnerabilities » Revivification of spiritual scars	» Without sufficient support, re-traumatization can occur

In this work of inner excavation, Toby strains to reach for the queer superpower of **No One Left Behind**, but without guidance or support he can't manage to heal or recover. He cannot make his way through his swamplands. Socially isolated, he writes drunk and high, taking uppers in the mornings and downers in the evening. The work of defrosting his frozen feelings of pain and loss and shame ultimately surpasses his courage and capacity. Though he finishes the first full draft of his story, he stops the work far too soon. Stubbornly insisting that his work is complete, Toby emails the overgrown mess of a script to everyone he knows, regretting this "slow suicide" almost immediately.[136]

Eric responds to Toby's email with an invitation to visit him at Walter's old house. When Toby arrives, he acknowledges the trouble he is in and asks for Eric's help. Offering Toby refuge from queer languishing in this safe house, Eric presents Toby with the box of his parents' things, saying, "I've been holding onto it all these years because I hoped that one day you'd be ready to look inside it."[137] Opening Pandora's box of mementos and memories, Toby once again faces his dilemma, heal or burn. In the end, Toby's demons got the better of him. "I can't," was all he wrote in his last note to Eric, before driving himself away from Walter's house and crashing explosively into a cement wall. Finally, Toby finished his efforts to flee himself. Though he once "shone with life," eventually he was "burned alive."[138]

Toby Darling plummets into many of the pitfalls associated with the ten queer superpowers that we have considered, but that does not account for his ultimate downfall. The queer superpowers represent handholds that we grasp onto as we face the challenges of life. Toby yearned to flourish, as anyone does, and like anyone who uses these queer superpowers, at times he inevitably tumbles into their associated pitfalls. Darling's downfall, however, results from staving off love so effectively that he ultimately lacks the power to move *through* rather than *around* his suffering. As his demons chase him, he just keeps running away. Bereft of love, he falls from languishing to perdition.

Heroes Journey from Languishing to Flourishing

To the extent that queer culture attends to personal development, the discussion typically focuses on authenticity. Coming out as ourselves seems to stand as our paradigm for personal growth, and we generously and compassionately support each other in the lifelong process of coming out. Yet, notwithstanding the importance of coming out or other forms of authenticity, too often the journey of queer flourishing both starts and ends with coming out. In the terrain of queer development that we have explored together, we have looked beyond the undoubtedly important move of coming out and living openly in our sexual orientation and gender, whatever they might be. This "field guide" to queer development means to serve some specific needs that arise from our passionate emphasis on authenticity in queer culture.

Examined in the light of adult developmental theory, we've seen that in the process of coming out, the very achievement of authenticity that marks our entry as members into queer culture requires attention to our sense of what truly fulfills us, no matter the feedback from society. To come out, we must break and meld, melt and re-form, the structures of personhood that straight culture imposes as normative. The coming out process looks alternatively immoral or amoral to mainstream culture. In its bucking of tradition and convention, it creates a gravitational pull in queer culture toward the so-called **Redefining** stage of development. Queer culture pulls LGBTQ+ people towards this stage, the beginning of post-conventional sense-making.

We've also discovered ten postures and patterns that gay, bi, and queer men commonly use in our quest to flourish. Together, these "queer superpowers" demonstrate some of the complexity of developmental journeys for LGBTQ+ adults. Yet, until we recognize the postures and patterns that we adopt in order to create a sense of safety and a sense of self, we are their prisoners. They subject us. The postures grip and hold us. The patterns hem us in. We unwittingly fuse with the masks we wear and forget that we are more than this or that persona, whether the **Best Little Kid** or the **Queen** or whatever. Besides attending to the pitfalls of the queer superpowers, we have also seen how overholding any of these developmental supports can keep us from growing. Even the gravitational force that draws us past the conventional stages can mire us in **Redefining** form of mind. We can become seekers who never find what we are looking for. Ever skeptical, we hold fast to nothing. Our very sense of meaning and purpose in life can dissolve together with the beehive of conventional compartments in which we used to dwell.

Now that you have read this book, I hope that you cannot unsee what you have seen in your developmental path. With its maps and field notes, this book means to help you see where you stand in the larger terrain of human development, how you have been traveling the path, and the value of staying on the journey. Setting up permanent camp in any of these waystations keeps us from moving forward. We make best use of the queer superpowers when we can consciously choose to take refuge in one or another for a time, like stopovers in Alpine huts over the course of an arduous trek.

Besides tumbling into the pitfalls of queer superpowers or overusing them, languishing presents yet another temptation and trouble. Flourish or languish, heal or burn, show up or ghost—these options present alternatives for what to make of ourselves and of our lives. In languishing, we shrink, deaden, and petrify. In ghosting, all parties involved become less. Aliveness diminishes. Avoiding love, we avoid ourselves and the swamplands we hold within.

Solitary hikers cannot make it through the trek. Whatever your sexual identity or gender, whatever the nature of your unique journey, I hope you now feel less alone and more connected, part of a great "chain of gay men" and queer folks and people of all sexual orientations and genders who pass on a life-giving inheritance, one to the next. Heroes journey together. We all need each other to face our demons and become ourselves. In these pages, I have shared much of my own story of powers and pitfalls, languishing and flourishing. I have focused on the journey we go on within ourselves while embedded in relationships, communities, networks, and societies. However, imagining the archetypal hero's journey as a solitary venture misses the vitality of love. Becoming more alive, that is, becoming more ourselves, is made possible by love. We vitally need loving relationships in order to be ourselves and to become ourselves more fully.

The venture of flourishing also requires more than giving and receiving love, as vital and necessary as that is. Flourishing requires courageously stepping into the yet unimaginable "what is to come," which is the literal meaning of *adventure*. Aliveness means showing up for what shows up, rather than hiding, evading, numbing, or deadening. Flourishing requires that we be present to what shows up in our world and to what shows up in ourselves. Flourishing demands a practice of noticing and reflecting. We must pay attention in order to purchase fuller presence. Paradoxically, this expansive process of becoming ourselves more fully demands that we exchange perspectives with other people. Lest we become isolated on an idiosyncratic island, we must tell others what we sense, and we must listen to what they sense. Love requires being seen and known, starting with seeing and knowing ourselves so that we can reveal ourselves to other people—especially our most tender and powerful parts. Most demanding of all, aliveness requires moving *through* rather than *around* "the swamplands of the soul, the savannas of suffering."[139]

We are all made to flourish. We need to love one another to make that flourishing possible. And nowhere do we more need love than when in the swamplands of the soul. Moving through the gamut of human suffering, we grow and expand, becoming ourselves ever more fully. Gay, bi, and queer men hold no monopoly on suffering, of course, any more than do our queer siblings across the LGBTQ+ rainbow of identities. The pitfalls of queer developmental journeys are eminently human, as are queer superpowers. Queer flourishing benefits all, because we are all weird and wonderful. All flourishing is queer, because to flourish, we all need to give and receive love against the grain and across adversity, that is, *queerly*. I hope that your commitment to life, to the aliveness made possible by love, has grown and deepened, as you have read these pages. You are made to flourish! Go forth—love and live!

What's Next?

Let's Journey on Together

You made your way to the end. Good work! How does it feel to be here? What's next now that you've read *Queer Flourishing*? What's moving in you now? What desires do you notice? Maybe it's time for a little break from so much introspection and deep reflection? Or perhaps it's time to immerse yourself in music or art or a forest or sea, and let all you've explored in yourself just swirl and resettle?

When you feel ready for more stimulation and support to help you grow, after whatever rest and recovery you need, what steps might you take then? If you've been reading *Queer Flourishing* by yourself, you might feel the urge to talk with others about some of your new perspectives. Some of what you're seeing differently about yourself and your life journey might feel incomplete. Your thoughts are still forming, and your new way of seeing your story is wanting to take shape.

While your experience of reading *Queer Flourishing* is still fresh, find a friend or other loved one to tell them about what you discovered through reading this book. What's shifting in your self-understanding? What parts of yourself have you become aware of? What well-worn stories of moments in your life seem most in need of revising? What chapter of life do you now find yourself in? What's happening at this moment in the epic journey of becoming yourself ever more fully?

Through my **coaching** practice, I companion and support individuals who yearn to grow as human beings and as leaders in the world. Over a number of months (usually six or more), I will help you move forward on your journey of personal expansion into greater flourishing. One-on-one coaching focuses where you need it to. Through the intensive support and stimulation of a coaching engagement, you'll get personalized attention and expert guidance to help you bring forth more of the person you yearn to be.

Beyond furthering your own development, how about using *Queer Flourishing* to create community? Or perhaps you wish to deepen the conversation in an existing community, whether that's a social group of friends, an Employee Resource Group of work colleagues, or fellow volunteers in some community organization.

Go to QueerFlourishing.com to find ideas and guidance for bringing together a group for one or more community conversations using *Queer Flourishing*. Whether you want to host a dinner party that takes the conversation deeper or create a book club that meets on an ongoing basis, the Flourishing Gays Community Guide will spur creative ideas and offer tips for facilitation.

You might want a group experience that cultivates flourishing at your organization. I can work with you hand-in-hand to **design and facilitate an interactive workshop** or **a talk or keynote speech**. Let's create what's needed to foster the kind of flourishing most needed in your organization—leadership development, better teamwork and community connection, a culture of greater inclusion, or whatever it might be. In corporate contexts, this kind of event typically sits at the intersection of leadership development and DEI (Diversity, Equity, & Inclusion). An infusion of queer flourishing can bring your event to life!

Finally, if you're a gay, bi, or queer man who has accomplished a great deal but is yearning for something more, then the **Heroes Journey** program might be for you. It combines the best of one-on-one coaching support with a powerful community of peers who companion each other.

GLOSSARY FOR
QUEER FLOURISHING:

Concepts in Adult Development Seen from LGBTQ+ Perspectives

This glossary is not ordered alphabetically, but in a logical sequence where the concepts build upon one another. Read the glossary from beginning to end, and come back to it for reference as needed.

Queer: Once a derogatory slur, today "queer" is commonly used to describe sexual orientations and gender identities that differ from standard straight norms and the gender binary. The word might derive from the German *quer*, meaning oblique, against the grain, odd. Queer is used by some (not all) individuals across the LGBTQ+ spectrum, more by younger generations than older. It accentuates the complex fluidity of gender and sexual identities, rather than their clearcut divisions and definitions. The term is also used in cultural discourse as an adjective to describe anything as related to LGBTQ+ people or their perspectives, such as queer politics, queer literature, queer theology, queer studies.

Flourishing: In the context of human development, flourishing refers to a condition of holistic well-being that continues to expand, grow, and generate in a dynamic process. Derived from the Latin *florere*, meaning to bloom, to blossom, to flower.

LGBTQ+ or LGBTQIA+: Acronym for lesbian, gay, bisexual, transgender, queer, questioning, intersex, asexual, and other non-standard sexual orientations and gender identities.

Personal growth: The process of becoming oneself more fully, through unfolding more of one's unique human potential. As we grow, how we make sense of reality changes and expands to encompass more of its complexity. In other words, personal growth refers to changes in our sense-making or meaning-making. Stress, confusion, and suffering consistently appear in this process of metamorphosis, shedding old skins and structures so as to grow new ones. While this process is invariably messy, at times difficult, and full of surprises, researchers of adult development have identified a number of patterns and dynamics that show up as human beings realize more of their unique potential.

No trophy awaits at some finish line in the journey of personal growth and development, yet engaging in the process of growing, at whatever degree of intensity, seems to be necessary for human beings to flourish. For this reason, people often describe periods of languishing or malaise by using metaphors of stuckness or stagnation, which emphasize the lack of movement. Deep desires, yearnings, and dreams make for one valuable source of indications for the possible directions and pathways for the movement needed for personal growth at a given moment in life.

Personal growth within an individual always and only occurs in the context of social groups and cultural systems.

Human beings need each other to be human and to become themselves more fully. Consequently, the meaning and thrust of personal growth for LGBTQ+ people has shifted and continues to evolve as societies change.

Personal growth for LGBTQ+ people used to commonly focus on suppression of deviance and conversion to normalcy. Deeper and wider understanding and acceptance of the variations in sexual orientations and gender identities and expressions has changed this context considerably in many societies, especially since the Sexual Revolution of the 1960s and the Stonewall Riots of 1969, which marked a watershed in the gay rights movement. Since that time, personal growth for LGBTQ+ people has focused primarily on coming out and integrating their non-normative sexuality orientation or gender identity or expression. More recently, thanks to ever greater acceptance in society, fewer LGBTQ+ adults need to hide or suppress themselves, and more are able sooner and more fully to integrate their sexual orientation and gender identity. As a result, what personal growth means for LGBTQ+ people today expands beyond coming out to include the full panoply of opportunities and challenges faced in adult life, as spouses, parents, employees, professionals, entrepreneurs, organizational leaders, political actors, artists, spiritual beings, etc.

Leadership development: The part of personal growth that relates to having an impact in the world. Since all human beings have some degree and kind of impact on the world around them, everyone is a leader, to whatever extent of consciousness or efficacy. Leadership development thus refers to the process of growing in the capacity to have greater and more intentional impact in the world.

Because of gendered and heteronormative expectations for leaders, LGBTQ+ people face particular challenges—and enjoy particular opportunities—in their development as leaders. The standard molds for leaders often do not apply to the gifts, talents, charisma, or personal style of LGBTQ+ adults. Challenges arise from this difference, in that LGBTQ+ leaders sometimes confound implicit standards and norms for leaders just by being themselves, and thus receive frequent and sometimes strong resistance or disapproval for their leadership approach. On the other hand, as an LGBTQ+ leader steps confidently and powerfully into their distinctive difference that crosses gender norms in creative and innovative ways, they can access unusually effective leadership capacities that surpass standard molds for leaders. Recognizing both these unique pitfalls and possibilities enables LGBTQ+ leaders to circumvent the former and seize on the latter to great effect.

Understory: The partially conscious, inner story we hold to make sense of ourselves, others, and the world. Whereas someone's backstory tells what external events happened earlier in their life—the when, where, and what of their history, a person's understory relates the why and how of who they are today. It relates the inner dynamics of their personality with the experiences they've had in their life and the sense they made of those experiences. The understory spans the conscious, subconscious, and unconscious. Uncovering and noticing more aspects of our understory through introspection and reflection increase self-awareness and self-possession, allowing us greater freedom and agency in choosing how to see and relate to reality. Exploring our understory is vital for personal growth and leadership development.

Aliveness: Beyond biological life, aliveness refers to awareness, activation, and integration of the diverse parts of the Self. Encompassing the light and joyful aspects of human experience as well as the heavy and painful aspects, aliveness can be extremely difficult and taxing at times. The opposite of aliveness is a deadened, numbed state of half-awake avoidance.

Languishing: A middle ground in mental health between flourishing and depression. Somone languishing may describe themself as aimless, joyless, empty inside, blah, ho-hum, stuck, stagnating, and/or discontented. Sticking to the routines of life, a person who's languishing might maintain normal function, but feel exhausted and drained, even lifeless. Self-limiting stories that a person tells themself can keep someone in this state by closing off possibilities for moving into a more natural state of greater aliveness.

For LGBTQ+ people, languishing sometimes gets expressed in characteristic manners. Drug and alcohol use can become avenues for artificially creating euphoric and otherwise altered states, in place of actual joy and overall emotional aliveness. Sexual self-expression might be shut down completely, or ramped up manically.

Escaping the sticky clutches of languishing takes courage to break out of well-worn paths, to face difficult situations and painful emotions, and to allow oneself to be vulnerable enough for love.

Closeting–coming out continuum: A fluid array of social positions for LGBTQ+ people in their self-disclosure of sexual orientation or gender identity. Because LGBTQ+ people are often an invisible minority in the sense that their non-normative sexual orientation or gender identity is not, in many cases, apparent, coming out is an ongoing experience. Whenever an LGBTQ+ person faces someone else for the first time, the choice whether and how much to conceal or disclose arises.

Because of the power of the gender binary and the prevalence of heteronormative assumptions, LGBTQ+ people must make a continuous series of decisions that cover or make manifest their LGBTQ+ identity. Some dress or speak in ways that make quite apparent their queerness, while others dress or speak in ways that make their queerness less discernible. For many different reasons, including safety, avoidance of discrimination, preservation of emotional energy, and needs for authentic self-expression, an individual can show up at various points on the closeting–coming out continuum in different moments or situations.

Adult development theory: Field of scholarly research focused on the ongoing process, after reaching physical adulthood, of human beings expanding their capacities and realizing their potential. When the field of developmental psychology began, it focused on the remarkably apparent transformations of consciousness that occur as children grow. Starting in the second half of the 20th century, researchers began to pay greater attention to the similarly dramatic transformations of mind that happen in different ways for adults.

Among the most striking differences in adult development as compared to children is the role of agency and choice. To a large extent, adults can choose to grow or not. They often stave off growing, clinging to their status quo. One enabling condition which especially supports adult development is a person's practice of simply noticing what is going on in themselves, a group, or their world. More systematically noticing becomes introspection and reflection. Experiences that stress but don't overwhelm make for another important enabling condition for adult development. Developmental relationships and communities, where members exchange diverse views and perspectives, are also crucial to support and catalyze adult development.

Subject-object shift: A change in consciousness or sensemaking that can be described as the most basic unit of human development.

When something is subject for us, it forms a background against which we see reality. What we are subject to forms the context in which we see and understand all else. Subject makes for the kind of consciousness we project outwards to structure our world and inwards to structure ourselves. Many beliefs, ideas, values, categories, and assumptions comprise this ground, and we are subject to these realities at each moment in our development. We lack a sense of choice and freedom to question, critique, or change that which is subject for us. That to which we are subject weaves the context of our lives and the reality in which we are currently embedded. It is the ground on which we stand, the stage on which we play, the background for the scenes of our lives. When we are subject to something, it defines us and our knowable world. It holds us rather than us holding it. We are subjected to its power. In a sense, we are a subject *of* that thing, that reality. It *subjects* us, and we are subjected to it. It makes us who we are. It makes us *a subject* and shapes our *subjectivity*. When we are subject to something, it has power over us that we cannot overcome, because we are not even able to truly see it as "a thing." It rather structures our very consciousness.

In contrast, what we hold as object populates our inner and outer reality, but does not define it. When something is object for us, it makes part of the contents of our consciousness. We grasp it with its limits and boundaries. We grasp these objects as separate from us. We can behold objects and accept or reject them. Our relationship to what's object for us is characterized by freedom, awareness, and choice. It is an item or aspect that we can see distinctly, in the context of our overall horizon of understanding. That which is object for us is a figure set against the background that frames and structures our consciousness.

Growing in awareness or consciousness can thus be described as a move of some aspect of reality from subject to object. At each subsequent stage, a person's purview expands, as that to which we were subject now becomes object which we *have*. In this way, our awareness can embrace more of reality, including more aspects of both our inner complexity and of the world outside ourselves. This so-called "subject-object shift" reorganizes, expands, and complexifies the reality that we construct through our meaning-making.[140]

Inner diversity and inclusion: A concept that evokes integration of key concepts from the fields of DEI (diversity, equity, and inclusion) and adult development, respectively. The process of human development can, for example, be described as an ongoing increase of diversity of realities and perspectives within a person's consciousness as well as an increase of fuller inclusion and integration of these realities into that person's consciousness, rather than ignoring, avoiding, or marginalizing those diverse realities. In this sense, DEI, which is also called JEDIB, brings a justice lens to adult human development. In each developmental stage, a person becomes conscious of realities which they previously could not see. For example, upon moving into Conformist mind, a person first fully sees and appreciates what marks belonging in social groups. Upon moving into Expert mind, a person first fully sees and appreciates what knowledge and skills distinguish them within social groups to which they belong. Upon moving into Achiever mind, they first fully see and appreciate what desires, values, and aspirations they themselves most want to honor and pursue to realize their vision and goals for life. Upon moving into Redefining mind, they first fully see and appreciate how thoroughly their cultural and social milieux have imbued in them values, beliefs, categories, and perspectives. Upon moving into Transforming mind, they first fully see and appreciate the mutual influences and effects between the whole and the parts of systems—which illuminates the never-ending dynamic of the developmental process itself. In all of these examples, a person can not only see and appreciate but also include into themselves and equitably integrate these new realities for the first time.

DEI, for its part, is enriched by a developmental lens. DEI initiatives aspire to catalyze learning, growth, and change in individuals and groups. Seeing these aims developmentally puts due emphasis on the shifts of perspective needed to achieve them, rather than solely emphasizing the acquisition of knowledge and skills, or other important objective metrics such as the portion of new hires or promotions allotted to historically marginalized social groups. Developmental DEI work changes how participants see themselves, others, and society, so that they can more effectively and more justly bridge social differences.

Stage of development, or developmental stage: A way of making sense of reality, including oneself, others, and the world. Synonymous with form of mind and developmental mindset. Each stage represents a major step in the capacity for noticing and responding to greater levels of complexity. The sequence of stages proceeds like an ever-widening spiral, which can hold more and more of what's real and true and possible. Each later stage encompasses and transcends the structures of all previous stages. Thus, no one can skip a stage, and as a person grows into a later stage, they retain all the previous stages.

Stage describes a kind of meaning-making; it doesn't describe any individual. Actual human beings operate from multiple stages of development at any given point in life, by consciously or, more often, unconsciously switching from one stage to another to make sense of reality in different ways at different moments in time.

Form of mind: Synonymous with stage of development and developmental mindset.

Mindset: Synonymous with stage of development and form of mind.

Pre-Conventional: Developmental period encompassing multiple stages of meaning-making or forms of mind before a person gains the capacity to internalize societal conventions. In this period of psychological childhood, cultural and societal norms, values, expectations, and rules have not yet become rooted in a person's inner world. In that sense, the person has not yet become a full member of society. In pre-conventional stages of development, a person might experience bullying for unselfconsciously talking or acting in ways that violate cultural gender norms.

Conventional: Developmental period encompassing multiple stages of meaning-making or forms of mind characterized by a person's capacity to internalize the conventions of their cultural milieu. This capacity marks the beginning of psychological adulthood and the possibility of joining a society as a full member. Internalizing heteronormativity and gender norms can lead to an experience of seemingly unresolvable tension due to the awareness of discrepancies between one's own preferences, tendencies, and mannerisms on the one hand and societal expectations on the other. Most adults operate primarily from a conventional mindset.

Post-Conventional: Developmental period encompassing multiple stages of meaning-making or forms of mind marked by a greater capacity for seeing and navigating complexity, within oneself and out in the world, thanks in part to significant subject-object shifts in the realm of societal and cultural conventions. In post-conventional developmental stages, the interplay between self and system becomes increasingly fascinating, and the boundary between them less and less definite.

Self-Protective Opportunist: Later Self-Sovereign mind. Term used to refer to the last pre-conventional developmental stage or mindset, characterized by a focus on self-oriented urges and power dynamics. Also known as late Self-Sovereign form of mind. Flourishing at this stage revolves around safety and security. The greatest fear is about physical pain and not getting basic needs met, and the highest dream is being so safe as not having to worry about harm or deprivation. A Self-Protective style of this mindset focuses on staying safe defensively, for example, through hiding, deferring, or dodging threats. An Opportunist style of this mindset focuses on staying safe through dominating less powerful others, for example, through swagger, aggression, or physical violence. Someone in a Self-Protective Opportunist mindset gets what they can, by whatever means possible. The queer superpowers of Chameleonic Passing, the Shield of Hypervigilance, and the Great Escape address the needs of this stage.

Self-Sovereign: Term for the pre-conventional developmental stage of meaning-making encompassing both the Self-Protective Opportunist mindset and an earlier mindset sometimes called the Impulsive stage.

Conformist: Early Socialized mind. Term used to refer to the early conventional developmental stage or mindset characterized by a focus on fitting into social groups. In contrast to earlier forms of mind whose boundaries cannot transcend themselves, Conformist mind gains the capacity to see others and one's relationship to them in new ways. Flourishing at this stage revolves around social belonging. The greatest fear is social excommunication or shunning, and the highest dream is finding one's people or chosen family. LGBTQ+ individuals can experience a split between their need for social inclusion and their emergent non-normative sexual and/or gender identities. The queer superpowers of Gaydar and Pride Tribe alleviate this tension.

Expert: Later Socialized mind. Term used to refer to the conventional developmental stage or mindset characterized by a focus on earning distinction within social groups through showing special knowledge and skill. Flourishing at this stage revolves around social recognition. The greatest fear of this mindset is some version of inadequacy, and the highest dream is superiority that yields social approval, particularly from certain important others. Jagged development often emerges in this stage for LGBTQ+ individuals as they fervently strive in certain arenas while trying to downplay queer personal attributes and avoid other arenas where their social difference is most apparent. The Best Little Boy/Girl/Kid queer superpower can help LGBTQ+ folks to address the most pressing needs and dilemmas of this stage.

Self-Conscious: Another term used to refer to the Expert stage of meaning-making.

Important others: Socialized mind imprints on certain people as role models and authorities. The worldview, values, manners, and even personal styles of these important others especially influence the person who holds them as such. Important others might be family members, mentors, peers, or public figures or celebrities whom the person has never even met.

Socialized: Term for the conventional developmental stage of meaning-making encompassing both the Conformist and Expert mindsets.

Achiever: Early Self-Authoring mind. Term used to refer to the last conventional developmental stage or mindset characterized by the capacity to be oneself in new and profound ways. While firmly embedded in conventional values, beliefs, assumptions, and expectations, Achiever mind begins to be able to construct an independent self, with ultimate decision rights over their own life. Flourishing at this stage revolves around being one's own person and achieving a kind of greatness that matters to them. The greatest fear might be the failure at realizing one's own unique vision, while the highest dream is making that vision a reality. Mainstream culture typically points to the Achiever mindset as the epitome of leadership.

From this high point of independent autonomy onwards, developmental journeys become more individualized and less prone to common patterns. LGBTQ+ individuals operating from this mindset might choose to embrace more or less recognizably queer attributes or personal styles, depending on the fit with the person's goals and vision. The Queen is a queer superpower meeting the needs of this mindset by exemplifying self-possession and haughty power.

Redefining: Later Self-Authoring. Term used to refer to the first post-conventional developmental stage or mindset characterized by the capacity to see systems and appreciate their complexity and power. Leaving the comfort of conventional meaning-making can be profoundly distressing, like leaving civilization for the wilderness. Flourishing at this stage revolves around courageous experimentation in the quest for authentic self-expression. The greatest fear is to be the perpetual wanderer, the seeker who never finds. The greatest dream aspires to disentangle and deprogram oneself from the limiting aspects of inculturation, so as to truly become oneself.

Straight mainstream culture can admire the spontaneity and creativity of people operating from Redefining mind, while also harboring suspicion and disapproval for their unusual choices and countercultural quirkiness. Queer culture offers LGBTQ+ individuals many resources and much encouragement to move towards Redefining mind. Attention to queer history and the lived experience of LGBTQ+ folks creates incentives and appreciation for flouting the conventions of straight society. The queer superpower of Second Adolescence gives LGBTQ+ folks a taste of the controlled coming apart of the self that is a hallmark of Redefining mind.

Self-Authoring: Term for a stage of meaning-making that straddles the conventional (Achiever) and post-conventional (Redefining).

Shadow: Those attributes, desires, needs, and other parts of ourselves that we do not want to have and that most of the time we strive to avoid noticing or acknowledging are indeed in us. Pet peeves, that which especially bothers us in other people, typically point to our own shadow material, which instead of recognizing in ourselves we tend to see and hate in other people. Swiss psychologist Carl Jung called this process "projection." Indicating our natural yearning for wholeness, what dwells in the shadow also appears in our dreams, fantasies, and unconscious behaviors.

Though we reject our shadow material as what we most want not to be, it paradoxically contains treasures of unrealized human potential. Consciously exploring and reclaiming shadow material bring us into greater wholeness as we allow ourselves capacities and qualities that previously we did not allow ourselves to bear or inhabit.

LGBTQ+ people might relegate to the shadow certain attributes which they associate with straight norms. Some gay men might, for example, dissociate from hard-edged attributes, such as their own strength, assertiveness, authority, or aggressiveness. Some queer women might similarly relegate the shadow soft qualities typical of feminine gender norms, such as gentleness, delicacy, and caretaking.

Self-Transforming: Term used to refer to a post-conventional developmental stage or mindset that grounds itself in the ever-shifting dynamics growth, change, and development—within the Self and in systems. Moving further beyond convention, Self-Transforming mind sees more of its own multiplicity and internal contradictions, including more of its shadow sides, which previously were to be avoided. The developmental process within oneself accelerates and an increasingly fascinating object of attention. Self-Transforming mind often gains greater interest in non-rational sources of knowledge and wisdom, such as dreams, fantasies, spirituality, and the occult. In this stage, individuals can paradoxically hold themselves more lightly while also at times do deep inner work, such as healing and integration of childhood trauma. Flourishing at this stage revolves around wholeness. The greatest fear could focus on existential aloneness, while the highest dream sees a reciprocal flourishing of Self in all and all in Self.

LGBTQ+ folks operating from a Self-Transforming form of mind have increasingly access to many versions of themselves, to such an extent that their way of being might seem inscrutable or unsettling to others. The queer superpower of No One Left Behind emerges to support the quest for wholeness through care for wounded parts of the Self.

Transforming: Another name used to refer to the Self-Transforming stage of meaning-making.

Queer superpower: A posture or pattern commonly appearing in LGBTQ+ people in order to handle the particular constellation of personal and social challenges of their lives at a given developmental stage. Queer superpowers are creative adaptations that ingeniously empower LGBTQ+ people with heroic capabilities, yet each superpower also brings treacherous pitfalls. The processes of personal growth and leadership development for LGBTQ+ people necessarily involves learning to employ their queer superpowers when they are fit for purpose—and to not employ these postures and patterns at other times, when they can be detrimental, self-limiting, or even self-destructive.

Chameleonic Passing: A queer superpower of the Self-Protective Opportunist mindset that shape-shifts to seek safety.

Shield of Hypervigilance: A queer superpower of the Self-Protective Opportunist mindset that looks at the world through the lens of threat, so as to be poised to avoid danger.

Great Escape: A queer superpower of the Self-Protective Opportunist mindset that, against all odds, ingeniously escapes existential threats.

Gaydar: A queer superpower of the Conformist mindset that sees queerness invisible to others.

Pride Tribe: A queer superpower of the Conformist mindset that creates a queer community of solidarity.

Best Little Boy/Girl/Kid: A queer superpower of the Expert mindset that achieves excellence in one or more socially approved domains.

Queen: A queer superpower of the Achiever mindset that claims self-determination and gains self-possession with regal dignity and authority.

Double Life: A queer superpower of the Achiever mindset that creates a second domain of life for free and queer self-expression.

Second Adolescence: A queer superpower of the Redefining mindset that allows a re-forming of the adult Self for the sake of greater authenticity and personal fullness.

No One Left Behind: A queer superpower of the Self-Transforming mindset that retrieves and cares for wounded parts of the Self for the sake of greater wholeness and integrity.

Jagged development: a personal profile in which some capacities or aspects of the self are highly developed and others much less so. Lacking sufficient support and social acceptance in teenage and young adult years, LGBTQ+ people might accentuate academic, athletic, artistic, or cultural development, while avoiding or not finding opportunity for relationships that foster sexual or certain kinds of social development. Jagged development could emerge as a consequence of reliance on The Shield of Hypervigilance or The Best Little Boy/Girl/Kid queer superpower. The Queen might solidify and cling to overdeveloped aspects while covering over underdeveloped capacities. Jagged development can contribute to circumstances that call for a Second Adolescence.

Fallback: The utterly common experience of a temporary and involuntary shift to an earlier and thus more limited form of meaning-making. While unsettling, fallback presents us with valuable information about smaller versions of ourselves, such as their needs, desires, fears, formative experiences, and unhealed wounds. Fallback can be triggered by threats, stress, and social context, such as an adult's holiday visit back their parents' home. In earlier developmental mindsets, we lack the capacity to notice or acknowledge fallback. In later stages, we grow in the capacity both to notice and appreciate with interest fallback as exceedingly valuable developmental opportunities to see our shadow material and possibly integrate more of it into our conscious Self.

LGBTQ+ adults might especially go into fallback in settings that resemble childhood experiences of bullying or social exclusion. Because LGBTQ+ people may have had difficulty finding many opportunities early in life for sexual expression in the context of dating relationships sanctioned by their parents and peers, sex itself might be a context that induces fallback. Instead of showing up in sex with personal resources such as responsibility, empathy, and generosity, a Self-Protective Opportunist or earlier version of themselves might take the lead in their sex lives.

Uplift or **springing forward**: A parallel to fallback in which a person temporarily visits a later developmental mindset. As with fallback, circumstances play an important part in developmental uplift. A person might find support in developmental scaffolding that creates a holding environment where more resource is available to them than in whatever developmental stage is currently their norm for making sense of reality. *Queer Flourishing* aims to serve as developmental scaffolding like this, especially for LGBTQ+ readers.

Bibliography

Alessi, Edward J. and James I. Martin. "Intersection of Trauma and Identity." *Trauma, Resilience, and Health Promotion in LGBT Patients: What Every Healthcare Provider Should Know.* Ed. Kristen L. Eckstrand and Jennifer Potter. New York: Springer International, 2017. Pp. 3–14.

Althaus-Reid, Marcella. *Indecent Theology: Theological Perversions in Sex, Gender and Politics.* London: Routledge, 2000.

Brokaw, Tom. *The Greatest Generation.* New York: Random House, 1998.

Cook-Greuter, Susanne. *Nine Levels of Increasing Embrace in Ego Development: A Full-Spectrum Theory of Vertical Growth and Meaning Making.* Prepublication version, 2013. Cook-greuter.com. 2 Jan 2021.

Cook-Greuter, Susanne. *Postautonomous Ego Development: A Study of Its Nature and Measurement.* Ph.D. Dissertation, Harvard University, 1999; Integral Publishers, 2010.

Crowley, Mart. *The Boys in the Band.* Introduction by Tony Kushner. New York: Samuel French, 1968; 2018.

Davis, Louanne. *Meditations for Healing Trauma: Mindfulness Skills to Ease Post-Traumatic Stress.* Oakland, CA: New Harbinger Publications, 2016.

Downs, Alan. *Velvet Rage: Overcoming the Pain of Growing Up Gay in a Straight Man's World.* Boston: Da Capo Press, 2005; 2006; 2012.

Emerson, Brian and Kelly Lewis, *Navigating Polarities: Using Both/And Thinking to Lead Transformation.* Washington, DC: Paradoxical Press, 2019.

Garvey Berger, Jennifer. *Changing on the Job: Developing Leaders for a Complex World.* Stanford University Press, 2012.

Glenn, William D. *I Came Here Seeking a Person: One Gay Man's Spiritual Journey.* New York: Paulist Press, 2023.

Goffman, Erving. *Stigma: Notes on the Management of Spoiled Identity.* New York: Touchstone, 1963.

Grant, Adam. "There's a Name for the Blah You're Feeling: It's Called Languishing." *New York Times*, 19 April 2021. Online. https://www.nytimes.com/2021/04/19/well/mind/covid-mental-health-languishing.html. Accessed 21 Oct 2021.

Heifetz, Ronald A. and Marty Linsky. *Leadership on the Line*: Staying Alive Through the Dangers of Leading. Boston: Harvard Business School Press, 2002.

Hobbes, Michael. "Together Alone: The Epidemic of Gay Loneliness." *Huffington Post.* 2 Mar 2017. Accessed 26 Apr 2021. https://highline.huffingtonpost.com/articles/en/gay-loneliness/

International Coaching Federation. "ICF Definition of Coaching." Coachfederation.org. 2 Jan 2021.

Jordan, Mark D. *The Silence of Sodom: Homosexuality in Modern Catholicism*. University of Chicago Press, 2000.

Johnson, Barry. *Polarity Management: Identifying and Managing Unsolvable Problems*. Amherst, MA: HRD Press, 1992; 1996.

Kegan, Robert. *The Evolving Self: Problem and Process in Human Development*. Cambridge, MA: Harvard University Press, 1982.

Kegan, Robert. *In Over Our Heads: The Mental Demands of Modern Life*. Cambridge, MA: Harvard University Press, 1994.

Kegan, Robert and Lisa Laskow Lahey. *Immunity to Change: How to Overcome It and Unlock the Potential in Yourself and Your Organization*. Boston, Massachusetts: Harvard Business Press, 2009.

Keyes, Corey L. M. "The Mental Health Continuum: From Languishing to Flourishing in Life." *Journal of Health and Social Research* 2002, Vol 43 (June): 207–222.

Kugle, Scott Siraj al-Haqq. *Living Out Islam: Voices of Gay, Lesbian, and Transgender Muslims*. New York: New York University, 2014.

Lansky, Sam. *The Gilded Razor*. New York: Gallery Press, 2016.

Lansky, Sam. *Broken People*. Toronto: Hanover Square Press, 2020.

Livesay, Valerie Townsend. *Exploring the Paradoxical Role and Experience of Fallback in*

Developmental Theory. Ph.D. Dissertation, University of San Diego, 2013.

Livesay, Valerie Townsend. *Leaving the Ghost Light Burning: Illuminating Fallback in Embrace of the Fullness of You.* San Marcos, California: Kairos, 2022.

Livesay, Valerie Townsend. "One Step Back, Two Steps Forward: Fallback in Human and Leadership Development." *Journal of Leadership, Accountability and Ethics* 12:4 (2015) 173–189.

Longo, F. Dominic. *Spiritual Grammar: Genre and the Saintly Subject in Islam and Christianity.* New York: Fordham University Press, 2017.

Lopez, Matthew. *The Inheritance.* London: Faber and Faber, 2018; 2019.

Louis, Édouard. *En finir avec Eddy Bellegueule.* Paris: Éditions du Seuil, 2014.

Louis, Édouard. *Histoire de la violence.* Paris: Éditions du Seuil, 2016.

Louis, Édouard. Trans. Michael Lucey. *The End of Eddy.* New York: Farrar, Straus and Giroux, 2017.

Louis, Édouard. Trans. Loren Stein. *History of Violence.* New York: Farrar, Straus and Giroux, 2018.

Meyer, I. H. "Prejudice, social stress, and mental health in lesbian, gay, and bisexual populations: conceptual issues and research evidence." *Psychological Bulletin* Sept 2003: 129(5) 674-697.

Nimmons, David. *The Soul Beneath the Skin: The Unseen Hearts and Habits of Gay* Men. New York, NY: St. Martin's Press, 2002.

Odets, Walt. *Out of the Shadows: Reimagining Gay Men's Live.s* New York: Farrar, Straus and Giroux, 2019.

Rooke, David and William R. Torbert. "Seven Transformations of Leadership." *Harvard Business Review.* April 2005.

Schmelzer, Gretchen. *Journey Through Trauma: A Trail Guide to the 5-Phase Cycle of Healing Repeated Trauma.* New York: Avery, 2018

Schwartz, Richard C. and Martha Sweezy. *Internal Family Systems Therapy*, Second Edition. New York: Guilford Press, 2020.

Talvacchia, Kathleen T. *Embracing Disruptive Coherence: Coming Out as an Erotic Ethical Practice.* Eugene, OR: Cascade Books, 2019.

Tolkien, J.R.R. *The Lord of the Rings.* Boston: Houghton Mifflin, 2004.

Torbert, Bill et al. *Action Inquiry: The Secret of Timely and Transforming Leadership.* Oakland, California: Berret-Koehler Publishers, Inc. 2004.

Van Der Kolk, Bessel. *The Body Keeps the Score: Brain, Mind, and Body in the Healing of Trauma.* New York: Penguin, 2014.

Wilkerson, Isabel. *Caste: The Origins of Our Discontents.* New York: Random House, 2020.

Yoshino, Kenji. *Covering: The Hidden Assault on Our Civil Rights.* New York: Random House, 2006.

Endnotes

1. The phrase comes from James Hollis, *Swamplands of the Soul: New Life in Dismal Places* (Toronto: Inner City Books, 1996).
2. Mart Crowley, *The Boys in the Band* (New York: Samuel French, 2018)
3. Édouard Louis, *En finir avec Eddy Bellegueule* (Paris: Éditions du Seuil, 2014).
4. Édouard Louis, *Histoire de la violence* (Paris: Éditions du Seuil, 2016).
5. Alan Downs, *Velvet Rage: Overcoming the Pain of Growing Up Gay in a Straight Man's World* (Boston: Da Capo Press, 2005; 2006; 2012) 3.
6. Walt Odets, *Out of the Shadows: Reimagining Gay Men's Lives* (New York: Farrar, Straus and Giroux, 2019).
7. John Reid [Andrew Tobias], *The Best Little Boy in the World* (New York: Ballantine, 1973; 1976); Mohsin Zaidi, *A Dutiful Boy: A Memoir of a Gay Muslim's Journey to Acceptance* (London: Square Peg, 2020).
8. Sam Lansky, *The Gilded Razor* (New York: Gallery Books, 2016).
9. Sam Lansky, *Broken People* (Toronto: Hanover Square Press, 2020).
10. William D. Glenn, *I Came Here Seeking a Person: One Gay Man's Spiritual Journey* (New York: Paulist Press, 2023)
11. Marcella Althaus-Reid, *Indecent Theology: Theological Perversions in Sex, Gender and Politics* (London: Routledge, 2000)

12. Mark D. Jordan, *The Silence of Sodom: Homosexuality in Modern Catholicism* (Chicago: University of Chicago, 2000).
13. Scott Siraj al-Haqq Kugle, *Living Out Islam: Voices of Gay, Lesbian, and Transgender Muslims* (New York: New York University, 2014).
14. David Nimmons, *The Soul Beneath the Skin: The Unseen Hearts and Habits of Gay Men* (New York, NY: St. Martin's Press, 2002).
15. Nimmons, *Soul Beneath*, 8.
16. Nimmons, *Soul Beneath*, 10.
17. Nimmons, *Soul Beneath*, 79.
18. Nimmons, *Soul Beneath*, 85.
19. Susanne R. Cook-Greuter, *Nine Levels of Increasing Embrace in Ego Development: A Full-Spectrum Theory of Vertical Growth and Meaning Making*, p. 2. Prepublication version, 2013. www.cook-greuter.com, accessed 2 Jan 2021.
20. The stage names here come from Robert Kegan and Susanne Cook-Greuter.
21. Cf. Jennifer Garvey Berger's practical and concise overview of adult development theory in Ch. 1 of *Changing on the Job: Developing Leaders for a Complex World* (Stanford University Press, 2012), with a definition of "subject" on p. 18. Robert Kegan and Lisa Laskow Lahey provide a valuable and succinct discussion of the subject-object relationship in *Immunity to Change: How to Overcome It and Unlock the Potential in Yourself and your Organization* (Boston: Harvard Business, 2009) 51–53.
22. Garvey Berger, *Changing on the Job*, 108–9.
23. At these later stages of ever-increasing inner diversity and inclusion, social categories like gender and sex, race and ethnicity, professional guild and place of origin define us less and less. We increasingly transcend and include our own and other affiliations and categorizations. Some researchers have identified additional developmental mindsets or stages beyond these that I have briefly described, but we will not address these in this book. In my own search and research, exploration and speculation, I have as of yet come upon no queer superpowers particular to the stages of

development that follow those described above. Undoubtedly, my own limits circumscribe my purview.

24. Cook-Greuter, *Nine Levels*, 35.
25. Some material in this chapter has been adapted from the previously published F. Dominic Longo, "Taking a Developmental Approach to Coaching Gay Men," *Coaching Wisdom: Voices of the Gay Coaches Alliance* (Gay Coaches Alliance, 2022), pp. 55–60. Used with permission.
26. Ronald A. Heifetz and Marty Linsky, *Leadership on the Line: Staying Alive Through the Dangers of Leading* (Boston: Harvard Business Press, 2002).
27. Zaidi, *A Dutiful Boy*, 66.
28. Zaidi, *Dutiful Boy*, 66–7.
29. Zaidi, *Dutiful Boy*, 223–4.
30. Reid [Tobias], *Best Little Boy*, 84.
31. Reid [Tobias], *Best Little Boy*, 12.
32. Reid [Tobias], *Best Little Boy*, 1.
33. Reid [Tobias], *Best Little Boy*, 243.
34. Cook-Greuter, *Nine Levels*, 19. From a study Cook-Greuter used in her dissertation of a population of 4510 individuals, including "priests and prisoners, accountants and artists, and subjects spanning ages 18–82 with the middle 35–65 being the most represented" (20).
35. David Rooke and William R. Torbert, "Seven Transformations of Leadership," *Harvard Business Review* (April 2005).
36. Kegan gives the section title "Evolutionary Truces" to Part One (Chs 1–3) of *The Evolving Self: Problem and Process in Human Development* (Cambridge, MA: Harvard University, 1982).
37. Cook-Greuter, *Nine Levels*, 16.
38. Cf. Discussion of "Developmental center-of-gravity vs. developmental range" in Valerie Townsend Livesay, *Exploring the Paradoxical Role and Experience of Fallback in Developmental Theory*, Ph.D. Dissertation (University of San Diego, 2013) pp. 93ff.

39. Valerie Townsend Livesay's dissertation and book on this topic are invaluable. *Leaving the Ghost Light Burning: Illuminating Fallback in Embrace of the Fullness of You* (San Marcos, California: Kairos, 2022).
40. J. R. R. Tolkien, *The Lord of the Rings* (Boston: Houghton Mifflin, 2004).
41. Cf Cook-Greuter, *Nine Levels*, 2–3.
42. Isabel Wilkerson, *Caste: The Origins of Our Discontents* (New York: Random House, 2020) 29.
43. Some material in this chapter has been adapted from the previously published F. Dominic Longo, "Taking a Developmental Approach to Coaching Gay Men," *Coaching Wisdom: Voices of the Gay Coaches Alliance* (Gay Coaches Alliance, 2022), pp. 55–60. Used with permission.
44. Crowley, *Boys*, 25.
45. Crowley, *Boys*, 27.
46. Crowley, *Boys*, 35.
47. Crowley, *Boys*, 36.
48. Crowley, *Boys*, 45.
49. Cook-Greuter, *Nine Levels*, 40.
50. "Carly" is a pseudonym.
51. Channing Gerard Joseph, "America's Black Queer History," lecture at the American Academy in Berlin, Online https://www.americanacademy.de/event/americas-black-queer-history/, accessed 30 August 2023.
52. Cook-Greuter, *Nine Levels*, 45.
53. I owe this neat phrasing to Jan Rybeck.
54. Kegan, *Evolving Self*, 222.
55. "In the empire of closets that is the modern Catholic church, no one knows more than a few of the compartments. The church is not one big closet. It is a honeycomb of closets that no one can survey in its entirety." Jordan, *Silence of Sodom*, 89.

56. Cook-Greuter, *Nine Levels*, 42.
57. Kegan, *The Evolving Self*.
58. Descriptions of Self-Authoring, Achiever mind (Stage 4) as self-governing and self-regulating make apparent a certain resonance with the Self-Sovereign (Stage 2). In both stages, the person errs on the side of greater independence and self-focus rather than greater inclusion of what exists outside their inner world. However, "the nature of their self-determination is as different as the control of one's behavior is from the control of one's self-definition" (Kegan 223). The child who arrives at the Self-Sovereign stage, which Kegan called "the Imperial Self" in his early work, has gained control over their own impulses and thus their behavior. Someone in Self-Authoring mind, on the other hand, has gained control over their self-definition. They have organized an internal administration for self-governance, complete with expression of direction, agenda, and purpose in life. For Jean Piaget, cognitive development reaches full adulthood at this stage, which Kegan calls Self-Authoring. For Piaget, this means acquiring the capacity for full formal operational thought, meaning the person embodies certain logico-deductive tenets. According to Cook-Greuter, those logico-deductive tenets posit the following relationships among elements: (1) causality is linear, (2) variables are independent, (3) boundaries of objects are closed, and (4) objects are separate from the observer" (Cook-Greuter, *Postautonomous Ego Development: A Study of Its Nature and Measurement*, Ph.D. Dissertation, Harvard University, 1999; Integral Publishers, 2010, p. 115). The person in this stage regards truth as accessible through what Descartes describes as "clear and distinct" perceptions. Here, one has the full capacity for logic, including testing hypotheses, making inferences and deductions, and reasoning *about* reasoning.
59. Cook-Greuter, *Nine Levels*, 17.
60. Cook-Greuter, *Nine Levels*, 45. This sense of guilt from betraying oneself gives Cook-Greuter reason to call this stage "Conscientious."
61. Kegan, *Evolving Self*, 245.

62. The origin of this adage is unknown.
63. Garvey Berger, *Changing on the Job* 186.
64. Kegan, *The Evolving Self,* 242.
65. These Redefining characteristics are described in Cook-Greuter, *Nine Levels,* 56, 57, 60. The claims about a link to queer cultures and LGBTQ+ representations are my own.
66. Cook-Greuter, *Nine Levels,* 58.
67. Cook-Greuter, Torbert, and other researchers see Redefining (demarcated by 4/5) as later Self-Authoring, a stage that follows Achiever (demarcated by 4).
68. "The transition from conventional to postconventional meaning making . . . signifies an overall, large-scale shift from increasing differentiation and the creation of an independent self-identity towards increasing integration and deconstruction of the separation developed in the first half of the growth trajectory." Cook-Greuter, *Nine Levels,* 51.
69. Heiftz and Linsky, *Leadership on the Line.*
70. Cook-Greuter, *Nine Levels,* 53.
71. Cook-Greuter, *Nine Levels,* 54.
72. Cook-Greuter, *Nine Levels,* 52.
73. Cook-Greuter, *Nine Levels,* 58.
74. Cook-Greuter, *Nine Levels,* 54.
75. Bill Torbert et al., *Action Inquiry: The Secret of Timely and Transforming Leadership* (Oakland, California: Berret-Koehler Publishers, Inc. 2004) 94.
76. Cook-Greuter, *Nine Levels,* 56.
77. Cook-Greuter, *Nine Levels,* 57–8.
78. Cook-Greuter, *Nine Levels,* 61.
79. Cook-Greuter, *Nine Levels,* 52.
80. Cook-Greuter, *Nine Levels,* 57.
81. Thanks to researcher Valerie Livesay for her important work on this topic.

82. Livesay, *Exploring the Paradoxical Role*, 244.
83. Livesay, *Exploring the Paradoxical Role*, 248.
84. I. H. Meyer, "Prejudice, social stress, and mental health in lesbian, gay, and bisexual populations: conceptual issues and research evidence," *Psychological Bulletin* Sept 2003: 129(5) 674–697.
85. Edward J. Alessi, and James I. Martin, "Intersection of Trauma and Identity," *Trauma, Resilience, and Health Promotion in LGBT Patients: What Every Healthcare Provider Should Know*, ed. Kristen L. Eckstrand and Jennifer Potter (New York: Springer International, 2017) 9.
86. Livesay, *Exploring the Paradoxical Role*, 249.
87. The concepts of inner exiles and protectors come from Richard C. Schwartz and Martha Sweezy, *Internal Family Systems Therapy*, Second Edition (New York: Guilford Press, 2020).
88. Gretchen Schmelzer, *Journey Through Trauma: A Trail Guide to the 5-Phase Cycle of Healing Repeated Trauma* (New York: Avery, 2018).
89. Schmelzer, *Journey Through Trauma*, 127.
90. Schmelzer, *Journey Through Trauma*, 4–5.
91. Translations are my own, but for convenience I also give the page numbers for the published English translation. Édouard Louis, *History of Violence*, trans. Lorin Stein (New York: Picador, 2018).
92. Louis, *Histoire de la violence* 81–2; *History of Violence* 77.
93. Louis, *Histoire de la violence* 52; *History of Violence* 48.
94. Schmelzer, *Journey Through Trauma*, 136.
95. Louis, *Histoire de la violence* 149; *History of Violence* 140.
96. Kegan, *The Evolving Self*, 41.
97. Cook-Greuter, *Nine Levels*, 9.
98. As a reminder, Kegan only gives names to the stages demarcated by whole numbers. All of his stages encompass multiple steps, which, taking the Self-Sovereign stage as an example, are demarcated 2, 2(3), 2/3, 3/2, and 3(2).

99. Kathleen T. Talvacchia, *Embracing Disruptive Coherence: Coming Out as an Erotic Ethical Practice* (Eugene, OR: Cascade Books, 2019) 85.
100. A great deal of research on Adverse Childhood Experiences (ACE) has been undertaken in the past several decades. Cf. the World Health Organization's ACE International Questionnaire at https://www.who.int/publications/m/item/adverse-childhood-experiences-international-questionnaire-(ace-iq). Accessed 30 March 2022.
101. Kenji Yoshino, *Covering: The Hidden Assault on Our Civil Rights* (New York: Random House, 2006).
102. While not yet able really to see or take on the perspectives of other people, the kid who has emerged from the magical, Symbiotic stage of early childhood has come to know himself as a distinct "realm." Like any sovereign king or queen, he recognizes that he has his own beliefs, feelings, opinions, and desires. He eventually also comes to see and know that other people have their own beliefs, feelings, opinions, and desires. He becomes especially aware of this when other people's interests interfere with his own. At times impetuous and tyrannical, and always egocentric in the truest sense, the so-called "Self-Sovereign" mind is focused on the question, "What's in it for me?" Avoiding the pains of losing while seeking the pleasures and rewards of winning, the person in the Self-Sovereign mind learns rudimentary rules of the game. He abides by these rules when he has to—and breaks them when he can get away with it.

    This Self-Sovereign stage identified by Kegan encompasses both the Impulsive stage (early Self-Sovereign) and the Self-Protective, Opportunist stage (later Self-Sovereign) identified by Cook-Greuter and others.
103. Cook-Greuter, *Nine Levels*, 24.
104. Cook-Greuter, *Nine Levels*, 25.
105. Michael Hobbes, "Together Alone: The Epidemic of Gay Loneliness" *Huffington Post* (2 Mar 2017) https://highline.huffingtonpost.com/articles/en/gay-loneliness/, accessed 26 Apr 2021.

106. Édouard Louis, trans. Michael Lucey, *The End of Eddy* (New York: Farrar, Straus and Giroux, 2017).
107. Cook-Greuter, *Nine Levels,* 63.
108. Kegan, *Immunity to Change,* 52.
109. Cook-Greuter, *Nine Levels,* 65.
110. Cook-Greuter *Nine Levels,* 66–7.
111. Cook-Greuter, *Nine Levels,* 67.
112. Adam Grant, "There's a Name for the Blah You're Feeling: It's Called Languishing," *New York Times*, 19 April 2021, https://www.nytimes.com/2021/04/19/well/mind/covid-mental-health-languishing.html, accessed 21 Oct 2021.
113. Grant, "There's a Name."
114. Corey L. M. Keyes, "The Mental Health Continuum: From Languishing to Flourishing in Life," *Journal of Health and Social Research* 2002, Vol 43 (June): 208.
115. Keyes, "Mental Health Continuum," 210.
116. Grant, "There's a Name."
117. Hollis, *Swamplands of the Soul.*
118. Center for Disease Control and Prevention, "Disparities in Suicide," https://www.cdc.gov/suicide/facts/disparities-in-suicide.html, accessed 8 Dec 2022.
119. Grant, "There's a Name."
120. Matthew Lopez, *The Inheritance* (London: Faber and Faber, 2018; 2019), Part One, Act I, Scene ii, 2. Eric Interlude, p. 26.
121. *The Inheritance,* Part One, I.iv, 8, p. 52.
122. *The Inheritance,* Part One, I.ii.2, p. 29.
123. *The Inheritance,* Part Two, III.iii.2. Walter's House, p. 285.
124. *The Inheritance,* Part One, I.v, p. 54.
125. *The Inheritance,* Part One, I.i, 1, p. 12.
126. *The Inheritance,* Part One, I.v, p. 55.
127. *The Inheritance,* Part One, Prologue, p. 7.

128. *The Inheritance*, Part Two, I.iii.3. Strand Bookstore, p. 190.
129. *The Inheritance*, Part Two, II.i.1 Beach on Fire Island, p. 221.
130. *The Inheritance*, Part One, Prologue, p. 10.
131. *The Inheritance*, Part One, II.v.2, p. 151.
132. *The Inheritance*, Part One, III.iv.3. Eric and Toby's Apartment, p. 140.
133. *The Inheritance*, Part One, III.iv.3. Eric and Toby's Apartment, p. 141.
134. *The Inheritance*, Part Two, I.v.1 Henry's Hamptons Beach House, p. 214.
135. *The Inheritance*, Part Two, III.i.1. A Hotel Room in Alabama, pp. 264-5.
136. *The Inheritance*, Part Two, III.i.3. Toby's Apartment, p. 270.
137. *The Inheritance*, Part Two, III.iii.2. Walter's House, p. 285.
138. *The Inheritance*, Part Two, III.iii. 2. Walter's House, p. 285 and 3. Walter's House, p. 287.
139. Hollis, *Swamplands*, 8.
140. Garvey Berger, *Changing on the Job*, 108–9.

Acknowledgements

Writing this book has been of a piece with creating a social enterprise called Flourishing Gays. What could it mean to bring queer perspectives to personal growth, leadership development, and coaching? Working out this question both in my client service and in my writing has required me to grow and learn a great deal over the past five years. Bringing *Queer Flourishing* into the world means putting what I've been learning in the service of a wider audience. I arrive to this point feeling immense gratitude for the many individuals and communities who supported my learning and writing.

First of all, the clients who came to Flourishing Gays for help taught me a great deal. Whether workshop participants or coaching clients or part of a Heroes Journey cohort, brave individuals across the gender spectrum have let me companion them for some stretch of their developmental journeys. CEOs and Founders have come to me knowing that Diversity, Equity, and Inclusion matter, but not knowing where to start. How to lead inclusively? How to grow into a bigger version of themselves, so as to make space for truly diverse perspectives and team members? Clients have trusted me to join them in exploring some of the most important and tender areas of their lives. In so doing, they allowed me to see new vistas with them.

Taking all I have learned, I have fashioned *Queer Flourishing* to give readers as much of the experience as possible of what live support and interaction can offer over time. Reading is no substitute for one-on-one coaching or facilitated group work, but I have done everything I can to give readers what I see my clients gain.

Numerous professional communities of practitioners have greatly enriched my life and learning in the fields of leadership development and coaching. I am first of all grateful to the Org Practice at McKinsey, which first introduced me to these fields some eighteen years ago. It is a great gift to still be working with numerous friends from the McKinsey office in Dubai, thanks to our former office head, Zafer Achi, who sponsored my affiliating with Cultivating Leadership (CL) some three years ago. As part of CL, I have found a truly developmental community of leadership development practitioners that spans the globe.

When I first left McKinsey and sought formal coach training, the Co-Active Training Institute wowed me with the deep learning that great coaching can spur. Through both their coaching workshops and year-long Leadership program, CTI took me to new places in my growth, and equipped me with new tools to lead others and to help others become themselves more fully. From the Magpies cohort, with whom I went through that Leadership program, I learned above all how much more compelling and effective a leader I am when I show up with my heart open. From the Mandrills cohort, whom I companioned as an assistant through that same program, I learned how to put my own ongoing growth in the service of others in their unique developmental journeys.

Jennifer Brown convened a community of DEI practitioners for weekly calls during the height of Covid isolation that made space for all of us to support each other and sense what those strange times required of us. This community, together with Jennifer's warm friendship and able mentorship, helped me find my place and how to contribute to the field of DEI.

Jan Rybeck first brought me the power of adult development theory by taking me through a sentence completion assessment developed by Susanne Cook-Greuter and based on Jane Loevinger's work. Through that debrief, Jan and I began a friendship and a collaboration that continue today.

Besides the colleagues and developmental communities that have nourished me as I have gestated *Queer Flourishing*, I wish to express great gratitude to all those who read versions of this manuscript or parts of it and shared feedback that helped me make it as compelling, useful, and accessible as possible.

Bill Glenn was my first reader and generous advocate in this project. He read multiple versions of virtually every part of this book over the several years of our friendship. He brought the wisdom of a retired psychotherapist, the life experience of a gay man who lived and loved in the Bay Area since the height of the AIDS crisis, and the kind insight of a soul mate who saw the best of what I have to give to others, even when I would lose sight of it myself. Michael Milano generously brought his wisdom and insight to this complete manuscript, and became my friend in the process. My dear friend and fellow Nebraskan-New Yorker of Sicilian heritage, Michael Pettinger, completed two rounds of professional editing, with the eye of a careful reader who is himself a highly accomplished gay man yearning for something more.

In addition, I received valuable feedback from others who read parts of various versions of the manuscript, namely: Bob Rosen, Jennifer Garvey Berger, Carolyn Coughlin, Patrick Nolan, Kathy Talvacchia, Martin Cho, Rebecca Scott, John McDargh, and Susan Palmer.

Sharing this manuscript with my beloved aunt and godmother, Marilyn Longo, followed by an hours-long conversation about all it brought up for her has been among the greatest gifts of this book project.

Though I was more than a year into the writing of this book when our relationship began, Martin Cho has given me the greatest gift of all, by sharing life with me. More than anyone else, his love throughout these years has made possible my aliveness.

Hire Dominic to Speak

Create greater aliveness in your next event by having Dominic as your keynote speaker. You can count on having a thoughtful and heart-full experience!

He speaks on a variety of topics including:

- **Queer Flourishing for All**: Flourishing expresses aliveness. Queer marks difference. Whatever our sexual orientation or gender identity, we can all benefit from greater aliveness and vitality. The lived experience of LGBTQ+ people can contribute to the greater flourishing of all people, whatever their sexual orientation or gender identity.

- **Queer Superpowers**: Adversity spurs creative adaptations that serve us immensely but also create pitfalls which we must learn to navigate for the sake of ongoing flourishing. Get a grip on your queer superpowers, so that they don't have their grip on you!

- **The Case for LGBTQ+ Leadership Development**: Most organizations don't yet offer LGBTQ-specific leadership development, so why should you?

- **Diversity & Inclusion, More than an HR Function**: The very process of growing and developing as human beings can be framed as a journey of inner diversity and inclusion. Just as organizations gain more perspectives as they hire and retain more diverse employees, so does any individual increase their own perspective-taking capacity by seeing and honoring more parts of themselves.

Get in touch through the Flourishing Gays website: FlourishingGays.com/contact-us

Connect with me on LinkedIn: LinkedIn.com/in/fdominiclongo/

Bring Queer Superpowers for Leaders to Your Organization

The Queer Superpowers for Leaders program draws on the distinctive life experiences of LGBTQ+ adults to build greater capacities to lead creatively, courageously, and authentically. It can be offered either for participants of all sexual orientations and gender identities, or exclusively for LGBTQ+ participants.

By bringing queer eyes to the research on adult development and leadership, this program empowers participants to see themselves and others more fully and more compassionately. Focusing on ten specific patterns and postures that commonly show up in LGBTQ+ lives, Queer Superpowers for Leaders builds self-awareness for greater freedom of thought, speech, and action. Participants make their learning practical, through continually applying new concepts to their own current real-life leadership challenges, in small and large group settings, so as to all learn from each other.

With these and other queer superpowers, program participants:

- Investigate how these and similar adaptive patterns show up in their own life
- Learn to make the most of these powers and avoid their pitfalls
- Apply their learning to current adaptive challenges they are facing as leaders
- Form a community of practice for exchange of perspectives, wider application of learning, and a sense of solidarity
- Support each other in reimagining and reconfiguring postures and patterns for more effective leadership and greater flourishing

More info at FlourishingGays.com/queer-superpowers

Heroes Journey Program for Gay, Bi, and Queer Men

You are a gay, bi, or queer man who has accomplished much of what you've set out to do. Perhaps you've got the shiny resumé, nice home, maybe even a devoted husband—and yet, something's missing. The goals that once drove you have lost their luster, and you're left wondering, "What's next?"

Do you ever . . .

- Feel unclear about your sense of purpose in work and life?
- Sense diminished passion, energy, drive, or motivation?
- Desire to make a greater contribution to the world?
- Crave more fulfilling and impactful relationships?

You're not alone. We've seen this struggle again and again, so we created a distinctive program to help you step more fully into life, purpose, and impact.

Heroes Journey is a personal growth and leadership development program for highly accomplished gay, bi, and queer men. Executive coaching, a Mastermind group, and interactive workshops enable cohort members to grow as inclusive leaders and holistically as human beings, learning from and with each other, and from expert faculty.

Chief benefits that participants receive from engaging in this program include:

- Become a more inspiring, authentic, and inclusive leader
- Clarify vision for contributing to your organization, field, and society
- Set the most personally meaningful goals for life and work
- Tap into passion and sense of purpose so as to pursue that vision and those goals
- Integrate developmental learning into daily life, at work and elsewhere
- Develop capacities for navigating complexity
- Identify limiting beliefs and assumptions about self, others, and the world
- Reconfigure patterns of thought and behavior so as to increase personal efficacy and professional impact, while deepening interpersonal relationships
- Practice skills of genuine curiosity, courage, care, and compassion in peer relationships
- Increase capacity for listening deeply and empathetically

More info at FlourishingGays.com/heroesjourney

What Heroes Journey Alumni Say

"I deeply cherish and value the experience of connecting with other gay men through Flourishing Gays. I was given the freedom to be less guarded and more vulnerable within the group, and with myself. The framework of Heroes Journey pushed me to challenge what wasn't working in my life, and, even more importantly, to question what was working. In doing so, I left my comfort zone and opened my mind to a radically different future. With this broader mindset, I've been able to create rewarding and rich personal and professional possibilities."

Chiedu Egbuniwe
Diversity, Equity, and Inclusion Strategist
Los Angeles, California

"I've spent much of my life lamenting the common childhood traumas of growing up in hiding followed by the turmoil of the coming out journey. As Dominic chaperoned me and a group of other gay leaders through Heroes Journey, I became empowered by acknowledging and cultivating the Queer Superpowers that I have adapted from those experiences and that enhance my leadership to this day. Dominic's laid-back style creates a comfortable milieu for self-exploration while diving into evidence- and research-based topics."

David Selander, MD, MBA
Executive Medical Director, Providence Swedish
Seattle, Washington

"I took part in Heroes Journey during a time in which I felt stagnant in my career. As an insecure gay boy who sought to be the 'Best Little Boy' proving I could get the most competitive jobs and schools, I found the program to be introspective. It helped me understand that my gay childhood served me well in getting to where I was, but to be a leader I had to give up some of these behaviors."

Dan Chen
Product Strategy, Google
New York, New York

Actionable Allies Program

Despite politicized critique of Diversity, Equity, and Inclusion (DEI) initiatives, many organizational leaders recognize the importance of recruiting, retaining, and promoting talented colleagues with diverse identities, whether that means women, people of color, LGBTQ+ folks, or diversity of other kinds. Beyond talent management concerns, many individuals feel a strong sense of personal alignment with values underlying DEI initiatives, such as justice, equity, diversity, inclusion, and belonging. Yet often professionals nonetheless are not sure how to put their values into action, especially at the office.

Does your team or organization ...

- Want to build *all* colleagues as inclusive leaders?
- Aspire to put your values into action?
- Already offer women, people of color, and LGBTQ+ colleagues specific leadership development support, and want something especially for men, white or straight colleagues?
- Want to learn how to act effectively as allies to one another, across social differences of all kinds?
- Need help to address sensitive topics of personal identity while maintaining helpful professional boundaries?
- Feel worried about saying the wrong thing, and so avoid saying anything, even when you sense bias in effect?

- Hope to create a culture where colleagues of all identities can make their greatest contribution and flourish?

The Actionable Allies program builds participants' capabilities in allyship, a crucial dimension of inclusive leadership. Participants become more ready to act in the moment amidst fast-flying social dynamics. Specifically, Actionable Allies serves the following objectives:

- Build a culture of inclusivity and create conditions for diverse talent to thrive
- Focus on allyship as a primary mode of inclusive leadership
- Turn your personal commitments to diversity, equity, and inclusion into more effective and impactful leadership in action

Participants come away with greater self-awareness, intercultural competence, empathy, and practical know-how for acting effectively in common real-world scenarios. Growing as inclusive leaders fills critical skill gaps in uniquely human capacities needed today more than ever.

For more info: FlourishingGays.com/allies

Bring Dominic to Your ERG

Is your Employee Resource Group (ERG) looking to:

- Create deeper connections among members in a safe container?
- Make a more meaningful contribution to members' development as leaders?
- Craft a strategic plan for greater impact within your organization?

Whether it's for a leadership development program of a few weekly sessions, a more substantive approach to community building, or strategic thought-partnership for building a new ERG or expanding the impact of existing groups, Dominic is ready to lend his expertise and experience. *Queer Flourishing* can easily be used to structure

small reading group sessions for colleagues to learn and grow together in an atmosphere of reflection and mutual support.
For more info: FlourishingGays.com/organizations

About the Author

Dominic Longo brings queer perspectives to leadership development and coaching. He founded Flourishing Gays as a social enterprise to create learning experiences that help clients grow into fuller versions of themselves, through special attention to the particularities of queer developmental journeys.

He believes that flourishing is what we are all made for, yet sees how myriad obstacles keep the weird and wonderful potential of every person pushed down in various ways. Dominic understands leadership development as the process of unlocking this potential within all of us to become more fully human and more fully alive.

On his own journey into greater wholeness and flourishing, Dominic's path has traversed scholarly and professional work across the United States, Middle East, and Europe.

Previously, as director of a university center for interreligious dialogue, Dominic supported students, faculty, and staff to bridge differences of culture and worldview. As a management consultant at McKinsey serving clients in the Middle East and the United States, Dominic designed and directed large-scale programs transforming organizational cultures and building capabilities. There he also founded an Employee Resource Group for allies of LGBTQ+ colleagues.

He is a Professional Certified Coach and holds a Ph.D. in Arabic and Islamic Studies from Harvard University. A citizen of the United States and Italy, Dominic grew up in Nebraska and now lives with his partner in New York City.

You can follow Dominic on social media:
LinkedIn: LinkedIn.com/in/fdominiclongo/
Instagram: Instagram.com/flourishinggays/
YouTube: YouTube.com/@flourishinggays

Dear reader,

Thank you for reading this book and joining the Publish Your Purpose community! You are joining a special group of people who aim to make the world a better place.

What's Publish Your Purpose About?
Our mission is to elevate the voices often excluded from traditional publishing. We intentionally seek out authors and storytellers with diverse backgrounds, life experiences, and unique perspectives to publish books that will make an impact in the world.

Beyond our books, we are focused on tangible, action-based change. As a woman- and LGBTQ+-owned company, we are committed to reducing inequality, lowering levels of poverty, creating a healthier environment, building stronger communities, and creating high-quality jobs with dignity and purpose.

As a Certified B Corporation, we use business as a force for good. We join a community of mission-driven companies building a more equitable, inclusive, and sustainable global economy. B Corporations must meet high standards of transparency, social and environmental performance, and accountability as determined by the nonprofit B Lab. The certification process is rigorous and ongoing (with a recertification requirement every three years).

How Do We Do This?
We intentionally partner with socially and economically disadvantaged businesses that meet our sustainability goals. We embrace and encourage our authors and employee's differences in race, age, color, disability, ethnicity, family or marital status, gender identity or expression, language, national origin, physical and mental ability, political affiliation, religion, sexual orientation, socio-economic status, veteran status, and other characteristics that make them unique.

Community is at the heart of everything we do—from our writing and publishing programs to contributing to social enterprise nonprofits like reSET (www.resetco.org) and our work in founding B Local Connecticut.

We are endlessly grateful to our authors, readers, and local community for being the driving force behind the equitable and sustainable world we are building together.

To connect with us online or publish with us, visit us at www.publishyourpurpose.com.

Elevating Your Voice,

Jenn T Grace

Jenn T. Grace
Founder, Publish Your Purpose

www.ingramcontent.com/pod-product-compliance
Lightning Source LLC
Chambersburg PA
CBHW061252230426
43665CB00026B/2907